# Praise for Cesare Casella and Italian Cooking For Dummies

"Cesare Casella demystifies the popular misconceptions of authentic Italian cooking and food traditions while retaining the romance that has made it the most desired food in America."

> — Paul Bartolotta,
> James Beard Award-Winning Chef of Spiaggi,
> Chicago

"*Italian Cooking For Dummies* is everything you ever wanted to know and much more about cooking delicious Italian food like a pro."

> — Charlie Palmer,
> Chef, Aureole, New York

"I was very lucky to have been born in an Italian household. What I admired most was the simplicity of my mother's cooking, even though it was for the entire family. After so many years, it is phenomenal to see how it is reproduced in this fantastic book."

> — Jean-Louis Palladin,
> Chef, Rio Suite Hotel, Las Vegas

**TM**

# BESTSELLING BOOK SERIES FROM IDG

# *References for the Rest of Us!*™

Do you find that traditional reference books are overloaded with technical details and advice you'll never use? Do you postpone important life decisions because you just don't want to deal with them? Then our *...For Dummies*® business and general reference book series is for you.

*...For Dummies* business and general reference books are written for those frustrated and hard-working souls who know they aren't dumb, but find that the myriad of personal and business issues and the accompanying horror stories make them feel helpless. *...For Dummies* books use a lighthearted approach, a down-to-earth style, and even cartoons and humorous icons to diffuse fears and build confidence. Lighthearted but not lightweight, these books are perfect survival guides to solve your everyday personal and business problems.

> *"More than a publishing phenomenon, 'Dummies' is a sign of the times."*
> — *The New York Times*

> *"...you won't go wrong buying them."*
> — *Walter Mossberg, Wall Street Journal, on IDG Books' ...For Dummies books*

> *"A world of detailed and authoritative information is packed into them..."*
> — *U.S. News and World Report*

Already, millions of satisfied readers agree. They have made *...For Dummies* the #1 introductory level computer book series and a best-selling business book series. They have written asking for more. So, if you're looking for the best and easiest way to learn about business and other general reference topics, look to *...For Dummies* to give you a helping hand.

**TM**

# IDG BOOKS WORLDWIDE

4/98

# by Cesare Casella and Jack Bishop

IDG Books Worldwide, Inc.
An International Data Group Company

Foster City, CA ♦ Chicago, IL ♦ Indianapolis, IN ♦ New York, NY

**Italian Cooking For Dummies**®

Published by
**IDG Books Worldwide, Inc.**
An International Data Group Company
919 E. Hillsdale Blvd.
Suite 400
Foster City, CA 94404
www.idgbooks.com (IDG Books Worldwide Web site)
www.dummies.com (Dummies Press Web site)

Library of Congress Catalog Card No.: 98-87101

ISBN: 0-7645-5098-5

Printed in the United States of America

10 9 8 7 6 5 4 3 2

1B/SX/QY/ZY/IN

Distributed in the United States by IDG Books Worldwide, Inc.

Distributed by Macmillan Canada for Canada; by Transworld Publishers Limited in the United Kingdom; by IDG Norge Books for Norway; by IDG Sweden Books for Sweden; by Woodslane Pty. Ltd. for Australia; by Woodslane (NZ) Ltd. for New Zealand; by Addison Wesley Longman Singapore Pte Ltd. for Singapore, Malaysia, Thailand, Indonesia and Korea; by Norma Comunicaciones S.A. for Colombia; by Intersoft for South Africa; by International Thomson Publishing for Germany, Austria and Switzerland; by Toppan Company Ltd. for Japan; by Distribuidora Cuspide for Argentina; by Livraria Cultura for Brazil; by Ediciencia S.A. for Ecuador; by Ediciones ZETA S.C.R. Ltda. for Peru; by WS Computer Publishing Corporation, Inc., for the Philippines; by Unalis Corporation for Taiwan; by Contemporanea de Ediciones for Venezuela; by Computer Book & Magazine Store for Puerto Rico; by Express Computer Distributors for the Caribbean and West Indies. Authorized Sales Agent: Anthony Rudkin Associates for the Middle East and North Africa.

For general information on IDG Books Worldwide's books in the U.S., please call our Consumer Customer Service department at 800-762-2974. For reseller information, including discounts and premium sales, please call our Reseller Customer Service department at 800-434-3422.

For information on where to purchase IDG Books Worldwide's books outside the U.S., please contact our International Sales department at 650-655-3200 or fax 650-655-3297.

For information on foreign language translations, please contact our Foreign & Subsidiary Rights department at 650-655-3021 or fax 650-655-3281.

For sales inquiries and special prices for bulk quantities, please contact our Sales department at 650-655-3200 or write to the address above.

For information on using IDG Books Worldwide's books in the classroom or for ordering examination copies, please contact our Educational Sales department at 800-434-2086 or fax 317-596-5499.

For press review copies, author interviews, or other publicity information, please contact our Public Relations department at 650-655-3000 or fax 650-655-3299.

For authorization to photocopy items for corporate, personal, or educational use, please contact Copyright Clearance Center, 222 Rosewood Drive, Danvers, MA 01923, or fax 978-750-4470.

# About the Authors

**Cesare Casella** was born in a small town outside Lucca, Italy. He grew up in and around his family's restaurant, called Il Vipore. As a young chef, he transformed Il Vipore into a world-class establishment, earning a well-deserved Michelin star. Since 1993, Casella has been working as a chef at several leading Italian restaurants in New York. He is the coauthor of *Diary of a Tuscan Chef.*

**Jack Bishop** is the author of several books on Italian food, including *The Complete Italian Vegetarian Cookbook, Pasta e Verdura,* and *Lasagna.* He is the senior writer for *Cook's Illustrated* and writes for various national magazines and newspapers. He has studied cooking in Italy.

*Photo Renate*

## About the Photographer

**Lou Manna** resides in New York City, where he runs his own studio on Fifth Avenue. Through his specialty in food photography, he has worked with numerous restaurants, renowned chefs, and food critics since 1975, including a long-standing collaboration with Craig Claiborne and Pierre Franey. He also contributed the color photography in *Desserts For Dummies* and *Grilling For Dummies* as well as 24 other books, most notably *The Four-Star Kitchen, A Plaza Wedding,* and *Cuisine Rapide.* Lou began his career as a photographer for *The New York Times* and since then has worked with other national publications, corporations, and leading agencies worldwide.

# ABOUT IDG BOOKS WORLDWIDE

Welcome to the world of IDG Books Worldwide.

IDG Books Worldwide, Inc., is a subsidiary of International Data Group, the world's largest publisher of computer-related information and the leading global provider of information services on information technology. IDG was founded more than 25 years ago and now employs more than 8,500 people worldwide. IDG publishes more than 275 computer publications in over 75 countries (see listing below). More than 90 million people read one or more IDG publications each month.

Launched in 1990, IDG Books Worldwide is today the #1 publisher of best-selling computer books in the United States. We are proud to have received eight awards from the Computer Press Association in recognition of editorial excellence and three from *Computer Currents'* First Annual Readers' Choice Awards. Our best-selling *...For Dummies®* series has more than 50 million copies in print with translations in 38 languages. IDG Books Worldwide, through a joint venture with IDG's Hi-Tech Beijing, became the first U.S. publisher to publish a computer book in the People's Republic of China. In record time, IDG Books Worldwide has become the first choice for millions of readers around the world who want to learn how to better manage their businesses.

Our mission is simple: Every one of our books is designed to bring extra value and skill-building instructions to the reader. Our books are written by experts who understand and care about our readers. The knowledge base of our editorial staff comes from years of experience in publishing, education, and journalism — experience we use to produce books for the '90s. In short, we care about books, so we attract the best people. We devote special attention to details such as audience, interior design, use of icons, and illustrations. And because we use an efficient process of authoring, editing, and desktop publishing our books electronically, we can spend more time ensuring superior content and spend less time on the technicalities of making books.

You can count on our commitment to deliver high-quality books at competitive prices on topics you want to read about. At IDG Books Worldwide, we continue in the IDG tradition of delivering quality for more than 25 years. You'll find no better book on a subject than one from IDG Books Worldwide.

John Kilculien
CEO
IDG Books Worldwide, Inc.

Steven Berkowitz
President and Publisher
IDG Books Worldwide, Inc.

*Eighth Annual Computer Press Awards ≥1992*

*Ninth Annual Computer Press Awards ≥1993*

*Tenth Annual Computer Press Awards ≥1994*

*Eleventh Annual Computer Press Awards ≥1995*

IDG Books Worldwide, Inc., is a subsidiary of International Data Group, the world's largest publisher of computer-related information and the leading global provider of information services on information technology. International Data Group publishes over 275 computer publications in over 75 countries. More than 90 million people read one or more International Data Group publications each month. International Data Group's publications include: **ARGENTINA:** Buyer's Guide, Computerworld Argentina, PC World Argentina; **AUSTRALIA:** Australian Macworld, Australian PC World, Australian Reseller News, Computerworld, IT Casebook, Network World, Publish, Webmaster; **AUSTRIA:** Computerwelt Osterreich, Networks Austria, PC Tip Austria; **BANGLADESH:** PC World Bangladesh; **BELARUS:** PC World Belarus; **BELGIUM:** Data News; **BRAZIL:** Annuário de Informática, Computerworld, Connections, Macworld, PC Player, PC World, Publish, Reseller News, Supergamepower; **BULGARIA:** Computerworld Bulgaria, Network World Bulgaria, PC & MacWorld Bulgaria; **CANADA:** CIO Canada, Client/Server World, ComputerWorld Canada, InfoWorld Canada, NetworkWorld Canada, WebWorld; **CHILE:** Computerworld Chile, PC World Chile; **COLOMBIA:** Computerworld Colombia, PC World Colombia; **COSTA RICA:** PC World Centro America; **THE CZECH AND SLOVAK REPUBLICS:** Computerworld Czechoslovakia, Macworld Czech Republic, PC World Czechoslovakia; **DENMARK:** Communications World Danmark, Computerworld Danmark, Macworld Danmark, PC World Danmark, Techworld Denmark; **DOMINICAN REPUBLIC:** PC World Republica Dominicana; **ECUADOR:** PC World Ecuador; **EGYPT:** Computerworld Middle East, PC World Middle East; **EL SALVADOR:** PC World Centro America; **FINLAND:** MikroPC, Tietoverkko, Tietoviikko; **FRANCE:** Distributique, Hebdo, Info PC, Le Monde Informatique, Macworld, Reseaux & Telecoms, WebMaster France; **GERMANY:** Computer Partner, Computerwoche, Computerwoche Extra, Computerwoche FOCUS, Global Online, Macwelt, PC Welt; **GREECE:** Amiga Computing, GamePro Greece, Multimedia World; **GUATEMALA:** PC World Centro America; **HONDURAS:** PC World Centro America; **HONG KONG:** Computerworld Hong Kong, PC World Hong Kong, Publish in Asia; **HUNGARY:** ABCD CD-ROM, Computerworld Szamitastechnika, Internetto online Magazine, PC World Hungary, PC-X Magazin Hungary; **ICELAND:** Tolvuheimur PC World Island; **INDIA:** Information Communications World, Information Systems Computerworld, PC World India, Publish in Asia; **INDONESIA:** InfoKomputer PC World, Komputek Computerworld, Publish in Asia; **IRELAND:** ComputerScope, PC Live!; **ISRAEL:** Macworld Israel, People & Computers/Computerworld; **ITALY:** Computerworld Italia, Macworld Italia, Networking Italia, PC World Italia; **JAPAN:** DTP World, Macworld Japan, Nikkei Personal Computing, OS/2 World Japan, SunWorld Japan, Windows NT World, Windows World Japan; **KENYA:** PC World East African; **KOREA:** Hi-Tech Information, Macworld Korea, PC World Korea; **MACEDONIA:** PC World Macedonia; **MALAYSIA:** Computerworld Malaysia, PC World Malaysia, Publish in Asia; **MALTA:** PC World Malta; **MEXICO:** Computerworld Mexico, PC World Mexico; **MYANMAR:** PC World Myanmar; **NETHERLANDS:** Computer! Totaal, LAN Internetworking Magazine, LAN World Buyers Guide, Macworld Netherlands, Net, WebWereld; **NEW ZEALAND:** Absolute Beginners Guide and Plain & Simple Series, Computer Buyer, Computer Industry Directory, Computerworld New Zealand, MTB, Network World, PC World New Zealand; **NICARAGUA:** PC World Centro America; **NORWAY:** Computerworld Norge, CW Rapport, Datamagasinet, Financial Rapport, Kursguide Norge, Macworld Norge, Multimediaworld Norge, PC World Ekspress Norge, PC World Nettverk, PC World Norge, PC World ProduktGuide Norge; **PAKISTAN:** Computerworld Pakistan; **PANAMA:** PC World Panama; **PEOPLE'S REPUBLIC OF CHINA:** China Computer Users, China Computerworld, China InfoWorld, China Telecom World Weekly, Computer & Communication, Electronic Design China, Electronics Today, Electronics Weekly, Game Software, PC World China, Popular Computer Week, Software Weekly, Software World, Telecom World; **PERU:** Computerworld Peru, PC World Profesional Peru, PC World SoHo Peru; **PHILIPPINES:** Click!, Computerworld Philippines, PC World Philippines, Publish in Asia; **POLAND:** Computerworld Poland, Computerworld Special Report Poland, Cyber, Macworld Poland, Networld Poland, PC World Komputer; **PORTUGAL:** Cerebro/PC World, Computerworld/Correio Informático, Dealer World Portugal, Mac*In/PC*In Portugal, Multimedia World; **PUERTO RICO:** PC World Puerto Rico, Computerworld Puerto Rico; **ROMANIA:** Computerworld Romania, PC World Romania, Telecom Romania; **RUSSIA:** Computerworld Russia, Mir PK, Publish, Seti; **SINGAPORE:** Computerworld Singapore, PC World Singapore, Publish in Asia; **SLOVENIA:** Monitor; **SOUTH AFRICA:** Computing SA, Network World SA, Software World SA; **SPAIN:** Communicaciones World España, Computerworld España, Dealer World España, Macworld España, PC World España; **SRI LANKA:** Infolink PC World; **SWEDEN:** CAP&Design, Computer Sweden, Corporate Computing Sweden, Internetworld Sweden, it.branschen, Macworld Sweden, MaxiData Sweden, MikroDatorn, Nätverk & Kommunikation, PC World Sweden, PCaktiv, Windows World Sweden; **SWITZERLAND:** Computerworld Schweiz, Macworld Schweiz, PCtip; **TAIWAN:** Computerworld Taiwan, Macworld Taiwan, NEW ViSiON/Publish, PC World Taiwan, Windows World Taiwan; **THAILAND:** Publish in Asia, Thai Computerworld; **TURKEY:** Computerworld Turkiye, Macworld Turkiye, Network World Turkiye, PC World Turkiye; **UKRAINE:** Computerworld Kiev, Multimedia World Ukraine, PC World Ukraine; **UNITED KINGDOM:** Acorn User UK, Amiga Action UK, Amiga Computing UK, Apple Talk UK, Computing, Macworld, Parents and Computers UK, PC Advisor, PC Home, PSX Pro, The WEB; **UNITED STATES:** Cable in the Classroom, CIO Magazine, Computerworld, DOS World, Federal Computer Week, GamePro Magazine, InfoWorld, I-Way, Macworld, Network World, PC Games, PC World, Publish, Video Event, THE WEB Magazine, and WebMaster; online webzines: JavaWorld, NetscapeWorld, and SunWorld Online; **URUGUAY:** InfoWorld Uruguay; **VENEZUELA:** Computerworld Venezuela, PC World Venezuela; and **VIETNAM:** PC World Vietnam.
5/7/98

# Dedication

To everyone who likes Italian food.

# Authors' Acknowledgments

The authors would like to thank Laura Pensiero for her invaluable assistance writing the recipes in this book.

Our gratitude to photographer Lou Manna for capturing many of Cesare's recipes on film, and to Liz Kurtzman for her funny and informative illustrations.

Thanks to the team at IDG, especially Sarah Kennedy and Holly McGuire, who set us on our way, and Kelly Ewing, our diligent project editor, who turned our manuscript into this book.

Agents Angela Miller and Mark Reiter deserve credit for putting us together as a team.

Thanks also to Bryan Miller for helping to formulate the original concept for the book.

# Publisher's Acknowledgments

We're proud of this book; please register your comments through our IDG Books Worldwide Online Registration Form located at http://my2cents.dummies.com.

Some of the people who helped bring this book to market include the following:

### Acquisitions, Development, and Editorial

**Senior Project Editor:** Kelly Ewing

**Acquisitions Editor:** Holly McGuire

**Copy Editors:** Ted Cains, Gwenette Gaddis

**General Reviewers:** Diana R. Conover, Jane Uetz Johnson

**Editorial Manager:** Colleen Rainsberger

**Editorial Assistant:** Darren Meiss

### Production

**Associate Project Coordinator:** Tom Missler

**Layout and Graphics:** Lou Boudreau, Linda M. Boyer, J. Tyler Connor, Angela F. Hunckler, Heather Pearson, Brent Savage, Deirdre Smith

**Proofreaders:** Christine Berman, Kelli Botta, Michelle Croninger, Mildred Rosenzweig, Rebecca Senninger, Janet M. Withers

**Indexer:** Sharon Hilgenberg

### Special Help

Paula Lowell; Constance Carlisle; Tina Sims; Monica Baig, Prop Stylist

---

### General and Administrative

**IDG Books Worldwide, Inc.:** John Kilcullen, CEO; Steven Berkowitz, President and Publisher

**IDG Books Technology Publishing:** Brenda McLaughlin, Senior Vice President and Group Publisher

**Dummies Technology Press and Dummies Editorial:** Diane Graves Steele, Vice President and Associate Publisher; Mary Bednarek, Director of Acquisitions and Product Development; Kristin A. Cocks, Editorial Director

**Dummies Trade Press:** Kathleen A. Welton, Vice President and Publisher; Kevin Thornton, Acquisitions Manager

**IDG Books Production for Dummies Press:** Michael R. Britton, Vice President of Production and Creative Services; Beth Jenkins Roberts, Production Director; Cindy L. Phipps, Manager of Project Coordination, Production Proofreading, and Indexing; Kathie S. Schutte, Supervisor of Page Layout; Shelley Lea, Supervisor of Graphics and Design; Debbie J. Gates, Production Systems Specialist; Robert Springer, Supervisor of Proofreading; Debbie Stailey, Special Projects Coordinator; Tony Augsburger, Supervisor of Reprints and Bluelines

**Dummies Packaging and Book Design:** Robin Seaman, Creative Director; Jocelyn Kelaita, Product Packaging Coordinator; Kavish + Kavish, Cover Design

◆

The publisher would like to give special thanks to Patrick J. McGovern, without whom this book would not have been possible.

◆

# Contents at a Glance

# Cartoons at a Glance

By Rich Tennant

"I'm pretty sure it's pizza dough that gets tossed, not pasta dough."

page 315

"We're making ladyfingers for the tiramisù, why?"

page 265

Who ordered the Shrimp alla Diavola?

page 179

"Relax - another helping of vermicelli, and I'll be done with your precious shredder."

page 299

"I just don't think asking for extra-virgin ketchup on your hamburger reflects a full appreciation of Italian cuisine."

page 7

"Unfortunately, he drives the car like he makes pasta- al dente."

page 95

"What my husband meant to say is he made a 'Caesar salad', not a 'Cesarean salad'."

page 37

"What 'ya mean you don't want espresso?"

page 333

Fax: 978-546-7747 • E-mail: the5wave@tiac.net

# Recipes at a Glance

### Fresh Pasta

### Risotto

### Polenta and Gnocchi

## Pizza, Calzone, and Focaccia

## Poultry

## Meat

## Seafood

## Vegetable Side Dishes

## Desserts

# Table of Contents

# Introduction

● ● ● ● ● ● ● ● ● ● ● ● ● ● ● ● ● ● ● ● ● ● ● ● ● ● ● ● ● ● ● ● ● ● ● ● ● ● ● ● ● ● ● ● ● ● ● ●

*E*verybody loves Italian food, and with good reason. Chefs have embraced Italian food because the cuisine emphasizes fresh ingredients at their peak. Doctors and nutritionists tout Italian food because of its reliance on vegetables, complex carbohydrates, and olive oil (rather than butter). And for most people, Italian food is appealing because it tastes great. Pasta and pizza have become two of the most popular dishes on the planet because they're versatile and delicious.

But the big secret about Italian cooking — one that your local Italian restaurant doesn't want to share — is the ease of preparation. The best Italian cooking has always taken place at home, not in restaurants. And this means Mom or Grandma does the cooking, not an army of chefs. Mom's or Grandma's kitchen was probably poorly equipped — yes, you can cook without a six-burner cooktop or granite countertops — and she had access to only local ingredients.

Despite these limitations (or maybe because of them), Italian mothers and grandmothers have created some pretty fabulous food. And the recipes could not be simpler. A super pasta sauce can be as simple as cooking some fresh tomatoes with garlic, basil, and olive oil. Preparing such a sauce is not much harder than opening a jar of spaghetti sauce, but the difference is like eating in a four-star restaurant after years of cafeteria food.

## About This Book

We didn't structure *Italian Cooking For Dummies* like a conventional cookbook. We've organized the book like a resource manual, with chapters that can stand alone as individual lessons on making fresh pasta, preparing risotto, or adapting pizza for home ovens. If stranded on a deserted island, you could read the book from start to finish. But most cooks want to dart around, reading relevant information that can help them prepare dinner that night or plan a party for the upcoming weekend. Use the Index in the back of the book and the detailed Table of Contents on the preceding pages as your guides. The list of recipes at the start of the book can also help you get your bearings.

# Conventions Used in This Book

Each recipe in this book assumes certain conventions about the following basic ingredients:

- ✔ All herbs are fresh unless otherwise noted.

- ✔ All milk is whole milk. You can substitute lowfat milk (but not skim milk because it has no fat) in most cases, but the dish won't taste as rich and creamy.

- ✔ All butter is unsalted (also called sweet). Salted butter can ruin desserts. It won't ruin savory dishes, but we prefer to add our own salt to dishes. Also, Italian cooks don't use margarine, and neither should you. It doesn't taste very good, and olive oil is a better option for cooks who would rather not use butter.

- ✔ All eggs are large.

- ✔ All salt is kosher. We prefer kosher salt to regular table salt. Table salt usually contains additives that prevent clumping. We find that kosher salt, which doesn't contain any additives, has a cleaner flavor. We also like the large kosher salt crystals, which are easy to pick up with your fingertips and sprinkle over food.

- ✔ All pepper is freshly ground. Preground pepper in a bottle or tin lacks the full flavor of black peppercorns you mill yourself.

- ✔ All flour is all-purpose unless otherwise noted.

- ✔ All olive oil is extra virgin unless otherwise noted.

- ✔ All onions are red unless otherwise noted. Yellow onions may be used, but red onions are more authentic.

In the recipes, we tell you when you need special tools or gadgets to make a dish. Otherwise, we assume that you already own the following equipment:

- ✔ Dry and liquid measures, as well as measuring spoons. Dry measures are made from metal or plastic and usually have handles. Wet measures are made from glass or plastic and have pour spouts.

- ✔ Mixing bowls, wooden spoons, a spatula, a colander, and a wire whisk.

- ✔ A selection of sharp knives, which makes cooking easier and safer. (Dull knives not only slow you down but are dangerous because the blade is more likely to slip and land in your hand.) A paring knife, chef's knife, and bread knife are essential. Most paring knives have short blades that measure about 4 inches long. Chef's knives come in a variety of sizes. Most cooks are comfortable with an 8-inch chef's knife. However, if your hands are on the large side, you may want a 10-inch chef's knife. With its serrated edge, a bread knife is the best way to saw through bread as well as sandwiches or focaccia. A chef's knife can mangle bread.

✔ Saucepans with covers in various sizes for making sauces and boiling vegetables. Saucepans have straight sides and a single handle. We call for three sizes of saucepans in recipes — small (about 1 quart), medium (2 to $2^1/_2$ quarts), and large (about 4 quarts).

✔ Skillets or omelet pans in various sizes for sautéing vegetables, meats, poultry, and fish and for preparing eggs. These pans usually have sloped sides and a single handle. In some cases, we like to transfer skillets from the stovetop to the oven. An ovenproof handle (made from metal, not plastic or wood) is necessary in these recipes. We call for three sizes of skillets in recipes — small (8 inches in diameter), medium (10 inches), and large (12 inches). We don't generally use pans with nonstick surfaces, but you may, especially if you want to keep the amount of fat needed to sauté foods to a minimum. (Just keep in mind that foods don't brown as well in nonstick pans.)

✔ A large kettle or pot for cooking pasta and making soup. This pot should have a cover and a capacity of 8 to 10 quarts.

✔ A jelly roll pan or other metal baking sheet for toasting bread slices, baking cookies, or roasting vegetables. We like a flat sheet with a small lip around the edge — a $^3/_4$-inch lip is pretty common. You can use any medium to large baking sheet, but we find that a pan that measures 15 inches long and 10 inches across is pretty useful.

✔ A metal roasting pan to hold a pork loin or a chicken. This pan should be about 2 inches deep and measure at least 13 inches long and 9 inches across. Larger pans are fine as well, as long as they fit comfortably in your oven.

# Foolish Assumptions

We have made some assumptions, which we hope aren't foolish, about you, the reader of this book. You probably know what grated cheese is and that pasta comes in many shapes and sizes. But you may not know the difference between Parmigiano-Reggiano and the cheese that comes in the little green can. Or maybe no one has ever explained to you why some recipes call for spaghetti and others for ziti.

*Italian Cooking For Dummies* provides answers to these questions, as well as explanations. Many Italian cookbooks assume that readers know the difference between Roman and Sicilian cuisine, that readers have traveled the backroads of Tuscany, and that olive oil is as familiar as water. While we assume that you know how to boil water and know the difference between pasta and pizza, we don't assume much more than that. Step-by-step, we explain how to make authentic Italian food at home, with detailed discussions about ingredients as well as techniques.

# How This Book Is Organized

*Italian Cooking For Dummies* follows the structure of an Italian meal, with sequential chapters on appetizers, soups, pastas, main courses, and desserts. The book begins with several chapters that explain basic principles of Italian cooking and discuss key ingredients and equipment. The book ends with several chapters on menu planning and other resources for discovering more about Italian food. In all, the book contains eight parts.

## Part I: What Is Italian Cooking?

This part defines the essence of Italian cooking, with its emphasis on spontaneity, flexibility, and freshness. We offer some explanations for the worldwide popularity of Italian food and tell you what's really Italian and what's not. This part also explains the various regional cuisines within Italy (Sicilian food is quite different from Tuscan food), as well as the traditional structure of an Italian meal and how that translates in other cultures. A detailed listing of key Italian ingredients, as well as some notes about unusual pieces of equipment, round out this part of the book.

## Part II: First Impressions

This part covers appetizers and some dishes that are traditionally served as first courses, including antipasti, salads, and soups. These dishes rarely make a complete meal but are components that Italian cooks use again and again when planning menus.

## Part III: The Grains: Pasta, Pizza, and Beyond

This part covers the carbohydrates that make Italian food so popular. The first two chapters explain the differences between fresh and dried pasta and show how each has a place in the Italian kitchen. Later chapters focus on *risotto* (the creamy rice dish that has become the darling of chefs), *gnocchi* (light Italian dumplings usually made from potatoes), and *polenta* (a fancy name for grits or cornmeal mush). This part ends with a discussion of bread dishes, including pizza, calzone, and focaccia.

## Part IV: The Main Event

This part covers the traditional main courses — chicken, beef, veal, lamb, pork, and seafood. Italians usually keep the main course quite simple. This part ends with a discussion of the vegetable side dishes that usually accompany main courses.

## Part V: La Dolce Vita

*La dolce vita* means "the sweet life." Italians certainly know how to eat, and enjoying dessert is no exception. This part covers desserts that Italian restaurant patrons may find familiar — gelato, biscotti, and tiramisù — as well as some little-known regional desserts. A chapter on coffee demystifies espresso-making at home and explains how to prepare cappuccino, lattes, and other Italian coffee drinks like a pro. We also discuss Italian after-dinner drinks and liqueurs, such as grappa, Frangelico, and amaretto.

## Part VI: Menus for Every Occasion

This part shows you how to combine the recipes in the rest of the book to create menus for a variety of occasions.

## Part VII: The Part of Tens

This part contains a variety of listings that take you to the next level. Want to find out more about key Italian phrases or Italian food on the World Wide Web or other cookbooks? These chapters can increase your knowledge with practical information that takes you out of the kitchen.

## Part VIII: Appendixes

This final part is a resource that explains Italian cooking terms and lists common substitutions and abbreviations.

# Icons Used in This Book

To make this book easier to use, we've included six icons in the margins to draw your attention to especially noteworthy material. Here's what the icons mean:

This icon highlights inside information, timesaving steps, and expert techniques from coauthor Cesare Casella or another Italian chef.

This icon alerts you to possible problems in executing a recipe. When possible, we provide solutions for fixing a dish if something has gone wrong.

This icon identifies the most important skills involved in Italian cooking and explains how to master them.

This icon steers you clear of potentially disastrous mishaps.

This icon highlights ideas so quick and simple that you save time and effort in the kitchen.

This geographical icon locates regional recipes within a map of Italy. Italy contains 20 separate regions, each with its own distinctive cuisine. This icon tells you where a dish originated.

# Where to Go from Here

Let's face it, Italian stuff is cool. Why do you think Hollywood loves Armani and Versace? Why do car freaks rave about the Ferrari? And think about Sophia Loren. Is there a sexier grandmother?

You may not be able to afford to dress or drive like an Italian (and you can forget about Sophia Loren), but you can eat like an Italian. This book shows you how. It's surprisingly simple. So read on to discover how to think like an Italian cook.

# Part I
# What Is Italian Cooking?

The 5th Wave    By Rich Tennant

"I just don't think asking for extra-virgin ketchup on your hamburger reflects a full appreciation of Italian cuisine."

# In this part . . .

*1* If you've ever eaten pasta or pizza (and who hasn't?), you already know something about Italian cooking. But real Italian cooking, as prepared by home cooks in Italy, is often quite different from the dishes you may enjoy at your local pizza parlor or pasta joint. This part of the book explains the philosophy behind great Italian cooking. (Don't worry, it's simpler than Plato and Aristotle.) We also discuss the ingredients — such as olive oil, balsamic vinegar, and Parmesan cheese — that make Italian cooking so distinctive.

# Chapter 1

# How to Think Like an Italian Chef

*1*f you think that Italian cooking is nothing more than tomato sauce and tiramisù, think again. Italian cooking is one of the world's great cuisines, with a tremendous diversity of flavors and methods of preparation. Many dishes are hundreds of years old, and some have their roots in the Roman Empire. Although Caesar and friends couldn't phone for takeout, they still enjoyed grilled flatbreads not all that different from modern-day pizzas.

Italians have a strong sense of this history, but the rest of the world (and that may include you) probably doesn't. Despite what you may think, Caesar salad wasn't named for the Roman emperor. In fact, Caesar salad isn't even Italian; it first appeared in Mexico in the 1920s. Spaghetti and meatballs was probably invented in Brooklyn, and tiramisù isn't the national dessert of Italy.

Okay, so you may not know what's really Italian and what's just an imitation. If the food tastes good, who really cares about its history and pedigree? Well, the quality of Italian food prepared outside Italy often isn't very high. In fact, some so-called Italian food is pretty awful. For many people, Italian food is fast food, akin to burgers and fries. Like anything that becomes overexposed (think Madonna), Italian cooking has become a victim of its own success.

Throughout this book, we want to help you understand what's really Italian and what's not. With that knowledge, preparing good Italian food is easy. In this chapter, we tell you everything you need to know to think like an Italian chef — and it's surprisingly simple stuff.

# All Cooking Is Local

Ready for your world to come crumbling down? There is no such thing as Italian cooking. Until the late 19th century, Italy wasn't even a unified country. Tremendous regional differences still persist today. Local traditions, coupled with the varying availability of ingredients, has shaped dozens, if not hundreds, of different styles of cooking, or *microcuisines*.

In the 1970s and 1980s, many Italian restaurants in North America and Europe introduced "northern Italian cuisine" to their patrons. They banished spicy tomato sauces and heavy lasagnes; instead they showcased rice dishes and refined pastas with cream sauces. Although this trend helped break the notion of one single Italian cuisine, it confused a lot of people. It left the impression that two Italian cooking traditions exist — one from the South, which is based on tomatoes and olive oil, and another from the North, where butter, cream, rice, homemade pasta, and polenta are king. Although you can find some truth in this generalization, it vastly oversimplifies the true nature of modern Italian cooking.

The Venetians eat quite differently from the Milanese. Both cities are in northern Italy, no more than a few hours apart by train. But the cuisines differ quite a bit. Milan is inland, near agricultural areas that produce rice, corn, and other grains. It's a wealthy city with a long history of meat cookery. Venice rests on the water, so seafood plays a major role in most meals. Venice also served as a crossroads for trade for centuries. You can still detect Mediterranean and Middle Eastern influences in local Venetian cooking today.

Even dishes common to both cuisines are often prepared differently. For example, Venetians tend to prepare a creamier, looser risotto, with grains floating in a sauce of cheese and butter. In Milan, the consistency is firmer and stickier.

This is just one example of the regional differences that still abound in modern Italian cooking. Italy has 20 regions, each with its own distinct personality and traditions. Sicily, for example, has a warm Mediterranean climate that supports the growth of citrus fruits. The island endured numerous invasions and immigrations of people from Greece and North Africa. Couscous, chiles, olives, and capers became important ingredients.

In north-central Italy, the state of Tuscany has a very different climate and topography. And even within Tuscany, there are important distinctions in cooking styles from the coast to the mountainous interior regions. Urban areas, such as Florence and Siena, have their own culinary traditions, many of which date back to the Renaissance.

As former U.S. Speaker of the House Tip O'Neill once said, "All politics is local." The same is true of Italian cooking. Each region has its own distinct tradition. Each is equally Italian, but none is the sole voice of Italian cooking.

# So Many Courses, So Little Time

The Italian meal is a celebration. Tradition dictates that the meal should take at least an hour or two to enjoy. It's a leisurely process, with several distinct courses. The meal, usually eaten at midday, gives families a chance to talk. Eating becomes a communal activity — a time to share news of the day while enjoying the fruits of the cook's labor.

To some extent, modern life has taken its toll on this tradition. Italians compete in a world economy, which means shorter lunches to keep up with developments in New York, Tokyo, or London. And while most Italians are holding fast to their culinary traditions, more and more young Italians are trying things like microwaved dinners and American fast food.

But tradition still remains, especially on weekends and holidays. Even during the week, many people go home for long lunches, and most business comes to a halt in the early afternoon, only to reopen again around three or four. (The Italians we know will give up an afternoon siesta to compete in the global economy, but they won't give up their midday bowl of pasta.)

## Five easy pieces

So what's the structure of the traditional Italian meal? There are actually five components. Not every meal contains all five, but many do.

- ✔ **The antipasto:** A traditional Italian meal starts with something to nibble on, called an *antipasto,* which translates into English as "before the meal." The antipasto may consist of a bowl of marinated olives and some fresh fennel for dipping in extra-virgin olive oil, with a wedge of fine Parmigiano-Reggiano and some bread. You can also serve drinks, such as wine, sparkling water, *prosecco* (the Italian equivalent of champagne), or cocktails (such as Campari and soda). You can serve this part of the meal at the table or, better yet, on the patio or in front of a roaring fire. (For more on antipasti, see Part II.)

- ✔ **The primo:** We know some non-Italian people who consider a pound of pasta dinner for two. The average American family feeds four from a pound of dried pasta. But in Italy, pasta is a first course, or *primo,* served as an appetizer, not as the main event. There, a pound of pasta yields six, or even eight, first-course portions. Soup, rice, and polenta are the other main options for the primo. (For first course ideas, see Part III.)

✔ **The secondo:** After the plates for the first course have been cleared, it's time for the main course (called *il secondo,* or second course). Chicken, meat, or fish are the usual choices, and portions are generally small. These main courses are usually fairly simple, especially if a rich pasta or rice dish precedes them. Italian cooks usually serve a grilled steak, a roast loin of pork, or maybe some sautéed fish. Sauces are usually light or nonexistent. (For more on the main course, see Part IV.)

✔ **The contorno:** A platter of vegetables usually accompanies the main course. This side dish highlights the simple goodness of the vegetable — for example, potatoes roasted with garlic and herbs, peas cooked with bacon and onion, or maybe some oven-roasted asparagus with olive oil and salt. The word *contorno* loosely translates as "contours" and refers to the fact that the vegetable course helps shape and define the meal. It's how the cook connects with the season. Asparagus, peas, and artichokes herald the arrival of spring. Peppers, eggplant, and tomatoes celebrate summer. Broccoli, cauliflower, and mushrooms signal the arrival of cooler fall weather. And carrots, winter squash, and Savoy cabbage round out a winter meal. (See Chapter 14 for more on vegetable side dishes.)

✔ **The dolce:** A *dolce,* or sweet, ends a traditional Italian meal. On most days, the dolce is a bowl of fruit. Some hard Italian cookies, called *biscotti,* and dessert wine for dunking is another option. Italians serve more elaborate cakes, tortes, and custards on special occasions. (See Part V for more information on sweet endings to your meal.)

## Assembling a menu

The structure of an Italian meal ensures that the meal is well balanced. No single component dominates. (Italians are aghast at the notion of serving each person a 12-ounce steak.) The pacing is leisurely so that you can fully enjoy and digest your food. The five-course meal also allows for a good balance of flavors, textures, and colors.

When assembling a menu, keeping all these things in mind is important. You don't want to serve mushroom toast as an antipasto, mushroom risotto as a primo, and then grilled mushrooms as a contorno, unless, of course, you were preparing a special mushroom harvest menu. The Italian chef thinks seasonally and also works with the available ingredients to achieve a varied menu that's still easy to prepare.

A sample menu in fall may look like this:

✔ **The antipasto:** Mushrooms look wonderful at the market but are very expensive, so maybe you buy just a little and serve on toast.

✔ **The primo:** You can continue the autumnal theme with squash-filled ravioli.

- ✔ **The secondo:** Because the ravioli are fairly rich, serving a simple secondo, maybe a roast loin of pork without any sauce, makes sense.

- ✔ **The contorno:** So far, you've served nothing green, so choose a contorno like Swiss chard or spinach that complements the pork but also rounds out the entire menu.

- ✔ **The dolce:** If you are choosing a fruit dessert, think apples or pears rather than strawberries. A nut dessert would also work fine in this menu.

Planning a traditional Italian meal is like putting together a jigsaw puzzle. Start with the facts that you can't change, such as your budget, the number of people coming to dinner, the amount of time you can devote to cooking, or the availability of ingredients. (See the section "The Three Tenets of Italian Cooking," later in this chapter, for more information.) These facts are the corner pieces of the puzzle, the ones you should put into place first. Perhaps you have a lot of tomatoes sitting on the counter, and they're looking very ripe. Or maybe you want to keep things light and avoid dishes with cream or butter. Next, you can start playing with the other components of the meal, making them fit as necessary. When you've struck the right balance, the result is a culinary mosaic, attractive to both the eye and the palate. (For menu ideas, see Part VI.)

## *Adapting this tradition for the 21st century*

Unfortunately, five-course meals aren't terribly practical, especially if you're pressed for time like most cooks we know. There is that thing called life, with jobs to do and kids to tend. For holidays, the traditional Italian meal structure may help, but day-in and day-out, most cooks need to assemble meals with fewer components. Italian cooking is flexible in this regard. Tradition dictates a certain course of action, but reality has a way of changing the rules.

So how can you make this structure work when you get home from work at 5:30 p.m. and the kids are screaming for dinner? Here are some lessons for making more with less. All these solutions attempt to accommodate the Italian preference for balance, while keeping your work to a minimum.

- ✔ **Serve a secondo with two contorni, making sure that the vegetables complement each other.** Oven-roasted mushrooms and sautéed spinach work together. However, you don't want to serve broccoli with the spinach — too much green.

- ✔ **Beef up the primo and forget about the secondo.** A double portion of pasta or risotto can make a meal, especially if accompanied by a vegetable side dish or salad.

✔ **Serve an antipasto or two and then skip right to the secondo.** This alternative is better for casual entertaining than for weeknight dinners, but it allows you to add some pacing to the meal without a lot of extra cooking or cleanup. You can always buy the antipasto — cheese, marinated olives, and so on — to save even more work.

✔ **Choose a few kinds of fruit and place them in an attractive bowl.** Italians know that fruit, if well presented, makes a light, but impressive, ending to a meal. You're already in the market to shop for dinner, and assembling a fruit bowl at home takes less than five minutes.

# The Three Tenets of Italian Cooking

Understanding the structure of an Italian meal is one part of the process. But how do you capture the style, the poetry, of Italian cooking? How do you think like an Italian chef?

To help, we've devised three simple rules. We call them the three tenets. No, we're not talking about the Three Tenors. We're talking philosophical beliefs, not opera singing. These tenets are a way of life. When you're in the kitchen or at the market and are trying to make a split-second decision, keep these points in mind.

Italians learn these rules as they grow up. They watch their parents and grandparents in the kitchen. For everyone who doesn't have the benefit of cultural osmosis, some practice is in order. Eventually though, these tenets become second nature.

## Be spontaneous

Accomplished Italian chefs are flexible and creative. They react to the situation at hand and adjust accordingly. To prevent making mistakes, think of a recipe as an outline. Make a dish once and then feel free to change nonessential elements as you like to make use of the ingredients on hand or accommodate other constraints, such as time or money. For example, after you master the technique of making a *frittata,* an Italian open-faced omelet, you can vary the flavorings and seasonings. The eggs are a constant, as is the cooking technique. But you can use sautéed onions rather than shallots or change cooked green beans to cooked asparagus if you like.

The trick to successful spontaneous cooking is knowing when to stop and when one change necessitates another. For example, if you don't have enough eggs, don't try to make a frittata with less. This is an egg dish after all, and if the recipe calls for six eggs, four eggs just won't work.

Spontaneous cooking also requires some common sense. Say you don't have fresh oregano, but you see a jar of dried oregano in the cupboard. You also know that for every teaspoon of fresh herb, you generally substitute one-quarter to one-third of a teaspoon. (See Chapter 2 for more information on using fresh and dried herbs.) But as you can see from the following example, a little knowledge can be dangerous.

A salad that calls for several leaves of fresh oregano isn't the place to get spontaneous and substitute dried oregano. Think ahead. Do you really want to eat tough, little bits of dried oregano in a salad? Of course not. (Another fresh herb, such as thyme or basil, would be a better substitute.) But say you're making a soup that calls for fresh oregano. This dish turns out fine with dried oregano because the tiny flakes soften and release their flavor into the liquid.

And remember, all cooks, even good ones, make mistakes occasionally. If you can learn from your mistakes, they're worth the inconvenience. If you continue to make the same mistakes over and over, then recognize your creative limitations and vow to follow recipes in both spirit and letter.

## Act seasonally

Italians approach shopping and menu planning quite differently than Americans do. With large refrigerators and crowded supermarkets, Americans try to shop once a week. They may make quick runs to convenience stores for bread or milk, but they generally purchase vegetables, meats, staples, and other items once a week. This makes menu planning a challenge, especially toward the end of the week when any "fresh" foods left in the refrigerator are looking old and tired.

Italians keep the kitchen stocked with certain staples — pastas, rices, cornmeal — but for the most part, they visit the market daily to pick up fresh fruits, vegetables, and meats. Italians have traditionally shopped this way, and because their refrigerators are about the size of a dishwasher, they still keep to this routine.

Because Italian cooks shop daily, they're more likely to plan menus seasonally. The Italian cook reacts to what looks good at the market and often composes a menu at the market, not at home. Shopping without a list may seem impossible (and it is if you expect to pick up a week's worth of groceries at one time), but it doesn't have to be. Shopping without a list (or with a minimal list that you change as you survey what's available) gives you flexibility and allows you to take advantage of the best seasonal produce. Shopping becomes an adventure, and you get a certain sense of pride and accomplishment (as well as excitement) when you purchase the first asparagus of spring, take them home, and turn them into a wonderful sauce for pasta or a base for a vegetable risotto.

If all this sounds hopelessly romantic, then think about this strategy. Keep your kitchen filled with basics. If you like pasta, keep an assortment of shapes on hand. If you like risotto, make sure you have some arborio rice in the cupboard. Use your weekly big marketing trips to stock up on these items, as well as meats and poultry, which can go in the freezer. Make sure that you always keep vegetables that last for weeks (like onions and garlic), as well as oils and vinegars, on hand. Then stop at a natural food store or produce market a couple of times a week and get inspired. The lines are shorter, and the produce is better at these stores. If you know that you have steak defrosting in the refrigerator, you can pick up zucchini, eggplant, peppers, onions, asparagus, or whatever looks good to round out the meal.

## Get fresh

Italian cooking has changed the way chefs around the world think about food. In most of Europe and North America, French cooking was the dominant force in professional kitchens for much of the last century. But tastes have changed in the past two decades. Diners and chefs have come to prefer fresher, bolder flavors. Unpretentious Italian cooking has whisked the heavy French sauces of past generations into the history books.

Why has Italian cooking been so successful? Because, above all else, Italian cooking stresses freshness. Why eat a tomato that has been shipped three thousand miles and gassed along the way to change its color from green to red? It may look pretty, but how does it taste? And why use dried herbs, which don't have all that much flavor, if the supermarket stocks a dozen fresh herbs? (Italians rarely use dried herbs, and neither do we.)

Good Italian cooking reveals the true essence of ingredients. It's honest and direct. No elaborate sauces mask inferior cuts of meat or tired vegetables. The ingredients should be as fresh as possible and should be presented with a minimum of fuss. Starting with less-than-fresh ingredients makes your work more difficult. Start with really fresh ingredients that taste good, and your work is almost done.

Putting freshness above all else makes your cooking pretty good. Adding some traditional Italian techniques (which we share with you in this book) makes your cooking great. All this sounds easy because it is.

# Chapter 2

# The Italian Kitchen: Ingredients and Equipment

*I*n this chapter, we detail most of the key ingredients that we use throughout this book, except for vegetables, rice, and pasta — all of which we devote individual chapters to. Here, we focus on the building-block ingredients used again and again in Italian cooking, offering tips on buying, storing, preparing, and using everything from fresh basil to Kalamata olives.

We also help you figure out what's important and what's not when shopping for Italian ingredients. In many ways, being a good shopper is the first step to becoming a good cook. Italian food is so simple that the quality of the ingredients really matters. If you do any Italian cooking, most of the ingredients that we talk about in this chapter quickly become essential.

Although Italian cooking relies on a wide array of sometimes unfamiliar ingredients, the equipment used in the Italian kitchen is fairly straightforward. If you cook at home, you probably already own the most essential pieces of equipment — knives, pots, pans, and cutting boards — that you need to make most Italian recipes. We tell you about some traditional Italian kitchen tools — ranging from the essential (a cheese grater) to the curious (a mortar and pestle) — that you can use in many recipes. (We discuss tools with very specific uses, such as pasta machines, in the appropriate chapters.)

# *Beyond Armani and Gucci: Where to Shop for Italian Ingredients*

Italians sure make shopping fun. What would fashion be without Armani and Gucci? Unfortunately, shopping for Italian ingredients isn't as easy as shopping for Italian designer suits, which you can find in malls across the globe. We often find ourselves scanning the shelves at a number of markets to find the exact ingredients that we need in the kitchen. Here are our thoughts on some possible sources. Take a look at the Yellow Pages and ask friends for specific suggestions.

- **Supermarkets:** The typical North American supermarket carries a fairly good range of basic Italian food products. Most supermarkets carry the important vegetables (garlic, onions, and tomatoes), herbs (everything from fresh sage to fresh mint in tiny plastic pouches, usually near bundles of parsley and basil), and olive oils. Some supermarkets may even carry a few Italian cheeses and a couple of brands of jarred olives.

- **Gourmet shops:** The prices may be high, but most gourmet shops have a better selection of extra-virgin olive oils and vinegars than your average supermarket. Gourmet shops are also good places to find two important Italian pork products: pancetta and prosciutto. If your supermarket doesn't carry dried porcini mushrooms or arborio rice, the local gourmet shop should. Many gourmet shops also marinate their own olives and sell them loose.

- **Italian markets and delicatessens:** Communities with large Italian-American populations usually have a couple of Italian markets that sell prepared foods. (You can pick up many good antipasti at these markets.) Most Italian markets also stock an excellent selection of meats and cheeses (some even make their own mozzarella). You may find some high-quality olive oils at reasonable prices. These markets are also your best bet for hard-to-find items like imported instant *polenta* or precooked and dried cornmeal.

- **Natural-food stores:** For vegetable lovers (and anyone who cooks Italian food should love vegetables), natural-food stores are often the best source for the freshest vegetables and fruits. Natural-food markets are more likely to stock local, organic produce and usually have a good supply of fresh herbs and grains, such as arborio rice, polenta, and dried beans.

# Essential Ingredients

Italian food relies on a number of key ingredients to give dishes their distinctive flavor. For example, just try to imagine Italian cooking without garlic, onions, and olive oil.

And sometimes the choices can be confusing. Some of these products are imported, and labels aren't always clear. In other cases, the choices are astounding. Decent cheese shops may carry a dozen or more Italian cheeses. Even the most basic supermarket stocks half a dozen or more olive oils, and some gourmet stores may have 20 or 30 different brands.

In the following sections, we show you how to choose quality Italian ingredients.

## Grate expectations: Cheeses for cooking and eating

Italians are rightly famous for their cheeses. Parmesan cheese is used the world over to flavor pasta dishes, as well as egg, rice, and meat dishes. When shopping for cheeses, here are some guidelines to help you:

- **Search for only fresh cheeses.** Shop from a store that handles the cheese properly and does a brisk business so that nothing sits around for very long. A wedge cut to order is fresher than a precut and wrapped wedge.

- **Taste everything before you buy.** Good cheese shops unwrap cheeses and cut off small slices for you to sample.

- **Buy Italian.** Many Parmesan and other Italian cheeses made in the United States, Argentina, Canada, Denmark, and Switzerland lack the full flavor of the original. Read labels, which usually cite the country of origin. If in doubt, ask someone.

You have hundreds of Italian cheeses to choose from. Most, however, aren't exported. The following sections describe some of the most popular and useful Italian cheeses. Some are sold in supermarkets. All are readily available at a good cheese shop or gourmet store.

### Fontina

Real Fontina cheese from Valle d'Aosta in the far north is rich and creamy with a buttery, nutty flavor. This is a fine eating cheese. (You would never eat some cheeses as is, like ricotta or mascarpone — they're just for cooking.) Let it come to room temperature, and it becomes soft. Fontina never gets runny like brie, but it shouldn't be firm, either. You can eat Fontina as is, or because it melts so well, you can use it in sandwiches or pizzas.

Avoid Fontina from other sources. Most supermarkets carry a rubbery, bland Fontina cheese from Denmark or Sweden with a texture more like Cheddar and absolutely no flavor.

### Gorgonzola

Italy's prized blue cheese can be made in various styles. Sometimes Gorgonzola is dry and crumbly and has an intense blue cheese flavor similar to Roquefort, a popular blue cheese from France. Although this aged cheese is fine for nibbling, when cooking we generally prefer a milder, creamier type of Gorgonzola called *dolce* or *dolce latte* — "sweet" or "sweet milk." The texture is creamy, and the distinctive blue cheese flavor isn't overpowering.

If you can't find Italian Gorgonzola dolce, you might try Saga Blue, a Danish blue cheese readily available in supermarkets. The flavor isn't as distinctive as Gorgonzola, but Saga Blue is milder and creamier than most supermarket blue cheeses.

### Mascarpone

This Italian version of cream cheese often appears in desserts. (It's essential in the trendy tiramisù.) You can also use Mascarpone to enrich pasta sauces or fillings. The imported and domestic versions of this fresh cheese are all pretty good and are sold in plastic tubs. Mascarpone has a light, creamy texture and buttery flavor. Don't try to substitute American cream cheese. The texture is much stiffer, and the flavor is quite different. Mascarpone has a short shelf life, so pay attention to expiration dates when shopping and try to use the cheese quickly.

### Mozzarella

You can find so many styles of this important Italian cheese that figuring out where to start may seem hard. The original mozzarella was made from the milk of water buffalo and was called *mozzarella di bufala,* which is fairly hard to find in Italy and downright scarce elsewhere. It tastes best when incredibly fresh (no more than a few days old) and doesn't ship all that well.

Most fresh mozzarella (the fresh cheese is packed in water, not shrink-wrapped) is made from cow's milk and called *fiore di latte*. The flavor is milky and sweet, and the texture is springy, yet yielding. You should eat this cheese as is, in a simple mozzarella, tomato, and basil salad (see Chapter 4) or perhaps marinated in olive oil and served as an antipasto. When cooked, it loses some of its delicacy.

When buying fresh mozzarella, try to get cheese that has been made that day. Mozzarella starts to go downhill after a day or two, and after three or four days, it's usually not worth eating. The cheese should look white and have a fresh, sweet smell. If the cheese smells at all sour or looks dried out, go to another shop. When you get fresh mozzarella home, use it immediately. If you must keep it for a few days, refrigerate the cheese in a container filled with enough very lightly salted water to cover the cheese.

Fresh mozzarella is made by hand and is usually sold in large balls that weigh between half a pound and one pound. You can also find smaller balls, usually no more than an ounce or two. Look for words that indicate size, such as *bocconcini* ("little mouthfuls") or *ciliegine* ("little cherries"), when shopping.

Of course, most of the world relies on shrink-wrapped versions of mozzarella cheese that are rubbery and bland. Never use these cheeses in a dish in which you don't cook the cheese. We prefer fresh mozzarella in pizzas, but you can use supermarket mozzarella in cooked dishes. When the cheese melts, the rubbery texture is less of a problem, and if you include other assertive ingredients (tomato sauce and pizza toppings), you may not notice that the cheese has no flavor.

### *Parmesan*

Parmigiano-Reggiano is the king of Italian cheeses. This name is given to the finest aged Parmesan cheese produced in the Parma area in northern Italy. Another Italian Parmesan cheese, called Grana Padano, is quite good, but nothing compares to the real thing.

Although you may balk at paying $12 a pound for Parmigiano-Reggiano, most recipes call for very little, and the cheese delivers a large impact. Freshly grated Parmigiano-Reggiano (don't buy pregrated cheese; it dries out and loses much of its flavor) has a rich, buttery, nutty flavor. It's so good that Italians often break off tiny pieces from a hunk of Parmigiano-Reggiano and eat the cheese with drinks as an appetizer.

When shopping for Parmigiano-Reggiano, try to buy small wedges (about half a pound is a good size for grating) that have been freshly cut from a whole wheel of the cheese. A whole wheel weighs at least 65 pounds and has the words *Parmigiano-Reggiano* stenciled on the rind. When buying wedges, check the rind to make sure that part of this stenciling appears — this is the only way to know that you're getting the real thing. You can wrap Parmigiano-Reggiano in waxed paper or plastic wrap and keep it in the refrigerator for several weeks, at least.

If Parmigiano-Reggiano is just too expensive for your budget, look for Grana Padano, an Italian cheese made in the same region but usually not aged quite as long. Although not as complex, this cheese is still quite delicious, and it often costs much less (sometimes half as much) than Parmigiano-Reggiano.

We're less impressed with Parmesan cheeses made in the United States and South America. They tend to be much saltier and lack the subtlety and flavor of the real thing. And as for grated Parmesan in a can, we'd rather sprinkle sawdust on our food!

### Pecorino

Pecorino is traditionally made from sheep's milk, although some manufacturers add some cow's milk to reduce the pungency or save money. In Italy, Pecorino is usually sold fresh or lightly aged and is served as an eating cheese. Young Pecorino isn't widely known elsewhere. Most of the exported Pecorino has been aged much longer. Like Parmesan, aged Pecorino is designed for grating, but it has a much saltier and more pungent flavor.

Most exported Pecorino is from the Rome area, hence the name Pecorino Romano. (Pecorino cheeses are also made in Sardinia, Sicily, and Tuscany.) Pecorino Romano is bone-white cheese that has an intense peppery flavor. Like Parmigiano-Reggiano, the words *Pecorino Romano* appear stenciled on the rind to make shopping for the authentic product easy. Many American-made Pecorino cheeses taste of salt and nothing else; you should avoid these American varieties.

Pecorino is best in dishes with assertive ingredients, such as capers, olives, or hot red pepper flakes. Pecorino also works well with vegetables like eggplant and zucchini. Pecorino is widely used in Sicilian and Sardinian dishes.

### Ricotta

Like mozzarella, ricotta should be freshly made and consumed within a few days. It should be creamy and thick, not watery and curdish like so many supermarket brands sold in plastic containers. In Italy, local cheese makers produce fresh ricotta with a dry, firm consistency (akin to goat cheese). The flavor is sweet and milky. This cheese is so perishable that it's rarely exported.

In the United States, you can get fresh, locally made ricotta in and near urban centers with large Italian-American populations. This cheese shares many qualities with the Italian versions. These U.S. versions are especially good in ricotta cheesecakes and pasta sauces or fillings, in which the cheese is the main ingredient.

You can use supermarket ricotta cheese, but it's bland and the texture mushy and unappealing. You might try draining supermarket ricotta in a fine-mesh strainer for an hour or two to remove some of the water. This can improve the texture, but you can't really do anything to improve its flavor.

# An ode to garlic and onions

Oh, how do we love garlic and onions? Let us count the ways. Well, if you read closely, you can see that more than half the recipes in this book contain one or both of these ingredients — and that makes a lot of ways.

Many Italian recipes begin by sautéing onions or garlic in olive oil. These two *alliums* (a family of vegetables that also includes leeks, chives, and scallions) provide the flavor base for pasta sauces, rice dishes, roasts, vegetable side dishes, and more.

Although many Americans fear that onions and, in particular, garlic give food a harsh, overpowering flavor, this rarely happens in good Italian cooking. Italian cooks use the onions and garlic like salt to help bring out the flavors in other ingredients. They are infrequently the focal point of a dish and should never be so prominent that they're objectionable.

You must use a light hand, especially with the garlic. Two cloves can make a pasta sauce delicious. Use eight cloves only if you're expecting vampires that night. Also, cooking garlic over moderate heat (not high heat — the garlic burns and becomes bitter) tames its flame and brings out its sweeter notes. You should finely mince garlic (smaller pieces cook evenly and are less likely to burn that larger pieces) and cook it until golden.

Cooking also changes the flavor of onions. The harshness fades, and the onions become sweeter as they start to color. The darker the onions become, the sweeter and more caramelized their flavor. Only when onions are burned do they become bitter.

When shopping for garlic, look for firm bulbs with no green sprouts or shoots. When shopping for onions, pick up red onions for most recipes. Yellow onions are also used (especially in the north), but red onions are the standard in most Italian recipes. Unless otherwise indicated, recipes in this book use red onions, although you can use yellow onions with a slight difference in flavor.

Store garlic and onions at room temperature. They should stay fresh for weeks.

To peel garlic, simply use the side of a chef's knife to crush the cloves and loosen the papery skin, as shown in Figure 2-1.

**Figure 2-1:**
Peeling
garlic.

Use the side of a large chef's knife to press down on a garlic clove and loosen the papery skin...

Im free!

To prepare an onion for cooking, follow these steps, as shown in Figure 2-2:

1. **To peel the onion, cut off the stem and cut the onion in half through the ends. Gently lift off the dry outer layers of skin.**

2. **Lay the halves down on a work surface. To chop or mince, make parallel lengthwise cuts, starting just in from the root end.**

   Keep the root end intact to keep the onion layers from separating.

3. **Turn the knife so that it's horizontal to the work surface and slice through the onion, again leaving the root end intact.**

   For small onions, one slice is fine; larger onions require several slices to produce finely minced pieces.

4. **Cut across the onion to turn out pieces of the desired size.**

### How to Mince an Onion

**1.** Cut off stem. Cut in half through the root. Peel off skin

**2.** Make parallel lengthwise cuts. don't cut through root end!

**3.** Cut horizontal slices from top to bottom. not all the way through!

**4.** Now cut crosswise

**Figure 2-2:**
Cutting an
onion.

## Herbs: The importance of being fresh

Dried herbs have almost no place in Italian cooking. Sure, Italian cooks use dried bay leaves to flavor soups and beans as they cook. And some Italian cooks may add a pinch of dried oregano to a tomato sauce as it cooks. But that's it. Otherwise, Italian cooks use fresh herbs. Why? Because fresh herbs taste a lot better than dried herbs do.

Fresh herbs have all their aromatic oils. Dried herbs are weak and often about as tasty as fallen leaves. If you have any doubts, rub a fresh sage leaf between your fingers. The aroma is intoxicating and immediately recalls the woods. Next, open a jar of dried sage. You can detect some aroma, but it's faint and one-dimensional.

Most supermarkets carry a half dozen or more fresh herbs. (See Figure 2-3 for help in identifying herbs that are not labeled in stores.) And if you do any gardening at all, we recommend throwing a few herbs in the ground every spring. It takes very little time, the plants require minimal mainte-nance, and you end up with a steady supply of fresh herbs all summer, at great savings. Put plants into the ground or in clay pots and make sure that they get a lot of sun and some water every day or two.

One final note about herbs: If you can't get the fresh herb specified in a particular recipe, think about using another fresh herb rather than the dried equivalent. A dish may not taste the same, but it can still turn out to be delicious. For example, a fresh tomato sauce with fresh basil is equally good with fresh mint or parsley, but dried basil adds little to the sauce.

Herbs do vary in intensity, so when substituting, try to pick something with a similar punch, or be prepared to adjust the amount of herb. We find that parsley and basil are the mildest herbs, and you can use them in the greatest amount. Mint, chives, and tarragon are more potent; you should use them

Figure 2-3: Fresh herbs are a key ingredient in Italian cooking.

with a lighter hand. Thyme, oregano, marjoram, and rosemary are the most potent — use them sparingly. Table 2-1 lists the most important herbs used in Italian cooking.

| Table 2-1 | | Favorite Herbs for Italian Cooking |
|---|---|---|
| *Herb* | *Italian Name* | *Description* |
| Basil | Basilico | Italy's best known herb, basil has a strong anise flavor. A must in pesto, basil is a natural with tomatoes. (Basil's sweetness works nicely with the acidity in the tomatoes.) Tarragon, which isn't widely used in Italy, has a similar anise flavor, and you can use it as a substitute. You can also use parsley in most recipes calling for basil. |
| Bay leaf | Alloro | Once sold only dried, this herb is increasingly available fresh as well. Dried leaves are often dropped into a pot of simmering beans or soup to impart their gentle aroma. You can use fresh leaves, which tend to be longer and thinner, in the same fashion. |
| Marjoram | Maggiorana | This herb is similar to oregano but milder in flavor. Popular in the Riviera, marjoram is good with meats and seafood. |
| Mint | Menta | You can find hundreds of kinds of mint. Some are mild and sweet; others spicy and hot. Mint is used more in southern Italy and has an intensity and freshness similar to basil, which is perhaps the best substitute. |
| Oregano | Origano | This herb has a potent aroma and flavor that predominates in much southern Italian cooking and is used commonly with tomatoes. |
| Parsley | Prezzemolo | This herb is the unheralded star of Italian cooking. Basil may get all the attention, but parsley is more widely used. Flat-leaf varieties have a stronger flavor than curly-leaf varieties. You can cook parsley with garlic and onions in olive oil to form the flavor base for many dishes. |
| Rosemary | Rosmarino | With rosemary's strong resinous (or pine) aroma and flavor, you must use it sparingly. The tough needles need time to soften, and you shouldn't add it to dishes that you don't cook. Rosemary is a natural with potatoes, chicken, lamb, and beef. |

| Herb | Italian Name | Description |
|------|--------------|-------------|
| Sage | Salvia | Sage is especially popular in Tuscany and other parts of central and northern Italy. Sage is pungent with a musty mint taste and has an affinity for butter sauces, as well as pork and chicken. |
| Thyme | Timo | Diminutive thyme leaves pack a surprising punch. Many varieties have a lemony flavor. Thyme isn't as widely used in Italy as other herbs. |

# You salty thing!

Italians use anchovies, capers, and olives to make simple dishes taste special. These ingredients are especially popular in southern Italy and add a salty, piquant flavor to dishes. Italian cooks commonly use them with tomatoes, either singly or in combination.

### Anchovies

Anchovies are small fish that are especially popular in Sicilian cooking. These fish are often filleted, packed in oil, and canned. This is the most common form found in North American markets. Try to pick brands with olive oil as the packing medium. The anchovies taste better, and you can use the oil. For example, in many recipes, you cook the anchovies fillets in oil (either from the can or fresh oil) and mash them until they dissolve. This way, the anchovies impart their briny, fishy flavor to a dish without diners having to encounter large chunks that could otherwise prove overwhelmingly salty.

### Capers

Capers are the preserved green flower buds of a bush that grows all around the Mediterranean. Capers are usually packed in a brine made with white vinegar, salt, and water, which acts as a preservative. Capers are also packed in salt, although this variety doesn't keep well ( brined capers stay fresh in the refrigerator indefinitely) and is hard to find.

You need to drain brined capers before use and rinse them to remove excess saltiness and the vinegar flavor. You must rinse salted capers thoroughly. Capers come in a variety of sizes — you can add very small whole capers to dishes; you should chop larger capers.

### Olives

You have dozens of varieties of olives to choose from, each with a different shape, size, and color. Unlike other fruits (olives are like cherries, a pitted fruit that arises from tree blossoms), you must cure olives before eating them. Straight from the tree, they're bitter and inedible.

When olives are picked before they fully ripen, the color is green. As olives ripen on the tree, they turn black or purple. After olives are harvested, all olives (whether they're picked green or black) are soaked in a weak alkali solution to remove some of the bitterness. They're then washed and put in a vinegar, salt, and water solution. (Some black olives are dry-cured in oil and salt. The result is a meaty, very salty olive, better for cooking rather than eating out of hand.)

Never buy canned olives, which usually come from California. These olives have been boiled and pitted, a process that strips all character from the olives and leaves them bland and mushy. Jarred imported olives are a fine choice, as are olives sold loose in brine at the deli counter. Of course, you must taste to find a variety and brand you like. We describe some of the most popular varieties in Table 2-2.

To remove olive pits, try using a cherry pitter, or place olives on a cutting board and use the side of a large chef's knife or cleaver to lightly crush the olives. After the olives have split, popping out the pit and chopping the flesh should be easy.

| Table 2-2 | Popular Olive Varieties |
|---|---|
| *Variety* | *Description* |
| Cerignola | This enormous olive from Apulia is sold both green and black. The green variety is actually an alluring blue-green color, and the flavor is mild and vegetal. When black, the flesh is softer and sweeter, and the pit is much easier to remove. Sometimes called Bella di Cerignola. |
| Gaeta | Gaeta is an excellent, small brownish black olive that can be hard to pit, but the flavor, which is reminiscent of nuts, is worth the effort. |
| Kalamata | A plump, purplish black Greek variety that is especially popular in U.S. markets and a good choice in most recipes calling for black olives. Can be fairly salty. Sometimes spelled Calamata. |
| Niçoise | This small, brownish purple variety grows in southern France. Removing the large pits from these chewy, flavorful olives is hard. Often, these olives are added whole to salads, and you must remove the flesh with your teeth before spitting out the pit. You can use this variety in place of Gaeta olives. |
| Oil-Cured | These wrinkled black olives have a meaty, chewy texture and are often very salty. They're popular in Sicily. |
| Sicilian Green | Sometimes called Sicilian Colossals, these oversized olives have a dense, somewhat sour or tart flesh. You can use other green olives, like the popular Manzanilla or Sevillano from Spain, in their place, but they are rarely as tart. |

One final tip: Always keep olives packed in their brine to keep them from drying out. Instead of draining them, we usually use a long spoon to fish out olives from the jar, one at a time. Rinsing brined olives to remove some of the vinegar before using them in recipes is also a good idea.

# Liquid gold: Olive oil or nothing

Perhaps more than any other ingredient, olive oil gives Italian cooking its distinctive flavor. Italian olive oils are rightly regarded as the world's finest, although excellent oils also come from Spain, Greece, North Africa, the Middle East, and California. But Italian oils set the standard. In fact, many oils with Italian names are actually made from olives grown elsewhere that are shipped to Italy for processing.

A lot has been written about olive oil in the past decade, and some of it has been quite confusing. Here's what we think you need to know.

When shopping, you're likely to encounter three types of olive oil: extra virgin, pure, and light. The first two names refer to grades. Extra-virgin oils are extracted from olives by cold mechanical pressure and have the best flavor and lowest acidity. Traditionally, the olives were placed between straw mats and ground between heavy stones powered by animals, much the way flour was once milled. Modern equipment has made the process faster, but without heat or solvents, the olives don't give up all their oil. When heat or solvents are applied to increase the yield, the oil is called "pure." Pure oils are relatively characterless.

The third kind of olive oil sold in the United States is called light olive oil. Despite the name, it has the same nutritional profile as other olive oils. However, this oil has been stripped of all flavor, hence the name "light." Brilliant marketers thought that the real stuff scared Americans because of its strong flavor. But that's the beauty of olive oil. Unlike corn or vegetable oil, it adds something to dishes besides fat and calories. If you want a bland oil, buy corn oil or canola oil. If you want olive oil, buy the real thing.

Olive oil can be refined and filtered (as are most extra-virgin oils sold in supermarkets, as well as all pure oils), or they can be left relatively untouched and sold with lots of sediment. Many premium Italian oils available in gourmet shops come to market this way. In general, the less the oil is processed, the more likely that the oil has captured all the nuances from the olives.

In our kitchens, we use extra-virgin olive oil for almost everything. (We use pure olive oil for deep-frying.) When sautéing, we turn to a relatively inexpensive extra-virgin olive oil from the supermarket. At $10 a liter, these oils aren't cheap, but they have much more character than pure oils. Many of these oils are bottled in Italy but aren't really Italian oils. But they're good enough for everyday use.

When using the oil raw (in salad dressing or to drizzle over a piece of cooked fish or some vegetables), we use an unrefined extra-virgin olive oil from a small Italian producer. Sometimes called estate oils, these oils represent the finest quality. They often cost $20 or $30 a liter or more, but the aroma and flavor are unmatched. Some of these oils are spicy, while others are gentle with the flavor of almonds, artichokes, or even flowers dominating.

When shopping for an estate oil, look to see whether the oil is clear or cloudy. A little cloudiness indicates that the oil hasn't been filtered excessively. Note that filtering does prolong shelf life, so make sure that you use unfiltered oils quickly, within six months. Also read the label. An oil made from Italian olives has a label that says "produced and bottled in Italy." If you don't see these words, assume that the manufacturer used some non-Italian olives, even if the label says "imported from Italy."

Color, which ranges from golden to green, indicates the type of olives and their ripeness but isn't a gauge of quality. If you can, try to smell an open bottle of the oil. An oil that smells good probably tastes good. You should also detect nuances when smelling the oil. Some oils smell like grass or herbs; others smell like almonds or flowers. Eventually, you find traits that you enjoy, but the important thing is that the oil has some character.

## *Pancetta and prosciutto*

Many Italian soups, pasta sauces, rice dishes, and stews rely on small amounts of pork to add flavor and richness. *Pancetta* (see Figure 2-4) is unsmoked Italian bacon that's salted and spiced and rolled up into a log that looks like salami. When sliced, you can see spirals of pink meat surrounded by milky white fat. You usually slice pancetta thin (like other cold cuts). For most recipes, you want to chop it quite fine as well.

American bacon is an imperfect substitute because it's smoked. If you can't find pancetta, try cooking strips of regular bacon in simmering water for a minute or two to remove some of the smoky flavor. More and more supermarkets carry pancetta, as do most gourmet stores and all Italian delis. If you like, you can freeze pancetta in small packages and just pull it out as needed.

*Prosciutto* (see Figure 2-4) is salted and air-cured ham. Like pancetta, you often cook prosciutto along with aromatic vegetables, such as onions and carrots, to establish a flavor base. Of course, you can also serve prosciutto as is for appetizers or use it in pizza toppings. *Prosciutto crudo* is the standard product that has been cured but not cooked. *Prosciutto cotto* has been cooked, like a boiled or Virginia ham. Unless a recipe says otherwise, use prosciutto crudo.

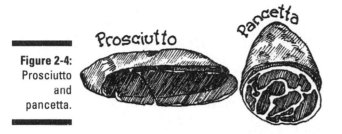

**Figure 2-4:**
Prosciutto
and
pancetta.

## *Flavor in a bag: Dried porcini mushrooms*

The porcini is a favorite mushroom, with a rich, earthy, meaty flavor. Italians enjoy this mushroom fresh as well as dried. In the United States, fresh porcini are expensive and extremely hard to find. However, most supermarkets and gourmet shops now sell dried porcini at reasonable prices.

Dried porcini come in small plastic packets, weighing between $1/2$ ounce and 2 ounces. When buying porcini, look for pieces that are large, thick, and tan or brown in color, rather than black. If the mushrooms are thin and brittle with lots of dust and crumbled pieces mixed in, find another source.

To reconstitute dried porcini, place the mushrooms in a small bowl and add just enough hot tap water to cover them. When the mushrooms have softened (about 20 minutes later), carefully lift the mushrooms from the liquid with a fork. Because all mushrooms grow in soil, they can be sandy. Usually, most of the grit falls into the soaking liquid. which is why you use a fork to lift the floating mushrooms from the liquid, without stirring up the grit at the bottom of the bowl. As a precaution, run your fingers over the softened porcini. If you feel any grit, rinse them under cold water. If the mushrooms feel clean, don't bother to rinse them because the water can wash away some of their flavor. The porcini are now ready for you to chop and add to dishes.

The soaking liquid is extremely flavorful; you should never discard it. However, you need to strain the grit from the liquid. The easiest way to do this is to line a small mesh strainer with a coffee filter or single piece of paper towel. Set the lined strainer over a measuring cup and pour the liquid through. Carefully discard the filter or paper towel (you should see the sediment) and then use the liquid along with the mushrooms. If, for some reason, you have leftover soaking liquid, place it in an ice-cube tray in the freezer. When frozen, pop out the cubes, put them in an airtight container, and use the cubes to perk up the flavor of sauces, soups, or stews.

## *Tomatoes*

Imagining Italian cooking without tomatoes is hard. "Red sauce" is almost synonymous with Italian cooking. Many people are surprised to discover that tomatoes originated in the New World and first came to Europe only after Columbus brought them back from the Americas. Eventually, Italians adopted tomatoes as their own, using them in everything from salads and soups to pasta sauces and pizzas. However, contrary to popular belief, most Italian dishes don't contain tomatoes.

Italians love tomatoes, but they hate bad tomatoes. Unfortunately, the tomato has been much abused in the name of progress. In order to keep our markets stocked with tomatoes 365 days a year, geneticists, farmers, and marketers have engineered tomatoes that look great but taste horrible. Most of the perfectly round, red orbs that fill supermarket bins are picked when green, shipped thousands of miles, and then gassed to turn them red. They are designed for the shopper who selects food based on appearance rather than flavor. Ugh!

We suggest that you buy local, in-season tomatoes for dishes in which you don't cook the tomatoes. If it's January and you live in New York or Toronto, please don't make a tomato salad with mozzarella and basil. Choose another recipe instead of trying to make this dish with tomatoes from Holland, Israel, Mexico, or a hothouse.

When we want the flavor of tomatoes out of season, we rely on canned tomatoes (at least they're picked ripe) or oval plum tomatoes, which are also called *Roma* tomatoes. Plum tomatoes are not as juicy as round (also called *beefsteak*) tomatoes and don't have as many seeds. Their flesh is usually quite firm (one reason we don't think that most plum tomatoes are worth eating raw), but they do add fresh tomato flavor and texture to cooked dishes.

When preparing tomatoes, remove the *core* — the small brown patch at the stem end. You can then slice or dice the tomatoes as needed. When cooking tomatoes, we often remove the peel first (the skin separates from the flesh and isn't terribly appealing) by submerging the tomatoes in simmering water for ten seconds and then peeling the skin with our fingers (see Figure 2-5). Summer tomatoes are often quite juicy, which can be a problem when adding them to cooked dishes. In some cases, we seed the tomatoes before chopping them.

**Figure 2-5:**
When using tomatoes in cooked dishes, the peels and seeds are often removed.

# Tools of the Trade: Some Unusual Italian Cooking Equipment

If you already do some cooking at home, you probably have the equipment you need to make most of the recipes in this book. (If you're wondering, check out our list of essential equipment in the Introduction.) As you become more sophisticated and adventurous about Italian cooking, you may want to get some specialty items, such as a pasta machine for making fresh egg pasta or a pizza peel for making homemade pizzas. We discuss these items in later chapters that focus on these dishes.

We want to tell you about a few pieces of equipment that have many uses in the Italian kitchen. Our grandmothers would have considered these items as essential as a knife and cutting board. A good *cheese grater* is still a must, but the invention of the food processor has made the mortar and pestle something of a culinary relic. A *mortar and pestle* grinds herbs, nuts, garlic, and oil into a beautiful pesto, but the process is so labor-intensive that few modern cooks ever bother. The *mezzaluna* is an Italian device for chopping and mincing, especially herbs and garlic. You can use a good chef's knife in its place, but the mezzaluna has such a long history in Italy that we think it's worth knowing about.

## Cheese grater

The three most common types of cheese graters are box, flat, and rotary (see Figure 2-6). You can grate Parmigiano-Reggiano and other hard cheeses on the fine holes of a four-sided, metal box grater. The box shape isn't the best for this job, and you may scrape your knuckles across the grater. However, the larger holes are ideal for shredding mozzarella and other soft cheeses. When buying a box grater, make sure to choose one made of sturdy, heavy-gauge stainless steel that doesn't bend under pressure.

**Figure 2-6:**
Three kinds
of graters
(box, flat,
and rotary).

When we grate Parmigiano-Reggiano and other hard cheeses, we prefer a flat or rotary grater. A flat cheese grater is simply a rectangular piece of metal with tiny holes. This tool is fine for grating small amounts of cheese (a quarter cup takes just a few minutes), but grating a cup or two can become a hassle.

A rotary grater makes quick work of hard cheeses. Rather than rubbing the entire wedge of cheese against tiny holes, you cut small nubs of cheese from the wedge. You place the pieces of cheese in a drum-shaped device and turn the crank. Within seconds, you can get mounds of fluffy, finely grated cheese. The process is quick and safe because your hands are far from the grating surface. Some models come with different inserts to control the size of the items that you're grating. Larger holes may be good for grating chocolate or nuts, but small holes are best for cheese.

Many modern cooks use a food processor to grate cheese. The shredding disk provides an excellent way to grate mozzarella and other soft cheeses. Just cut the mozzarella into chunks and push them through the feed tube into the spinning disk.

Unfortunately, the metal blade of a food processor doesn't really grate hard cheeses like Parmigiano-Reggiano. Instead, it cuts them into tiny pebbles, much larger than a flake of grated cheese. We prefer a fluffy, powdery mound of grated cheese from a grater. It melts better than the larger pebbles produced by a food processor.

## Mortar and pestle

For centuries, Italian cooks have used small stone, wood, or ceramic bowls (or *mortars*) and rounded pestles to crush nuts, herbs, or spices. A marble bowl and pestle (see Figure 2-7) is easy to clean, doesn't absorb flavors, and usually has a rough finish that helps crack and grind basil leaves or pine nuts. Porcelain mortars and pestles are less expensive, and as long as they're quite thick (so they won't crack), they make a good second choice. Wooden mortars tend to absorb flavors, which can be a problem when, for example, you grind nuts for a cake, and they come out with a faint garlic smell.

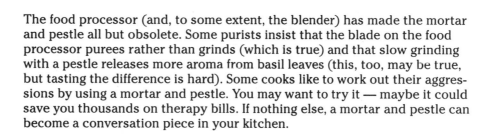

**Figure 2-7:**
A marble mortar and pestle.

The food processor (and, to some extent, the blender) has made the mortar and pestle all but obsolete. Some purists insist that the blade on the food processor purees rather than grinds (which is true) and that slow grinding with a pestle releases more aroma from basil leaves (this, too, may be true, but tasting the difference is hard). Some cooks like to work out their aggressions by using a mortar and pestle. You may want to try it — maybe it could save you thousands on therapy bills. If nothing else, a mortar and pestle can become a conversation piece in your kitchen.

## Mezzaluna

This Italian chopping tool usually has two curved, crescent-shaped blades that are attached to two handles at either end (see Figure 2-8). A mezzaluna (the name translates as "half moon") is ideal for chopping onions or mincing parsley. The two handles ensure smooth, even rocking with minimal pressure. The blades may range in length from 5 inches to more than a foot. An average and useful size is around 7 or 8 inches. Although some versions have just one blade, a double-bladed mezzaluna works more quickly and is easier to control.

**Figure 2-8:**
A
mezzaluna.

# Part II
# First Impressions

The 5th Wave    By Rich Tennant

"What my husband meant to say is he made a 'Caesar salad', not a 'Cesarean salad'."

# In this part . . .

In this part, we cover dishes that you can use to start a meal, including appetizers, salads, and soups. Italian appetizers, called *antipasti,* offer a remarkable selection of small bites, using seafood, meats, vegetables, cheeses, eggs, and bread. Italians often eat salads after the main course, but salads are equally appropriate as a first course, which is traditionally where a salad is served in many other countries, including France and the United States. Italians always serve soups as a first course at the table.

# Chapter 3
# Before the Meal: Antipasti

*J*ust as Rome is the cradle of Western civilization, the antipasto marks the birth of civilized dining. No doubt that cavemen and cavewomen ate dinner as quickly as possible — there were fires to build and mastodons to hunt. Eating was something you did to stay alive.

The role of food in human culture has changed over the millennia. For much of the world, cooking is now a recreational activity, something you do when you have the time. Eating has become something pleasurable and even sensual. A leisurely two-hour dinner may be fun, but it's not terribly efficient.

The *antipasto,* which translates in Italian as "before the meal," signals a more leisurely approach to eating dinner. If you're used to gobbling down takeout in the car, this concept may seem alien. But if you prefer to celebrate the communal aspect of eating, the antipasto is essential.

Nibbling on something light as you have a drink and talk with family and friends is the key to unwinding from the stress of the day. It's also a way to connect with others. In culinary terms, the antipasto stimulates your senses so that you're ready to enjoy the meal that follows.

# What Is an Antipasto?

So what exactly is an antipasto? Does anything served before dinner qualify?

Technically, yes. If you open up some longnecks and sit around eating peanuts and talking for ten minutes before dinner, that's an antipasto. Putting the nuts in a bowl is a true mark of civilized behavior.

Italians may laugh at the notion of beer and nuts, but this duo actually meets many of the criteria for a good antipasto. Just check out the list in the following section.

## Four rules for making an antipasto

Rules, especially culinary ones, are meant to be broken. But the following guidelines apply to most antipasti:

- ✔ **Keep it light.** Remember that dinner is just minutes away. You don't want to fill up now. A few bites for each person is just fine.

- ✔ **Keep it portable.** Antipasti are often served away from the table. If you want to relax on the sofa or on the porch with drinks, the antipasti should be something small and relatively easy to handle. You can use a plate if you like, but ideally you have the antipasto in one hand and a glass of good wine (champagne is even better) in the other. Toast covered with cheese, tomatoes, or beans is a perfect example of a portable antipasto.

- ✔ **Keep it flavorful.** Something salty, something aromatic, or something a bit spicy can take the edge off hunger pangs. Flavorful foods also stimulate the taste buds, readying them for the feast to follow. Avoid mind-numbingly spicy foods. Three-alarm salsa may sound good, but if the antipasto scorches your palate, you may not enjoy the dinner.

- ✔ **Keep it brief.** The antipasto course shouldn't last a long time. Otherwise, you may eat too much and drink too much. If you find it hard to get up off the couch, your antipasto course has gone on long enough. Thirty to 60 minutes is the usual length of time for the antipasto course.

## Antipasti at home

Restaurants tend to put out dozens of antipasti, with platters of marinated vegetables, salamis, cheeses, and grilled seafood. It looks appetizing but intimidating. Surely someone spent all day just making these delicious morsels.

At home, Italians rarely put out such a spread. (Holidays and parties are an exception.) One antipasto, or maybe two for a really fancy meal, is fine. Dinner is still the priority and should receive the lion's share of your attention.

For this reason, most antipasti are simple to prepare. French chefs are wont to make appetizers with several components — tiny pastry shells, a seafood concoction in a rich sauce, and a garnish of caviar. Italians take a simpler approach, one that even the novice cook, working without a chef, can pull off.

# Common Antipasti

Italians use a variety of ingredients to make antipasti. We've grouped the antipasti into a number of categories based on their main ingredients.

## Antipasti from the garden

Vegetables are a mainstay in many antipasti, which makes sense in a culture that places such a high value on freshness and lightness. Many vegetable antipasti are marinated. The vegetable is cooked, dressed with a vinaigrette (for more information on dressings, see Chapter 4), and set aside at room temperature to marinate for a couple of hours.

Don't let vegetables marinate for too long, or they may become mushy. Marinated vegetables should be consumed the day they are prepared. Cover them with plastic wrap and let them marinate on the counter at room temperature. Marinating at room temperature also ensures that the vegetables are the correct temperature when you serve them.

### Marinated Zucchini

In southern Italy, zucchini, eggplant, and even small fish are fried to seal in flavor and then pickled in a vinegar solution. The result is light and refreshing.

*Italian recipe name:* *Zucchine alla Scapece*

*Preparation time:* *15 minutes*

*Cooking time:* *15 to 25 minutes (plus 1 hour marination)*

*Yield:* *6 servings*

*(continued)*

*4 cups peanut oil*

*6 small zucchini, cut into strips roughly ¹/₈-inch thick and 4 inches long*

*1 cup red wine vinegar*

*Salt and pepper to taste*

*5 cloves garlic, peeled and thinly sliced*

*3 sprigs fresh mint*

*1* Heat the peanut oil in a heavy pot over medium-high heat until the oil is hot (about 350°). Add the zucchini in 5 or 6 batches, cooking until the strips are golden — about 3 to 4 minutes for each batch. Sandwich the zucchini slices between paper towels to drain very well and then transfer to a roasting dish or a serving platter with sides.

*2* In a small pan over medium heat, combine the vinegar, salt and pepper, and garlic. Bring nearly to a boil and add the mint. Drizzle the vinegar solution over the zucchini. Marinate for 1 to 2 hours. Serve at room temperature.

You can also use raw vegetables in an antipasto. In the spring, Roman cooks pile baby fava beans, still in their furry pods, into a bowl. They place top-quality extra-virgin olive oil and coarse salt in two separate bowls. Everyone gathers around the table and shells their own beans, dipping them in the oil and sprinkling them with salt. You can also add a hunk of Pecorino cheese to this spread.

**TOQUE TIP**

When choosing a particular vegetable antipasto, think seasonally. Often, the antipasto sets the tone for a meal. So, in spring, consider serving asparagus as an antipasto. In summer, peppers, eggplant, or tomatoes make sense. During the fall and winter, think about mushrooms, fennel, and leafy greens, such as spinach.

## Vegetables with Hot Anchovy Dip

*Bagna Cauda,* which translates as "warm bath," comes from the Piedmont, where it is traditionally prepared in the winter. You heat garlic and anchovies in a mixture of olive oil and white wine to create a pungent dip for raw vegetables. The flavor is delicious but intense. We have a friend whose children refuse to go school whenever their father prepares Bagna Cauda. They think their hair and clothes smell like garlic, and they are probably right.

***Italian recipe name:*** *Bagna Cauda*

***Preparation time:*** *20 minutes*

***Cooking time:*** *50 minutes*

***Yield:*** *8 to 12 servings*

*1¹/₂ cups olive oil*

*3 cloves garlic, peeled and thinly sliced*

*1 cup white wine*

*¹/₃ cup anchovy fillets (two 2-ounce cans), drained*

*2 cups water*

*Salt and pepper to taste*

*Assorted seasoned raw vegetables*

**1** In a medium saucepan over medium heat, cook the olive oil and the garlic together for about 5 minutes. Carefully add the wine and cook at a low boil for another 5 minutes; make sure that you don't let the mixture come to a full boil. Add the anchovies and water and cook, stirring occasionally, for 40 more minutes or until the anchovies have dissolved into a paste. Skim the surface fat off with a ladle and discard. Season to taste with salt and pepper.

**2** Transfer the hot Bagna Cauda mixture to a serving bowl, preferably terra-cotta. To keep the dip hot, set the terra-cotta serving bowl over a small flame or use a fondue pot. Dip slices of raw vegetables into the Bagna Cauda; celery, red and yellow peppers, cabbage, artichokes, cauliflower, broccoli, scallions, carrots, and fennel are the most common choices in Piedmont, but most any raw vegetable is delicious.

## Portobello with Radicchio

Italians use fresh porcini mushrooms in this dish. Unfortunately, porcini mushrooms rarely make it out of Italy, so use meaty portobello mushrooms instead. You can roast or grill the mushrooms, depending on the time of year and your preference.

**Italian recipe name:** *Portobello con Radicchio*

**Preparation time:** *15 minutes*

**Cooking time:** *15 to 18 minutes*

**Yield:** *4 servings*

*5 tablespoons olive oil plus 1 tablespoon for baking sheet (if roasting mushrooms in the oven)*

*2 tablespoons white wine*

*2 cloves garlic, peeled and finely chopped*

*1 tablespoon chopped fresh parsley, or 1 teaspoon dried parsley*

*1 tablespoon chopped fresh oregano, or 1 teaspoon dried oregano*

*Juice of ¹/₂ lemon (about 1¹/₂ tablespoons)*

*Salt and pepper to taste*

*4 large or 8 small portobello mushrooms, stems removed*

*1 head radicchio, core discarded and leaves sliced into long strips*

*(continued)*

*1* Preheat grill to medium-high or oven to 375°.

*2* Whisk together 3 tablespoons olive oil, the white wine, garlic, parsley, oregano, lemon juice, and salt and pepper in a medium bowl. Set aside.

*3* Place the mushrooms on a plate and season with 2 tablespoons olive oil and salt and pepper.

*4* Place the mushrooms on the grill or on a baking sheet rubbed with 1 tablespoon oil. If grilling, cook for about 3 minutes per side, brushing with the dressing mixture occasionally. If using the oven, brush the mushrooms with the dressing (to keep them from drying out) and roast for about 7 minutes per side. The total cooking time depends on the thickness of the mushrooms; whether you grill or roast the mushrooms, they should be lightly brown and tender.

*5* On a server plate, spread out the radicchio and place the portobellos, either whole or sliced, on top. Serve the mushrooms drizzled with the remaining dressing.

# How'd that mushroom get so big?

Portobello mushrooms are the darlings of chefs (because they look so impressive) and vegetarians (because they're so meaty). But where did these gigantic mushrooms come from? Are they on steroids?

Portobellos (see figure) are nothing more than overgrown cremini mushrooms, another popular variety in Italy and now around the world. Creminis look like regular white button mushrooms, except they're light brown in color and have a much stronger flavor. If you can find creminis, use them as your basic mushroom when cooking. Like white button mushrooms, you should wipe creminis clean (or rinse under cold, running water if really dirty) before using them. You should also trim a thin slice from the end of the stem, which invariably is tough and a bit dried out.

When cremini mushrooms grow to much larger sizes, they're called portobello mushrooms. Each mushroom weighs several ounces (some even weigh half a pound), and the cap spans at least 4 inches, if not more.

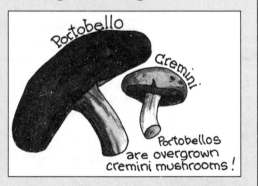

Portobellos require some different handling. The stems are usually quite tough and inedible. You can add them to stock, but when grilling, roasting, or sautéing portobellos, trim the stems flush with the cap. Tender black gills cover the underside of the cap. To keep moisture in the mushrooms, try grilling or roasting them with the gills facing up, away from the heat source.

## Sicilian Eggplant Relish

This recipe is one of Sicily's most famous dishes. You cook eggplant with other vegetables (in this case, onions, celery, and an assortment of peppers) in a sweet-and-sour tomato sauce that's flavored with vinegar and sugar. This version is lighter and easier than the traditional recipe, in which you fry the eggplant separately and then add it to the cooked vegetables. You can also mix this sauce into risotto or serve it with pasta.

You can serve this dish with bread or crackers for dipping, or your guests may eat it with a fork.

**Italian recipe name:** *Caponata*

**Preparation time:** *15 minutes*

**Cooking time:** *1 hour, 5 minutes*

**Yield:** *6 to 8 servings*

*¹/₄ cup olive oil*

*2 medium onions, diced*

*6 celery stalks, diced*

*1 small red bell pepper, seeded and diced*

*1 small yellow bell pepper, seeded and diced*

*1 small green bell pepper, seeded and diced*

*¹/₄ cup sugar*

*5 tablespoons red wine vinegar*

*2 medium eggplants, peeled and cut into ¹/₂-inch cubes*

*2 large tomatoes, diced*

*1¹/₂ cups water*

*1 cup pitted black olives*

*2 tablespoons chopped capers, drained*

*2 tablespoons chopped fresh basil, or 2 teaspoons dried basil*

*2 tablespoons chopped fresh parsley, or 2 teaspoons dried parsley*

*Salt and pepper to taste*

**1** In a large skillet, heat the olive oil over medium heat. Add the onion, celery, and peppers and cook for 10 minutes, stirring frequently.

**2** Sprinkle the sugar over the vegetables and stir in the vinegar. Cook for 5 minutes, until the vinegar has been almost completely absorbed.

**3** Add the eggplant and cook, covered, for another 15 minutes. Add the tomatoes and water and simmer, uncovered, for another 20 minutes.

**4** Stir in the olives and capers. Simmer for 10 minutes and then add the basil and parsley. Cook for 2 to 3 minutes more. Adjust the seasoning with salt and pepper. Serve warm or at room temperature.

# Olives as an antipasto

Olives are a common ingredient on the antipasto table. Occasionally, you use them to flavor dishes, such as Caponata (see preceding recipe). More often, you serve them separately in a small bowl.

Italians don't use canned or pitted olives. They serve the real thing, pits and all. We suggest that you put out a separate bowl in which guests can discard the pits. It's not terribly elegant, but pitted olives are bland and mushy and can't compete with the real thing.

To use olives as an antipasto, you can marinate them in olive oil and perhaps season them with crushed garlic cloves, hot red pepper flakes, lemon zest, or fresh herbs. Then you can serve the marinated olives with drinks. Think of olives as the Italian equivalent of a bowl of nuts.

We always keep a jar of marinated olives in the refrigerator. The cold causes the oil to congeal, so about an hour before we need the olives, we remove the jar from the refrigerator and let the oil return to a liquid state. (This also takes the chill off the olives.) If you're in a rush, set the container with the olives in some hot water.

You can buy several kinds of olives and marinate them yourself. Try to find olives in a variety of shapes and color. (For more information on individual varieties, see Chapter 2.) Note that olives can be either brined in a vinegar solution or dry-cured with salt. Brined olives are plump and juicy and are generally the better choice in most situations, including antipasti. Cured olives are wrinkled and look shriveled. They're quite chewy and meaty (almost like jerky) and very salty, making them better for cooking than eating out of hand.

Of course, you can buy marinated olives from a gourmet shop, supermarket, or Italian deli. Either way, the olives stay fresh for weeks, if not longer, in the refrigerator.

## Asparagus with Parmesan

This is one of those simple dishes (see photo in color section) that tastes like it took a lot of work but is actually quite easy. Asparagus spears are boiled, oiled, and then baked with a light dusting of cheese. In some places, this dish is prepared with eggs. Before adding the cheese and placing the asparagus in the oven, break 1 egg on top of each bunch of asparagus.

*Italian recipe name:* Asparagi alla Parmigiana

*Preparation time:* 15 minutes

*Cooking time:* 18 minutes

*Yield:* 4 servings

1 pound asparagus (about 16 pieces), ends trimmed, stems peeled with a vegetable peeler if asparagus is thick

3 tablespoons olive oil

$^1/_4$ cup grated Parmigiano-Reggiano

Salt and pepper to taste

*1* Preheat oven to 375°.

*2* Place the asparagus in a large pot with boiling, salted water. Cook until just tender, 3 to 5 minutes depending on the thickness of the asparagus. Drain. Transfer asparagus spears to a large bowl filled with ice water and let them cool, about 2 to 3 minutes. Drain again.

*3* Separate the asparagus into 4 separate bunches on a baking sheet (so that you can easily lift each serving from the pan when done). Drizzle the asparagus with the olive oil, sprinkle on the Parmigiano-Reggiano, and season with salt and pepper.

*4* Place the baking sheet in the oven and cook for 5 to 8 minutes until the asparagus is hot and the Parmigiano-Reggiano begins to brown. With a spatula, transfer each bunch of asparagus to a serving plate. Serve immediately.

## *A toast to start*

In Italy, many meals begin with toasted slices of bread. Stray slices of stale bread often get recycled into diminutive toasts that are rubbed with garlic, brushed with olive oil, and lightly topped with anything from tomatoes to chicken livers.

## A toast by any other name

Toast goes by many names in various regions of Italy. *Bruschetta* is the most common name, but the terms *crostini* and *fettunta* are also used. You can use all three terms interchangeably; however, you should be aware of some slight differences between them.

Bruschetta comes from the Italian word *bruscare,* which means "to roast over coals." Traditionally, Italians grilled all toast, including bruschetta, over a live fire. Of course, you can use the broiler or a toaster. Bruschetta is often cut from large round loaves of bread, but this isn't a hard-and-fast rule. When made with larger pieces of toast, bruschetta should be eaten with a knife and fork and may, in fact,

become a light meal, especially if you serve it with salad.

Crostini, literally "little crusts" or "toasts," is generally cut from baguettes or other narrow loaves and is rarely more than 2 inches in diameter. Crostini is always an appetizer, eaten out of hand along with a drink. Crostini is similar to the French canapé.

Fettunta translates as "oiled slices." Residents of Tuscany frequently use this term to describe this type of toast. Other more obscure names also exist, including *panunto,* or "oiled bread," and *soma d'ai,* or "brushed with garlic." Whatever you call them, these toasts make excellent antipasti.

The bread doesn't have to be stale, but it should be grilled or toasted. To make garlic toast, simply rub a peeled garlic clove over the hot toast. The craggy surface of the toast pulls off bits of the garlic. For a mild garlic flavor, rub lightly. For a real hit of garlic, rub vigorously several times. You can omit the garlic, but it's a nice touch, especially with a vegetable or bean topping.

As with the garlic, the olive oil is optional. Many recipes call for drizzling the oil over the toast to moisten it. If the topping is already moist or has plenty of oil in it, you can omit this step.

If you choose to add the oil, we find that a pastry brush (or a clean paint brush) is best for even coverage of the toast.

Although the topping gives the toast character, these antipasti start with bread. Stale bread is fine, but squishy loaves are not. Hearty country loaves with a good crust and chewy crumb are essential.

## Bruschetta with White Beans

Although we prefer to cook our own dried beans, you can use canned beans to make this recipe (see photo in color section). Just make sure that you drain them into a colander and rinse off the gelatinous packing liquid.

**Italian recipe name:** *Fettunta con Cannellini*

**Preparation time:** *15 minutes*

**Cooking time:** *5 minutes (excludes cooking time for beans)*

**Yield:** *4 servings*

8 slices country white bread (Italian or French bread)

4 cloves garlic, peeled

2 cups cooked cannellini beans (see Chapter 14 for a recipe)

2 tablespoons vinegar

$^1/_2$ cup olive oil

Salt and pepper to taste

$^1/_4$ cup chopped tomatoes (optional)

1 tablespoon chopped fresh parsley (optional)

*1* Preheat oven to 350°.

*2* Arrange the bread slices on a baking sheet and place in the oven. Allow them to lightly toast for about 5 to 7 minutes and then remove the baking sheet from the oven. Rub the bread slices with the garlic cloves.

*3* In a large mixing bowl, mix together the cannellini beans, vinegar, olive oil, salt and pepper, tomatoes, and parsley.

4 Spoon the cannellini mixture on top of the toasted bread pieces and place these bruschetta on a large serving plate or 2 each on 4 salad plates.

## Bruschetta with Tomatoes

This dish is a classic summertime favorite (see photo in color section). However, it depends on really ripe tomatoes. Give this recipe a try when it's local tomato season; otherwise, you may want to make something else.

***Italian recipe name:*** *Bruschetta al Pomodoro*

***Preparation time:*** *15 minutes*

***Cooking time:*** *5 minutes*

***Yield:*** *4 servings*

***Special tool:*** *Food processor*

*3 medium tomatoes, chopped*

*6 cloves garlic, peeled and crushed*

*12 whole basil leaves*

*Pinch of hot red pepper flakes*

*Pinch of black pepper*

*Salt to taste*

*3 tablespoons balsamic vinegar*

*3 tablespoons red wine vinegar*

*$^2/_3$ cup olive oil*

*8 slices country white bread (Italian or French bread)*

1 Preheat oven to 350°.

2 Place the tomatoes, garlic, basil, red pepper flakes, black pepper, salt, balsamic vinegar, and red wine vinegar in a food processor.

3 Run the food processor for a few seconds and then shut it off. Repeat this procedure 2 to 3 times. The resulting mixture should be somewhat chunky rather than a smooth puree.

4 Add the olive oil and pulse a few more times. Adjust seasoning with salt as needed and stir.

5 Arrange the bread slices on a baking sheet and place in the oven. Allow the slices to lightly toast for about 5 to 7 minutes and then remove from the oven.

6 Spoon the tomato mixture on the toasted bread and serve.

## Roman Style Toasts

For this Roman favorite, slices of cheese are skewered along with slices of bread, flavored with a pungent sauce, and then baked just until the cheese starts to melt. Think of this as grilled cheese on a stick with garlic, capers, and anchovies.

*Italian recipe name:* Crostini alla Romana

*Preparation time:* 10 to 15 minutes

*Cooking time:* 15 minutes

*Yield:* 4 servings

*Special tools:* 4 skewers

7 slices country white bread (French or Italian bread), cut into 28 $^1/_2$ x 2-inch pieces

12 ounces mozzarella, sliced into 24 $^1/_2$ x 1$^1/_2$-inch squares

5 tablespoons olive oil

12 fillets of anchovies (about 1 can), drained and chopped

2 tablespoons chopped capers, drained

3 cloves garlic, peeled and chopped

2 tablespoons white wine

Salt and pepper to taste

*1* Preheat oven to 375°.

*2* Prepare the skewers by starting with a piece of bread and then alternating 1 piece of mozzarella with 1 piece of bread. When finished, each skewer should have 7 pieces of bread and 6 pieces of mozzarella (make sure that a slice of bread is at both ends). Place prepared skewers on a baking sheet.

*3* In a small saucepan, combine the olive oil, anchovies, capers, garlic, white wine, and salt and pepper. Simmer for 3 minutes over low heat, stirring occasionally, until the anchovies dissolve.

*4* Spoon 2 tablespoons anchovy sauce on each skewer and bake for 3 minutes. Turn the skewers and spoon the remaining sauce over them. Bake for another 3 to 5 minutes or until the cheese starts to melt.

## *Crostini with Chicken Livers*

This classic Tuscan recipe can be made quicker and lighter if you like (see photo in color section). Instead of dipping the slices of bread in chicken stock and then frying them, you can simply toast the bread slices and then spread the chicken liver mixture on top. If toasting the bread, cut the slices about ¹/₂-inch thick. In either case, you can make the chicken liver spread in advance and refrigerate it for several days. However, wait to fry or toast the bread until just before you're ready to serve the crostini.

*Italian recipe name:* *Crostini di Fegatini alla Toscana*

*Preparation time:* *15 minutes*

*Cooking time:* *35 to 40 minutes*

*Yield:* *8 servings*

*Special tools:* *Food processor, kitchen tongs*

| | |
|---|---|
| *2 tablespoons olive oil* | *¹/₂ cup white wine* |
| *1 pound chicken livers, rinsed and drained* | *1 tablespoon chopped fresh parsley* |
| *1 medium onion, chopped* | *Salt and pepper to taste* |
| *3 cloves garlic, peeled and chopped* | *2 cups peanut oil* |
| *1 sprig fresh sage* | *2 cups homemade chicken stock or canned chicken broth* |
| *¹/₂ tablespoon flour* | |
| *¹/₃ cup chopped anchovies (two 2-ounce cans, oil drained)* | *One 10- to 12-inch loaf Tuscan bread (or Italian bread), cut into ³/₄-inch-thick slices* |
| *2 tablespoons capers, drained* | |

**1** Heat the olive oil in a medium skillet for 1 to 2 minutes. When hot, add the chicken livers, onion, garlic, and sage and sauté over medium-high heat for about 10 to 12 minutes, until the livers release their liquid and it evaporates.

**2** Add the flour, anchovies, capers, and wine and then stir. Cook for 5 minutes. Add the parsley and salt and pepper.

**3** Puree the liver mixture in a food processor and then return the mixture to the skillet. Cook at a gentle simmer over low-medium heat for 5 minutes. Set aside.

**4** Heat the peanut oil in a medium skillet until hot.

**5** Pour the broth into a medium-sized bowl and quickly dip the bread in the broth; the bread should be damp but not saturated with liquid. Carefully place the bread in the

*(continued)*

hot oil for 2 to 3 minutes. Using kitchen tongs, check the underside of the bread; when the bread is lightly golden, turn it over. Cook for another 1 to 2 minutes and then transfer to a large plate lined with paper towels.

*6* Spread the liver mixture over the bread slices and serve immediately.

# *The incredible egg*

The *frittata,* an open-faced omelet that doesn't require any complicated folding or flipping, is a standard item on the antipasto table. To make a frittata, you lightly beat the eggs in a bowl with seasonings, pour them into a hot skillet, and cook them over gentle heat until the bottom is golden brown and the eggs are mostly set except for the top. At this point, you place the skillet in a hot oven or under the broiler to brown the top.

We usually choose the broiler for browning the top of the frittata. Although the danger of burning the frittata is real, this method takes just a minute or two. A hot oven takes longer (up to ten minutes), but the chance of burning the top is greatly diminished. If you're the kind of cook who burns food often (because the phone is always ringing or the kids are always fighting), go with the oven.

After the top is browned, you can serve the frittata immediately or allow it to cool to room temperature. The simplest serving method is to cut wedges straight from the pan. To get fancy, loosen the whole frittata from the pan with a spatula and then invert the frittata onto a platter. You can bring the whole frittata to the table.

A note about choosing a skillet: Italian grandmothers might laugh, but a nonstick skillet makes the whole process much easier and ensures that the cooked frittata comes out of the pan without tearing or sticking. Because the frittata will go under the broiler, choose a pan with a metal handle.

The seasonings can be as simple as salt and pepper, herbs, and grated cheese (usually Parmigiano-Reggiano). Most frittatas are a bit more elaborate and incorporate cooked vegetables. You can use other cheeses, especially grated Pecorino, as well as meats, especially pancetta or prosciutto.

The frittata is open to countless variations. Here are some quick, simple ideas. Start with 6 beaten eggs seasoned with salt and pepper to taste, a few tablespoons of grated cheese, and some minced fresh herbs if desired. Add any of the following ingredients alone or in any combination to the egg mixture. Then cook in a hot, oiled skillet as directed in the Italian Style Mushroom Omelet recipe.

✔ Chop and sauté several onions or shallots until golden.

✔ Chop several handfuls of arugula, spinach, Swiss chard, or other tender leafy greens.

✔ Boil 1 to 2 cups of bite-sized pieces of asparagus, broccoli, cauliflower, or green beans in salted water until tender and then drain.

✔ Cut 1 or 2 bell peppers into thin strips and sauté until tender.

✔ Cut several zucchini into small pieces and sauté until tender.

✔ Add up to 1 cup ricotta cheese for an extra-fluffy texture.

✔ Fry up to 1 cup bite-sized pieces of pancetta or prosciutto until crisp.

## Italian Style Mushroom Omelet

This dish is equally good as a lunch entree or as a light dinner. Unlike a French or American omelet, you should cook the Italian frittata through. The eggs should be soft but not runny. You can serve this dish warm or at room temperature.

**Italian recipe name:** *Frittata di Funghi*

**Preparation time:** *10 minutes*

**Cooking time:** *25 to 30 minutes*

**Yield:** *4 servings*

*4 tablespoons olive oil, divided*

*1/2 cup chopped red onion*

*3 cloves garlic, peeled and chopped*

*1 teaspoon chopped fresh oregano*

*1 teaspoon chopped fresh parsley*

*1 medium red bell pepper, seeded and chopped*

*2 cups sliced mushrooms (any mix of at least two of the following: domestic, shiitake, cremini, or oyster)*

*Salt and pepper to taste*

*6 large eggs*

*2 tablespoons grated Parmigiano-Reggiano (optional)*

*1* Place 2 tablespoons olive oil, the onion, and garlic in a medium skillet and cook over medium heat for 2 to 3 minutes. Stir in the oregano, parsley, and bell pepper and cook for another minute. Then add the mushrooms and salt and pepper. Sauté the mushrooms for 15 to 20 minutes, stirring occasionally, or until the mushrooms are tender and most of the liquid has evaporated. Let cool.

*2* Preheat broiler.

*(continued)*

**3** In a medium mixing bowl, combine the cooled mushrooms, eggs, and Parmigiano-Reggiano. Mix well.

**4** Heat the remaining 2 tablespoons olive oil in the nonstick skillet.

**5** Add the egg mixture and cook for 2 minutes, stirring for the first minute, until the eggs begin to set. Cook for another 1 to 2 minutes, until the bottom of the eggs just begins to brown. (Lift the eggs gently with a spatula to check the bottom.)

**6** Slide the skillet onto the top rack about 5 inches under the broiler and cook for 2 to 3 minutes, just until the top browns. Cut into 4 wedges and serve warm or at room temperature.

# Antipasti from the sea

The antipasto course is a good place to use seafood, especially if you're trying to keep to a budget. A little seafood goes a long way as an appetizer. Grilled seafood makes an excellent summertime antipasti. Italians make good use of bivalves — clams, mussels, and oysters — in antipasti, as well as other exotic sea creatures, such as octopus and squid.

Purchase bivalves from a reputable source, and your prep time should be minimal. A quick wash to remove any grit from the exterior should be sufficient.

Octopus and squid require a lot of cleaning. You can save a few bucks and do this yourself, or you can ask your fishmonger to clean them. Unless you like handling slimy, smelly innards, we suggest spending the extra bucks. Squid and octopus aren't exactly flying off the shelves and are pretty cheap either way.

The biggest mistake that novice cooks make when preparing seafood antipasti is overcooking. Squid and octopus become tough and rubbery if you leave them on the grill for too long, and clams, mussels, and oysters dry out after just a few minutes of cooking. Read recipes carefully and watch the clock.

### Grilled Shrimp

Italians sometimes eat very small shrimp raw — an Italian version of sushi. We recommend cooking the shrimp, but don't overcook them. You want the shrimp to be tender and fresh. You can cook the shrimp in their shells or peeled. If cooked in their shells, the shrimp become messy to eat but are a bit moister. If you think that your family and friends would rather not peel cooked shrimp at the table, then do it yourself before combining the shrimp with the other ingredients.

*Italian recipe name:* Gamberetti alla Griglia

*Preparation time:* 15 minutes

*Cooking time:* 6 to 12 minutes

*Yield:* 4 servings

1¹/₂ pounds medium shrimp, peeled

2 tablespoons olive oil

2 tablespoons white wine

1 sprig fresh rosemary, or ¹/₂ teaspoon
dried oregano

Salt and pepper to taste

1 lemon, cut into wedges

*1* Preheat grill to medium-high or oven to 375°.

*2* Combine all ingredients (except lemon wedges) in a large mixing bowl and toss well. Allow the flavors to blend together for about 10 minutes.

*3* If you're using a grill, remove the shrimp from the marinade mixture and place them in a wire basket on the grill. Cook for about 2 to 3 minutes per side until the shrimp are pink and firm. If you're using the oven, spread the shrimp, along with the marinade mixture, on a baking sheet and cook for 10 to 12 minutes, mixing occasionally. Again, the shrimp will be pink and firm when they're thoroughly cooked. Serve with lemon wedges.

## Peppered Mussels

This simple dish is among our favorites from Naples (see photo in color section). Most mussels are now farmed in seabeds and come to market quite clean. Simply wash the mussels with a scrub brush and pull off any weedlike material that hangs from the shells. This part of the mussel is called the beard, and it's often, but not always, removed during processing.

*Italian recipe name:* Pepata di Cozze

*Preparation time:* 30 minutes

*Cooking time:* 12 minutes

*Yield:* 4 servings

4 pounds mussels

¹/₃ cup white wine

¹/₄ cup finely chopped fresh parsley

5 cloves garlic, peeled and finely chopped

³/₄ teaspoon salt

1 teaspoon pepper

*(continued)*

*1* Clean the mussels, removing the beard and scrubbing the shells with a clean scrub brush.

*2* Place the mussels and wine in a large pot over medium heat and cook for about 10 minutes, covered, until the mussels have opened. Discard any mussels that remain closed.

*3* Add the parsley, garlic, and salt and pepper. Stir to combine. Continue cooking for 2 minutes and then turn off the heat and set aside, covered, for 2 to 3 minutes.

*4* Serve hot in large soup or pasta bowls with a side plate for the shells.

## Broiled Squid

Fried calamari is a restaurant dish. At home, it's easier and less smelly to broil the squid. Make sure that you buy fully cleaned squid.

***Italian recipe name:*** *Calamari alla Griglia*

***Preparation time:*** *15 minutes*

***Cooking time:*** *8 to 15 minutes (depends on cooking method selected)*

***Yield:*** *4 servings*

*$^1/_2$ cup bread crumbs*

*2 cloves garlic, peeled and finely chopped*

*$^1/_2$ tablespoon finely chopped fresh rosemary, or $^1/_2$ teaspoon dried rosemary*

*$^1/_2$ tablespoon finely chopped fresh thyme, or $^1/_2$ teaspoon dried thyme*

*$^1/_2$ tablespoon finely chopped fresh sage, or $^1/_2$ teaspoon dried sage*

*$^1/_2$ tablespoon finely chopped fresh oregano, or $^1/_2$ teaspoon dried oregano*

*$^1/_4$ cup olive oil*

*$1^1/_2$ pounds squid, cleaned, cut into $^1/_4$-inch rings*

*2 medium tomatoes, cut into $^1/_4$-inch-thick slices*

*Salt and pepper to taste*

*1 bunch arugula, washed and trimmed*

*1* Preheat the broiler. If you plan on baking the squid, preheat oven to 375°.

*2* In a medium bowl, combine the bread crumbs, garlic, herbs, and olive oil. Stir with a wooden spoon until the mixture is somewhat sticky.

**3** Add the squid to the bowl and gently stir until all the rings are coated with the bread crumb mixture. Arrange the squid on a baking sheet and broil for 3 to 4 minutes per side until lightly browned. To cook in the oven, arrange the squid on a baking sheet and bake for 12 to 15 minutes, turning occasionally. Again, the squid turns light brown and becomes crunchy when done.

**4** Arrange the tomato slices on 4 plates and spoon the squid on top. Season with salt and pepper. Garnish with the arugula leaves.

## Stuffed Oysters, Taranto Style

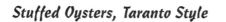

Oysters are tricky to work with. Don't attempt to open oysters yourself; ask your fishmonger to open them. Doing this safely and efficiently takes years of practice. You can also make this southern Italian dish with littleneck or cherrystone clams, if desired. You should get the clams opened at the fish store as well.

***Italian recipe name:*** *Ostriche alla Tarantina*

***Preparation time:*** *15 minutes*

***Cooking time:*** *15 to 20 minutes*

***Yield:*** *4 servings*

*6 tablespoons bread crumbs*

*4 to 6 tablespoons olive oil, divided*

*5 cloves garlic, peeled and chopped*

*3 tablespoons chopped fresh parsley*

*3 tablespoons grated Parmigiano-Reggiano*

*1 teaspoon chopped fresh thyme, or*
*¹/₂ teaspoon dried thyme*

*Salt and pepper to taste*

*24 oysters with shells (or substitute clams)*

*1 lemon, cut into wedges*

**1** Preheat oven to 375° or preheat broiler (oven rack should be 3 to 4 inches from heat).

**2** In a mixing bowl, combine the bread crumbs, 2 tablespoons olive oil, garlic, parsley, Parmigiano-Reggiano, thyme, and salt and pepper. Mix well.

**3** Pack the bread crumb mixture into neat mounds over the oysters in the half-shells and then place the shells on a baking sheet. Sprinkle with 2 tablespoons olive oil. Bake 15 to 20 minutes or broil 3 to 4 minutes until golden brown and crisp. Serve warm with lemon wedges.

## *Meat and cheese antipasti*

Cured meats and cheeses are another important category of antipasti. An Italian deli, called a *salumeria,* carries dozens of salamis and cheeses, as well as prosciutto. Although the home cook can embellish these store-bought ingredients, for the most part, meat and cheese antipasti involve little preparation.

Italy produces literally hundreds of cheeses; most varieties never leave Italy. A small handful — no more than a dozen — are available internationally, and of those, only a few are commonly used as antipasti. Here's a list of our favorite cheeses to serve as antipasti. (For more information on buying cheese, see Chapter 2.)

- **Mozzarella:** Use only fresh, creamy, homemade mozzarella. Avoid rubbery, shrink-wrapped versions at all costs, especially if you're not going to cook the cheese. You can marinate tiny mozzarella balls, often called *bocconcini* (or "little mouthfuls") in extra-virgin olive oil that has been spiked with hot red pepper flakes.

- **Parmigiano-Reggiano:** A hunk of Parmigiano-Reggiano is perfect for nibbling on with drinks and olives. Use a short, broad-bladed knife with a pointed end to furrow into the cheese and break off irregular chunks (see Figure 3-1). You should eat only the finest Parmigiano-Reggiano this way. You may enjoy good Pecorino in the same fashion.

- **Gorgonzola:** This is Italy's famed blue cheese. You can find numerous styles of Gorgonzola — from the creamy, mild *latte dolce,* or "sweet milk," to crumbly, aged versions that are quite potent and usually very salty. We generally prefer the milder, creamier cheeses when planning an antipasto.

- **Other creamy cheeses:** You can serve other creamy cheeses with bread or crackers. Italian Fontina has a mild, buttery, even nutty flavor. Taleggio is a buttery, sometimes runny, cheese with a rind — think of this as brie, but with a funkier aftertaste.

**Figure 3-1:**
Cutting
Parmigiano-
Reggiano.

A broad-bladed knife can be used to dig into a hunk of Parmigiano-Reggiano and break off hunks for nibbling with drinks.

In addition to cheeses, your local gourmet shop or Italian market should carry a selection of cured pork products, including salami and prosciutto. A platter of cured meats is a commonly offered antipasto in northern Italy. You may serve these meats singly or in combination, allotting $1/2$ to 1 ounce per person. Here are several possible choices; note that you can find dozens more.

- **Salami** is dry cured sausage made from minced lean meat and pork fat. The meat is usually all pork, but occasionally some beef is added. The meat and fat may be seasoned with garlic, fennel seeds, chiles, or even white wine. Salamis are cured for several months and sometimes up to a year. You can ask the butcher to slice the salami for you or simply cut it yourself into slices or small cubes.

- **Mortadella** is Italy's answer to bologna. Pork is beaten into a smooth puree that is light and airy. This pink puree is seasoned, often with warm spices like cinnamon and nutmeg. Mortadella looks like oversized bologna studded with cracked peppercorns and large cubes of creamy white fat. Mortadella originally hails from the city of Bologna. Although bland bologna takes it name from this city as well, mortadella is much more complex. Never spicy like salami, it nonetheless is richly seasoned and delicious.

- **Coppa** is cured pork shoulder sold in thick, short logs. The meat should be rosy-colored and well-marbled with fat. The meat is seasoned with salt and black pepper, as well as with an aromatic spice like cinnamon or nutmeg.

- **Bresaola** is salted, air-dried, and pressed beef that you slice very thin and serve with a drizzle of olive oil and lemon juice. Originally from Lombardy, this cured beef is popular throughout Italy now.

- **Prosciutto** is salted and air-dried fresh ham. Called *prosciutto crudo* in Italian, this product has been cured but not cooked. (The term *prosciutto cotto* refers to cooked ham, not unlike boiled ham.) Prosciutto crudo is not smoked. The flavor is simply the ham plus the seasonings, usually salt and black pepper. The butcher must slice the prosciutto paper-thin so that pieces melt in your mouth. Italian prosciutto from the Parma region is now available around the globe. It may cost a few dollars more per pound than domestic products, but it's money well spent. You may eat prosciutto as is or with fruit, especially melon and figs (see photo in color section). (You don't need a recipe for this; just serve thinly sliced prosciutto with halved fresh figs or chunks of peeled canteloupe or honeydew melon.)

In addition to cured meats, Italians also enjoy thin-sliced, raw beef as an antipasto. Beef carpaccio is a common appetizer in Italian restaurants. Layer thin pieces of tender beef over a bed of salad greens, moisten the beef with olive oil and lemon juice, and serve with pieces of Parmigiano-Reggiano. The cut of beef must be tender. Filet mignon is a good choice, as is top round.

## Raw Beef Salad

If you like, have your butcher slice the beef for this salad on his slicing machine. Tell the butcher that you're making carpaccio and that you need the filet mignon sliced paper-thin. The slices should be just thick enough to hold together without shredding. If you decide to do this yourself, put the meat in the freezer for 30 minutes to make it firmer and easier to slice. Then, after slicing the meat, pound the slices between pieces of plastic wrap with a heavy mallet or the bottom of a heavy pan to get them really thin.

Don't be put off by the number of different herbs called for in this recipe. Just use whatever herbs you have.

**Italian recipe name:** *Carpaccio*

**Preparation time:** *20 minutes*

**Cooking time:** *None*

**Yield:** *4 servings*

*2 scallions, finely chopped (white part only)*

*$^1/_4$ teaspoon finely chopped fresh thyme, or $^1/_8$ teaspoon dried thyme*

*$^1/_4$ teaspoon finely chopped fresh chervil, or $^1/_8$ teaspoon dried chervil*

*$^1/_4$ teaspoon finely chopped marjoram, or $^1/_8$ teaspoon dried marjoram*

*$^1/_4$ teaspoon finely chopped basil, or $^1/_8$ teaspoon dried basil*

*$^1/_4$ teaspoon finely chopped fresh chili pepper, or $^1/_8$ teaspoon dried chili powder*

*$^1/_2$ cup olive oil*

*Juice of 1 lemon (about 3 tablespoons)*

*Pepper to taste*

*4 cups arugula, washed, trimmed, and dried*

*$^3/_4$ pound filet mignon*

*2 ounces Parmigiano-Reggiano, shaved into thin slices*

*1* In a small bowl, mix together the scallions, thyme, chervil, marjoram, basil, chili pepper, olive oil, lemon juice, and pepper.

*2* Arrange the arugula in neat mounds on the center of 4 plates.

*3* Slice the meat as thin as possible; you should have at least 12 slices. Place the meat between 2 sheets of waxed paper or plastic wrap and pound with a meat mallet or the bottom of a heavy pan. The meat should be even in thickness (paper-thin). Drape 3 slices of meat over each mound of arugula and drizzle with the dressing.

*4* Arrange Parmigiano-Reggiano cheese shavings on top and serve.

# Chapter 4

# Salads

**M**aking a good salad should be easy, but not mindless. You may think that preparing salad means opening a bag of prewashed lettuce and tossing it in a large bowl with some bottled dressing. You can make salad this way, but will it taste great? Not likely.

Salad gets a bit more respect in Italy. It's still easy to prepare, but the quality of the ingredients is much higher. You won't find packages of "Italian seasonings for dressing" (which taste too much like grass) or bland greens. Salad shouldn't be something you eat to pass the time, waiting for the dinner to be served. It should have its own character and be packed with flavor.

A good salad begins with fresh leafy greens or perhaps some cooked potatoes, sliced fennel and oranges, or steamed mussels. The dressing can be as simple as a drizzle of extra-virgin olive oil and some good vinegar. Of course, you can get fancier by adding herbs, garlic, or other seasonings, but at heart, Italian dressings are ridiculously easy.

Two kinds of salads are popular in Italy — leafy salads and room-temperature vegetables, seafood, or meat dressed with oil and vinegar. Leafy salads are so simple that you don't really need a recipe. They're a place for improvisation and creativity, as long as you follow some basic rules about handling greens and dressing them. Room-temperature salads, with cooked vegetables, seafood, or meat, require more attention to detail. This chapter explains how to prepare both types of salad. No more salad from a bag!

# The Marriage of Oil and Vinegar

As with most marriages, a dressing is only as strong as the two partners — in this case, oil and vinegar. In Italy, extra-virgin olive oil is the first (and in most cases the only) choice for salad. If you can afford a bottle of cold-pressed Italian olive oil, this is the place to use it. (For more information on buying and using olive oil, see Chapter 2.)

## Vinegar 101

Although the oil may be the flashy member of the duo, the vinegar is just as important. Here's a rundown on the choices:

- **Red wine vinegar:** The better the red wine, the better the vinegar. Imported red wine vinegar tends to be slightly more acidic than domestic brands, but either makes a dressing with a strong kick. Like wine, good red wine vinegar is full-bodied and complex.

- **White wine vinegar:** Less full-bodied than vinegar made with red wine, white wine vinegar is still fairly acidic. When you don't want a pink dressing (for example, a dressing made with red wine vinegar dyes cauliflower and other white foods), use white wine vinegar. Don't buy distilled white vinegar, which is made from grains, not wine, and has little flavor.

- **Citrus juice:** Many Italian salad dressings don't contain any vinegar. Before juicing lemons or oranges, think about grating some of the peel and adding a little to the dressing. The zest boosts the citrus flavor without altering the acid-to-oil ratio. If you can get your hands on some ruby red blood oranges, use them in dressing. Their musky, sweet-and-sour flavor and unusual red color are not to be missed.

- **Balsamic vinegar:** Balsamic vinegar has a rich brown color and sweet, woody flavor that comes from aging in casks. Many recipes call for half balsamic vinegar and half red wine vinegar. This ratio helps balance the sweetness of the balsamic vinegar and keeps it from overpowering other ingredients.

### Avoiding fake balsamic vinegar

You say you've tried balsamic vinegar and can't figure out what all the fuss is about. Odds are good that you've been taken and haven't purchased real balsamico.

# Balsamic vinegar

Balsamic vinegar is the trendy condiment of choice for everything from salad dressings to sauces. However, most Americans would be surprised to learn that they have never tasted "real" balsamic vinegar. Even more shocking, balsamic vinegar is more popular in the United States than in Italy, where its culinary uses are actually quite limited. Contrary to what the chef at your local restaurant may think, balsamic vinegar is not Italy's answer to soy sauce. Balsamic vinegar has very specific uses. One of those is salad dressing.

Until 20 years ago, balsamic vinegar was an obscure condiment from the Emilia-Romagna region of north-central Italy. It was made at home, as it had been for centuries, by wealthy families and served mostly as a digestive after dinner. This artisanal product starts with the unfermented juice of local white grapes, which is then aged for decades in wood casks. Barrels of vinegars were often passed down from one generation to the next, sometimes as part of a dowry. (We'll take cash, thank you.) Production has always been extremely limited and costs have always been prohibitive. Traditional balsamic vinegar is a labor of love, not a money-making venture.

All this changed when savvy Italian marketers realized that Americans would buy endless amounts of sweet-and-sour commercially made balsamic vinegar. Although fewer than 10,000 bottles of traditional balsamic vinegar are released every year, annual American consumption of balsamic vinegar now stands at several million bottles. To turn a family tradition into an international business, manufacturers first had to create the supply to meet the demand. The solution — sell a compromised product.

Many cheap brands of balsamic vinegar are simply red wine vinegar with caramel added for color and sweetness. If a bottle of "balsamic vinegar" costs $2, you can be sure it has not been aged and isn't the real thing.

While the real thing can cost upwards of $50 an ounce, a happy middle ground is available. Unaged balsamic vinegar is harsh and unpleasant, but aging for 12 or more years makes the product costly to produce. The solution some companies have adopted is aging for several years in wood. The resulting vinegar has a gentle sweetness combined with a low-to-moderate acidity; a complex, woody bouquet and flavor reminiscent of fruit; and a dense, syrupy consistency — all qualities that are revered in traditional balsamic vinegar. A small bottle costs $5 or $10, but remember that a little goes a long way. When shopping, read labels carefully. Vinegars that are aged usually say so.

Even quality commercial balsamic vinegars are not used straight in salad dressings in Italy, but are usually combined with red wine vinegar. Other traditional uses — such as sprinkling over steamed asparagus, sliced Parmesan, or vanilla gelato — require very small quantities. Italians do not generally cook with balsamic vinegar because heat destroys its subtle qualities. To use balsamic vinegar in savory foods, add a few drops to a sauce just before serving or drizzle some over a piece of grilled fish.

### Why some balsamico costs $150 a bottle

So why does a 3-ounce bottle of traditional aged balsamic vinegar cost $150? The answer is low yield and high storage fees. A typical vineyard acre may produce enough grape juice to make 800 gallons of wine vinegar. After the juice from those same grapes has been cooked down and aged, during which time massive evaporation occurs, just 20 or 30 gallons of balsamic vinegar remain. High storage costs (just keeping water that long is expensive) add to the final price, which is rarely less than $60 per bottle (see Figure 4-1) and can climb to $200.

**Figure 4-1:**
Aged balsamic vinegar.

Aged balsamic vinegar is usually sold in small flasks that resemble perfume bottles.

Is any vinegar worth that much? Traditional balsamic vinegar has a high viscosity, intense but pleasant sweetness, heady aroma, and minimal acidity — all traits that easily distinguish it from commercial vinegars. These characteristics also restrict its uses. Wealthy Italians sip traditional balsamico after dinner or sprinkle a few drops over sliced strawberries. For most other culinary purposes, a good commercial balsamic vinegar will do just fine. But be prepared. When dining with the Duke and Duchess of Mantua, they may just serve you a spoon of balsamic vinegar after dinner.

# Making dressing

Like oil and water, oil and vinegar would rather remain separate. Put them together in a bowl, and the oil rises to the top and the vinegar sinks to the bottom. Use a colored vinegar, such as red wine vinegar, and you actually see the red vinegar layer on the bottom and the oil on top.

But mixing the oil and vinegar together is essential for making an emulsion, a scientific term that refers to any mixture of liquids that don't ordinarily combine. Salad dressing is an emulsion. The French call this cold sauce vinaigrette, and so does much of the rest of the world.

To make a vinaigrette, start by beating (with a fork or small wire whisk) the vinegar, salt and pepper, and any other seasonings (mustard, spices, and so on) together in a bowl until smooth. Drizzle in the oil and beat until the dressing is smooth. Use a light hand with seasonings — a pinch of salt and pepper is fine and a teaspoon of mustard is plenty. As for the amount of oil, use 2 to 4 tablespoons oil for every tablespoon of vinegar. Of course, taste the dressing (dip a piece of lettuce into the bowl if you like) and adjust the seasonings and amount of oil to suit your personal tastes.

Vinaigrette can be set aside at room temperature for several hours or refrigerated for several days. However, after several minutes, the emulsion breaks and the oil and vinegar separates. Simply whisk again right before drizzling over greens and the vinaigrette is as good as new.

The following tomato and cheese salad is dressed with Italy's simplest and most common vinaigrette, made with red wine vinegar, salt and pepper, and olive oil. This dressing complements almost any salad ingredients.

## Tomato and Mozzarella Salad, Capri Style

This classic Italian salad works well as a light lunch or as an appetizer (see photo in color section). This summer dish depends on ripe tomatoes, fresh basil, and good-quality fresh mozzarella cheese. You can add sliced red onions as well.

*Italian recipe name:* Insalata Caprese

*Preparation time:* 10 minutes

*Cooking time:* None

*Yield:* 4 servings

*(continued)*

*1 tablespoon red wine vinegar*

*Salt and pepper to taste*

*2 tablespoons olive oil*

*2 cups arugula, washed (optional)*

*2 large ripe tomatoes, cut into $^1/_4$-inch-thick slices*

*$^3/_4$-pound mozzarella, cut into $^1/_4$-inch-thick slices*

*8 leaves basil, finely sliced, or 2 table-spoons dried oregano*

*1* Prepare the dressing, whisking together the vinegar and salt and pepper in a small mixing bowl. Slowly whisk in the oil until the dressing is smooth. Set aside.

*2* Line 4 plates with the arugula leaves. Arrange alternating slices of tomato and mozzarella over the arugula to form a circle.

*3* Sprinkle the salad with basil and drizzle with the prepared dressing. Serve immediately after the salad is dressed.

## The real mozzarella di bufala

A lot of restaurants make a big deal about their mozzarella. Menus shout about cheese that comes from Italy. And this mozzarella certainly was never shrink-wrapped. The original mozzarella was made in the countryside of Campania and Latium from water buffaloes (see figure), a cousin to the American bison. In those regions, cheese is still sometimes made from water buffalo's milk rather than cow's milk, hence the name mozzarella di bufala. This cheese is prized for its intense flavor, porcelain white color, and compact but moist texture. Don't cook with this cheese. Heat destroys all the subtleties that cost so much money. It's shown to its best advantage when served fresh in salads, such as Tomato and Mozzarella Salad, Capri Style.

This highly perishable cheese is sometimes shipped by air. However, it's not a very good traveler. After a few days, the delicate, sweet flavor and creamy texture are lost. If you have a good Italian market or cheese shop that imports mozzarella di bufala, ask when their shipment arrived before buying. If the answer is

A water buffalo makes the world's best mozzarella.

last week, stick with fresh mozzarella made closer to home. (See Chapter 2 for more information on buying mozzarella.)

# Leafy Salads

In Italy, leafy salads are served after dinner and before dessert. This may be one reason why bitter greens, such as arugula and radicchio, are so popular. The assertive flavor of the salad cleanses the palate and acts as a transition between the main course and dessert.

You can also serve bold greens American style, before dinner. Their strong flavors stimulate the appetite, and you don't need to consume tremendous quantities to quell hunger pangs. Can you say that about iceberg lettuce with store-bought dressing?

Don't drown greens with too much dressing. Add just enough dressing to coat the greens. They should glisten with just the lightest sheen of oil and vinegar. Never add so much dressing that the leaves become soggy. Tastes vary, but we generally use $^1/_4$ cup of dressing per 8 cups of salad greens — enough salad for four servings.

For the dressing to cling to greens, they must be perfectly dry. Oil and vinegar will slide off wet lettuce leaves and pool up at the bottom of the salad bowl. Yuck!

A salad spinner (shown in Figure 4-2) does a good job of drying greens, but it doesn't hurt to then pat greens with paper towels to remove all traces of moisture.

**Figure 4-2:**
A salad spinner makes drying greens quick and foolproof.

salad spinner

## Gosh, those greens are bitter

Italians find the bitter bite of peppery arugula or sharp radicchio refreshing. But fill a bowl with too much arugula, radicchio, and endive, and eating salad can become a test of machismo.

If you are not so wild about bitter greens, we know of several ways to keep the punch under control:

- **Mix bitter greens (such as arugula, radicchio, endive, and chicory) with milder greens (such as leaf lettuces).** Salads will have some bite, but they won't be so assertive that kids will run from the table.

- **Dress bitter greens with a dressing that is low in acidity.** A sharp, acidic dressing makes the greens taste even more bitter. Try using lemon juice in place of vinegar (it has half the acidity), or make sure to use a high ratio of oil-to-vinegar in your dressing, at least 4 parts oil to 1 part vinegar.

## A guide to salad greens

A good *insalata mista,* or mixed salad, has a balance of colors, textures, and flavors. For example, red radicchio leaves and white Belgian endive perk up any all-green salad. Or mix really crunchy greens like endive or chicory with something soft and tender like escarole. And remember, a little bitter radicchio or arugula is nice, but make sure that you add something mild in the salad bowl, such as spinach or leaf lettuce.

Here are some notes on our favorite salad greens (see Figure 4-3):

- **Arugula:** This tender, dark green leaf ranges from faintly peppery to downright hot. Arugula from the garden or a farmers' market is usually hotter than the varieties sold in supermarkets. Taste before adding to the salad bowl and adjust the proportion of arugula according to intensity. Also called rocket, especially in California.

- **Belgian endive:** This crisp and crunchy chicory is grown without light, hence the pale yellow and white color of the leaves. Fairly bitter, so use sparingly.

- **Bibb lettuce:** This mild lettuce has medium-green leaves that are extremely tender. Similar to Boston lettuce.

- **Boston lettuce:** Like Bibb lettuce, Boston is very mild tasting and very tender. Medium-green color and compact, round head resembles a rose.

- **Chicory:** Also called curly endive, this green has curly, cut leaves that form a loose head in the shape of a sunburst. The leaves are bright green and bitter. Outer leaves can be quite tough and should be discarded. Chicory is also the name for a family of bitter greens that include endive, escarole, frisee, and radicchio.

- **Dandelion:** Dandelion greens are long and have ragged edges. They are bitter and can be used interchangeably with arugula. Young, small dandelion greens are best in salads. Older leaves are tougher and should be cooked.

**Figure 4-3:**
Favorite
salad
greens.

✔ **Escarole:** With its long ribs and ruffled leaves, escarole looks like leaf lettuce. However, the flavor is more intense (escarole is related to radicchio and endive) but not bitter or overpowering.

✔ **Frisee:** This miniature green has spike-shaped leaves and a rich flavor that is reminiscent of nuts. Fairly crunchy, this chicory can be slightly bitter.

✔ **Leaf lettuce:** Also called looseleaf lettuce, this designation applies to several varieties, including red leaf, green leaf, red oak, and lolla rossa. All grow in a loose rosette shape, not a tight head. Leaves are ruffled and soft but a bit crunchy in places. Flavor is mild but not boring. Extremely versatile and a favorite.

- ✓ **Mesclun:** A mix of baby greens that originally hails from the south of France, classic mesclun contains herbs and edible flowers. Today, markets label any mixture of baby greens mesclun. Often includes baby versions of cooking greens, such as baby beet greens, baby chard, and baby kale.

- ✓ **Radicchio:** Several varieties of this red chicory are available. The most common variety has a compact, round head of magenta leaves streaked with white ribs. Other varieties popular in Italy include Treviso, with long, tapered leaves.

- ✓ **Romaine lettuce:** Long, broad leaves that shade from dark green on the outside of the head to pale green in the crisp heart. Also called Cos lettuce, this variety is crunchy and has a fairly strong earthy or mineral flavor. Romaine lettuce is essential in Caesar salad, which (despite its name) is not Italian. Caesar salad was invented by a chef in Tijuana, Mexico, in the 1920s.

- ✓ **Spinach:** Flat-leaf spinach sold in bundles is better for salads than the curly variety sold in cellophane packages. The leaves are less fibrous and more moist.

- ✓ **Watercress:** With its small leaves and long, thick stalks, watercress has a distinctive look. It requires some work to prepare because the tough stalks must be removed one at a time. Flavor is mildly spicy, similar to arugula.

## Adding herbs to the salad bowl

Italian cooks often add fresh herbs to a leafy salad. Whole leaves of basil and parsley are most common, but mint, tarragon, oregano, or thyme also are possible choices, especially if used in small quantities. Just make sure that the herbs are really fresh and thoroughly washed to remove any dirt. You can put herbs in a salad spinner with greens and then dry thoroughly.

### Mushroom Salad

Italians love cremini mushrooms. They look like regular white button mushrooms that have been painted light brown. However, their flavor is much stronger and woodsy. Prepare them like regular white mushrooms by trimming a thin slice from the stem and then wiping them clean with a paper towel. If the mushrooms are really dirty, you can rinse them under cold running water. Just make sure to dry them thoroughly, or they will become soggy.

***Italian recipe name:*** *Insalata di Funghi*

***Preparation time:*** *15 to 20 minutes*

***Cooking time:*** *None*

***Yield:*** *4 to 6 servings*

3 tablespoons lemon juice

$^1/_2$ cup olive oil

2 teaspoons finely chopped fresh oregano

1 tablespoon finely chopped fresh Italian parsley, or 1 teaspoon dried parsley

4 cups cleaned and sliced cremini (or regular) mushrooms

Salt and pepper to taste

40 arugula leaves, washed

1 head radicchio, sliced into long strips

3 ounces Parmigiano-Reggiano, shaved into thin strips (see Figure 4-4)

**1** In a large bowl, whisk together the lemon juice, olive oil, oregano, and parsley. Add the mushrooms. Season with salt and pepper. Mix well.

**2** Arrange arugula and radicchio on a large serving plate or on 4 to 6 salad plates. Neatly mound the mushroom mixture on top and sprinkle with the Parmigiano-Reggiano shavings.

**Figure 4-4:**
Shaving a hunk of Parmigiano-Reggiano.

# Salad without dressing

We aren't suggesting that you eat undressed greens. Rabbits might like to chew on plain lettuce, but most people we know like their greens to dress for dinner. But we can recommend a simple solution when you don't feel like whisking oil, vinegar, and seasonings together to make a vinaigrette.

Some Italian cooks drizzle a favorite vinegar directly over a bowl of greens, sprinkle with salt, drizzle with olive oil, and then toss. No shaking up dressing in a little jar or whisking involved.

Because the oil and vinegar are not mixed, the flavor of the vinegar stands out, and the greens taste a bit sharper. Some people like this unadulterated hit of vinegar. Others may want to use a bit less vinegar than usual to keep the acid under control. Of course, if you're weary of vinegar, make a vinaigrette. The vinegar is broken into small droplets coated with oil that are harder for our tongues to detect.

## Fennel and Orange Salad

Fennel, a popular vegetable in Italy, is eaten raw in salads or cooked and served as a side dish. Raw fennel is crunchy like celery but has a sweet licorice flavor. This dish is Sicilian in origin and has the exotic, sweet flavors that are typical of the local cooking (see photo in color section).

**Italian recipe name:** *Insalata di Finocchi e Aranci*

**Preparation time:** *15 minutes*

**Cooking time:** *None (1 hour marination)*

**Yield:** *4 to 6 servings*

*2 small fennel bulbs, stems discarded; bulbs halved, cored, and thinly sliced*

*3 oranges, peeled and sectioned*

*2 tablespoons olive oil*

*2 teaspoons vinegar*

*1 tablespoon chopped parsley*

*Salt and pepper to taste*

*8 or 12 leaves of a colorful lettuce, such as red leaf*

**1** In a bowl, combine all the ingredients (except lettuce) and let the mixture marinate for 1 hour.

**2** Place 2 lettuce leaves on each salad plate and divide the Fennel and Orange Salad over the top.

To section an orange, use a sharp paring knife to trim a piece from either end so that the fruit will sit flat on a cutting board. Trim the peel and white pith with the knife. Many salad recipes call for sectioning a peeled orange. This process removes the stringy white membranes that hold each section in place. Simply cut along each side of the membrane, working the knife beneath the membrane and down toward the center of the fruit (see Figure 4-5). Section the fruit over a bowl to catch any juices.

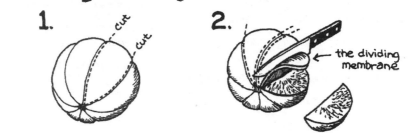

**Sectioning an Orange to Eliminate Membranes**

**Figure 4-5:**
Sectioning
an orange.

# *Hearty Salads*

Many Italian salads don't contain a single leafy green. In other cases, the greens are merely a bed for the "main" ingredients. Italians enjoy all kinds of room-temperature foods, including vegetable, seafood, or chicken salads bound with dressing. For most of these recipes, the main ingredient is cooked, dressed, and then cooled to room temperature.

Leafy salads are light and refreshing, but composed salads are generally more substantial and are designed to make a light meal or lunch, especially if they contain meat or seafood. (No, you don't need a music degree, but often you do need to assemble or compose the elements in these recipes on a plate rather than tossing them in a salad bowl.) Composed salads are especially appealing during warm weather — that's why they're popular in Italy. You can also served a composed salad as an antipasto.

## Tuscan Bread Salad

Italians cooks are thrifty by nature. They find uses for everything, including stale bread, which gets used in delicious summer salads. Bread that is too fresh makes the salad soggy, and bread that is too hard doesn't soften up enough. To take the guesswork out of this dish, we suggest toasting slices of fresh Italian bread in a 300° oven until dry but not brown, about 5 to 7 minutes (see photo in color section). If you have some stale bread on hand, you can use it instead, but be prepared to adjust the marinating time to achieve the right texture. You can add canned tuna and/or anchovies to make this salad more substantial.

*Italian recipe name:* *Panzanella*

*Preparation time:* *20 minutes*

*Cooking time:* *None (1 hour marination)*

*Yield:* *4 to 6 servings*

*(continued)*

*6 slices Italian bread, toasted and cut into
$^{1}/_{2}$-inch cubes*

*4 ripe tomatoes, cut into 1-inch cubes*

*2 stalks celery, cut crosswise into $^{1}/_{2}$-inch
pieces*

*1 medium onion, peeled and thinly sliced*

*1 small cucumber, skinned, seeded, halved
lengthwise, and cut into $^{1}/_{8}$-inch crescents*

*$^{3}/_{4}$ cup olive oil*

*$^{1}/_{2}$ cup red wine vinegar*

*1 cup fresh basil, sliced into long
ribbons*

*Salt and pepper to taste*

**1** Combine all ingredients in a large bowl, toss, and let sit for 1 hour.

**2** Serve at room temperature.

## Lentil Salad

In Umbria, the farmers grow especially small and flavorful lentils. Unfortunately, these lentils are not exported. You can use regular supermarket brown lentils in this recipe, but if you make it with green lentils from France, called lentils du Puy, the results are especially good. These tiny green lentils hold their shape well and are excellent in salads like this one.

***Italian recipe name:*** *Insalata di Lenticchie*

***Preparation time:*** *15 minutes*

***Cooking time:*** *None (30 minutes marination)*

***Yield:*** *4 to 6 servings*

*$2^{1}/_{2}$ cups cooked lentils (see Chapter 14)*

*1 medium onion, peeled and chopped*

*2 shallots, finely chopped*

*1 tomato, chopped*

*2 tablespoons chopped parsley*

*$^{1}/_{2}$ cup olive oil*

*$^{1}/_{4}$ cup wine vinegar*

*Salt and pepper to taste*

**1** Combine all ingredients in a small bowl.

**2** Allow flavors to combine for at least 30 minutes before serving. Serve at room temperature.

## Italian Potato Salad

This is a popular summertime dish in Italy because it can be eaten at room temperature. With their gold flesh and buttery flavor, Yukon Gold potatoes are especially good in this recipe, but any potato will work fine.

***Italian recipe name:*** *Insalata di Patate*

***Preparation time:*** *15 minutes*

***Cooking time:*** *48 minutes (plus 1 hour marination)*

***Yield:*** *4 servings*

| | |
|---|---|
| *7 medium potatoes, peeled* | *1 tablespoon chopped garlic* |
| *Salt and pepper to taste* | *¹/₂ cup olive oil* |
| *2 tablespoons chopped parsley* | *¹/₄ cup red wine vinegar* |

**1** Place the potatoes in a large pot and cover with cool water. Add salt and pepper. Bring to a boil and then reduce heat to medium and cook for 45 minutes or until the potatoes are tender but still slightly firm and unbroken. Drain potatoes, discarding the water and returning the potatoes to the pot.

**2** Place the pot over medium heat for 2 minutes to evaporate the remaining water from the potatoes.

**3** Remove the pot from the heat and cut the potatoes into bite-sized pieces (about 1¹/₂ inches) and place in a large bowl. Add remaining ingredients and toss gently. Cover and let stand for 1 hour to blend flavors. Serve at room temperature.

## Capon Salad

This recipe comes from Mantua in Lombardy and dates back to the Renaissance when Spanish nobility married into local families. The combination of sweet and sour shows the Spanish influence on this dish. Traditionally, this salad is made with the breast of a capon, which is larger than a chicken. If you can order capon from your butcher, great. If not, use the largest chicken breast you can find.

***Italian recipe name:*** *Insalata di Cappone*

***Preparation time:*** *20 minutes*

***Cooking time:*** *30 minutes (plus 2 hours marination)*

***Yield:*** *4 servings*

*(continued)*

*¹/₂ cup white wine*

*2 teaspoons sugar*

*¹/₄ cup raisins (light or dark)*

*2 quarts chicken broth (homemade or canned)*

*1¹/₂ pounds capon breast (or chicken breast)*

*2 tablespoons red wine vinegar*

*Juice from ¹/₂ lemon (about 1¹/₂ tablespoons)*

*2 celery stalks, finely sliced*

*2 tablespoons pine nuts*

*2 tablespoons olive oil*

*Salt and pepper to taste*

*1 apple, peeled and thinly sliced*

*8 lettuce leaves, such as red leaf*

*1* In a small bowl, combine the wine, sugar, and raisins. Let stand for about 10 minutes, until the raisins become soft.

*2* In a medium saucepan over medium-high heat, bring the broth to a boil. Place the capon breast in the broth and lower the heat so that it gently boils. Cook for 30 minutes. Turn off the heat and allow the capon breast to cool in the broth.

*3* Remove the capon breast from the broth and shred it into bite-sized pieces. Place the breast meat in a large bowl.

*4* Add the raisin mixture, red wine vinegar, lemon juice, celery, pine nuts, and olive oil. Season with salt and pepper. Toss well. Cover and refrigerate for 2 hours.

*5* Add the apple slices. Toss well. Place 2 lettuce leaves on each plate and place a neat mound of capon salad on top.

 **Salmon Salad**

Nothing is worse than a salmon salad with bones, so make sure to buy a salmon fillet rather than a salmon steak for this recipe (see photo in color section). As an added precaution, run your fingers over the surface of the fillet to feel for any stray bones. They will be white and thin and can be removed by hand or with tweezers if necessary. The vinaigrette for this dish is a bit unusual because it contains white wine. Choose something fruity and then serve the same wine with the salad.

***Italian recipe name:*** *Insalata di Salmone*

***Preparation time:*** *30 minutes*

***Cooking time:*** *20 minutes*

***Yield:*** *4 servings*

4 cups vegetable broth (canned or homemade) or water

1 carrot

2 stalks celery, cut in $^1/_4$-inch pieces

$^1/_2$ yellow bell pepper, cut in $^1/_4$-inch pieces

$^1/_2$ red bell pepper, cut in $^1/_4$-inch pieces

2 zucchini, cut in $^1/_8$-inch slices

12 ounces salmon fillet

3 tablespoons olive oil

1 tablespoon vinegar

Juice of $^1/_2$ lemon (about $1^1/_2$ tablespoons)

1 clove garlic, peeled and finely chopped

3 tablespoons white wine

Salt and pepper to taste

8 lettuce leaves, preferably Boston

*1* In a large skillet, bring the vegetable broth to a boil. Add the carrot and cook, covered, for 5 minutes. Transfer the carrot from the broth to a medium mixing bowl. Let cool and slice into $^1/_6$-inch pieces. Set aside. Reserve the cooking liquid in the skillet.

*2* Add the celery, yellow pepper, red pepper, and zucchini to the bowl.

*3* Return the vegetable broth to a boil. Reduce heat so that the mixture gently simmers and add the salmon. Cook for about 12 minutes and then turn off the heat and allow the salmon to cool in the vegetable broth. Remove and discard the skin from the salmon, flake the salmon, and add it to the bowl with the vegetables.

*4* In a small mixing bowl, prepare the dressing by whisking together the oil, vinegar, lemon juice, garlic, wine, and salt and pepper. Add the dressing to the salad and gently stir to evenly coat. Adjust seasoning with salt and pepper, if necessary.

*5* On a large serving plate or 4 serving dishes, decoratively place the lettuce leaves. Neatly mound the salmon salad on top.

## Ligurian Style Tuna Salad with Vegetables

If you eat in French restaurants, you probably already know this dish as Niçoise salad. This Italian version comes from Genoa, which is just south of the French border. If you like, serve the salad with quartered hard-boiled eggs, using 1 egg per person. Italians usually use canned tuna packed in oil. Tuna packed in water works as well.

***Italian recipe name:*** *Insalata di Tonno alla Ligure*

***Preparation time:*** *15 minutes*

***Cooking time:*** *10 to 12 minutes*

***Yield:*** *4 servings*

*(continued)*

*2 medium potatoes, peeled and cut into 1-inch cubes*

*4 ounces French green beans, ends trimmed*

*1 head lettuce, preferably Boston*

*1 cucumber, sliced crosswise into ¹/₄-inch slices*

*2 large ripe tomatoes, each cut into 6 pieces*

*24 pitted olives*

*10-ounce can of tuna, drained*

*8 fillets of anchovies, drained*

*8 fresh basil leaves, or 1 teaspoon dried basil*

*4 tablespoons olive oil*

*2 tablespoons red wine vinegar*

*Salt and pepper to taste*

*1* Place the potatoes in a medium saucepan and cover with water. Bring to a boil and cook until potatoes are tender but still firm, 10 to 12 minutes. During the last 5 minutes of cooking, add the green beans. Drain, rinse under cold water, and then drain again.

*2* Divide the lettuce leaves neatly among 4 plates or use them to line the bottom of a serving tray.

*3* Arrange the green beans, potatoes, cucumber, tomatoes, olives, tuna, anchovies, and basil on top of the lettuce.

*4* Prepare the salad dressing: In a small bowl, whisk together the olive oil, vinegar, and salt and pepper. Drizzle the dressing over the salad and serve.

# Chapter 5

# Soup's On

## In This Chapter

▶ Making soup, Italian style

▶ Using stock versus water

▶ Boosting flavor with cheese rinds and dried mushrooms

▶ Making soup a meal with pasta, rice, beans, and bread

### Recipes in This Chapter

▶ Chicken Stock

▶ Fish Stock

▶ Vegetable Stock

▶ Chicken Soup with Pasta and Eggs

▶ Onion Soup

▶ Pasta and Bean Soup

▶ Lentil Soup

▶ Vegetable Soup, Genovese Style

▶ Tuscan Bread and Tomato Soup

▶ Second Day Vegetable Soup with Bread

🍴 🥄 🍲 🧄 🌿 🥕

Few dishes capture the essence of Italian cuisine like a bowl of hot soup. Soup in Italy is a humble dish, with its roots in *la cucina povera,* or the cooking of the poor. In not-too-distant times, soup was considered a meal. Historically, Italian cooks would cobble together nourishing, tasty suppers out of a few vegetables and maybe some beans or stale bread. These soups are generally thick, and never pureed. Rich cream soups are a rarity in Italy, at least in traditional home cooking.

*Zuppa* (zoop-pa) is the Italian word for soup. If you eat in Italian restaurants, you may recognize the term *zuppa di pesce.* With several kinds of seafood, this soup bespeaks of abundance. However, most Italian soups prepared at home are much simpler and less costly to make. For example, Pappa al Pomodoro, a traditional summer soup from Tuscany, is nothing more than ripe tomatoes simmered with water, basil, garlic, and olive oil and then thickened with leftover bread to create a thick, paplike texture (like baby food). Despite these humble ingredients, Pappa al Pomodoro is one of the most beloved dishes in Tuscany.

This chapter focuses on simple recipes that rely on beans, pasta, bread, and vegetables to create hearty, delicious soups that reveal the artistry and magic of Italian home cooking.

# *Making Soup — The Basics*

Making soup requires very little equipment and allows for plenty of latitude in the kitchen. You can often use vegetables, herbs, and beans interchangeably. If spinach is unavailable, you can use chard or kale (or even arugula) instead. Likewise, you can enrich a soup thickened and made hearty with pasta with rice instead. Soup-making is ideal for the cook who prefers not to follow rules.

That said, you need to know general procedures and have certain pieces of equipment. Soup requires a pot of some sort. A pot with a heavy bottom is preferable because many recipes call for sautéing onions and other vegetables in fat before adding the liquid ingredients. If you make soup in small batches, a 4- or 5-quart pot will suffice. For larger batches, a 6- to 8-quart pot will be better.

When choosing a pot size, make sure that the ingredients will not come too close to the top. Nothing is worse than a boil-over that spills precious soup onto the range top.

In many recipes, you will need a pot with a cover. The cover allows the cook to control the rate at which the liquid evaporates. When soup is cooked uncovered, much of the stock or water evaporates, and the result is a thick soup. Of course, if you want something more brothy, you can opt to leave the cover on.

Whether the cover is on or off, keep the liquid at a modest simmer. In most recipes, we recommend that you heat the liquid until it reaches a boil and then reduce the temperature to a simmer. (When the surface is covered with large popping bubbles, the soup is at a boil. When the soup is at simmer, small bubbles should rise gently to the surface.) Simmering, rather than boiling, ensures that vegetables, beans, and other ingredients soften without disintegrating.

In most recipes, we suggest that you season throughout the cooking process. When making soups, you need to be careful, though, not to add too much salt at the start. This is especially important in soups that are cooked uncovered. As the liquid reduces, what tastes like the right amount of salt becomes more concentrated in the remaining liquid, and the soup may be too salty by the time it's ready to be served. Go lightly at the start with the salt and then adjust the seasoning after the soup has cooked down sufficiently.

When soup is ready, it's time to dig out a ladle from the drawer; it's so much quicker and neater than using a spoon or pouring the soup straight from the pot. If you like your soup especially hot, use ovenproof ceramic soup bowls and warm them in a 200° oven for 10 minutes. (The bowls will be hot, so use oven mitts to handle them and warn diners that the bowls are hot.) The heat from the bowls will keep the soup piping hot, right to the last spoonful.

Most soups work well as leftovers, reheated the next day. Soups with pasta, rice, and bread are the exceptions. These ingredients become mushy if reheated. Although these soups taste fine, the texture is not as appealing as when freshly made. In general, you can keep soups in the refrigerator for up to two days. If you want to store soup longer, place it in airtight containers and pop the containers in the freezer. Make sure to leave some headroom at the top of the containers because the soup will expand slightly as it freezes. Soup can be kept in the freezer for several months. Defrost frozen soup in the refrigerator before reheating.

Soup should be reheated over medium-low heat and stirred often to prevent the bottom from scorching. Sometimes the texture of the soup seems quite thick when it's being reheated. Thin the soup with water or stock until the desired consistency is achieved and adjust the seasoning if needed.

# Making Stock

Many Italian soups use water as their base, while others start with meat, chicken, fish, or vegetable stock. Stock is made by simmering bones, scraps of meat, parts with little use (like chicken backs or fish heads), and/or chopped vegetables and herbs in water. The solids flavor the water to create a rich base, called stock, that can be used to make soups or sauces.

Some cooks are under the misconception that the stock pot is the place to use limp vegetables, old scraps of meat, and other kitchen leftovers. However, stock tastes only as good as the ingredients used to make it. Meat should be fresh and trimmed of as much fat and gristle as possible. Vegetables should be fresh and clean. Although stock is the perfect place to use up a stray onion or carrot, don't add anything to the stock pot that you would not consider fresh enough to eat.

You can control the intensity of the stock in several ways. At the outset, you can change the ratio of solids to liquid. In general, you want to add enough water to cover the solid ingredients by an inch or two. Add more water, and the resulting stock will be weak, which may be fine for risotto but is not appropriate for brothy soup that needs a potent stock. If the solids are just barely covered with water, the stock will be more intense in flavor.

After the solids and water are in the pot, bring everything to a boil and then reduce the heat to a gentle simmer. As the solids cook, they may throw off some impurities in the form of foam, which should be skimmed off with a spoon and discarded.

After the solid ingredients have given up their flavor, the contents of the stock pot are poured through a mesh strainer set over a clean container or pot. (This flavor-finding mission happens quickly — in less than an hour — for vegetables and fish; for chicken and meat, this process can take two or three hours.) The strainer traps the solids. To release as much flavor as possible from the solids, press down on them with the back of a large spoon to squeeze out their juices. A French strainer, called a chinois, has a conical shape that makes it especially easy to extract every last bit of flavor from the stock ingredients (see Figure 5-1).

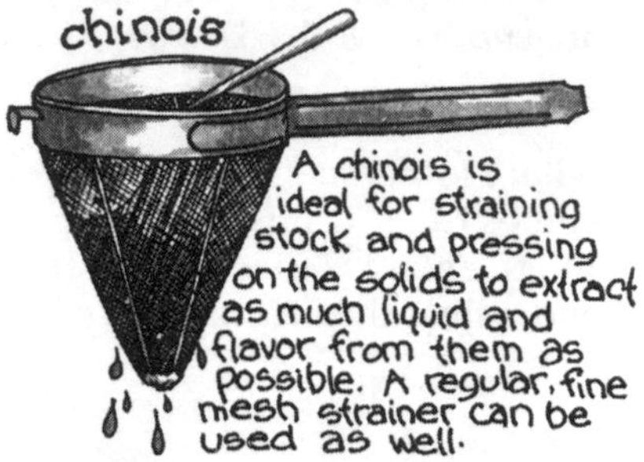

**Figure 5-1:** A chinois.

To intensify the flavor of a finished stock, place the strained liquid back over the heat and cook until reduced to the desired consistency. Because stock is often reduced, salt is generally not added until the stock is ready to be used. When the stock is done, it should be cooled until the fat congeals on top. This fat can be removed with a spoon or skimmer and discarded.

Defatted stock should be placed in an airtight container and refrigerated for up to three days or frozen for up to several months. When freezing stock, divide a single batch into several smaller containers so that you can pull out just as much as you need when making recipes in the future. Or, freeze stock in ice cube trays and store the frozen cubes in plastic bags.

## Stock portfolio

Cooks who want to plan strategically for the future should keep chicken, fish, and vegetable stock in the freezer. Stock on hand is the culinary equivalent of owning a diversified portfolio of stocks, bonds, and mutual funds.

✔ **Chicken stock:** Chicken stock is by far the most versatile stock. It's rarely inappropriate (beef stock in fish soup is odd, but

chicken stock will taste just fine) and is often the best choice. Use backs, necks, wings, or even drumsticks to make stock. In most cases, the chicken should be balanced with a handful or two of chopped vegetables (onion, carrot, and celery are the usual choices) and perhaps 1 or 2 bay leaves, several peeled garlic cloves, and a dozen or so whole black peppercorns. You can also add some whole parsley sprigs. The chicken is essential; the vegetables are nice but optional.

To make about 2 quarts chicken stock, start with 3 pounds chicken parts (remove any fat and skin first) in a pot and cover with 2¹/₂ quarts water. Add vegetables and herbs and simmer for at least 2 hours to extract the full flavor from the chicken.

✔ **Fish stock:** Fish stock has limited uses (for chowders, other fish soups, and seafood risotto), but it can make a good dish great, adding depth of flavor and intensity. Fish stock is usually made from scraps such as heads, bones, and tails from fish, as well as shells from lobster or shrimp. Avoid oily fish, such as salmon, which makes the stock too fishy. Fish with mild, white, flaky flesh, such as red snapper or flounder, are best for stock. Make sure that innards and gills don't go into the stock pot because they impart an off flavor.

To make about 2 quarts fish stock, place 2 pounds fish heads, bones, tails, and fins in a pot and cover with 2 quarts water. Add aromatics like bay leaves, parsley, and thyme sprigs, and whole black peppercorns and simmer for about 30 minutes to extract the flavor from the fish. (Do not cook too long, or the stock will become too fishy.) Many chefs use a little wine along with water as the liquid. The acidity from the wine balances the fish flavor nicely. If you want to use white wine, add 1 cup for every 2 quarts water. You can add a halved lemon as well.

✔ **Vegetable stock:** Some chefs argue that light vegetable dishes, such as an asparagus risotto, are overwhelmed by rich chicken stock and that a milder vegetable stock is the better route. Other chefs find vegetable stocks insipid and prefer to use chicken stock in most every application, other than seafood soups. One camp appreciates the mild sweetness of good vegetable stock, while the other camp wishes vegetable stock were richer and stronger tasting, like chicken stock.

We tend to agree that vegetable stock is nice in certain applications where chicken stock can overwhelm the flavor of vegetables. However, you must use good vegetable stock. Throwing a chicken into a pot with some water produces good stock. Add some aromatic vegetables such as onions and carrots, and you have great stock. Vegetable stock requires more thought and more work.

To coax flavor from the vegetables, we recommend that you sauté them in a little olive oil before adding the water. Using lots of vegetables (at least a cup of chopped vegetables for every cup of water) is imperative. Leeks, onions, carrots, and celery are a must. Typical seasonings include fresh herbs (especially thyme, basil, and parsley sprigs), dried bay leaves, and whole black peppercorns. Add potatoes to give the stock some body, peeled garlic cloves for some intensity, a little dried porcini for some earthy flavor and color, and a chopped tomato or two for color. Finely chop all vegetables so that they release as much flavor as possible.

To make about 2 quarts vegetable stock, place 10 cups finely chopped vegetables in a pot along with 2 tablespoons olive oil. Sauté until the vegetables are golden, 10 to 12 minutes. Add 10 cups water and then simmer until the vegetables have given up their flavor, about 1 hour. When straining the stock, press firmly on the vegetables to extract all their juices.

## Chicken Soup with Pasta and Eggs

At its simplest, stracciatella is just eggs cooked in chicken stock. It's not all that different from the egg drop soup served at your local Chinese restaurant. In fact, this soup will even look like Chinese egg drop soup — with egg "rags" obvious. We like to add a little orzo, a tiny pasta shaped like rice, or broken spaghetti, but the pasta isn't essential. This recipe is typical of the cooking from the Jewish ghetto in Rome. High-quality homemade chicken stock really makes a difference in a such a simple dish. Some Roman recipes for stracciatella add the juice of half a lemon to the egg mixture. The acidity helps balance some of the richness from the chicken stock, eggs, and cheese.

***Italian recipe name:*** *Stracciatella*

***Preparation time:*** *5 minutes*

***Cooking time:*** *10 minutes*

***Yield:*** *4 servings*

*4 cups homemade chicken stock or canned chicken broth, divided*

*¹/₄ cup orzo or spaghetti, broken into 1-inch pieces*

*2 eggs*

*3 tablespoons grated Parmigiano-Reggiano*

*Salt and pepper to taste*

*1 tablespoon chopped fresh chives*

*1* Transfer ¹/₄ cup stock to a small bowl. Set aside. Pour the remaining stock into a medium saucepan and bring to a boil. Add the pasta and reduce the heat so that it gently boils.

*2* Add the eggs, Parmigiano-Reggiano, and salt and pepper to the reserved stock. Beat with a whisk for about 2 minutes. Slowly add the egg mixture to the simmering stock and pasta, stirring constantly. Continue to simmer for 8 minutes. Season with salt and pepper.

*3* Before serving, add the chives. Top with additional grated cheese, if desired.

# Using Water Rather than Stock

Many Italian peasant soups call for water. These recipes originated in times or places when meat was scarce. Because you don't need to make any stock, these recipes are appealing to modern cooks. Over the years, Italian cooks have found ways to make these simple soups rich in flavor.

## What about canned broth?

We always have some stock in the freezer, ready to flavor a quick soup, pasta sauce, or risotto. However, stock requires some planning, and you may not always have some on hand. Clearly, this happens very often, and that's why canned broths and bouillon cubes are so popular. (We don't know why, but when you cook chicken in water yourself, this resulting liquid is called stock. If you buy the same thing in a can, it's called broth.)

Italians are more likely to use a bouillon cube (called a *dado* in Italian) than canned broth. In the United States, we find that the bouillon cubes have an off-taste, and we generally avoid them. Canned broths, especially those that are low in sodium, are decent, if not great.

The flavor of chicken seems to translate best in canned broth. Canned beef broths have little meat flavor, and canned vegetable stocks are usually overly sweet. Remember you can always use water in an Italian soup if you have any doubts about the quality of canned broth. For more information, see the "Using Water Rather than Stock" section. (No one makes canned fish broth. Bottled clam juice is the usual substitute.)

First and foremost, start with cold, clean water. Hot water may seem like a timesaver, but it often picks up a metallic flavor in the water heater and should not be used when cooking soup or anything else, including tea or pasta. Also, make sure that all the ingredients that go into a water-based soup are extremely fresh and flavorful. Good chicken stock can compensate for lackluster vegetables better than plain water.

Besides using good ingredients, many Italian cooks rely on a number of flavor boosters when making water-based soups:

- Save the rinds from Parmigiano-Reggiano (they can be kept in the freezer in a zipper-lock bag for months) and add one rind to a pot of minestrone or other soup that can be served with grated cheese. The rind softens, but doesn't fall apart, as the soup cooks. When you're ready to serve the soup, just remember to fish out the rind and discard it. The cheese rind gives soups a rich buttery, nutty flavor.

- Soak some dried porcini mushrooms in hot water for 20 minutes, or until soft. Add the mushrooms and the strained soaking liquid to any soup that calls for mushrooms, and you'll get a heartier, fuller flavor.

- Sauté pancetta along with some vegetables in a little olive oil to heighten the flavor of the soup. The pancetta adds a salty, subtle pork flavor that is welcome in most soups.

✔ Swirl pesto or another herb paste (you can use something as simple as chopped fresh rosemary and minced garlic bound with olive oil) directly into the soup pot after the heat has been turned off. Even better, dollop a little pesto into each soup bowl just before serving. The heat releases the flavor of the basil and garlic, stimulating the olfactory senses as well as the taste buds.

✔ Grate some fresh cheese, especially Parmigiano-Reggiano or Pecorino Romano, directly into individual soup bowls.

✔ Drizzle high-quality extra-virgin olive oil into soup bowls at the table. Again, the heat of the soup releases the aroma from the oil and heightens the flavor of the soup.

## Onion Soup

Onion soup is made throughout Italy. Traditionally, a pot of onion soup would simmer gently on the stove all day. If eaten for lunch, it would be brothy. Later in the day, after the soup had cooked down, the consistency was more stewlike. This version is somewhere in between.

In the north, bowls of onion soup are usually sprinkled with grated Parmigiano-Reggiano just before serving. In the south, cheese is not added to the soup. The cheese is optional in this recipe, so do as you like.

**Italian recipe name:** *Zuppa di Cipolle*

**Preparation time:** *15 minutes*

**Cooking time:** *2 hours, 30 minutes*

**Yield:** *4 to 6 servings*

*$^1/_4$ cup olive oil*

*6 medium red onions, peeled, halved, and then sliced $^1/_8$- to $^1/_4$-inch thick*

*6 cloves garlic, peeled and thinly sliced*

*1 celery stalk, finely chopped*

*1 medium carrot, chopped*

*8 slices of pancetta or bacon (about 4 ounces), finely chopped*

*1 teaspoon crushed red pepper flakes*

*1 tablespoon red wine vinegar*

*1 cup white wine*

*Salt and pepper to taste*

*$2^1/_2$ quarts water or homemade vegetable stock*

*$^1/_4$ cup grated Parmigiano-Reggiano (optional)*

**1** In a large soup pot, heat the olive oil over medium heat. Add the onions, garlic, celery, carrot, pancetta, and red pepper flakes. Cook for 10 to 12 minutes, stirring occasionally, until the onions are soft.

**2** Add the vinegar and wine. Cook until the liquid has almost completely evaporated, about 5 minutes.

**3** Season with salt and pepper. Add the water or broth and bring to a boil. Reduce the heat and simmer, loosely covered, for 2 hours; the onions will have "melted."

**4** Adjust the flavor with salt and pepper, if necessary. Sprinkle with Parmigiano-Reggiano cheese before serving. Serve in large soup bowls.

# Creating Hearty Soups with Pasta, Rice, Beans, and Bread

Many Italian soups are made especially hearty by adding pasta, rice, beans, or bread to the pot. The texture becomes thick — almost stewlike — and these soups, which are usually vegetable-based, become a complete meal. You can add a salad or vegetable side dish, but otherwise these soups are one-dish meals.

## Pasta and rice in the pot

Pasta is almost always added when the soup is nearly done. The pasta should still be a bit al dente, not mushy or falling apart, when the soup is served. Tiny pasta shapes may need as little as 5 or 10 minutes of cooking; thicker shapes may need to simmer for 15 minutes.

The soup should be fairly brothy when the pasta is added. If the soup has cooked down, add a little water or stock, and return the liquid to a boil before adding the pasta.

Rice is treated in the same fashion as pasta. It should be cooked in the soup pot for as long as it takes to soften the grains. In general, 20 minutes is enough time. Regular long-grain rice is fine, but if you have some arborio rice (see Chapter 8) on hand, use it in soups. The grains will remain slightly chewy and are less likely to fall apart.

Both pasta and rice thicken soups by absorbing excess liquid as they soften and by throwing off some starch that gives body to the remaining liquid. As the pasta and rice cook, add more water if the soup is becoming too thick.

# Beans in the pot

Dried beans can be cooked right in the soup. The starch that the beans give off as they soften gives the soup body. If cooked long enough, the beans fall apart and make an especially thick, almost creamy, soup.

You can cook dried beans separately and then add them to the soup pot about five minutes before serving, simply to heat them through. (See Chapter 14 for more on dried beans.) You can also use canned beans, which have been drained and rinsed, in this kind of recipe.

## Pasta and Bean Soup

If pressed for time, place all the ingredients for the soup in the pot — except the pasta — and simmer until tender. Cook the pasta in the soup until al dente and serve. Whether making the quick or regular version of this recipe, you can sprinkle each serving of the soup with 1 tablespoon grated Parmigiano-Reggiano cheese.

***Italian recipe name:*** *Pasta e Fagioli*

***Preparation time:*** *20 minutes (plus overnight soaking for dried beans)*

***Cooking time:*** *2 hours*

***Yield:*** *6 to 8 servings*

***Special tool:*** *Food processor*

*$^1/_2$ cup dried cranberry beans*

*$^1/_2$ cup dried kidney beans*

*$^1/_2$ cup dried pinto beans*

*2 medium potatoes, peeled and diced*

*5 cloves garlic (3 cloves peeled and crushed; 2 cloves peeled and minced)*

*1 sprig fresh rosemary plus 1 tablespoon chopped fresh rosemary*

*1 sprig fresh sage plus 2 teaspoons chopped fresh sage*

*4 quarts cold water*

*1 tablespoon salt*

*$^1/_2$ cup olive oil, divided*

*4 ounces (about 8 slices) pancetta or bacon*

*1 small onion, peeled and chopped*

*1 leek, white part only, thoroughly rinsed and chopped*

*1 small celery stalk, chopped*

*1 medium carrot, chopped*

*$^1/_4$ teaspoon hot red pepper flakes*

*$^1/_2$ cup white wine*

*6 tablespoons tomato paste*

*$^1/_2$ pound dry short-cut pasta, such as pennette*

*Salt and pepper to taste*

*1* Rinse the beans, picking through them to remove any pebbles. Soak the beans overnight in a medium bowl with 5 cups cold water. Drain.

*2* Put the beans in a large soup pot with the potatoes, crushed garlic, rosemary sprig, and sage sprig. Add the water and bring the mixture to a boil. Add the salt and reduce the heat to a low boil. Cook, covered, until the beans are soft enough to crush easily between 2 fingers, about 40 to 45 minutes.

*3* Transfer half of the bean mixture to the bowl of a food processor. Puree until smooth. Return the bean puree to the soup pot.

*4* Heat $^{1}/_{4}$ cup olive oil in a medium skillet. Add the pancetta, minced garlic, chopped rosemary, chopped sage, onion, leek, celery, carrot, and red pepper flakes. Cook over medium heat, stirring occasionally, until the onion is soft and the mixture just starts to brown, about 12 to 15 minutes.

*5* Add the wine to the vegetables and cook until the liquid is completely absorbed, about 2 to 3 minutes.

*6* Transfer the contents of the skillet to the soup pot with the beans. Add the tomato paste. Stir to combine. Bring the soup mixture to a boil and then reduce the heat to maintain a low boil. Cook for 40 minutes, stirring occasionally.

*7* Add the pasta to the soup. Cook for another 8 to 12 minutes (depending on the cooking time of the pasta; check package instructions). Adjust the consistency of the soup as desired, adding up to 2 more cups of water. Adjust seasoning with salt and pepper. Serve soup hot, drizzled with remaining $^{1}/_{4}$ cup olive oil.

## Lentil Soup

Unlike other dried legumes, lentils are never soaked and are always cooked in the soup pot with the other ingredients. Lentil soup is a traditional dish for an Italian New Year's Eve celebration. Lentils are thought to bring good luck and money in the new year.

***Italian recipe name:*** *Zuppa di Lenticchie*

***Preparation time:*** *20 minutes*

***Cooking time:*** *40 to 45 minutes*

***Yield:*** *8 servings*

*(continued)*

*2 tablespoons olive oil*

*1 medium onion, peeled and chopped*

*1 medium carrot, peeled and chopped*

*2 celery stalks, chopped*

*4 cloves garlic, peeled and chopped*

*4 sprigs fresh sage, chopped, or 1 teaspoon dried sage*

*2 cups white wine*

*16-ounce can chopped Italian plum tomatoes, drained*

*1¹/₂ cups or 10 ounces dried green or brown lentils*

*2 medium potatoes, peeled and cut into 1-inch chunks*

*4 slices of pancetta (optional)*

*2 quarts cold water*

*Salt and pepper to taste*

**1** Heat the olive oil in a large saucepan. Add the onion, carrot, celery, garlic, and sage and cook over medium heat, stirring frequently, until the onion is translucent, about 7 minutes.

**2** Add the wine and cook until it reduces or evaporates completely.

**3** Add the tomatoes and cook for 5 more minutes and then add the lentils, potatoes, pancetta (if using), and water. Bring the mixture to a boil, reduce the heat, and simmer for 20 minutes. Test the lentils to see whether they're cooked; they should be tender but still have a slightly firm bite.

**4** Season the soup with salt and pepper. If a slightly creamy texture is desired, puree half of the soup in a food processor, return the puree to the saucepan, and simmer for another 5 minutes, stirring frequently.

## Vegetable Soup, Genovese Style

Minestra is another Italian word for soup. The word minestrone translates as "big soup" and refers to the fact that this soup is packed with vegetables. Each region in Italy has its own version of this classic vegetable soup. In Milan, minestrone usually contains more pancetta, cabbage, and squash and may be enriched with rice rather than pasta. In the Italian Alps, chestnuts are sometimes added, and in Tuscany black cabbage, a dark purple variety not widely available elsewhere, is a must for minestrone.

This version of minestrone comes from Genoa, where pesto or fresh basil is added to the soup. To make this soup heartier, add a handful or two of pasta about 5 minutes before the peas and pesto go into the pot. Small pasta shapes — such as elbows, ditali, or tiny shells — work best.

***Italian recipe name:*** *Minestrone alla Genovese*

***Preparation time:*** *30 minutes (plus overnight soaking time for dried beans)*

***Cooking time:*** *1 hour, 15 minutes*

***Yield:*** *6 servings*

*1 cup dried cannellini beans, or one 16-ounce can cannellini beans*

*2 tablespoons olive oil*

*4 slices pancetta or bacon (about 2 ounces), diced (optional)*

*1 medium onion, peeled and chopped*

*4 cloves garlic, peeled and minced*

*3 medium carrots, chopped*

*5 celery stalks, chopped*

*1 small fennel bulb, cored and diced*

*Pinch of dried red pepper flakes*

*1 cup white wine*

*3 medium potatoes, peeled and diced*

*3 cups shredded cabbage*

*1 cup canned Italian plum tomatoes*

*Salt and pepper to taste*

*2¹/₂ quarts cold water*

*12 asparagus spears, cut into 1-inch pieces*

*2 small zucchini, diced*

*¹/₂ cup frozen peas*

*1 cup diced green beans*

*¹/₄ cup Pesto (see recipe in Chapter 6), or 1 cup finely chopped fresh basil*

*1 cup grated Parmigiano-Reggiano*

*1* Pick over the dried beans to remove broken beans and pebbles and place the beans in a pot or bowl with 5 cups cold water. Soak them for at least 4 hours, preferably overnight. Drain.

*2* In a large soup pot, combine the olive oil, pancetta, onion, garlic, carrots, celery, fennel, and red pepper flakes. Cook over medium heat, stirring often, for about 10 minutes. Add the wine and continue cooking until most of it has evaporated, about 5 minutes.

*3* Add the potatoes, cabbage, tomatoes, and cannellini beans, stirring to combine. Season with salt and pepper. Add 2¹/₂ quarts water. Bring to a boil, reduce the heat, and simmer for 30 minutes. Add the asparagus, zucchini, and green beans and cook for another 30 to 35 minutes; the cannellini beans should be cooked to the point where they can easily be crushed between two fingers. Add the peas and pesto or basil and cook for 5 more minutes. Adjust the seasoning, if necessary, with salt and pepper. Serve hot or cold sprinkled with Parmigiano-Reggiano cheese.

# Bread in soup

Everyone knows that bread makes a great accompaniment to a bowl of soup. Italians take this logic one step further and actually add bread to the soup as it cooks. Stale cubes or slices soften in the pot and give soup heft and texture. Some cooks prefer to let the bread swell but still retain its shape. Others like the bread to fall apart. Depending on the size of the pieces and how stale they are, bread cubes require 5 to 10 minutes of cooking to soften and 30 to 40 minutes to fall apart.

As with pasta and rice, bread absorbs liquid and makes soups very thick. Make sure that the soup is still brothy when adding bread and thin out the texture before serving, if desired.

Most recipes calling for bread rely on country white bread. You can use a baguette or sourdough bread. However, avoid breads with seeds or nuts, which will float free in the soup.

## Tuscan Bread and Tomato Soup

This classic summertime soup is made in Tuscany with fresh ripe tomatoes (see photo in color section). In the winter, Tuscans make a similar soup called *pancotto,* or "cooked bread," which is brothier and contains a little tomato paste or canned tomatoes. However, Pappa al Pomodoro is about the tomatoes, so use the sweetest, ripest tomatoes you can find. The bread cubes in this recipe are cooked for a fairly long time and will fall apart to create a thick, porridgelike consistency, hence the name for the soup, which translates as "tomato pap."

***Italian recipe name:*** *Pappa al Pomodoro*

***Preparation time:*** *15 minutes*

***Cooking time:*** *1 hour*

***Yield:*** *4 servings*

*¹/₂ cup olive oil, divided*

*1 leek, white part only, thoroughly rinsed and chopped*

*1 small red onion, peeled and chopped*

*6 cloves garlic, peeled and chopped*

*¹/₂ cup white wine*

*¹/₂ cup chopped fresh basil, divided, or 1 tablespoon dried basil and 1 teaspoon dried oregano*

*1¹/₂ pounds ripe tomatoes (about 5 medium), peeled, seeded, and chopped, or one 20-ounce can of plum tomatoes*

*2 cups cold water*

*1¹/₂ cups cubed bread (1-day-old Italian country, or semolina bread)*

*Salt and pepper to taste*

*¹/₂ cup grated Parmigiano-Reggiano*

*1* In a large saucepan, heat ¹/₄ cup olive oil over medium heat. Add the leek, onion, and garlic and cook until the vegetables just start to brown, about 5 minutes. Do not allow the garlic to burn.

*2* Add the wine and maintain a low boil until it reduces to about 1 tablespoon of liquid, 5 to 8 minutes.

*3* Add ¹/₄ cup basil, the tomatoes, and water. Bring the mixture to a boil, reduce the heat, and simmer uncovered for 15 minutes. Add the bread. Cook, stirring occasionally, for another 20 minutes.

*4* Season the soup with salt and pepper, add the remaining ¹/₄ cup basil, and cook for 10 more minutes.

*5* Serve hot drizzled with the remaining ¹/₄ cup olive oil. Sprinkle with the Parmigiano-Reggiano cheese.

## Second Day Vegetable Soup with Bread

The name for this Tuscan soup literally translates as "reboiled" or "recooked." Traditionally, this soup is made from leftover vegetable soup. To stretch the leftovers, bread is added. The result is a thick, stewlike vegetable soup. Tuscans have become so enamored of this soup that they often make it from scratch, as we have.

Until this century, most Italians did not have an oven at home. If they needed to bake something, they would take a pot down to the local bakery and use the ovens after the bread for the day was made. We like the idea of baking soup, but you may simmer it on top of the stove if you prefer.

***Italian recipe name:*** *Ribollita*

***Preparation time:*** *20 minutes*

***Cooking time:*** *1 hour, 15 minutes*

***Yield:*** *6 servings*

*(continued)*

*8 slices pancetta or bacon (about 4 ounces), chopped*

*1 medium red onion, peeled and chopped*

*1 leek, white part only, rinsed well and chopped*

*1 cup chopped carrot*

*1 cup chopped celery*

*¹/₄ cup plus 2 tablespoons olive oil, divided*

*2 cups shredded Savoy cabbage*

*1 bunch (about 8 ounces) kale, rinsed thoroughly and chopped*

*1 bunch (about 8 ounces) Swiss chard, rinsed thoroughly and chopped*

*1 zucchini, sliced into ¹/₄-inch rounds*

*3 medium tomatoes, peeled, seeded, and diced*

*2 medium potatoes, peeled and diced*

*1¹/₂ cups dried cannellini beans, soaked and cooked (see Chapter 14), or one 16-ounce can cannellini beans, drained and rinsed*

*2 quarts water or homemade vegetable stock*

*5 slices Tuscan bread, each slice about 1-inch thick, toasted and brushed with garlic*

*Salt and pepper to taste*

*6 scallions, chopped*

*1 cup white wine*

**1** Preheat the oven to 350°. In a large, oven-safe soup pot or saucepan, combine the pancetta, onion, leek, carrot, celery, and ¹/₄ cup olive oil. Cook over medium-high heat, stirring occasionally, until the vegetables just begin to brown, about 5 minutes.

**2** Add the cabbage, kale, Swiss chard, zucchini, tomatoes, potatoes, and cooked cannellini beans. Cook, stirring often, for 5 minutes, and then add water or vegetable stock and the bread. Season with salt and pepper. Stir well, add the wine, cover, and cook for 5 minutes. Transfer the pot to the oven. Bake for 1 hour, stirring occasionally, until the beans and vegetables are soft. Spoon into hot soup bowls and sprinkle with the remaining 2 tablespoons olive oil and the scallions.

# Part III
# The Grains: Pasta, Pizza, and Beyond

The 5th Wave    By Rich Tennant

"Unfortunately, he drives the car like he makes pasta—al dente."

# In this part . . .

In this part of the book, we cover the carbohydrate-based dishes that have made Italian cooking so famous. We discuss dried and fresh pasta, along with rice, *polenta* (a cornmeal-based dish), and dumplings called *gnocchi*. Breads play an important role in Italian cooking, so we also include recipes for pizza, calzone, and focaccia in this part of the book.

# Chapter 6

# Dried Pasta

## In This Chapter

▶ Choosing dried pasta over fresh

▶ Buying dried pasta

▶ Cooking dried pasta

▶ Matching dried pasta shapes with sauces

▶ Saucing without a recipe

*1*t's hard to imagine Italian cooking without pasta. The average Italian consumes more than 60 pounds of pasta a year. Traditionally, pasta is served in small portions as a first course — often no more than 2 ounces. Divide 60 pounds by 2 ounces and that means the average Italian is eating pasta every day.

Pasta is Italy's leading culinary ambassador. Various sources attribute the origins of pasta to either China or Italy. Some scholars believe that Marco Polo or another traveler brought back knowledge of pasta from China in the Middle Ages. Other researchers believe that the Etruscans, a people who inhabited Italy more than 2,000 years ago, first learned to turn flour and water into the noodles we now call pasta.

Either way, we associate Italian food with pasta and pasta with Italian food. And although this book demonstrates that Italian cooking is more than just pasta (and pizza), pasta deserves its esteemed reputation.

# When You Should Use Fresh Pasta

Some chefs and food writers argue that the only pasta worth eating is fresh pasta. That's like saying you should only eat fresh local tomatoes at their peak of ripeness and then do without any tomatoes (canned or fresh) for the rest of the year. Fresh pasta is wonderful, and everyone should make it a couple of times a year. (For more information on making and saucing fresh pasta, see Chapter 7.) But can you live off fresh pasta alone? Hardly.

For the average Italian cook, fresh pasta is reserved for very specific uses and special occasions. Grandma makes her noodles for lasagne — she would never dream of using lasagne noodles from a box — or maybe she goes to the local pasta shop and buys fresh tagliatelle to toss with butter, cream, grated cheese, and some shaved fresh porcini mushrooms. In these dishes, fresh pasta makes a world of difference. Its softness and suppleness combined with its mild eggy flavor are divine. Make these recipes once with fresh pasta, and you'll never use dried pasta in these dishes again.

# When You Should Just Buy Dried Pasta

Day in and day out, the average Italian cook uses dried pasta. It's the first choice in Italian homes. And we can find plenty of reasons why dried pasta should be the first choice in your home.

- **It's cheap.** A pound of dried pasta feeds four as a main course or eight as an appetizer and costs less than a dollar. Sauces add to the cost, but as long as you avoid pricey ingredients like shellfish, the total cost of a pasta dinner is usually under $5.

- **It's versatile.** Many Italians eat pasta every day and claim to never tire of it. The variety of shapes — you can find literally hundreds — and sauces keep pasta from becoming boring. Because it is relatively bland, pasta takes on many guises — herbaceous and garlicky when served with pesto sauce; spicy and salty when sauced with tomato, anchovies, and capers; and light and fresh when sauced with grilled vegetables and olive oil.

- **It's always available.** Even when the cupboard is quite bare, most cooks are likely to have the ingredients for a pasta dinner on hand. Take some spaghetti, add a little oil and garlic, and you have the makings of a classic Italian dish. For cooks who hate to shop, pasta is a valued ally. It stays "fresh" for years, if stored in its box in a cool, dry pantry. Did you ever throw out spaghetti because it was past its prime?

- **It's quick.** Depending on the size and shape, dried pasta cooks up in as little as 5 minutes. Even the thickest shapes are done in 12 minutes. Many sauces can be prepared in the time it takes to bring the water to a boil and cook the pasta. Pasta makes the 20-minute meal a reality.

Don't think of dried pasta as something you cook when you don't have the time to make it fresh. Dried and fresh pasta are really two separate animals, each with its own uses. For the vast majority of recipes, dried pasta is actually preferable. Its springy texture is a better foil for all but the most delicate, creamy sauces.

# Buying Pasta

What you do at home when cooking pasta is certainly more important than what happens at the supermarket. It wasn't always this way, but most pasta manufacturers use similar ingredients and equipment, so the days of bad pasta are over. That said, keep these points in mind when shopping for dried pasta.

## Does brand matter?

Many cooks swear by one particular brand of pasta. They would never consider using anything other than something imported from Italy. Other cooks buy whatever is on sale, claiming that all pasta is the same. Who's right?

We are going to be diplomatic and say that both camps are right. The differences among brands of pasta are fairly slight. After the pasta is sauced, tasting any differences in wheat or water quality is difficult. Italian companies often buy their wheat from abroad, relying on sources in the United States and Canada. No company imports water to make pasta (although that sounds like a business to us — boutique dried pasta made with the finest spring water from the Alps), and it's hard to imagine that water really makes that big a difference.

All dried pasta may taste the same, but some brands do seem to cook up slightly better than others. (Italian pasta companies say that they slow-dry their pasta for a superior product. Some companies also use higher grades of wheat, which can make a difference in the way the pasta cooks up.) A good pasta will remain firm even when slightly overcooked. Some brands seem to go from too firm to too soft in a matter of seconds. But much of this is subjective and has to do with the skill of the cook.

Many cooks swear by Italian brands. We use them in our kitchens. They may cost an extra 50 cents per pound, but we like using a product with history. We've had good results with non-Italian brands, but given our backgrounds, we prefer to stick with the Italian brands our families have always used.

## *What about shapes?*

Okay, so the brand you buy isn't all that critical. What about the shape? Do you need to stock your pantry with a hundred shapes?

Of course not. Italians are a creative people — think of Michelangelo or Leonardo DaVinci — and many dried pasta shapes are the product of some overactive imaginations. That said, shape does matter. So does size.

Certain sauces work best with certain shapes. (See "The Marriage of Sauce and Noodle," later in this chapter, for some rules for matching sauces and pasta shapes.) If a recipe calls for linguine, you can use spaghetti, but ziti may not work well.

Keeping several shapes in your pantry is a good idea. Maybe something long and thin like spaghetti or linguine as well as something short and tubular like penne and ziti. Test-cook a variety of shapes to find those that you like. Eventually, you'll probably pick a few that become standard items in your house. Other shapes may make guest appearances when a recipe specifically calls for them. (See Figure 6-1 for illustrations of some particularly common shapes.)

# *Cooking Dried Pasta*

Cooking dried pasta seems easy enough. Bring water to a boil, add the pasta, and drain when tender. And although cooking pasta is easy, this simple operation has a right way and a wrong way. If your pasta sticks together or seems mushy, you probably are making some simple mistake that can be easily corrected. Italian cooking also calls for a lot of improvisation. However, cooking pasta is formulaic. Here are the secrets, spelled out in clear English.

## *Into boiling water*

Abundant boiling water is key to cooking pasta properly. Dried pasta needs room to swell and rehydrate. If you cook pasta in a small pot or in a small amount of water, the pieces are likely to stick together. Give pasta some room, and it will behave nicely.

Start with cold water. Hot tap water will come to a boil more quickly but usually picks up some odd flavors from your water heater. One pound of pasta requires a minimum of 4 quarts water. In order to leave room for the pasta and prevent boil-overs, start with a 6-quart pot. An 8-quart pot is even better.

**Figure 6-1:**
Common
pasta
shapes.

If cooking half a pound of pasta, you still need at least 3 quarts of water, and 4 quarts is best. If cooking more than a pound of pasta, use two pots. Even if you own a pot large enough to hold 8 quarts of water and 2 pounds of pasta, we don't recommend cooking pasta in this manner. The water will take forever to come to a boil. After the pasta is added, the water will take too long to come back to a boil, slowing your cooking time.

# What's that pasta shape?

Pasta comes in hundreds of shapes. This list gives a brief description of the most common shapes.

- **Agnolotti:** Filled fresh pasta shaped like half moons.

- **Bucatini:** Long, fat strands that look like spaghetti but are hollow.

- **Capelli d'angelo:** Long and extremely thin. Name translates as "angel's hair."

- **Cappellini:** Slightly thicker than angel hair pasta but still very thin, long strands.

- **Conchiglie:** Shell-shaped pasta that comes in a variety of sizes. Oversized shells, called conchiglioni, are often stuffed and baked.

- **Ditali:** Tiny tubes often used in soup. Name translates as "thimbles."

- **Farfalle:** Bow-tie-shaped pasta. Name translates as "butterflies."

- **Fettuccine:** Long, flat strands of egg noodles.

- **Fusilli:** Corkscrew shape that comes in varying lengths.

- **Lasagne:** Long, wide sheets of pasta that are layered with sauce and cheese and baked.

- **Linguine:** Long, thin ribbons. Similar to spaghetti except strands have flat sides as well as rounded ones.

- **Orecchiette:** Small bowl-shaped pasta. Name translates as "little ears."

- **Orzo:** Shaped like extra-long grains of rice. Often used in soup.

- **Pappardelle:** Long, flat noodle that is two to three times as wide as fettuccine. Often cut into shorter pieces for easier eating.

- **Pastina:** Any of the tiny pasta added to soup, including ditalini (little thimbles), perline (little pearls), and stelline (little stars).

- **Penne:** Medium-length tubes with ends cut on an angle. Can be ridged. Name translates as "quills."

- **Ravioli:** Stuffed pasta shaped like square pillows. Edges are often ruffled.

- **Rigatoni:** Fat, squat tubes with grooved exterior.

- **Rotelle:** Small wheels.

- **Ruote:** Wheels.

- **Spaghetti:** Long, thin strands. Name comes from the word "spago," meaning string or cord.

- **Tagliatelle:** Long, flat strands that are slightly wider than fettuccine.

- **Taglierini:** Similar to tagliatelle but cut narrower.

- **Tortellini:** Stuffed pasta shaped like fat rings. Often used in soups.

- **Trenette:** Long-strand pasta shape that is similar to linguine.

- **Vermicelli:** Long, very thin strands that are thinner than spaghetti. Name translates as "little worms."

- **Ziti:** Narrow tubes of medium length. Similar to penne except ends are not cut on an angle.

## Adding some salt

After the water comes to a rolling boil (the surface of the water should be moving or "rolling" with large bubbles), it's time to add salt. Much of the world has become salt-phobic. But Italians know that salt is essential to cooking pasta.

If you simply boil spaghetti in plain water, it will cook up bland. Salting the water makes dried pasta (which does not contain any salt) taste better. If you are concerned about your salt intake, go lightly on the salt in the sauce. But whatever you do, don't skimp on the salt in the pasta pot.

So how much salt is enough for 4 quarts water? Some Italian cooks add as much as 3 tablespoons of coarse or kosher salt. Remember that your pot contains a lot of water, and almost all of the salt goes down the drain with the cooking water. Adding $1/4$ teaspoon salt to 4 quarts water is like dropping 1 hot red pepper flake into a pot of tomato sauce. In order to season the pasta properly, you must add at least $1^1/_2$ tablespoons salt for every 4 quarts water.

## Forget the oil

Many pasta cooks outside of Italy add oil to the water to keep the pasta from sticking together. As long as you have started with enough water, adding oil is totally unnecessary. Although oil does keep strands from sticking together, using it has a downside. The oil will make the pasta slick. When you go to sauce the drained pasta, the sauce will have a hard time clinging to the noodles. Good dried pasta has a slightly rough surface to which sauce can cling. Oil the pasta, and you've made proper saucing impossible.

## Forget the clock

Many novice cooks read package instructions and watch the clock when cooking pasta. Neither is helpful. Every stove cooks differently, and individuals can have different opinions about how soft they like their pasta. You must taste the pasta in order to figure out when it is ready to hit the colander. Residual heat will cause pasta to continue to soften as it sits in the colander and later gets sauced, so take the pot off the flame about 30 seconds before you think that the pasta will be perfectly cooked.

# What is al dente?

Al dente, the Italian term that translates as "to the tooth," is a state of mind as much as a cooking term. When a recipe says "cook until golden brown," most cooks can agree when something looks golden brown. Al dente is another matter. Even within Italy, regional differences abound. Cooks in southern Italy often pull pasta off the heat a minute or two before their brethren in the north. We have eaten pasta in Italy that was so undercooked that it was still a bit crunchy in the center. The chef may think that his pasta is al dente, but we never serve pasta that crunches when chewed.

For us, the pasta should not be chewy or raw tasting. It should be tender throughout, while still possessing some bite or spring. If the pasta is soft or mushy, it's clearly overcooked. The more experience you have cooking pasta, the more you will develop an innate sense of al dente.

Think of al dente this way. When you first got your driver's license, you probably were speeding all the time. You had no way to judge the speed of the car unless you looked down at the speedometer. But the more you drive, the more you know how fast you are going without having to watch the dashboard. It just feels like you're going 40 miles an hour. Of course, you can misjudge your speed if you're not paying attention. The same is true of cooking pasta. But if you stay close to the pasta pot and fish out strands occasionally, you will know when the pasta is done.

# Drain, don't shake

How you drain your pasta is an often overlooked source of problems. No one likes watery pasta that dilutes the sauce and makes a mess in bowls. However, bone-dry pasta is equally problematic. Thick sauces or sauces based on olive oil will have a hard time coating long strands of pasta unless the noodles are moist. Many recipes even call for reserving some of the cooking water and adding it to the pasta and sauce if the mixture looks too dry.

When the pasta is cooked, we fish out some cooking water in a measuring cup and set it aside as an insurance policy. We then pour the pasta and water into a large colander in the sink to let the water drain out. Don't shake the colander — a little water clinging to the noodles is fine. Then toss the pasta and sauce in a warm serving bowl. A bowl that has been warmed in a 200° oven for 10 minutes usually works well. The heat of the bowl prevents the pasta from cooling off too quickly. After the sauce evenly coats the noodles, we divide portions among individual bowls.

## Serving pasta

In Italy, pasta is usually served in wide, shallow bowls, like the one shown in Figure 6-2. Flat plates are not ideal because the pasta can slide onto the floor. We also use the side of the bowl to help twirl long strands onto a fork.

**Figure 6-2:**
A pasta
serving
bowl.

Serve pasta in a
wide shallow bowl
like this...

Pasta is a first course in Italy, eaten in very small portions. The first course is followed by meat, chicken, or fish. Most of the recipes in this chapter call for 8 ounces of dried pasta, which yields four appetizer portions.

If you like, you can serve pasta as a main course. Eight ounces of dried pasta yields two main-course servings. All the recipes in this chapter can be doubled to yield four main-course servings.

# The Marriage of Sauce and Noodle

Hundreds of pasta shapes are out there, so how do you know which one will work best with your favorite sauce? This section provides some guidelines. But you won't find hard-and-fast rules here. If you serve spaghetti with a chunky vegetable sauce, the world will keep spinning. But we do tell you some good and not-so-good pairings.

In general, the consistency of the sauce determines which pasta shape is most appropriate. For example, that chunky vegetable sauce works nicely with large rigatoni that can trap pieces of vegetables inside individual pieces of pasta. However, that same sauce will just sit on top of thin strands of spaghetti. You will eat pasta in one bite, sauce in another. Ideally, you want to get the pasta and sauce onto the fork at the same time. These pasta shapes and sauces work well together:

- Long, thin strands, like linguine and spaghetti, are the best choice for smooth sauces, such as pesto, or those with very finely chopped ingredients.

- Long, wide noodles, such as fettuccine or tagliatelle, are especially good with creamy sauces. These shapes can tolerate slightly larger chunks but in general are best with smooth or relatively smooth sauces.

- Short, narrow, tubular shapes, such as penne and ziti, are good with sauces that have small-to-medium-sized pieces of vegetables or other ingredients. If the chunks will fit inside a penne noodle, then this shape is appropriate.

- Small, open shapes with crevices or pockets, such as farfalle and orecchiette, are good with moderately chunky sauces. These shapes can trap and hold bits of sauce.

- Large, open shapes, such as large shells, or wide tubes, such as rigatoni, are best with the chunkiest sauces.

# Pasta without Tomatoes?

The world tends to think of pasta and tomatoes as an inseparable unit. However, hundreds of pasta sauces do not contain a speck of tomato. In fact, because the tomato was not introduced in Italy until about 500 years ago (Columbus brought them back from the Americas), pasta with tomato sauce is actually a "new" invention. This section provides some of our favorite simple sauces without tomatoes.

### Spaghetti with Garlic, Oil, and Chiles

This spaghetti recipe is the simplest pasta dish imaginable (see photo in color section). The key is getting the garlic to turn a rich golden-brown color without burning it. If the garlic turns completely brown, the flavor will be bitter.

*Italian recipe name:* *Spaghetti Aglio, Olio, e Peperoncino*

*Preparation time:* *5 minutes*

*Cooking time:* *15 minutes*

*Yield:* *4 servings*

| | |
|---|---|
| 6 tablespoons olive oil | Salt and pepper to taste |
| 6 cloves garlic, peeled and sliced | $1^1/_2$ tablespoons kosher salt |
| Pinch of hot red pepper flakes | $^1/_2$ pound spaghetti |
| $^1/_2$ cup white wine | 2 tablespoons chopped fresh parsley |

**1** Heat the olive oil in a large skillet. Add the garlic and red pepper flakes and cook over medium heat until the garlic just starts to brown, about 2 minutes. Add the wine, season with salt and pepper, and cook for another 2 minutes.

**2** In a large pot, bring 4 quarts water to a boil. Add the kosher salt and pasta, mix well, and cook until the pasta is al dente.

**3** Drain the spaghetti. Place it in a large deep bowl. Pour the oil from the pan over the spaghetti, sprinkle with parsley, stir well, and serve immediately.

## Trenette with Pesto, Genovese Style

The basil sauce in this recipe comes from the sunny Ligurian coast. The local basil has a more complex, balanced flavor than the basil grown elsewhere. Adding a little parsley and chervil to the sauce mimics the flavor of the Ligurian basil. Unlike basil, these herbs don't turn brown when pureed, so this pesto does a better job of retaining its bright green color than an all-basil pesto. Be sure to use fresh herbs with this recipe; if you try to use dried herbs to make pesto, you'll end up with a flavorless mess that tastes like grass from your backyard.

In Genoa, they add some cubed potatoes and green beans to the pasta pot. You can leave them out, but they make this dish especially delicious and hearty. Also, unless you like a lot of sauce on your pasta, you'll probably want to freeze a third of it to use later.

**Italian recipe name:** *Trenette con Pesto alla Genovese*

**Preparation time:** *10 minutes*

**Cooking time:** *10 minutes*

**Yield:** *4 servings*

*(continued)*

$^1/_4$ *cup pine nuts*

*6 cloves garlic, peeled and crushed*

*2 cups fresh basil leaves*

$^1/_4$ *cup fresh parsley leaves*

$^1/_4$ *cup fresh chervil*

$^1/_4$ *cup grated Parmigiano-Reggiano*

*1 cup olive oil*

*Salt and pepper to taste*

$1^1/_2$ *tablespoons kosher salt*

$^1/_2$ *pound trenette pasta (or substitute linguine, fettuccine, or spaghetti)*

*1 small potato, cut into small cubes*

$^1/_4$ *pound green beans, cut in 1-inch pieces*

*1* Preheat the oven to 375°. Spread the pine nuts on a small baking sheet and place in the oven. Bake the pine nuts until they're lightly brown, 3 to 5 minutes. Let the nuts cool slightly.

*2* Place the garlic, basil, parsley, chervil, pine nuts, and Parmigiano-Reggiano in the bowl of a food processor. With the motor running, slowly drizzle the olive oil through the feed tube to the bowl and process until smooth. Transfer the pesto to a large bowl and stir in salt and pepper to taste. Set aside.

*3* In a large pot, bring 4 quarts water to a boil and add the kosher salt.

*4* Add the pasta, potato, and green beans to the boiling water, mix well, and cook until al dente. Drain. Add the pasta and vegetables to the bowl with the pesto sauce. Stir to combine. Serve immediately.

## Pasta Wheels with Walnut Sauce

The combination of creamy Mascarpone cheese and walnuts in this recipe is delicious. If you can't find Mascarpone, use ricotta cheese instead. Because ricotta is not as creamy, save some of the pasta cooking water to thin the sauce.

***Italian recipe name:*** *Ruote con Salsa di Noci*

***Preparation time:*** *10 minutes*

***Cooking time:*** *20 minutes*

***Yield:*** *4 servings*

*¹/₃ cup olive oil*

*1 clove garlic, peeled and minced*

*1¹/₂ cups finely chopped, shelled walnuts*

*1 cup Mascarpone cheese*

*1¹/₂ tablespoons kosher salt*

*¹/₂ pound wheel or ruote pasta*

*Salt and pepper to taste*

*¹/₂ cup grated Parmigiano-Reggiano*

*1 tablespoon chopped fresh parsley*

**1** Heat the olive oil in a large skillet or medium saucepan. Add the garlic and cook over medium heat until the garlic turns golden, about 1 minute. Because the garlic is finely minced, you must watch it carefully so that it doesn't burn.

**2** In a large pot, bring 4 quarts water to a boil. Add the kosher salt and pasta, mix well, and cook until al dente.

**3** Add the walnuts to the pan, cook for 2 to 3 minutes, stirring, and then remove from heat. With a wooden spoon, stir in the Mascarpone. Return the pan to low heat.

**4** Season the sauce with salt and pepper and add the Parmigiano-Reggiano and parsley. Serve with the pasta immediately.

## Orecchiette with Broccoli Rabe

Orecchiette pasta, which translates as "little ears," does a good job of catching bits of the broccoli rabe (see photo in color section). To save time, cook the broccoli and pasta in the same water. Put the broccoli rabe into the pot first, fish it out with a slotted spoon or sieve, and then add the pasta. As an added benefit, the broccoli rabe flavors the water, which in turn flavors the pasta as it cooks.

***Italian recipe name:*** *Orecchiette con Cime di Rabe*

***Preparation time:*** *10 minutes*

***Cooking time:*** *12 minutes*

***Yield:*** *4 servings*

*1 large bunch broccoli rabe, washed, cleaned, tough stems discarded, and florets separated from stems*

*1¹/₂ tablespoons kosher salt*

*¹/₂ pound orecchiette*

*¹/₄ cup olive oil*

*6 cloves garlic, peeled and crushed*

*Pinch of hot red pepper flakes*

*Salt to taste*

*¹/₄ cup grated Parmigiano-Reggiano (optional)*

*(continued)*

*1* In a large pot, bring 4 quarts water to a boil. Add the broccoli rabe and kosher salt and cook for 5 minutes. Using a slotted spoon or small sieve, remove the broccoli rabe from the pot and transfer to a small bowl. Add the pasta to the boiling water, mix well, and cook until the pasta is al dente.

*2* Place the olive oil, garlic, and red pepper flakes in a large skillet or medium saucepan and cook over medium heat until the garlic turns golden, about 2 minutes. Add the broccoli rabe to the skillet and cook for another 5 minutes, stirring occasionally. Season with salt.

*3* Drain the pasta and add it to the skillet with the broccoli rabe. Stir to combine. Serve immediately sprinkled with Parmigiano-Reggiano cheese.

## Pasta with Eggs and Bacon

The origins of this very popular pasta dish are not clear. Some sources indicate that *carbonara* originated right after World War II, when the egg and bacon rations of American GIs were turned into a pasta sauce. Other sources say that coal miners *(carbonari)* made this dish. Either way, this dish has become extremely popular throughout Italy. Onions are a delicious addition to the sauce, but they're optional in this recipe.

***Italian recipe name:*** *Penne alla Carbonara*

***Preparation time:*** *15 minutes*

***Cooking time:*** *15 minutes*

***Yield:*** *4 servings*

| | |
|---|---|
| *¹/₄ cup olive oil* | *1¹/₂ tablespoons kosher salt* |
| *1 medium onion, diced (optional)* | *¹/₂ pound penne* |
| *4 slices pancetta or bacon (about 6 ounces), diced* | *2 eggs* |
| | *3 tablespoons heavy cream (optional)* |
| *Pinch of hot red pepper flakes* | *¹/₄ cup plus 2 tablespoons grated Parmigiano-Reggiano, divided* |
| *1 cup white wine* | |
| *Salt and pepper to taste* | *2 tablespoons chopped fresh parsley* |

*1* Place the olive oil, onion (if using), pancetta, and red pepper flakes in a large skillet and cook over medium heat, stirring occasionally, until the onion is soft — about 10 minutes. Pour the wine into the pan and let it reduce for 3 minutes. Season with salt and pepper. Remove from heat.

**2** In a large pot, bring 4 quarts water to a boil. Add the kosher salt and the penne, mix well, and cook until the pasta is al dente.

**3** Drain the pasta and add it to the skillet.

**4** In a large bowl, mix together the eggs, cream (if using), $1/4$ cup Parmigiano-Reggiano cheese, and parsley. Slowly add this mixture to the skillet with the onion and pasta. Mix well. Cook over low heat, stirring constantly, for 2 to 3 minutes to heat the eggs through. Do not boil. Sprinkle with the remaining 2 tablespoons Parmigiano-Reggiano cheese and serve immediately.

## Spaghetti with Clams

Authentic Spaghetti with Clams is made with fresh clams that are served in the shell with the pasta (see photo in color section). Therefore, you need to use the smallest clams possible. In Italy, they often use clams the size of an adult fingernail. Manila or New Zealand clams are best. In a pinch, you can use small littlenecks.

***Italian recipe name:*** *Spaghetti con Vongole*

***Preparation time:*** *10 minutes*

***Cooking time:*** *15 minutes*

***Yield:*** *4 servings*

$1/4$ *cup plus 1 tablespoon olive oil*

*4 cloves garlic, peeled and chopped*

*3 tablespoons chopped fresh parsley, divided*

*Pinch of hot red pepper flakes*

$1/4$ *cup plus 2 tablespoons white wine*

*60 Manila or New Zealand small clams, rinsed*

*Salt to taste*

$1^1/2$ *tablespoons kosher salt*

$1/2$ *pound spaghetti*

**1** Place the olive oil, garlic, $1^1/2$ tablespoons parsley, and red pepper flakes in a large skillet. Cook over medium heat, stirring occasionally, until the garlic turns golden, about 3 minutes.

**2** Add the wine and clams to the skillet and season with salt. Cook, covered, until the clams open, about 5 minutes. Discard any clams that have not opened.

**3** In a large pot, bring 4 quarts water to a boil. Add the kosher salt and the spaghetti, mix well, and cook until al dente.

**4** Drain the pasta and add it and the remaining $1^1/2$ tablespoons parsley to the saucepan with the clams. Mix. Serve immediately.

# Pasta with Tomatoes

Although you can make plenty of pasta sauces without tomatoes, many of the most popular Italian sauces do contain tomatoes, and for good reason. The tomato has a bright, sweet, slightly acidic flavor that perks up bland pasta. The juicy consistency means that tomatoes can be turned into a liquidy sauce, perfect for coating strands of pasta.

Traditionally, tomatoes were available fresh for just a few short months in the summer and fall in Italy. (Jets, which can bring tomatoes from the other side of the world to market, have changed this, of course.) Italians learned to extend the tomato season by turning the abundance of fresh tomatoes into a variety of processed products.

Canned tomatoes are the most popular processed tomato product. Unlike many other canned fruits and vegetables, tomatoes retain most of their important qualities when canned. In fact, they're our first choice in pasta sauces unless really good fresh tomatoes are available. (Note that only one of the recipes in this section relies on fresh tomatoes.) Here's the rundown on the various forms of processed tomatoes:

- **Whole peeled tomatoes packed in juice:** This is the closest to fresh tomatoes. Whole tomatoes are steamed to remove their skins and then packed in tomato juice. The tomatoes can be chopped and used like fresh tomatoes in any cooked dish. Don't throw away the juice. Sometimes it is added when extra liquid is needed. For example, many soups with canned tomatoes use both the solids and the liquid.

- **Whole peeled tomatoes packed in puree:** Some manufacturers pack their whole peeled tomatoes in thick tomato puree instead of tomato juice. The puree, which is the consistency of tomato sauce and has a strong cooked flavor, is not as useful as fresh-tasting tomato juice, so we prefer to buy tomatoes packed in juice.

- **Diced tomatoes:** Peeled tomatoes are diced and then packed with a little tomato juice. Often manufacturers add seasonings — a little basil and garlic, for example. This product is often called stewed tomatoes. The idea is that the contents of the can are sauce-ready; you can simply heat and serve without any further chopping. We prefer to add our own seasonings and usually stick with whole tomatoes.

- **Crushed tomatoes:** Crushed tomatoes, sometimes called ground tomatoes, are useful in recipes where you want a smooth texture and you want it fast. You could buy whole peeled tomatoes, dice them yourself, and then simmer until they fall apart. But why not save time and buy whole tomatoes that have been put through a crushing device and broken into tiny bits at a factory?

At its best, a can of crushed tomatoes is nothing more than whole peeled tomatoes. Some companies don't do a very good job of peeling, and you may see lots of pieces of skin in inferior brands. In addition, many companies add tomato puree to add body to the crushed tomatoes, which can be watery. Tomato puree takes away from the fresh flavor of good crushed tomatoes. A little tomato puree is fine, but make sure that tomatoes, not tomato puree, are the first ingredient on the label.

- **Tomato paste:** Paste is thick enough to stand up on a spoon. It is made from tomato juice that is seasoned with salt, spices, and often sugar and then reduced to a thick, smooth consistency. Paste can add tomato color and flavor when a lot of liquid isn't needed. For example, paste is the best way to get tomato flavor into fresh egg pasta. Paste is usually sold in small cans. You may also see double-concentrated tomato paste in tubes like those used for toothpaste. This product comes from Italy and is very thick and very intensely flavored. As little as a few teaspoons can flavor a whole pot of soup or stew.

- **Tomato puree:** Puree is similar to paste, except that the tomato liquid has not been concentrated as much. Puree usually has the consistency of jarred tomato sauce. It has a strong cooked flavor, and we don't generally use it.

- **Tomato sauce:** This is sauce in a jar. Although not terrible, jarred sauce is often too sweet (many brands add sugar or corn syrup) and too bland. This is also sometimes known as spaghetti sauce.

- **Sun-dried tomatoes:** Italian housewives used to slice tomatoes, place them on mesh racks, and dry them under the hot summer sun for several days. Today, commercial outfits dry tomatoes inside (fewer bugs) into leathery tomato slices. Technically, they are not sun-dried, just dried, but the former name is so much more romantic that it has stuck. When dried, the flavor is especially intense, without any of the cooked flavor of paste. Sun-dried tomatoes come in two forms: loose in packages or marinated in olive oil.

Sun-dried tomatoes packed loose can be kept on the shelf indefinitely. To use the tomatoes, you must rehydrate them in hot water until tender (a 5- or 10-minute bath usually does the job) and then chop them. Sun-dried tomatoes add a real jolt of tomato flavor, so use them sparingly. They can be added to a sauce made with canned tomatoes for extra tomato flavor.

Sun-dried tomatoes are also sold marinated in olive oil. They come packed in jars, which must be refrigerated after opening. Like plain sun-dried tomatoes, marinated sun-dried tomatoes have an intense, fresh tomato flavor. However, their texture is soft, and they can be used as is without soaking. Often marinated sun-dried tomatoes contain more than just oil and tomatoes. Some brands have herbs and garlic for added flavor.

## "Angry" Penne

Plenty of hot red pepper flakes makes a spicy, or "angry," pasta sauce.

*Italian recipe name: Penne all'Arrabbiata*

*Preparation time: 10 minutes*

*Cooking time: 30 minutes*

*Yield: 4 servings*

2 tablespoons olive oil

4 cloves garlic, peeled and minced

1 teaspoon hot red pepper flakes

$^1/_3$ cup white wine

2 cups canned plum tomatoes

Salt to taste

$1^1/_2$ tablespoons kosher salt

$^1/_2$ pound penne

3 tablespoons chopped fresh parsley

4 tablespoons grated Parmigiano-Reggiano (optional)

**1** Place the olive oil, garlic, and red pepper flakes in a large skillet or medium saucepan. Cook over medium heat until the garlic turns golden, about 2 minutes. Pour the wine in the pan and continue cooking until it has almost completely evaporated. Add the tomatoes, lightly crushing them with a wooden spoon. Season with salt. Cook at a low boil, stirring often, for 20 to 25 minutes, until the sauce thickens slightly.

**2** In a large pot, bring 4 quarts water to a boil. Add the kosher salt and pasta, mix well, and cook until al dente.

**3** Drain the pasta. Add the pasta and parsley to the pan with the sauce. Stir to combine. Sprinkle with Parmigiano-Reggiano cheese and serve immediately.

## Pasta with Tomato and Basil Sauce

With garlic, basil, and canned tomatoes, this slow-simmered sauce is a classic. If you have ripe, fresh tomatoes, this recipe is even better.

*Italian recipe name: Pasta Pomodoro e Basilico*

*Preparation time: 10 minutes*

*Cooking time: 1 hour, 5 minutes*

*Yield: 8 servings*

*¹/₃ cup plus 2 tablespoons olive oil, divided*

*4 cloves garlic, peeled and chopped*

*1 medium onion, chopped*

*Pinch of hot red pepper flakes*

*16 fresh basil leaves, chopped, plus 16 whole leaves, or 1 tablespoon dried basil plus 2 teaspoons dried oregano, divided*

*¹/₃ cup white wine*

*28-ounce can plum tomatoes, not drained*

*¹/₂ cup water*

*Salt and pepper to taste*

*1¹/₂ tablespoons kosher salt*

*1 pound pasta such as spaghetti, fettuccine, or linguine*

*¹/₂ cup grated Parmigiano-Reggiano*

**1** In a large saucepan, place ¹/₃ cup olive oil, the garlic, onion, red pepper flakes, and half the chopped basil and cook over medium heat for 5 minutes. Add the wine and cook for 2 to 3 minutes, reducing it by half. Add the tomatoes and water, stir, and then simmer for 40 to 45 minutes, stirring occasionally.

**2** Season the tomato sauce with salt and pepper and add the remaining chopped basil. Simmer for 10 minutes.

**3** In a large pot, bring 4 quarts water to a boil. Add the kosher salt and pasta, mix well, and cook until al dente.

**4** Drain the pasta. Add the pasta, 2 tablespoons olive oil, whole basil leaves, and the Parmigiano-Reggiano cheese to the pan with the sauce. Mix well. Cook for 1 minute. Serve immediately.

## Shells with Uncooked Tomato Sauce

Raw tomatoes are too juicy to use as is in a tomato sauce. To draw off some of their moisture, set diced tomatoes in a colander and sprinkle them with salt.

Because all the ingredients in this simple dish are raw, quality is very important (see photo in color section). In Italy, Pasta alla Checca is very popular in the summertime because tomatoes are at their peak. You can serve this dish hot or at room temperature.

***Italian recipe name:*** *Pasta alla Checca*

***Preparation time:*** *20 minutes (plus 2 hours for tomatoes to drain)*

***Cooking time:*** *10 minutes*

***Yield:*** *4 servings*

*(continued)*

*4 medium tomatoes, diced*

*3 tablespoons kosher salt*

*$^1/_2$ pound shell pasta (or substitute penne or fusilli)*

*$^1/_4$ cup chopped fresh basil, or 2 table-spoons dried basil plus 1 teaspoon dried oregano*

*2 cloves garlic, peeled and chopped*

*$^1/_2$ teaspoon hot red pepper flakes*

*$^1/_4$ cup olive oil*

*$^1/_4$ cup grated Parmigiano-Reggiano (optional)*

**1** Place the tomatoes in a colander and sprinkle them with $1^1/_2$ tablespoons kosher salt. Let the tomatoes drain for 2 hours, stirring occasionally.

**2** In a large pot, bring 4 quarts water to a boil. Add the remaining kosher salt and pasta, mix well, and cook until the pasta is al dente.

**3** Transfer the tomatoes to a large serving bowl. Add the basil, garlic, red pepper flakes, and olive oil. Mix well. Drain the pasta and add it to the fresh tomato sauce. Add the cheese (if using). Mix and serve.

## What about pasta salad?

You may be wondering where the pasta salad recipes are. Well, Italians don't eat pasta salad, which is actually an American invention. Adding mayonnaise to cold pasta is a sure way to send your Italian friends packing.

Cold pasta salad in a no-no in Italy, but it is perfectly acceptable to let some pasta dishes cool to room temperature before serving. Shells with Uncooked Tomato Sauce or Trenette with Pesto, Genovese Style are often eaten at room temperature in the summer. Oil-based sauces are good candidates for eating at room temperature. (Sauces with butter or cream must be eaten hot.)

## Rigatoni with Eggplant

This recipe hails from Sicily. Traditionally, the eggplant is salted to remove some of the bitterness and then deep-fried. The fried slices of eggplant are then combined with the cooked pasta and tomato sauce. This version has a number of innovations. We like the slightly bitter flavor of eggplant and don't bother with salting. To make the dish lighter, we sauté the eggplant with the other vegetables used to make the tomato sauce. (See Figure 6-3 to find out how to cube the eggplant.) Feel free to freeze half the sauce to use later.

**Italian recipe name:** *Pasta alla Norma*

**Preparation time:** *20 minutes*

**Cooking time:** *45 minutes*

**Yield:** *4 servings*

*¹/₄ cup olive oil*

*5 cloves garlic, peeled and chopped*

*1 medium onion, chopped*

*1 teaspoon hot red pepper flakes*

*1 teaspoon chopped fresh thyme, or ¹/₄ teaspoon dried thyme*

*1 teaspoon chopped fresh oregano, or ¹/₄ teaspoon dried oregano*

*¹/₄ cup white wine*

*1 large eggplant, cut into ¹/₂-inch pieces (about 5 cups)*

*14-ounce can plum tomatoes*

*¹/₂ to 1 cup water (depending on how much moisture is needed)*

*¹/₄ cup chopped fresh basil, or 1 tablespoon dried basil*

*2 tablespoons chopped fresh parsley, or 2 teaspoons dried parsley*

*Salt and pepper to taste*

*1¹/₂ tablespoons kosher salt*

*¹/₂ pound rigatoni*

*¹/₄ cup grated Parmigiano-Reggiano*

**1** In a large saucepan, heat the olive oil, garlic, onion, and red pepper flakes and cook over medium heat for 2 to 3 minutes. Add the thyme and oregano, cook for 1 to 2 minutes, and then add the wine. Allow the wine to reduce slightly. Stir in the eggplant and lower the heat to low-medium. Cover and cook, stirring occasionally, until the eggplant becomes soft and its juices have evaporated, about 20 minutes.

**2** Add the tomatoes and water to the saucepan. Simmer for 15 minutes. Add the basil and parsley and season with salt and pepper. Cook for 3 to 4 minutes.

**3** While the sauce simmers, bring 4 quarts water to a boil. Add the kosher salt and rigatoni, mix well, and cook until al dente.

**4** Drain the pasta. Add the pasta and Parmigiano-Reggiano cheese to the pan with the sauce. Mix well. Serve immediately.

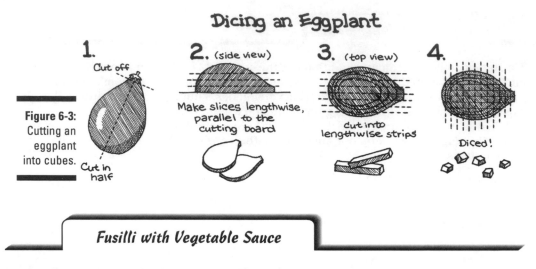

## Dicing an Eggplant

Figure 6-3: Cutting an eggplant into cubes.

1. Cut off / Cut in half

2. (side view) Make slices lengthwise, parallel to the cutting board

3. (top view) cut into lengthwise strips

4. Diced!

---

### Fusilli with Vegetable Sauce

A rich meat sauce with bits of ground beef is a favorite throughout Italy. (See the recipe in Chapter 7.) However, many poor country cooks couldn't afford the ingredients for a real meat sauce and made this approximation with vegetables ground by hand to resemble meat, hence the name *finto sugo,* or "fake sauce" (see photo in color section). A food processor makes the consistency smoother, but the flavor is the same.

***Italian recipe name:*** *Fusilli al Finto Sugo*

***Preparation time:*** *5 minutes*

***Cooking time:*** *1 hour, 20 minutes*

***Yield:*** *8 servings*

| | |
|---|---|
| $^1/_3$ cup olive oil | $^1/_2$ cup white wine |
| 2 medium onions, diced | 4 cups (2 16-ounce cans) plum tomatoes |
| 5 cloves garlic, peeled and chopped | $^1/_2$ cup water |
| 2 medium carrots, diced | Salt and pepper to taste |
| 5 celery stalks, diced | $1^1/_2$ tablespoons kosher salt |
| 1 teaspoon hot red pepper flakes | 1 pound fusilli |
| 1 cup chopped fresh basil, or 2 tablespoons dried basil, divided | $^1/_4$ cup grated Pecorino cheese |
| 2 tablespoons chopped fresh parsley, or 2 teaspoons dried parsley, divided | |

*1* In a large saucepan, place the olive oil, onions, garlic, carrots, celery, red pepper flakes, $^1/_2$ cup basil, and 1 tablespoon parsley. Cook over medium heat, stirring often, for 15 minutes.

**2** Add the wine and cook until it almost completely evaporates, about 5 minutes.

**3** Pour the tomatoes and water into the saucepan, stir, and simmer for 40 minutes. Remove from heat and stir in the remaining $^1/_2$ cup basil and 1 tablespoon parsley.

**4** Using a food processor or blender, puree the tomato sauce in batches. Return the tomato puree to the saucepan, season with salt and pepper, and simmer for another 20 minutes, or until slightly thickened.

**5** While the sauce simmers, bring 4 quarts water to a boil in a large pot. Add the kosher salt and fusilli, mix well, and cook until al dente.

**6** Drain the pasta and add it to the pan with the sauce. Stir to coat the pasta evenly with the sauce and add the Pecorino cheese. Serve immediately.

## Penne with Tomatoes, Capers, Anchovies, and Olives

This dish comes from Rome, and the name comes from the Italian word *puttana,* or prostitute. Some sources believe that the name refers to the fact that the dish can be thrown together with pantry staples. Other sources mention the strong, salty flavor. In any case, this dish is extremely popular in Italy, especially as a late-night snack.

***Italian recipe name:*** *Pasta alla Puttanesca*

***Preparation time:*** *15 minutes*

***Cooking time:*** *35 to 40 minutes*

***Yield:*** *4 servings*

$^1/_4$ *cup olive oil*

*4 cloves garlic, peeled and chopped*

*1 teaspoon hot red pepper flakes*

*5 anchovy fillets, chopped*

$^1/_2$ *cup white wine*

*16 black olives, pitted*

*2 tablespoons capers, drained and chopped*

*2 cups plum tomatoes, fresh or canned, peeled and chopped*

$^1/_2$ *cup water*

$^1/_2$ *cup chopped fresh parsley, or 1 tablespoon dried parsley*

$1^1/_2$ *tablespoons kosher salt*

$^1/_2$ *pound penne*

*Salt to taste*

*(continued)*

**1** In a large saucepan, heat the olive oil. Add the garlic and cook over medium heat until golden, about 1 minute. Add the red pepper flakes and anchovies, stir, and cook for another 2 minutes. Pour in the wine. Let it reduce slightly and then add the olives, capers, tomatoes, and water. Cook at a low boil for 25 to 30 minutes, stirring occasionally. During the last 2 minutes of cooking, add the parsley to the sauce.

**2** While the sauce cooks, bring 4 quarts water to a boil in a large pot. Add the kosher salt and penne, mix well, and cook until al dente.

**3** Drain the pasta and add it to the pan with the sauce. Season with salt and stir. Serve immediately.

## Pasta with Tuna

Canned tuna in olive oil makes an especially delicious addition to a basic tomato sauce. The tuna will soak up most of the liquid in the sauce. To keep the pasta from becoming too dry, reserve some of the pasta cooking water and use it to moisten the cooked pasta as you toss it with the sauce.

***Italian recipe name:*** *Pasta con Tonno*

***Preparation time:*** *10 minutes*

***Cooking time:*** *15 minutes*

***Yield:*** *4 servings*

| | |
|---|---|
| *¹/₄ cup olive oil* | *1¹/₂ cups canned plum tomatoes, peeled and chopped* |
| *3 cloves garlic, peeled and minced* | *Salt to taste* |
| *¹/₄ cup white wine* | *2 tablespoons kosher salt* |
| *3.5-ounce can of tuna (olive oil packed), drained* | *¹/₂ pound pasta (fusilli, shells, or penne)* |
| *2 tablespoons capers, drained and chopped* | *3 tablespoons chopped fresh parsley, or 1 tablespoon dried parsley* |
| *¹/₂ teaspoon hot red pepper flakes* | |

**1** Place the olive oil and garlic in a large skillet or medium saucepan and cook over medium heat until the garlic turns golden, about 2 minutes.

**2** Add the wine and cook until it has almost completely evaporated, 3 to 5 minutes. Add the tuna, capers, red pepper flakes, and tomatoes. Simmer 5 minutes, uncovered, and then season with salt.

**3** In a large pot, bring 4 quarts water to a boil. Add the kosher salt and pasta, mix well, and cook until al dente.

*4* Drain the pasta, reserving 1 cup of the cooking liquid. Add the pasta and parsley to the pot with the sauce and place it over medium heat. Stir or toss the pasta with the sauce and cook for 3 minutes. If the pasta becomes a little dry or begins to stick to the pot, add a little bit of the reserved cooking liquid; add more liquid depending on how dry the pasta becomes. Serve immediately.

## Spaghetti with Shrimp

In Italy, this dish is made with langostines that are kept in their shell. If you can find these crustaceans at your local seafood market, use them.

You can peel and devein shrimp in one easy motion with a cheap plastic deveiner (see Figure 6-4). Simply insert the pointed end of the deveiner into the back of the shrimp and push to pull the black vein out of the shrimp. The deveiner will also loosen the shell, which will fall off under cold, running water.

***Italian recipe name:*** *Spaghetti con gli Scampi*

***Preparation time:*** *15 minutes*

***Cooking time:*** *20 minutes*

***Yield:*** *4 servings*

*3 tablespoons olive oil*

*3 cloves garlic, peeled and chopped*

*¹/₂ cup white wine*

*1¹/₂ cups (14-ounce can) plum tomatoes*

*Salt and pepper to taste*

*¹/₂ pound medium shrimp, peeled, deveined, and halved lengthwise*

*2 tablespoons chopped fresh parsley, or 1 tablespoon dried parsley*

*1¹/₂ tablespoons kosher salt*

*¹/₂ pound spaghetti*

*1* Place the olive oil and garlic in a large skillet or medium saucepan and cook until golden, about 2 minutes. Pour the wine into the pan and continue cooking until it has almost completely evaporated. Add the tomatoes, lightly crushing them with a wooden spoon. Season with salt and pepper. Simmer for 15 to 20 minutes, until the sauce thickens slightly. Add the shrimp and parsley and cook until the shrimp are pink, 3 to 5 minutes.

*2* In a large pot, bring 4 quarts water to a boil. Add the kosher salt and pasta, mix well, and cook until al dente.

*3* Drain the pasta and add it to the pan with the sauce. Stir to coat the pasta evenly with the sauce. Serve immediately.

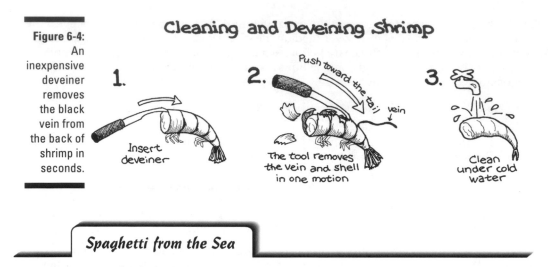

**Figure 6-4:**
An inexpensive deveiner removes the black vein from the back of shrimp in seconds.

### Spaghetti from the Sea

This recipe contains clams, mussels, shrimp, and scallops for a delicious taste of the sea (see recipe in color section). The shrimp and scallops can overcook easily, so add them to the sauce just before it is done.

*Italian recipe name:* Spaghetti allo Scoglio

*Preparation time:* 20 minutes

*Cooking time:* 30 minutes

*Yield:* 4 servings

$^1/_4$ cup olive oil

4 cloves garlic, peeled and chopped

Pinch of red pepper flakes

2 tablespoons chopped fresh parsley, or 2 teaspoons dried parsley

$^1/_4$ cup white wine

1 pound clams

1 pound mussels, scrubbed, beards removed

$1^1/_2$ cups (14-ounce can) plum tomatoes, lightly crushed

Salt to taste

$^1/_4$ pound medium shrimp, peeled and deveined

$^1/_4$ pound bay or sea scallops

$1^1/_2$ tablespoons kosher salt

$^1/_2$ pound spaghetti

**1** Place the olive oil, garlic, red pepper flakes, and parsley in a large skillet or medium saucepan and cook over medium heat until the garlic turns golden, about 2 minutes. Pour the wine into the pan and cook for another minute. Add the clams, mussels, and tomatoes. Cook at a low boil, stirring occasionally, for 15 minutes. Discard any mussels or clams that don't open.

**2** Season the seafood/tomato sauce with salt and add the shrimp and scallops. Cook for 5 minutes.

**3** In a large pot, bring 4 quarts water to a boil. Add the kosher salt and pasta to the boiling water, mix well, and cook until al dente.

**4** Drain the pasta and add it to the pan with the sauce. Stir to coat the pasta evenly with the sauce. Serve immediately.

# Spaghetti and meatballs is not Italian

Almost every Italian restaurant outside of Italy has spaghetti and meatballs on the menu. But ask a waiter in Italy for spaghetti and meatballs, and he will just stare at you. Even if you practice your best Italian and ask for *spaghetti con polpettine,* your request will be denied.

Italians eat meatballs. The Italian word for meatballs is *polpettine.* Small balls of seasoned ground beef, veal, and/or pork are sometimes added to soups. And oversized meatballs are sometimes served with a tomato sauce as a second course, after pasta, rice, or soup. But spaghetti and meatballs is as American as apple pie.

Italians certainly like meat and tomatoes as a sauce for pasta. However, they prefer to add the meat in small pieces, such as ground beef, sausage meat that has been removed from its casings and crumbled, or diced pancetta. Large meatballs just sit on top of the spaghetti, and the ladle of smooth tomato sauce doesn't help matters. The sauce and pasta flavors never really marry. If the meat is ground and then cooked in tomato sauce, it can be combined with fettuccine. Each mouthful will contain meat, tomatoes, and pasta.

The recipes for Rigatoni with Sausage and Peas and Bucatini with Tomatoes, Onions, and Pancetta in this chapter and the Meat Sauce recipe in Chapter 7 are good examples of how meat can be used in a pasta sauce.

# Ten great pasta sauces in ten minutes

Some pasta sauces are so simple that you don't need a recipe. We are deliberately vague about quantities when explaining the following ideas. These sauces are so simple that you can't really make them wrong — so get creative and do your own thing.

All these sauces can be prepared in the time it takes to cook the pasta. All will sauce half a pound of pasta.

**Spaghetti with Garlic, Parsley, and Pecorino:** Sauté several cloves of minced garlic in several tablespoons of olive oil. Add a handful of minced fresh parsley and a little crushed red pepper flakes and then toss with cooked spaghetti and some grated Pecorino cheese.

**Fettuccine with Butter and Pine Nuts:** Toast several tablespoons of nuts in a dry skillet. (You can use chopped walnuts rather than pine nuts, if you like.) When the nuts are fragrant, transfer them to a bowl. Melt at least half a stick of butter in the empty skillet. Toss with cooked fettuccine, toasted nuts, some grated Parmigiano-Reggiano, and pepper. Best with fresh pasta.

**Linguine with Olives:** Pit and chop a large handful of black and/or green olives. Combine with several tablespoons of olive oil, a little minced garlic, a pinch of hot red pepper flakes, and some minced fresh herbs. Toss the olive mixture with cooked pasta.

**Spaghetti with Olive Oil, Lemon, and Garlic:** Sauté several cloves of minced garlic in a couple of tablespoons of olive oil. Add the grated zest from a lemon and toss with cooked pasta.

**Spaghetti with Pancetta, Pecorino, and Pepper:** Sauté several slices of diced pancetta in a little olive oil until lightly crisped. Toss with cooked pasta, lots of freshly ground black pepper, and a half cup or more of grated Pecorino cheese. Reserve some cooking water to moisten the pasta, if necessary.

**Fettuccine with Butter and Cream (Fettuccine Alfredo):** Heat several tablespoons of butter and about half a cup of cream in a large skillet just until the cream starts to simmer. Add cooked fresh pasta to the skillet and then add plenty of grated Parmigiano-Reggiano. Cook over low heat for a minute, tossing until the sauce coats the noodles.

**Spaghetti with Herbs:** Sauté a few minced garlic cloves in several tablespoons of olive oil. Add a tablespoon or two of minced mixed herbs (basil, parsley, thyme, mint, and so on) and toss with cooked pasta.

**Penne with Ricotta and Peas:** Sauté a minced onion in several tablespoons of olive oil. Add a handful or two of frozen peas and cook just until warm. Thin a half cup or so of ricotta cheese to sauce consistency with some pasta cooking water. Combine the pea mixture, thinned ricotta, and several tablespoons of grated Parmigiano-Reggiano cheese with cooked pasta.

**Linguine with Raw Tomatoes and Pesto:** Chop several ripe tomatoes and combine with several tablespoons of pesto sauce. Toss with cooked pasta.

**Penne with Tomatoes, Onion, and Butter:** Sauté a minced onion in a few tablespoons of melted butter. Add some chopped canned tomatoes and simmer until tender. Toss with cooked pasta and serve with grated cheese.

## Rigatoni with Sausage and Peas

This recipe takes its name from the *butteri,* men who ride horses to herd cattle in Tuscany (see photo in color section). This hearty dish has long been popular with these Italian "cowboys."

This recipe calls for ground sausage meat. You can use an equal amount of link sausage, but you will have to remove the meat from the casings. (See Figure 6-5.)

*Italian recipe name: Rigatoni alla Buttera*

*Preparation time: 15 minutes*

*Cooking time: 1 hour, 15 minutes*

*Yield: 6 servings*

| | |
|---|---|
| *3 tablespoons olive oil* | *14-ounce can plum tomatoes* |
| *1 medium onion, chopped* | *1/4 cup water* |
| *3 cloves garlic, peeled and chopped* | *Salt and pepper to taste* |
| *2 tablespoons chopped fresh rosemary, or 2 teaspoons dried rosemary* | *Pinch of ground nutmeg* |
| *2 teaspoons chopped fresh thyme, or 1/2 teaspoon dried thyme* | *Pinch of ground cinnamon* |
| | *Pinch of ground cloves* |
| *1 tablespoon chopped fresh parsley, or 1 teaspoon dried parsley* | *1/2 cup frozen peas* |
| *4 slices pancetta or bacon (about 2 ounces)* | *1/4 cup heavy cream (optional)* |
| | *1 1/2 tablespoons kosher salt* |
| *Pinch of hot red pepper flakes* | *3/4 pound rigatoni* |
| *1/2 cup red or white wine, divided* | *1/2 cup grated Parmigiano-Reggiano* |
| *1/2 pound ground pork sausage* | |

*1* Place the olive oil, onion, garlic, rosemary, thyme, parsley, pancetta, and red pepper flakes in a large skillet or medium saucepan. Cook over medium heat until the onion is soft and translucent, about 5 minutes.

*2* Add 1/4 cup wine and cook until it has almost completely evaporated, 3 to 5 minutes.

*3* Add the sausage and cook for 10 minutes, stirring often. Pour in the remaining 1/4 cup wine, cook for 5 minutes, and then add the tomatoes, water, salt and pepper, nutmeg, cinnamon, and cloves. Simmer, uncovered, for 30 minutes stirring frequently.

*(continued)*

*4* Add the peas to the sauce and season with salt and pepper. Stir well and cook for 5 more minutes. Remove from heat, stir in the cream, and set aside.

*5* In a large pot, bring 4 quarts water to a boil. Add the kosher salt. During the last 5 minutes that the sauce simmers, add the pasta to the water, mix well, and cook until al dente.

*6* Drain the pasta and add it to the pan with the sauce. Sprinkle with the Parmigiano-Reggiano cheese. Stir to coat the pasta evenly with the sauce. Serve immediately.

**Figure 6-5:** Removing meat from sausage casings.

Use a knife to slit the casing on the end of the link...

...and then squeeze the sausage meat out with your hands!

## Bucatini with Tomatoes, Onions, and Pancetta

This recipe is one of the most popular pasta dishes in Italy (see photo in color section). Originally, the dish called for pig's cheek. Because this cut is so fatty, no olive oil was used. Leaner pancetta (or American-style bacon) is now the standard ingredient in this recipe, along with some olive oil to crisp the bacon.

*Italian recipe name:* Bucatini all'Amatriciana

*Preparation time:* 15 minutes

*Cooking time:* 45 minutes

*Yield:* 4 servings

2 tablespoons olive oil

4 cloves garlic, peeled and chopped

1 medium onion, sliced

Pinch of hot red pepper flakes

1 teaspoon chopped fresh rosemary, or
$^1/_4$ teaspoon dried rosemary

8 slices pancetta or bacon (about
4 ounces)

1 cup white wine

$1^1/_2$ cups (14-ounce can) plum tomatoes

Salt to taste

$1^1/_2$ tablespoons kosher salt

$^1/_2$ pound bucatini pasta

$^1/_4$ cup grated Pecorino cheese

**1** Heat the olive oil in a large skillet or medium saucepan. Add the garlic, onion, red pepper flakes, rosemary, and pancetta and cook over medium heat until the onion is soft, about 10 minutes. Pour the wine into the pan and continue cooking until it has almost completely evaporated. Add the tomatoes, lightly crushing them with a wooden spoon. Season with salt. Simmer for 30 minutes, until the sauce thickens slightly.

**2** In a large pot, bring 4 quarts water to a boil. Add the kosher salt and pasta, mix well, and cook until al dente.

**3** Drain the pasta and add it to the pan with the sauce. Sprinkle with the Pecorino cheese. Stir to coat the pasta evenly with the sauce. Serve immediately.

# Chapter 7

# Fresh Pasta

## In This Chapter

▶ Making fresh pasta

▶ Using a pasta machine

▶ Cooking and saucing fresh pasta

▶ Filling fresh pasta

*F*resh pasta is a project, but, oh, what fun. If you liked working with Play-Doh as a kid, you'll enjoy turning flour and eggs into thin ribbons of dough for fettuccine or see-through sheets for lasagne. But be warned: Don't plan on serving fresh pasta on a weeknight after a long day at work or taking care of your kids — at least, not if you want to make the pasta yourself.

Most Italian towns, no matter how small, have a shop, called a *pastificio,* that makes fresh fettuccine, tagliorini, ravioli, and agnolotti. These pastas are prepared every day and sold fresh. If you want to make the recipes in this chapter but don't have the time to make your own fresh pasta, go to a gourmet store or pasta shop that makes its own pasta every day.

But whatever you do, please, please, don't buy the so-called "fresh" pasta sold in the refrigerated case at the supermarket. This pasta is expensive and cooks up mushy and tasteless. Fresh pasta was never meant to sit for weeks in the supermarket. It may be edible for weeks or months (at least according to the sell-by dates stamped on most packages), but it's not fresh in the truest sense of the word. Fresh pasta loses its flavor and delicate texture very quickly, so either make it yourself or buy it from someone who makes it fresh every day, like people do in Italy.

# Making Pasta Yourself

Traditionally, certain dishes require fresh pasta. For example, filled pastas, such as ravioli, must start with fresh pasta. For other dishes, such as lasagne, you have a choice of fresh or dried pasta.

Although dried lasagne noodles and fettuccine exist, the fresh versions are far superior. Fresh noodles actually absorb some of the creamy sauces that are usually served with these pasta shapes. In contrast, butter, cheese, and cream sauces slide right off dried pasta. The delicate egg flavor of fresh pasta also complements these kinds of delicate, creamy sauces. If you want to make the dishes we discuss in this chapter, we really urge you to use fresh pasta.

Making pasta at home was once a challenge. The dough had to be kneaded by hand and then rolled out with much finesse into thin sheets that you then cut into the appropriate shape. You can still make pasta this way, but two modern inventions (the food processor and pasta machine) have made fresh pasta much more accessible, even for novices. Here's what you need to know.

## Choosing the ingredients

Fresh pasta requires only four ingredients — flour, eggs, olive oil, and salt. Flour produces fresh noodles that are delicate yet elastic enough to stretch and roll out. Unbleached flour is the closest thing to the flour used to make fresh pasta in Italy, although bleached flour, which has been treated with chemicals to make it whiter, also works.

The other main ingredient is eggs. Use the freshest eggs possible because they provide pasta with most of its flavor. And a tiny bit of olive oil can be used to make the dough more supple and flavorful. A pinch of salt adds flavor as well. The flour and eggs are essential, but you can consider the oil and salt optional but recommended.

You can flavor egg pasta in numerous ways. (For more information, see the sidebar "Flavoring egg pasta" later in this chapter.) However, many of these flavorings are for cosmetic rather than flavor reasons. For example, tomato paste can dye fresh egg pasta a beautiful orange-red color. But close your eyes, and you won't be able to taste the difference between plain and tomato pasta.

Some flavorings do provide subtle flavors that you can detect if the sauce is especially delicate. (For example, a plain cream sauce shows off the flavor of saffron or black pepper pasta.) However, after you put a spicy tomato sauce on any flavored pasta, you taste the sauce, not the pasta. Flavor fresh pasta if you like, but realize that flavoring is mostly an aesthetic decision.

# Flavoring egg pasta

You can add two types of flavoring agents to pasta dough. Relatively dry ingredients, such as flour, spices, and herbs, are easy to work with because they don't affect the ratio of flour to eggs.

However, after you add something moist, such as cooked spinach, the dough becomes stickier and harder to work with. You can add more flour, but we suggest avoiding this problem by making sure that all moist additions to pasta dough are as dry as possible. This means adding tomato paste, not fresh tomatoes, to pasta dough or squeezing every last bit of water out of cooked spinach leaves.

We have listed the following flavorings in order of ease. (By the way, you can make chocolate pasta, but it's not Italian. We have chosen traditional flavorings.) Start with things like herbs and black pepper because they don't make the dough harder to work with. After you feel like you have mastered the art of making fresh pasta, try spinach or tomatoes.

You can add all the following ingredients to the recipe for Fresh Egg Pasta, later in this chapter. Add dry ingredients along with the flour; add wet ingredients to the food processor along with the last egg.

✔ **Black pepper:** Coarsely ground black pepper gives egg pasta a mild spiciness and speckled appearance. Use $1\frac{1}{2}$ teaspoons coarsely ground black pepper.

✔ **Saffron:** Saffron threads dye fresh pasta a brilliant yellow-orange color and give it a mild, earthy flavor. Saffron pasta is especially good with tomato-cream sauces. Use $\frac{1}{4}$ teaspoon crumbled saffron threads.

✔ **Fresh herbs:** Finely minced herbs add fresh green color as well as subtle flavor to egg pasta. Use 2 tablespoons minced fresh parsley, basil, mint, sage, thyme, oregano, or marjoram.

✔ **Whole wheat flour:** Whole wheat flour produces a hearty pasta suitable for chunky meat and vegetable sauces made with olive oil rather than butter. Because it contains more gluten, whole wheat dough takes a minute or two longer to knead into a smooth ball. Replace $1\frac{1}{2}$ cups flour with an equal amount of whole-wheat flour.

✔ **Buckwheat flour:** Buckwheat pasta is a specialty of the Lombardy region. It's traditionally served with hearty sauces made with leafy greens, cabbage, and potatoes. It has a wholesome, nutty flavor and chewy texture. Buckwheat flour isn't actually made from grain; it's made from the seed of a plant in the rhubarb family. Replace $\frac{1}{2}$ cup flour with an equal amount of buckwheat flour.

✔ **Tomatoes:** Tomato paste dyes fresh pasta a pale orange color but adds little or no flavor. Use 2 tablespoons tomato paste and be prepared to add an extra $\frac{1}{4}$ cup flour to keep the dough from becoming too sticky.

✔ **Spinach:** Spinach adds no flavor but gives a good color to fresh pasta. Spinach noodles are appropriate in most recipes that call for fresh pasta. Because flavor is not an issue, start with frozen chopped spinach. Put half of a 10-ounce package in some boiling water and cook 2 to 3 minutes until tender. Drain the spinach in a colander, pressing on it with the back of a large spoon to remove as much water as possible. Place the spinach on a cutting board and finely chop it. Press the spinach with your hands, tilting the board over the sink to drain off any remaining liquid. You should have about $\frac{1}{3}$ cup finely chopped spinach. Squeezing out all the liquid you can is imperative, or the dough becomes sticky.

## Making the dough

Before the invention of the food processor, making the dough for fresh pasta took about 20 minutes. With the food processor, it takes about 1 minute. For history buffs, here's how to make it the old-fashioned way (see Figure 7-1).

1. **Place the flour in a pile on the counter.**

2. **Hollow out the center of the pile so that the flour is shaped into a ring.**

    It looks like the top of a volcano.

3. **Crack the eggs and place them in the center of the ring. Add the oil and salt to the eggs.**

4. **With a fork, slowly incorporate some of the flour into the eggs.**

    Don't break through the wall of flour and let the eggs run all over the counter!

# Making Pasta the Old-Fashioned Way

**1.**
Start with the flour in a pile on the counter.

**2.** *like the top of a volcano!*
Hollow out the center so it's shaped into a ring.

**3.**
Crack the eggs and place them in the center of the ring with the oil and salt.

**4.**
With a fork, slowly incorporate some of the flour into the eggs.....

☆ **CAREFUL...**
...without breaking through the wall of flour so the eggs don't run all over the counter!!

**5.**
When enough flour has been worked into the eggs so that they won't run away, you can start kneading...

**6.**...first to work in the rest of the flour, and then to knead the dough. Pasta dough must be smooth and well-kneaded, so work the dough for at least 10 minutes!

(When the dough is as smooth as a baby's bottom, you are ready to roll.)

*ready to roll, baby!*

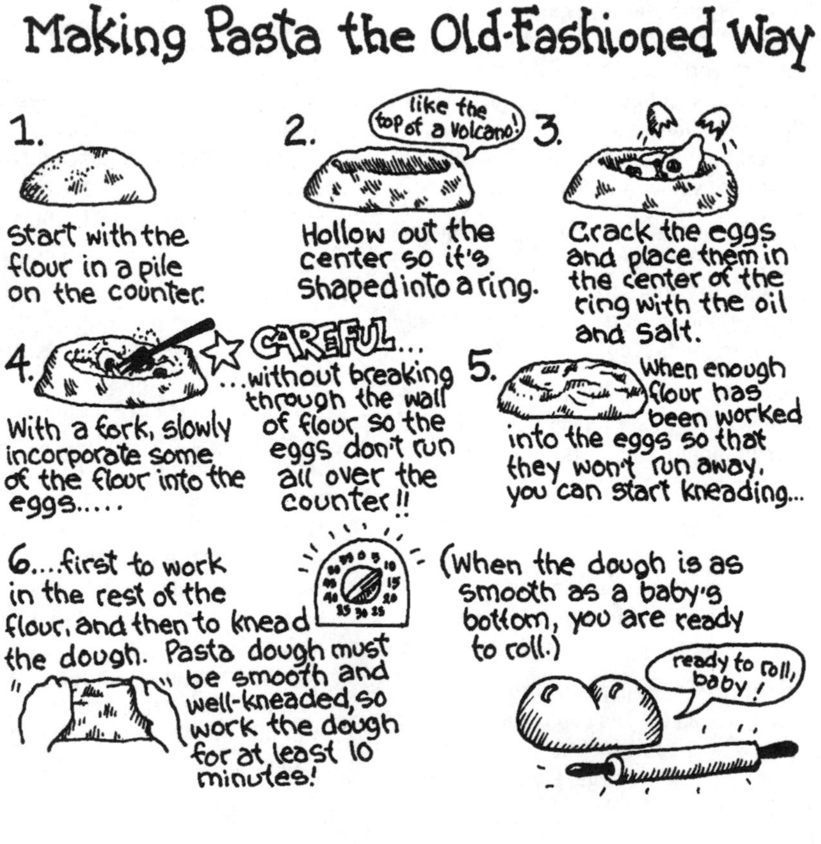

**Figure 7-1:**
Making pasta the old-fashioned way.

5. **When you've worked enough flour into the eggs so that they won't run away, start kneading to work in the rest of the flour and then to knead the dough.**

   Pasta dough must be very smooth and well kneaded, so work the dough by hand for at least 10 minutes. When the dough is as smooth as a baby's bottom, you are ready to roll.

The modern method, of course, is much simpler. Just place the flour in a food processor, turn on the machine, add the eggs, and wait about ten seconds. You should still knead the dough by hand after it comes together in the food processor. But this takes only a minute or two, no longer.

## Rolling and cutting the dough

After you've kneaded the pasta dough, it's time to rock and roll. (Well, you can skip the rock part, but you must roll.) Traditionally, Italian home cooks would use a rolling pin or even a wine bottle. However, stretching the dough out this way is very hard. The dough is tough and resists your best efforts. In the end, pasta rolled with a rolling pin is usually too thick.

We prefer using a manual pasta machine (see Figure 7-2). It rolls the pasta to an even thickness, and you can get the sheets of pasta quite thin. This machine also cuts the pasta. Most models can cut the pasta into fettuccine or spaghetti. The wider fettuccine cutters usually work a little better.

In addition to pasta machines that you crank by hand, you can find several electric extruders on the market. Basically, these are a food processor and pasta machine in one. You put the ingredients in the machine and then press a button to knead and then extrude a variety of shapes.

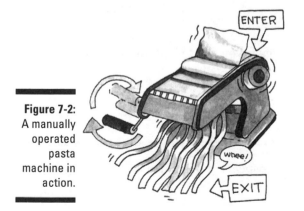

**Figure 7-2:**
A manually operated pasta machine in action.

Unfortunately, most electric pasta machines don't work all that well, and we don't think that they're worth the $200 or so that most companies charge. For that money, you can buy a food processor (for about $150) and a manual pasta machine (for about $40), and the food processor has hundreds of uses. An electric pasta machine is good for only one thing.

A manual pasta machine produces two shapes — fettuccine or spaghetti. However, you can take the long sheets of dough and cut them to make lasagne noodles. Or take those long sheets and cut them with a knife into long, wide ribbons to make pappardelle or squares for ravioli or tortellini.

After you have cut out the pasta shape, you need to be careful to keep the individual pieces separated. Letting them dry for a half hour or so helps. You can keep fresh pasta on clean kitchen towels at room temperature for several hours before cooking. For longer storage, place the pasta in a zipper-lock plastic bag and freeze it for up to one month. Don't defrost frozen fresh pasta. Simply take the pasta out of the freezer and dump it into a pot of boiling water. The cooking time is a minute or two longer than for fresh pasta.

## Cooking and saucing fresh noodles

Cooking fresh pasta takes less time than you may think. After the water returns to a boil (it takes a minute or two, depending on how much pasta you've added to the pot and how high the heat is), the pasta may be almost done. Start tasting, and just before you think that the pasta is done (it should be cooked through and tender but still have some chew and elasticity), drain it quickly and get it sauced.

Even more so than dried pasta, fresh pasta goes from perfectly cooked to soggy and overcooked very quickly. After the pasta goes into the pot, stay close (no phone calls, please) and taste the pasta often to make sure that you catch it at just the right moment.

Because fresh pasta cooks so quickly, you must finish the sauce before the pasta goes into the pot.

### Fresh Egg Pasta

Making your own pasta is surprisingly easy, especially if you use a food processor and manual pasta machine.

***Italian recipe name:*** *Pasta all'Uovo*

***Preparation time:*** *50 minutes*

***Cooking time:*** *None*

***Yield:*** *6 servings*

***Special tools:*** *Food processor, manual pasta machine*

*2$^{1}$/$_{4}$ cups flour plus flour for dusting work surface and pasta*

*3 eggs*

*Pinch of salt*

*$^{1}$/$_{2}$ tablespoon olive oil*

*1* Place the flour in the bowl of a food processor. With the motor running, add the eggs 1 at a time and then add the salt and olive oil. Process for 10 more seconds.

*2* Transfer the dough to a flat, flour-dusted surface. Knead it until it forms a smooth, firm ball, about 5 minutes. Place it in a bowl, cover it with a kitchen towel, and set aside for about 30 minutes.

*3* Divide the dough into 5 balls. With the palm of your hand, flatten each ball. Set the wheel for the rollers of the pasta machine on the widest setting. Turning the handle, roll the dough through. Lightly dust the pasta with flour and fold it into thirds. Roll it through the machine again. Repeat this 3 more times, folding the dough each time.

*4* Continue rolling the pasta through the machine, dusting it with flour, but no longer folding it in between rolling. Make the opening smaller each time, until you have a long sheet of pasta that is about $^{1}$/$_{16}$-inch thick. It's now ready to be cut into different shapes with the pasta machine.

## Four sauces for fresh pasta

Our favorite way to enjoy fresh fettuccine or tagliorini is with butter, cheese, and white truffles. But you can't always get (or afford) white truffles. So here are some other ideas for saucing fresh noodles:

✔ Leave out the truffles and just coat the pasta with melted butter and lots of freshly grated Parmigiano-Reggiano cheese.

✔ Try a simple tomato sauce, such as that used in the Pasta with Tomato and Basil Sauce in Chapter 6. Use butter instead of olive oil when making the sauce and stir a little heavy cream into the finished sauce, if you like.

✔ Try Pesto (see Chapter 6) with fresh pasta. Again, enrich the pesto with several tablespoons of cream if you like.

✔ Use Italy's famed meat sauce, Ragù di Carne, over fettuccine as in lasagne. (See recipe later in this chapter.)

# Other Uses for Fresh Pasta

You can treat fresh pasta like dried pasta — that is, cut into noodles, cooked, and drained. However, you can also use fresh pasta in baked pasta dishes like lasagne or in filled pastas like ravioli.

## Lasagne

Make lasagne with dried noodles if you must, but try it with fresh noodles and you really notice the difference. The result is a much lighter, more delicate dish.

In Bologna, lasagne is made with a rich meat sauce. The layers are bound together with a creamy white sauce, called bechamel, and the cheese is Parmigiano-Reggiano. Italians in this region don't use mozzarella or ricotta, which are used primarily in lasagne recipes from southern Italy and the United States.

### Bechamel Sauce

You can use this creamy white sauce as a binder in many baked pasta dishes. When making this sauce, you must whisk constantly to prevent the formation of lumps.

***Italian recipe name:*** *Bechamela*

***Preparation time:*** *5 minutes*

***Cooking time:*** *9 minutes*

***Yield:*** *1 quart*

| | |
|---|---|
| *8 tablespoons butter* | *Pinch of ground nutmeg* |
| *¹/₂ cup flour* | *Salt and white pepper to taste* |
| *1 quart warm milk* | |

**1** In a heavy saucepan, melt the butter. Add the flour and cook, stirring, over low heat for 4 minutes. Increase the heat to medium and gradually add the milk, stirring constantly with a whisk.

**2** Continue whisking the sauce as it gently boils, about 5 minutes. Add the nutmeg and salt and pepper. Stir well and remove from heat. Use immediately or store in a bowl with plastic wrap touching the surface of the bechamel so that a skin doesn't form on top. Store, refrigerated, for up to 2 days.

## Meat Sauce

This sauce requires very gentle simmering to produce a finely textured, sweet meat sauce that's rich and delicious. You can use the sauce in baked pasta dishes, such as lasagne, or tossed with fresh fettuccine. This sauce stores well, frozen in small containers, for up to 3 weeks.

**Italian recipe name:** *Ragù di Carne*

**Preparation time:** *25 minutes*

**Cooking time:** *3 hours*

**Yield:** *8 servings*

*¹/₄ cup olive oil*

*1 large onion, peeled and chopped*

*3 celery stalks, chopped*

*1 medium carrot, chopped*

*5 cloves garlic, peeled and minced*

*³/₄ pound ground pork*

*³/₄ pound ground beef*

*4 thin slices of pancetta or bacon, minced*

*4 thin slices of prosciutto, minced*

*2 cups dry red wine*

*28-ounce can whole Italian tomatoes, undrained*

*2 cups water*

*Salt to taste*

*¹/₂ teaspoon hot red pepper flakes*

*¹/₄ teaspoon black pepper*

*Pinch of allspice*

*Pinch of nutmeg*

*Pinch of cloves*

*Pinch of cinnamon*

**1** In a large pot, heat the olive oil over medium heat. Add the onion, celery, carrot, and garlic and cook, stirring often, until the vegetables are tender, about 15 minutes.

**2** Add the pork, beef, pancetta or bacon, and prosciutto and cook, stirring frequently, for another 10 minutes.

**3** Add the wine and cook for about 5 minutes. Add the tomatoes and water and simmer, covered, for 50 minutes.

**4** Season with the salt, red pepper flakes, black pepper, and spices and then stir. Simmer, stirring occasionally, for 90 more minutes, until the sauce is thick and flavorful. Check the sauce during cooking. If it thickens too quickly, add a little bit of water (about ¹/₂ cup at a time) and continue cooking. Adjust seasoning with salt, if necessary.

### Lasagne

Lasagne is a lot of work, but you can make the Meat Sauce and Bechamel Sauce in advance. You can assemble the entire lasagne, wrap it tightly in foil, and then refrigerate it for up to 1 day before baking.

***Italian recipe name:*** *Lasagne*

***Preparation time:*** *25 to 30 minutes (excludes time for preparation of Meat Sauce, Bechamel Sauce, and pasta)*

***Cooking time:*** *35 minutes*

***Yield:*** *12 servings*

| | |
|---|---|
| *2 recipes Fresh Egg Pasta* | *1 recipe Bechamel Sauce* |
| *2 tablespoons butter, for greasing the baking dish* | *1 cup grated Parmigiano-Reggiano* |
| *1¹/₂ recipes Meat Sauce* | |

**1** Preheat oven to 375°.

**2** Prepare the pasta. Cut the rolled pasta dough into 8 x 6-inch sheets. Precook the pasta sheets in salted boiling water for 1 minute and then transfer to a large bowl of cold water. After the pasta has cooled, remove the squares and place them on a large platter. Set aside.

**3** Butter the bottom and sides of a 9 x 13-inch baking dish. Spread a layer of the meat sauce, about ¹/₂ cup, on the bottom of the dish.

**4** Line the baking dish with a layer of pasta. Evenly spread a layer of bechamel over the pasta, followed by meat sauce, and then sprinkle with about ¹/₄ cup cheese. Cover with a layer of pasta, bechamel, meat sauce, and cheese. Repeat this process 3 more times. The top layer should have bechamel, meat sauce, and cheese.

**5** Bake for 30 to 35 minutes until bubbly and slightly browned on top. Remove from oven, let cool for 10 minutes, and serve.

# Filled pastas

You can use fresh pasta to make filled pastas, such as ravioli, agnolotti, and tortellini (see Chapter 6 for definitions). Ravioli are the easiest filled pasta to make because they aren't shaped by hand but rather cut into squares.

To make ravioli, you should leave the pasta dough in long sheets. You then dot the filling — spinach and cheese is popular, as is plain cheese — along the length of the pasta sheet. Lay a second sheet over the first and then cut out the ravioli with a scalloped cutter (see Figure 7-3).

If you work quickly, the pasta retains enough moisture to seal on its own. However, as a safety measure, you may want to brush an egg wash over the edges of the pasta sheets to make sure that they stick together. If the edges don't seal properly, the ravioli can open up when boiled. To make an egg wash, beat an egg with a tablespoon or so of water and then use a pastry brush to moisten the edges of the pasta sheets just before you place the second sheet over the filled first sheet.

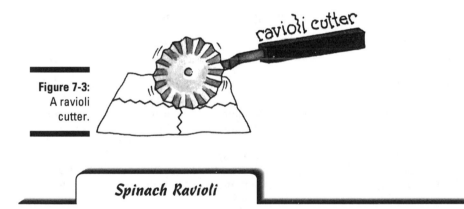

**Figure 7-3:**
A ravioli
cutter.

### Spinach Ravioli

You must squeeze all the moisture out of the cooked spinach or the filling becomes watery. Serve these ravioli with the Meat Sauce from the recipe earlier in this chapter or the Tomato and Basil Sauce from Chapter 6 (see photo in color section). Or simply serve the ravioli with some melted butter and grated Parmigiano-Reggiano cheese. If you like, warm several minced sage leaves in the melted butter.

*Italian recipe name:* Ravioli di Spinaci

*Preparation time:* 45 minutes

*Cooking time:* 8 minutes

*Yield:* 4 servings

*Special tools:* Ravioli cutter, strainer-skimmer

1 recipe Fresh Egg Pasta

1 cup ricotta

$^1/_2$ cup grated Parmigiano-Reggiano

$^1/_2$ cup cooked spinach, fresh or frozen, water thoroughly squeezed out after cooking

1 egg

1 tablespoon chopped fresh parsley, or 1 teaspoon dried parsley

1 tablespoon chopped fresh thyme

Pinch of ground nutmeg

Pepper to taste

$1^1/_2$ tablespoons salt

Flour for dusting work surface

**1** Prepare the pasta. Let it rest, wrapped and refrigerated, for 30 minutes.

**2** To prepare the filling, combine all ingredients (except salt) in a medium bowl. Mix well and set aside.

**3** Lay the pasta sheets out on a flat, flour-dusted surface. Place $^1/_2$ tablespoon dots of the spinach filling, about 3 inches apart, on the bottom layer and fit a second layer of pasta over the first. With your fingers, press down lightly to seal the sheets together and remove any air. Use a scalloped cutter to cut out the ravioli squares.

**4** In a large pot, bring 4 quarts water to a boil. Add the salt and half the ravioli. (You should cook the ravioli in 2 batches.) Gently boil for 2 to 4 minutes, until the ravioli rise to the surface. Place the ravioli in a pan, mix with any sauce that you like, and serve.

# Chapter 8

# Risotto: Worth the Work

*P*asta gets all the attention, at least when it comes to Italian cooking and carbohydrates. But rice is an important starch, especially in northern regions of Italy. Most of this rice is turned into a dish called *risotto* (ree-**zaw**-toh).

Most rice dishes around the world are fairly similar. You take the rice, add a set amount of liquid, bring it to a boil, cover, and simmer until the grains have absorbed all the liquid and are tender. This is rice as a side dish.

Italians prepare risotto in a different fashion. The rice is sautéed in a bit of fat for several minutes and then stirred constantly as hot stock is added in increments — not all at once. The result is a creamy, hearty rice porridge, not unlike rice pudding in consistency. Of course, you don't make risotto with sugar or milk. However, it does get some dairy creaminess from butter and cheese.

Like pasta, Italians serve risotto in small portions as a first course. You can also serve risotto as a light main course. Like pasta, rice is a blank canvas that you can flavor in countless ways. Risotto has a special affinity for vegetables. For vegetarians, risotto offers a good break from a steady pasta diet. But risotto is so delicious, everyone wants to eat it.

## Start with the Right Rice

To make risotto, you must start with Italian-grown rice. Other kinds of rice simply don't have the right balance of starches to produce the correct texture. You can use several Italian rices to make risotto, but arborio rice is the most widely available.

This medium-grain rice is pearly white and has several unique properties. First and foremost, this rice can hold its shape, even after prolonged simmering. (In contrast, regular long-grain rice falls apart into mush if substituted in a risotto recipe.) In addition to a firm texture, arborio rice slowly releases starches as it cooks. These starches help create the creamy texture that is the hallmark of good risotto.

You may use other Italian rices, including vialone nano and carnaroli, in risotto. Vialone nano is popular in the Veneto. It tends to cook up firmer than arborio rice. Carnaroli is a relatively new strain developed in the last 50 years. It cooks up firmer than either arborio or vialone nano, but releases plenty of starch to form a creamy sauce.

Vialone nano and carnaroli are very popular in Italy but are hard to find elsewhere. They tend to be more expensive than arborio as well. If you see either of these rices, give them a try. Otherwise, stick with arborio rice, which has become a staple in most supermarkets.

# Stir Crazy

Buying the right rice is the first step to making great risotto. The second important element is the cooking process. Here's what you need to know.

Most risotto recipes begin by sautéing onions in a little fat. Some recipes use olive oil, others butter, and still others a combination of the two. After the onion is golden, you add the rice. You toast the rice in the fat to bring out its flavor. The rice doesn't actually brown, but you should smell a "toasty" aroma as the rice cooks in the fat.

You can use a wooden spoon to stir the rice as it cooks, but a flat wooden spatula (see Figure 8-1) does the best job of freeing the rice grains from the surface of the saucepan and keeping them from burning. The sharp edges on a wooden spatula are also better to get into the "corners" of the saucepan where the bottom meets the side.

After you've toasted the rice, add a little white wine to the saucepan to build flavor. Simmer the wine just until the alcohol aroma fades and the liquid has reduced slightly, no more than a minute or two.

**Figure 8-1:**
A flat wooden spatula.

At this point, the rice is ready for some hot liquid. In most rice recipes, you add all the liquid at once. For risotto, you add the liquid in increments. Also, this liquid must be hot. As soon as the rice has absorbed the liquid, it's time to add more.

 Because so little liquid is in the saucepan, you must stir the rice constantly with a wooden spoon or spatula to keep it from sticking. Stirring also helps release the starches from the rice and builds creaminess. Don't walk into another room or set the table when making risotto.

As soon as the grains have swollen and become tender but firm (they should be just slightly chewy), stop adding the hot liquid. At this point, remove the saucepan from the heat and beat in a little butter and grated Parmigiano-Reggiano cheese. The butter and cheese make the texture especially creamy and boost the flavor. They also absorb some of the liquid in the saucepan and make the texture of the risotto less runny.

To serve, ladle the risotto into wide, shallow bowls, like those used to serve pasta. Although it may look awfully moist, you can eat properly cooked risotto with a fork. You may sprinkle on extra grated cheese at the table, if you like.

## Dado is not a painter

The choice of cooking liquid affects the flavor of the risotto. Restaurants widely use chicken stock. Occasionally, Italian chefs use fish stock when making a seafood risotto or a vegetable stock when making a delicate vegetable risotto.

But what should the home cook use, especially if you have no stock on hand? In Italy, many home cooks turn to *il dado,* or the bouillon cube. They drop a cube into a pot of simmering water and, in seconds, have the liquid that they need for risotto.

They don't have canned broth in Italy, but you can use this product rather than homemade stock, if you like. Pick a low-sodium brand and dilute it with water to keep the flavor from overpowering the other elements in the risotto.

You can also make risotto with water. The dish may not be as flavorful, but it still tastes good, especially if you use plenty of other potent ingredients (such as cheese). Whatever liquid you use, keep it at a gentle simmer in a small saucepan and ladle it into the rice saucepan as needed.

You may find that you have a little extra liquid when the rice is done. Resist the temptation to add it to the saucepan. When the rice tastes tender but firm, stop adding liquid. Likewise, if you run out of stock and the rice is still crunchy, just add hot water until the rice is properly cooked.

## Parmesan Risotto

This is the most basic risotto, flavored with onion, stock, and grated cheese. Many Italian restaurants use veal stock in this recipe. Good chicken stock is equally delicious.

***Italian recipe name:*** *Risotto alla Parmigiana*

***Preparation time:*** *10 minutes*

***Cooking time:*** *25 minutes*

***Yield:*** *4 servings*

*6 tablespoons butter, divided*

*1 small onion, chopped*

*1¹/₄ cups Italian rice (arborio, carnaroli, or vialone nano)*

*³/₄ cup white wine*

*4 cups simmering chicken stock or water, divided*

*Salt and pepper to taste*

*¹/₄ cup grated Parmigiano-Reggiano*

**1** In a medium saucepan with a heavy bottom, heat 3 tablespoons butter. Sauté the onion over medium heat for 2 to 3 minutes until limp. Add the rice and cook for 1 to 2 minutes, stirring constantly, "toasting" the rice.

**2** Pour the wine in the saucepan and cook for 1 to 2 minutes until it reduces slightly.

**3** Stir in 1 cup simmering stock or water, season with salt and pepper, and bring to a boil. Simmer, stirring frequently. When most of the liquid has been absorbed, add another cup of simmering stock. Continue adding small ladles of stock as the rice absorbs the liquid. After 15 minutes, taste a grain of rice. It should be tender but firm; the mixture should have movement, but no excess liquid. If it requires more cooking, add a touch more liquid and cook for another 1 to 2 minutes.

**4** Remove from heat and whip in the remaining 3 tablespoons butter and Parmigiano-Reggiano cheese. Adjust the seasoning with salt and pepper, if necessary. Serve immediately.

## Saffron Risotto, Milan Style

This golden risotto gets its beautiful color and earthy flavor from a pinch of saffron threads. Saffron dyes everything that it touches a brilliant yellow-orange color. Artisans working on the Duomo in Milan used saffron to paint frescos. Some ended up in rice, or at least that's the story behind the origins of the dish. To release their flavor, crush the saffron threads in your fingers right over the saucepan (see Figure 8-2). Italian restaurants make this dish with veal stock and the marrow from veal shank bones. Because most home cooks probably don't have these ingredients on hand, use chicken stock and pancetta instead. You can serve this recipe on its own or as an accompaniment to Braised Veal Shanks (see Chapter 12).

***Italian recipe name:*** *Risotto alla Milanese*

***Preparation time:*** *15 minutes*

***Cooking time:*** *25 minutes*

***Yield:*** *4 servings*

| | |
|---|---|
| *¹/₄ cup olive oil* | *¹/₂ cup white wine* |
| *4 tablespoons butter, divided* | *4 cups simmering chicken stock or water, divided* |
| *1 small onion, chopped* | |
| *2 tablespoons chopped marrow or pancetta* | *¹/₄ teaspoon saffron threads* |
| | *Salt and pepper to taste* |
| *1¹/₄ cups Italian rice (arborio, carnaroli, or vialone nano)* | *¹/₄ cup grated Parmigiano-Reggiano* |

*1* In a medium saucepan with a heavy bottom, heat the olive oil and 2 tablespoons butter. Sauté the onion and the marrow or pancetta over medium heat for 2 minutes. Add the rice and cook for 1 to 2 minutes, stirring constantly, "toasting" the rice.

*2* Add the wine and cook for about 2 minutes.

*3* Stir in 1 cup simmering stock or water. Crumble and add the saffron and season with salt and pepper. Simmer, stirring frequently. When most of the liquid has been absorbed, add another cup of stock. Continue adding small ladles of stock as the rice absorbs the liquid. After 15 minutes, taste a grain of rice; it should be tender but firm. The mixture should have movement, but no excess liquid. If the rice requires more cooking, add a touch more liquid and cook for another 1 to 2 minutes.

*4* Remove from heat and whip in the Parmigiano-Reggiano cheese and remaining 2 tablespoons butter. Adjust the seasoning with salt and pepper, if necessary. Serve immediately.

**Figure 8-2:**
Crumbling
saffron
threads.

Rub the saffron between your fingers right over the pot to release its full flavor.

## White Wine Risotto

Here, you use white wine in much greater quantities than most risotto recipes for a delicious flavor that complements the rice and vegetables. To keep this dish vegetarian, we use vegetable stock or water. You can use chicken stock instead, if you like.

***Italian recipe name:*** *Risotto al Vino*

***Preparation time:*** *15 minutes*

***Cooking time:*** *35 minutes*

***Yield:*** *4 servings*

*3 tablespoons olive oil*

*1 medium onion, chopped*

*2 garlic cloves, peeled and chopped*

*1 medium carrot, chopped*

*2 celery stalks, chopped*

*1 sprig fresh thyme, or 1 teaspoon dried thyme*

*$^1/_2$ teaspoon red pepper flakes*

*$1^1/_4$ cups Italian rice (arborio, carnaroli, or vialone nano)*

*2 cups white wine*

*3 cups simmering vegetable stock or water, divided*

*Salt and pepper to taste*

*2 tablespoons chopped fresh parsley, or 2 teaspoons dried parsley*

*3 tablespoons grated Parmigiano-Reggiano*

*1* In a large saucepan with a heavy bottom, heat the olive oil. Add the onion, garlic, carrot, celery, thyme, and red pepper flakes and cook over low-medium heat, stirring frequently. To achieve the most concentrated flavor, be patient and allow the vegetables to *sweat*, or slowly cook; the onion should be soft and translucent after about 10 minutes.

*2* Add the rice and cook for 1 to 2 minutes, stirring constantly, "toasting" the rice.

*3* Add the wine and reduce the heat to maintain a simmer. Cook for about 5 minutes until the rice has absorbed almost all the wine.

*4* Add 1 cup simmering stock or water and cook, stirring, until the rice absorbs the liquid, another 3 to 5 minutes. Continue adding the simmering liquid, $^1/_2$ cup at a time, until the rice is tender but firm; the total cooking time of the rice should not exceed 15 minutes. The rice should have movement but no excess liquid. If it requires more cooking, add a touch more liquid and cook for another 1 to 2 minutes.

*5* Season with salt and pepper. Remove from heat and stir in the parsley and Parmigiano-Reggiano cheese. Serve immediately.

## Gorgonzola Risotto

A mild or sweet Gorgonzola, usually labeled Gorgonzola dolce, is essential in this rich, creamy risotto. An aged, crumbly blue cheese is too pungent and overwhelms the other flavors.

***Italian recipe name:*** *Risotto al Gorgonzola*

***Preparation time:*** *10 minutes*

***Cooking time:*** *30 minutes*

***Yield:*** *4 servings*

*4 tablespoons olive oil, divided*

*2 cloves garlic, peeled and finely chopped*

*$^3/_4$ cup white wine, divided*

*6 ounces sweet Gorgonzola cheese*

*4 cups simmering chicken or vegetable stock or water, divided*

*1 small onion, chopped*

*$1^1/_4$ cups Italian rice (arborio, carnaroli, or vialone nano)*

*Salt and pepper to taste*

*2 tablespoons chopped fresh parsley, or 2 teaspoons dried parsley*

*5 tablespoons grated Parmigiano-Reggiano*

*(continued)*

*1* In a small saucepan with a heavy bottom, heat 2 tablespoons olive oil. Add the garlic and cook over medium heat for 1 to 2 minutes until limp. Reduce the heat to low and add ¼ cup wine. Cook for 3 to 4 minutes. Add the Gorgonzola and 1 cup simmering stock or water. Simmer, stirring, until the mixture is creamy and smooth, about 5 minutes. Keep the Gorgonzola sauce warm.

*2* In a medium saucepan with a heavy bottom, heat the remaining 2 tablespoons olive oil. Sauté the onion over medium heat for 2 to 3 minutes until limp.

*3* Add the rice and cook for 1 to 2 minutes, stirring constantly, "toasting" the rice.

*4* Add the remaining ½ cup wine and reduce the heat to maintain a low boil. Cook for about 3 minutes until the rice has absorbed almost all the wine.

*5* Add 1 cup simmering stock or water and cook, stirring, until the rice absorbs the liquid, another 3 to 5 minutes. Add another cup of stock or water and continue stirring. When this liquid is almost absorbed by the rice, stir in half of the Gorgonzola sauce and another ½ cup stock or water. After 5 minutes, add the remaining Gorgonzola sauce. Add stock or water as needed, until the rice is tender but firm; the total cooking time of the rice should not exceed 15 minutes. The rice should have movement but not excess liquid. If the rice requires more cooking, add a touch more liquid and cook for another 1 to 2 minutes.

*6* Season with salt and pepper. Remove from heat and stir in the parsley and Parmigiano-Reggiano cheese. Serve immediately.

## Butternut Squash Risotto

Butternut squash needs a long cooking time to soften properly (see photo in color section). For that reason, you add the squash right after the rice. Butternut squash can be tricky to peel and dice. Try using a sturdy vegetable peeler to remove the tan skin. A paring knife also works. After you've removed the skin, cut the squash in half lengthwise with a cleaver or heavy knife. Make sure to scrape away and discard any seeds and stringy fibers before dicing the peeled squash. (See Figure 8-3 for information on handling this vegetable.)

*Italian recipe name:* Risotto con la Zucca

*Preparation time:* 15 minutes

*Cooking time:* 40 minutes

*Yield:* 4 servings

**Figure 8-3:** Preparing butternut squash.

A Butternut Squash Requires Some Muscle to Peel and Cut

(hi-ya!)

Cut the squash in half lengthwise with a chef's knife.

Scoop out seeds and strings.

Then dice!

3 tablespoons olive oil

1 medium onion, chopped

2 cloves garlic, peeled and chopped

3 tablespoons white wine

5 fresh sage leaves, chopped, or 2 teaspoons dried sage

1¼ cups Italian rice (arborio, carnaroli, or vialone nano)

1 pound butternut squash, peeled, seeded, and cut into 1-inch cubes (about 3 cups)

Salt and pepper to taste

4 cups simmering vegetable stock or water, divided

2 tablespoons chopped fresh parsley, or 2 teaspoons dried parsley

¼ cup grated Parmigiano-Reggiano

**1** In a medium saucepan with a heavy bottom, heat the olive oil. Add the onion and garlic and cook over medium heat for 2 to 3 minutes until limp.

**2** Add the wine and sage and cook for 3 to 4 minutes. Add the rice and cook for 1 minute. Add the squash and salt and pepper and cook, covered, for 12 minutes.

**3** Add 1 cup simmering stock and cook, stirring, until the rice absorbs the liquid, another 3 to 5 minutes. Continue adding the simmering liquid, ½ cup at a time, until the rice is tender but firm; the total cooking time of the rice should not exceed 15 minutes. The rice should have movement but no excess liquid. If it requires more cooking, add a touch more liquid and cook for another 1 to 2 minutes.

**4** Remove from heat and whip in the parsley and Parmigiano-Reggiano cheese. Adjust the seasoning with salt and pepper, if necessary. Serve immediately.

## Vegetable Risotto

You use nine vegetables in this attractive and satisfying risotto, each adding a different color, texture, and flavor. The various vegetables go into the saucepan at different times to ensure that you cook each one properly.

***Italian recipe name:*** *Risotto Primavera*

***Preparation time:*** *10 minutes*

***Cooking time:*** *25 minutes*

***Yield:*** *6 servings*

*¹/₂ cup olive oil*

*1 medium onion, chopped*

*1 medium carrot, chopped*

*2 celery stalks, diced*

*4 fresh sage leaves, chopped, or 2 teaspoons dried sage*

*12 asparagus spears, tough ends snapped off and discarded, spears cut into 1-inch pieces, and tips reserved separately*

*1 yellow or red bell pepper, seeded and diced*

*1²/₃ cups Italian rice (arborio, carnaroli, or vialone nano)*

*1 cup white wine*

*7 cups simmering vegetable stock or water, divided*

*36 green beans (string beans), trimmed and halved crosswise*

*¹/₂ cup fresh or frozen peas*

*1 medium tomato, diced (seeds removed before dicing)*

*1 medium zucchini, diced*

*12 fresh basil leaves, coarsely chopped, or 2 teaspoons dried basil*

*2 tablespoons chopped fresh parsley, or 2 teaspoons dried parsley*

*¹/₃ cup grated Parmigiano-Reggiano*

*Salt and pepper to taste*

**1** In a medium saucepan with a heavy bottom, heat the olive oil. Add the onion, carrot, celery, and sage and cook over medium heat, stirring often, 2 to 3 minutes. Add the asparagus spears and bell pepper pieces and cook for 1 minute. Add the rice and cook for 1 to 2 minutes, stirring constantly, "toasting" the rice.

**2** Add the wine and cook, stirring constantly, for 1 to 2 minutes.

## Other simple ideas for flavoring risotto

You can flavor risotto in hundreds of ways. Almost any vegetable is appropriate. You can cook sturdy vegetables that can withstand prolonged cooking (onions, fennel, cabbage) before the rice. Add delicate green vegetables, like peas and asparagus, toward the end of the cooking time to preserve their freshness.

Here are some simple ideas for creating your own risotto recipes.

✔ Cook a little diced pancetta in the fat along with the onions.

✔ Use red wine rather than white wine. The red wine dyes the rice a pretty mauve color.

✔ Add the liquid used to rehydrate porcini mushrooms in place of some of the hot stock.

✔ Along with some butter, finish the risotto with a few tablespoons of heavy cream for extra richness.

**3** Stir in 2 cups simmering stock and the green beans. Reduce the heat so that the rice/vegetable mixture remains at a low boil. Stir often. After 3 minutes, add the peas and the asparagus tips, and 2 more cups of stock. Continue cooking for 10 to 11 minutes, stirring frequently and adding more liquid in $1/4$ cup batches as necessary. Taste a grain of rice; it should be tender but firm. The mixture should have movement but no excess liquid. If the rice requires more cooking, add a touch more liquid and cook for another 1 to 2 minutes.

**4** Remove from heat. Stir in the tomato, zucchini, basil, parsley, and Parmigiano-Reggiano cheese. Adjust the seasoning with salt and pepper, if necessary. Serve immediately.

# *Italian Rice Beyond Risotto*

Risotto is the first and best use for arborio and other Italian rices. However, you can also use these rices in salads, side dishes, and soups.

For rice salad and side dishes, boil Italian rice as if it's pasta (in an abundance of salted water). When the grains are tender but still firm, drain the rice and season. If making a salad, add a vinaigrette, let the rice cool, and add chopped vegetables, herbs, and olives. For side dishes, toss the drained rice with butter and herbs, or perhaps a spoonful of pesto (refer to Chapter 6).

## Rice and Peas

This Venetian dish is a thick rice and pea soup that you eat with a spoon. Although you toast the rice as if making risotto, you add all the liquid at once and don't stir the rice as it simmers. In some (but not all) parts of the Veneto, pancetta is added, but you can omit this ingredient, if you prefer.

**Italian recipe name:** *Risi e Bisi*

**Preparation time:** *15 minutes*

**Cooking time:** *30 minutes*

**Yield:** *4 servings*

*2 tablespoons olive oil*

*2 tablespoons butter*

*1 medium onion, chopped*

*1¹/₄ cups Italian rice (arborio, carnaroli, or vialone nano)*

*4 slices of pancetta or bacon, diced (optional)*

*¹/₂ cup white wine*

*1¹/₂ cups fresh or frozen peas*

*Salt and pepper to taste*

*5 cups simmering vegetable or chicken stock*

*2 tablespoons chopped fresh parsley, or 3 teaspoons dried parsley*

*2 tablespoons grated Parmigiano-Reggiano*

**1** In a medium saucepan with a heavy bottom, heat the olive oil and butter. Add the onion and cook over medium heat 2 to 3 minutes until limp, stirring often. Add the rice and "toast" it, stirring constantly, about 2 minutes.

**2** Add the pancetta. Cook for 2 minutes. Add the wine and cook for 1 to 2 minutes. Add the peas and season with salt and pepper.

**3** Stir in the simmering stock and bring the mixture to a boil. Reduce the heat and simmer for 14 to 15 minutes. Taste a grain of rice; it should be tender but firm. The mixture will be runny. If the rice is too firm, simmer for another 1 to 2 minutes.

**4** Remove from heat. Stir in the parsley and Parmigiano-Reggiano cheese. Adjust the seasoning with salt and pepper, if necessary. Serve immediately.

# Chapter 9
# Polenta and Gnocchi

*P*asta and risotto are the most common first courses in Italy. Soup is another popular choice. But two other options — neither of which is well known outside of Italy — are also worth discussing.

*Polenta* is cornmeal cooked into a creamy porridge. Think grits, with an Italian name. Polenta may look like a hot breakfast cereal, but polenta is actually a base for savory sauces. You can spoon almost any stewlike mixture of vegetables or meat over creamy polenta.

*Gnocchi* are tender, light dumplings made from potatoes, ricotta cheese, or semolina. Unlike many other dumplings, gnocchi are never heavy or leaden. You cook and serve them like ravioli or filled pasta — boiled just until tender, drained, and then sauced with something fairly simple, such as a good tomato sauce or maybe some butter and cheese.

This chapter explores these two first courses and explains how to make them at home. If you like something simple but a bit unusual, then you need to add polenta and gnocchi to your repertoire.

## Polenta: Italian for Grits

Polenta (poe-**len**-tah) has long been a staple food for many northern Italians because it's hearty, filling, and inexpensive. In recent years, polenta has become hip, thanks to the efforts of some non-Italian chefs. Some trendy restaurants in London, New York, and Toronto charge $20 or more for a bowl of cornmeal mush!

So, just what is polenta? Basically, it's grits, Italian style. Polenta is the Italian word for cornmeal. In Italy, cornmeal is generally yellow, not white as is common in the American South. Polenta is also the Italian word for the dish made by simmering cornmeal in liquid (usually water) to produce a thick porridge.

You can serve polenta two ways. You can ladle the soft, creamy porridge that comes right out of the pot into bowls and top with a sauce. You can put almost any sauce on polenta that you would on pasta — everything from a pat of butter and some grated Parmigiano-Reggiano cheese to tomato sauce.

You can also serve polenta firm, usually in squares or rectangles, under roasted game birds or some sausages. To make firm polenta, pour the hot porridge into a greased baking sheet and let it cool. As the polenta cools, it solidifies. When it reaches room temperature, turn the polenta out of the pan and slice it. Use the polenta in baked casseroles or broil, grill, or sauté the slices and use them as a starch accompaniment to any number of meat dishes.

You prepare both kinds of polenta (soft and firm) in the same way, using the same cornmeal and cooking technique. The only difference is how you handle the cooked polenta.

## Choosing the right cornmeal

Good polenta starts with the right grind of cornmeal. Italians use yellow cornmeal that has been ground coarse. Fine cornmeal, with a texture akin to table salt, makes polenta that's gummy. To make your polenta have better consistency, start with cornmeal that's ground to the texture of granulated sugar.

In addition to getting the right grind, try to buy stone-ground cornmeal, which is made from the whole grain. Called *polenta integra* in Italian, this cornmeal contains both the germ and the bran and has a richer corn flavor. Look for the words "stone-ground" or "whole-grain" on labels when you buy domestic cornmeal or buy polenta in see-through packages. Whole-grain cornmeal is speckled with light and dark bits of grain. A uniformly yellow cornmeal probably doesn't contain any of the flavorful bran.

## Making polenta, step by step

Making polenta sounds easy — bring water to a boil in a deep saucepan, add the cornmeal, and cook. However, you need to avoid several potential pitfalls when making polenta. The first pitfall is lumps. Adding cornmeal to boiling water almost always results in little lumps. No matter how fast you stir, pesky lumps form.

## Polenta in an instant

In addition to regular Italian polenta (which is just cornmeal ground to make the dish polenta), you may also see imported products labeled instant or quick-cooking polenta. Like instant rice, instant polenta has been cooked and then dried. Instant polenta is prepared like regular polenta, but the cooking time is just 5 minutes — not the usual 40 minutes or more.

So, how does instant polenta taste? It doesn't have the smooth, buttery corn flavor of polenta made from regular cornmeal. However, in a pinch, it's more than adequate. The texture can be a bit gritty, which is more of a problem when you want to serve polenta in a soft, creamy mound. If you cool instant polenta for use in casseroles, the gritty texture is harder to detect.

To avoid those lumps (which are caused when heat sets the starches and causes the granules to clump together), add the cornmeal to cold water. Bring the cornmeal, water, salt, and oil to a boil, reduce the heat, and then simmer, stirring often to ensure that the polenta doesn't stick.

Italian cooks use a wooden spoon to stir because polenta tends to stick to metal. Simmering polenta also tends to splatter. To protect your hands, use a long wooden spoon and cook the polenta in a deep 4-quart saucepan.

## *Polenta, soft and creamy*

When the polenta achieves the proper consistency, you should ladle it into bowls, sauce it, and serve it. The recipes that follow offer some concrete ideas for saucing polenta. Here are some other possibilities:

- ✔ Almost any tomato sauce you might consider putting over pasta works over bowls of polenta. Hearty sauces, with chunks of vegetables and/or meat, are best. A mushroom ragù or bolognese sauce is ideal.

- ✔ Almost any cheese works as a topping for polenta. Place a thick slice of Gorgonzola dolce over a bowl of creamy polenta. Or dollop some Mascarpone over polenta. Or stir some ricotta and grated Pecorino cheese right into the polenta.

- ✔ Drizzle some high-quality extra-virgin olive oil over soft polenta. Minced fresh herbs, such as basil, parsley, sage, and thyme, work nicely with the oil.

- ✔ It may not be very traditional, but soft polenta makes a great breakfast cereal. Serve with honey or maple syrup and a pat of butter on a cold winter morning.

In addition to these ideas, here are some recipes worth trying.

## Basic Polenta

You must keep a close eye on the pot, stirring often with a wooden spoon to prevent the polenta from scorching.

*Italian recipe name:* *Polenta*

*Preparation time:* *5 minutes*

*Cooking time:* *45 to 50 minutes*

*Yield:* *8 servings*

| | |
|---|---|
| *2 quarts cold water* | *1 tablespoon salt* |
| *2 cups coarsely ground cornmeal* | *2¹/₂ tablespoons olive oil* |

Combine the water, cornmeal, salt, and olive oil in a large saucepan. Turn the heat to medium and cook, stirring constantly. When the polenta begins to boil, lower the heat to a simmer and continue cooking, stirring often, for 40 to 45 minutes. It should be the consistency of soft ice cream and pull away from the sides of saucepan. If it is too stiff, add a little hot water.

## Polenta with Vegetables

Serve a medley of vegetables over a mound of fluffy polenta to make an excellent first course for a spring meal (see photo in color section).

*Italian recipe name:* *Polenta con Verdure*

*Preparation time:* *25 minutes*

*Cooking time:* *45 to 50 minutes*

*Yield:* *6 to 8 servings*

1 recipe Basic Polenta

$^1/_4$ cup olive oil

2 cloves garlic, peeled and chopped

1 medium onion, peeled and diced

1 carrot, peeled and diced

2 celery stalks, diced

1 yellow bell pepper, cut into long thin strips

1 teaspoon chopped fresh sage, or 1 teaspoon dried sage

1 teaspoon chopped fresh thyme, or $^1/_2$ teaspoon dried thyme

Salt and pepper to taste

$^1/_2$ cup white wine

8 asparagus spears, stems cut into 1-inch pieces, tips reserved seperately

24 green beans, cut into 1-inch pieces

1 zucchini, diced

2 medium tomatoes, diced

$^1/_2$ cup chopped fresh basil, or 1 tablespoon dried basil

$^1/_2$ cup water

**1** Prepare the vegetable sauce before or during the preparation of the polenta: In a medium-sized pan, heat the olive oil over medium heat. Add the garlic, onion, carrot, celery, yellow pepper, sage, and thyme and cook, stirring often, until the vegetables soften, 8 to 10 minutes.

**2** Season with salt and pepper and add the wine. Simmer until the wine is reduced by half, about 3 minutes, and then add the asparagus spears and beans. Cook, stirring frequently, for 10 minutes.

**3** Add the zucchini, tomatoes, asparagus tips, basil, and water and continue cooking for another 10 minutes. Adjust the seasoning with salt and pepper.

**4** Serve the vegetable mixture over a generous mound of polenta.

# Polenta as a building block

You can serve polenta straight from the pot, when it's soft and creamy, or you can pour it into a greased baking pan, let it cool, and cut it into squares to use in casserole-type dishes.

## Baked Polenta with Meat

This layered casserole is sometimes called polenta lasagne, with the rounds or squares of cooled polenta taking the place of the pasta.

***Italian recipe name:*** *Polenta Pastizzada*

***Preparation time:*** *15 minutes*

***Cooking time:*** *25 minutes (plus 45 to 50 minutes to cook the polenta)*

***Yield:*** *6 to 8 servings*

*1 recipe Basic Polenta*

*¹/₄ cup butter divided*

*4 cups Meat Sauce (see Chapter 7)*

*¹/₂ cup grated Parmigiano-Reggiano*

*1* Preheat oven to 375°.

*2* Pour the hot polenta into a large, shallow baking pan. The polenta should be ³/₄ to 1-inch thick. Set aside to cool.

*3* Using 2 tablespoons butter, grease an 8 x 8 x 1.5-inch baking pan. When the polenta is at room temperature, cut out even circles or squares and place half of them, touching one another, on the bottom of the pan. Top with half the meat sauce and half the grated cheese. Place the remaining polenta over the meat sauce and cheese and top with the remaining meat sauce followed by the remaining cheese. Dot the top with the remaining 2 tablespoons butter and place the pan in the oven. Bake until heated through and lightly browned, about 20 minutes.

*4* Cut large pieces and place them on serving plates or place the pan in the center of the table to eat "family style."

# Gnocchi: Little Dumplings

Gnocchi (**gnoh**-key) are little Italian dumplings that are formed by hand, boiled until tender, and then served with sauce. Several kinds of gnocchi are made in Italy.

✔ Potato gnocchi are the most popular type of gnocchi. They're made with potatoes, flour, eggs, and salt. Cooked spinach may be added for color and a little flavor. Even with spinach, potato gnocchi are fairly bland, making them a good backdrop for almost any sauce.

✔ Ricotta gnocchi are creamy and softer than those made with potatoes. They generally contain ricotta, flour, and salt. Most recipes contain some grated Parmigiano-Reggiano cheese as well. Minced herbs or spinach are other common additions. Simpler sauces, such as butter and cheese or tomato-cream sauces, work best with these gnocchi.

✔ Semolina gnocchi are a specialty of Rome. They're made with semolina, milk, and butter. They're usually shaped into thin rounds, rather than the traditional gnocchi shape, and baked rather than boiled. They're usually baked with butter and cheese, so there's no need to sauce them.

## *Potato gnocchi*

Although potato dumplings are made throughout Europe, potato gnocchi are quite different from those made in Central Europe. For example, German dumplings are usually quite large (about the size of an egg or larger) and heavy. In contrast, Italian dumplings are small (usually about the size of a large grape) and light.

Many other European dumplings float in soup. (Actually, most of those dumplings are so leaden that they don't really float.) Italians prepare dumplings like fresh pasta. The are boiled in abundant water and served with sauce. The texture should be light and ethereal.

Making potato gnocchi isn't complicated, but several important steps are necessary for good results:

✔ Boil the potatoes with their skins on. This keeps the potatoes from becoming mushy or soggy.

✔ Peel the potatoes as soon as you can and put them through a ricer to eliminate all lumps. Don't let the potatoes cool too much before peeling them or your gnocchi will be gluelike.

✔ Roll the dough into long logs (about 10 to 15 inches) or ropes on a floured counter.

✔ Cut the long ropes into 1-inch pieces and roll each piece off the tines of a fork (see Figure 9-1). The fork imprints each piece of the dough with fine lines and crevices. The sauce has an easier time clinging to these crevices, so don't skip this step.

✔ Boil gnocchi in batches to prevent them from sticking together. About a minute after they float to the top, use a skimmer, small mesh strainer, or slotted spoon to fish out the gnocchi and transfer them to a platter or individual bowls. Toss with sauce and serve immediately.

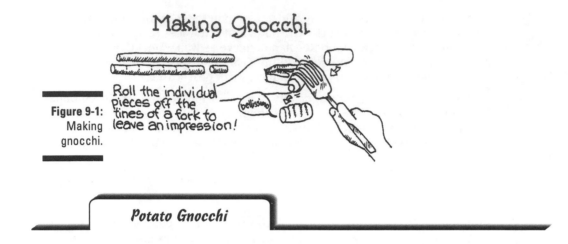

**Figure 9-1:**
Making
gnocchi.

*Making Gnocchi*

Roll the individual pieces off the tines of a fork to leave an impression!

(bellissimo)

### Potato Gnocchi

You can serve potato gnocchi with many of the same sauces you use on pasta, including Meat Sauce (refer to Chapter 7) as well as Tomato and Basil Sauce and Pesto Sauce (both in Chapter 6). Use about $1/4$ cup sauce per serving of gnocchi. In some regions of Italy, ricotta cheese replaces part or all of the potatoes in this recipe.

***Italian recipe name:*** *Gnocchi di Patate*

***Preparation time:*** *40 minutes*

***Cooking time:*** *25 to 30 minutes*

***Yield:*** *8 servings*

***Special tool:*** *Ricer*

| | |
|---|---|
| *4 medium russet potatoes, unpeeled (2 pounds)* | *1³/₄ cups flour plus flour for dusting work surface (you may not need all of it)* |
| *3 eggs, lightly beaten* | *1¹/₂ tablespoons kosher salt* |
| *Salt and pepper to taste* | |

**1** Place the potatoes in a medium pot and cover them with cold water. Add a touch of salt to the water and bring it to a boil. Reduce the heat to a simmer and cook until the potatoes are tender when pierced, but are still firm. Drain.

**2** When the potatoes are cool enough to handle, peel them. Using a ricer, squeeze the potato flesh into a mound on a smooth, flat surface. It's important to do this when the potatoes are still hot; otherwise, the gnocchi become gluey when cooked. Allow the riced potatoes to cool.

**3** Form a well in the center of the potatoes and add the eggs and salt and pepper. Mix to combine. Sift in 1¹/₂ cups flour. Mix until you have a sticky ball. Add more flour if the dough is too wet to knead. Knead the dough until it's smooth and all ingredients are well incorporated. Lightly dust the work surface with flour and then roll out the gnocchi dough so that it forms a 1¹/₂-inch-diameter log. Cut into 1-inch pieces. Take each piece and roll it off a fork so that the grid impression remains (refer to 9-1).

*4* In a large pot, bring 4 quarts water to a boil. Add the kosher salt and a fourth of the gnocchi. Using a strainer/skimmer, transfer the gnocchi to a warm plate or serving platter about 1 minute after they float to the surface. Toss with some warmed sauce (see suggestions earlier in this recipe). Repeat 3 times with the remaining gnocchi. Serve immediately.

## Spinach Gnocchi

Spinach gnocchi may look quite different from regular potato gnocchi, but their flavor is fairly similar. Use any of the sauces mentioned in the Potato Gnocchi recipe, about ¹/₄ cup per serving.

***Italian recipe name:*** *Gnocchi Verdi*

***Preparation time:*** *1 hour*

***Cooking time:*** *30 to 35 minutes*

***Yield:*** *8 servings*

***Special tool:*** *Ricer*

*4 medium russet potatoes, unpeeled (2 pounds)*

*Salt and pepper to taste*

*1 pound fresh spinach, stems removed, leaves rinsed*

*¹/₄ cup water*

*2 eggs, lightly beaten*

*1³/₄ cups flour plus flour for dusting work surface (you may not need all of it)*

*¹/₂ cup grated Parmigiano-Reggiano*

*Pinch of ground nutmeg*

*1¹/₂ tablespoons kosher salt*

*1* Place the potatoes in a medium pot and cover them with cold water. Add a touch of salt to the water and bring it to a boil. Reduce the heat to a simmer and cook until the potatoes are tender when pierced, but are still firm. Drain.

*2* While the potatoes cook, prepare the spinach. In a large saucepan, place ¹/₄ cup water and the spinach. Season with salt and cook over medium heat, covered, for 5 to 6 minutes. Drain. When the spinach cools slightly, using both hands, squeeze out any excess water, and then chop the spinach and set it aside.

*3* When the potatoes are cool enough to handle, peel them. Using a ricer, squeeze the potato flesh into a mound on a smooth, flat surface. It's important to do this when the potatoes are still hot; otherwise, the gnocchi become gluey when cooked. Allow the riced potatoes to cool.

*(continued)*

**4** Form a well in the center of the potatoes and add the eggs, spinach, and salt and pepper. Mix to combine. Sift in 1¹/₂ cups flour and add the Parmigiano-Reggiano cheese and nutmeg. Mix well. Add more flour if the dough is too wet to knead. Knead the dough until it's smooth and all ingredients are well incorporated. Lightly dust the work surface with flour and roll out the gnocchi dough so that it forms a 1¹/₂-inch-diameter log. Cut it into 1-inch pieces. Take each piece and roll it off a fork so that the grid impression remains (refer to Figure 9-1).

**5** In a large pot, bring 4 quarts water to a boil. Add the kosher salt and a fourth of the gnocchi. Using a strainer or skimmer, transfer the gnocchi to a warm plate or serving platter about 1 minute after they float to the surface. Toss with some warmed sauce. Repeat 3 times with the remaining gnocchi. Serve immediately.

## Semolina gnocchi

Semolina is the pale yellow grain milled from the heart of durum wheat berries, the same kind of wheat used to make pasta. Look for semolina in health food stores, gourmet shops, or Italian markets, where it may be called semolino, the Italian name for this grain. Semolina flour, which is used to make dried pasta, is much finer and can't be used to make gnocchi.

### Semolina Gnocchi, Roman Style

Semolina gnocchi are prepared more like polenta. In this case, semolina (not cornmeal) is cooked into a thick porridge and then cooled and cut into small rounds, which are layered with butter and cheese and baked. Semolina gnocchi are a specialty of Rome.

**Italian recipe name:** *Gnocchi alla Romana*

**Preparation time:** *10 minutes*

**Cooking time:** *1 hour, 20 minutes*

**Yield:** *4 servings*

*1 quart milk*

*1¹/₄ cups semolina*

*Salt and pepper to taste*

*2 egg yolks*

*4 ounces prosciutto, chopped (optional)*

*6 tablespoons grated Parmigiano-Reggiano, divided*

*¹/₂ cup butter (1 stick), divided*

*1* Preheat oven to 400°.

*2* In a medium saucepan with a heavy bottom, heat the milk over medium-low heat. When it begins to boil, add the semolina in a steady stream while stirring. Season with salt and pepper. Reduce the heat and cook at a low boil, stirring frequently, 10 minutes.

*3* Remove from heat and beat in the egg yolks, prosciutto, 4 tablespoons Parmigiano-Reggiano cheese, and $1/4$ cup butter. If you have a large marble surface, pour the hot mixture over the marble and spread it out so that it is about $1/2$-inch thick. Otherwise, spread the semolina over a large cutting board lined with parchment paper. Allow the semolina to cool completely, about 45 minutes. Using a 2- to 3-inch circular cookie cutter, cut the semolina into small circles. Try to cut the circles as close together as possible to obtain the most gnocchi.

*4* Grease an 8 x 8 x 2-inch baking dish with 2 tablespoons butter. Place the semolina circles next to each other (overlapping a little bit) to line the bottom of the pan. Sprinkle with the remaining 2 tablespoons Parmigiano-Reggiano cheese and dot with the remaining 2 tablespoons butter. Bake until heated through and lightly browned, about 15 minutes.

# Chapter 10

# Pizza, Calzone, and Focaccia: Breads of Distinction

*I*talians love good bread. Even small villages have a bakery that turns out loaves in a variety of shapes, sizes, and flavors. Luckily, the quality of Italian bread has risen dramatically in recent years in the United States. Many artisanal bakers, devoted to small production and high quality, are now working in big cities, as well as in small towns. Buying decent bread is becoming pretty easy. Unless you're a real baking fan, we think it's best to leave bread to the professionals.

Flatbreads, such as pizza and focaccia (foe-**cah**-cha), and their folded and stuffed cousins called calzones, are another matter. You can get pizza almost everywhere by just making a phone call. Calzones are almost as easy to buy, and focaccia is fast becoming a regular item in many markets.

However, these breads are rarely made right. At least, they're rarely made as they are in Italy. In this chapter, we define these breads (what is the difference between pizza and focaccia, anyway?) and explain how to make them yourself, the right way.

# Some Quick Definitions

Here are some quick definitions to keep in mind.

- **Pizza:** A thin, round disk of dough that's topped fairly generously (often with tomatoes and cheese) and then baked.

- **Calzone:** A thin, round disk of dough that's covered with cheese and other fillings on one half, folded over, sealed tightly, and then baked. The filling is inside the dough, not on top.

- **Focaccia:** A puffier piece of dough (usually rectangular) that's dimpled with fingertips, covered with oil and kosher salt, and then baked. Although pizza and calzone are usually eaten as a meal, focaccia is eaten as a snack. It can be topped with vegetables and cheese, and the toppings are usually fairly light. Focaccia bakes up chewier and higher, and you can split the pieces in horizontal halves to make sandwiches.

# Pizza at Home

Pizza originated in Naples, but it's now a staple throughout Italy. Students and others on the go may grab a piece of pizza for lunch. Pizza is also popular at night, especially as a light dinner after a traditional multicourse lunch.

Italians generally eat less pizza per sitting than Americans. The pizzas themselves are lighter, without so much cheese and other toppings. Italians recognize that pizza is still a bread dish and that the crust must be good and crisp.

# The dough

Good crust begins with the right dough. Pizza dough is basically regular bread dough with oil added for suppleness. Many novice cooks think that making pizza dough is hard. It's not. Keep these points in mind and success is guaranteed:

- Yeast likes warm water, but hot water kills the yeast. Use water that feels a bit warmer than your body temperature; or better still, pull out an instant-read thermometer and make sure that the water temperature is between 105° and 115°.

- Yeast likes a little sugar. You can leave this ingredient out, but the yeast takes longer to work its magic — and who wants to wait any longer than is necessary to eat pizza?

- Pizza dough can be made to work around your schedule. Cool temperatures slow down the rising process. For example, you can put the dough right into the refrigerator after making it in the morning, let it rise all day in the refrigerator, and then let the dough rise a bit longer on the counter after you get home from work. Pizza dough can even be frozen in an airtight container. Just let it rise fully, freeze for up to one month, and then let the dough come to room temperature before stretching.

✔ Mixing dough in a bowl with a wooden spoon is just fine for pizza dough. If you own a food processor or standing mixer (a handheld mixer is too wimpy to handle bread dough), use them to save time.

✔ To speed rising, tightly cover the bowl containing the dough with plastic wrap and place the bowl in a warm area, away from open windows and other drafts.

✔ Let the dough rest a bit before stretching it. Resting allows the gluten in the dough to relax and makes rolling much easier.

## Basic Pizza Dough

Pizza dough can be made by hand or with the help of a large food processor or standing mixer. To use a food processor, combine the yeast, water, and oil until smooth, add the flour and salt, and process until the dough comes together in a ball. In a standing mixer, the process is the same as outlined in this recipe, except that the paddle attachment does the mixing and the dough hook does the kneading.

**Italian recipe name:** *Pasta per la Pizza*

**Preparation time:** *10 minutes (plus rising time of 1 hour, 15 minutes)*

**Cooking time:** *None*

**Yield:** *Two 12-inch pizzas or four 8-inch pizzas*

| | |
|---|---|
| *1 package active dry yeast* | *1 teaspoon sugar* |
| *1¹/₂ cups warm water* | *2 tablespoons olive oil plus olive oil for greasing bowl* |
| *3³/₄ cups flour, divided, plus flour for dusting work surface* | *2 teaspoons salt* |

**1** In a large mixing bowl, combine the yeast and water. Wait 2 to 3 minutes for the yeast to rise and then add ¹/₂ cup flour and sugar. Mix well. Add the olive oil, salt, and remaining 3¹/₄ cups flour. With your hands or a large wooden spoon, work the ingredients together. Transfer the dough to a smooth flour-dusted surface and knead it until the dough is smooth, about 5 minutes. If the dough becomes sticky when kneading, gradually add up to another ¹/₄ cup flour. Place in a large bowl that's been lightly greased with olive oil. Cover tightly with plastic wrap and allow to double in size, about 1 hour.

**2** Divide the dough into 2 pieces (or 4 pieces if making individual pizzas) and roll them into balls. Rest the dough for 15 minutes before using for pizza or calzone.

## Making a pie

ESSENTIAL SKILL

You've got the dough, so now you can turn it into pizza. The process consists of four steps: rolling the dough, transferring the dough to a pizza pan or baking sheet, topping the dough, and baking the pizza.

1. **Rolling is actually stretching; simply place the ball of dough on a floured counter or work surface and flatten it with your hands.**

   Keep stretching and pressing down on the dough until it reaches the desired size. You can use a rolling pin if you like, but this tool isn't essential.

2. **Transferring the dough to a pizza pan is pretty simple; slide your hands underneath the dough and lift it onto an oiled pan.**

   For large 12-inch pizzas, we recommend using a perforated pizza pan (see Figure 10-1) that allows heat to attack the bottom of the crust, ensuring that it becomes crisp in the oven. Cook individual pizzas (about 8 inches each) on flat baking sheets.

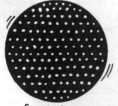

**Figure 10-1:** The tiny holes help ensure a crisp crust.

A perforated pizza pan makes a crisp crust !

3. **Now place your toppings on the dough.**

   Toppings on traditional Italian pies are generally light. Italians are aghast at American pizzas with a pound of meat and cheese. And putting cheese in the crust is a totally foreign idea.

4. **After the dough has been topped, put it in the oven immediately; bake until the cheese turns golden brown in spots and the edge of the crust looks golden brown.**

   If you have any doubts, carefully lift up the crust with a metal spatula (plastic can melt) to see whether the bottom of the crust is lightly browned. You can put two pizza pans or two baking sheets in the oven at the same time, but you may need to reverse their positions in the oven halfway through the baking time to ensure even cooking.

(Clockwise from top)
Crostini with Chicken Livers,
Bruschetta with Tomatoes, Bruschetta
with White Beans (all in Chapter 3)

Fennel and Orange Salad
(Chapter 4)

(Top to bottom)
Asparagus with Parmesan,
Peppered Mussels
(both in Chapter 3),
Salmon Salad (Chapter 4)

(Clockwise from top-right) Tuscan Bread Salad (Chapter 4), Tuscan Bread and Tomato Soup (Chapter 5), Tomato and Mozzarella Salad, Capri Style (Chapter 4), Prosciutto with Melons (Chapter 3)

(Top to bottom)
Polenta with Vegetables (Chapter 9),
Butternut Squash Risotto (Chapter 8)

(Bottom-right) Spinach Ravioli (Chapter 7); Different types of pasta (Counterclockwise from top-right)... Lasagne, Tagliatelle Pasta, Taglierini Pasta, Angel Hair Pasta, Ravioli, Potato Gnocchi, Spinach Gnocchi

Bucatini with Tomatoes, Onions, and Pancetta
(Chapter 6)

(Top to bottom)
Shells with Uncooked Tomato Sauce,
Fusilli with Vegetable Sauce (both in Chapter 6)

(Top to bottom) Rigatoni with Sausage and Peas, Spaghetti with Garlic, Oil, and Chiles, Orecchiette with Broccoli Rabe (all in Chapter 6)

(Top to bottom)
Spaghetti with Clams, Spaghetti
from the Sea (both in Chapter 6)

(Clockwise from top)
Red Snapper with
Vegetables (Chapter 13),
Foccaccia with Onions
(Chapter 10), Grilled
Soft-Shell Crabs with
Salad, Halibut with
Peas and Scallions
(both in Chapter 13)

Swordfish with Tomatoes and Oregano
(Chapter 13)

(Clockwise from top-right)
Chicken Cutlets with Artichokes (Chapter 11),
Stewed Potatoes (Chapter 14),
Baby Chicken with Lemon, Chicken
Cutlets with Tomato and Basil
Salad (both in Chapter 11)

(Top to bottom)
Sautéed Pork Chops with
Tomatoes and Olives, Sausage
and Beans (both in Chapter 12),
Stewed Peppers (Chapter 14)

(Clockwise from top) Grilled Steak, Florentine Style (Chapter 12), Sautéed Broccoli Rabe (Chapter 14), Chicken under a Brick (Chapter 11)

(Clockwise from top)
Tiramisù, Biscotti, Roasted Fruit
(all in Chapter 15)

## Stone baking

For the crispiest crusts, bake all pizzas and breads on a ceramic baking or pizza stone. These stones, which cost about $15, are sold in kitchenware stores. They come in a variety of shapes and sizes. Large rectangular stones are the easiest to work with when making pizza.

Stones conduct heat much better than metal baking sheets and allow the home cook to create a "brick-oven" effect at home. Just put the stone on the bottom rack of a 500° oven

and allow it to heat for 30 minutes before sliding the unbaked pizza on top.

If using a stone, you want to roll the dough out on a pizza paddle with a long handle (called a *pizza peel*) or on a flat rimless baking sheet. After the pizza is topped, gently and carefully slide the pie onto the stone and close the oven. Baking stones work so well that they may shave a few minutes off the baking time in the recipes in this chapter.

After the pizza comes out of the oven, wait a minute or two to allow the bubbling cheese to solidify again. Then use a pizza wheel (see Figure 10-2) to cut the pie into wedges and serve.

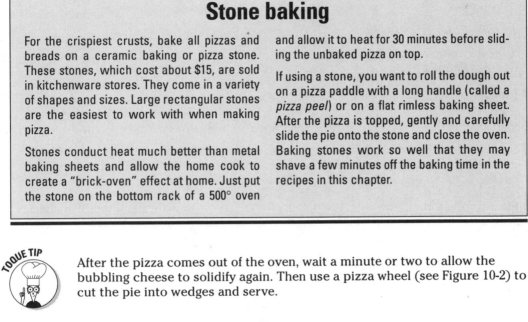

**Figure 10-2:** A pizza wheel.

The handle on a pizza wheel gives you the leverage you need to cut through the toppings and crust on the first try!

## Pizza with Tomato and Mozzarella

This basic recipe is open to countless variations. Some of our favorite pizza toppings are in the sidebar "Pizza variations," later in this chapter, but feel free to create your own variations. You need 1 prepared recipe of Basic Pizza Dough.

***Italian recipe name:*** *Pizza Margherita*

***Preparation time:*** *10 minutes*

***Cooking time:*** *15 minutes*

***Yield:*** *4 servings*

*(continued)*

*Olive oil for greasing pizza pans*

*¹/₄ cup flour*

*1 recipe Basic Pizza Dough*

*1¹/₂ cups Tomato and Basil Sauce (refer to Chapter 6)*

*2 cups shredded mozzarella cheese*

*2 teaspoons dried oregano*

*Salt and pepper to taste*

*1* Preheat oven to 450°.

*2* Lightly oil two 12-inch perforated pizza pans or 2 large baking sheets.

*3* Spread the flour out on a flat surface. Press each ball of dough out to form a 12-inch circle for 2 large pies or an 8-inch circle for 4 individual pies. Transfer the dough circles to the prepared pans.

*4* Evenly spread the sauce over the dough circles. Then top with the mozzarella cheese. Sprinkle the oregano over the top, season with salt and pepper, and place the pans in the oven.

*5* Bake for 12 to 15 minutes, turning the pans occasionally, until the cheese is bubbly and the crusts are cooked. Wait 2 to 3 minutes and serve.

## White Pizza with Arugula

Pizza doesn't always mean tomatoes. This "white" pie is topped with cheese and showered with fresh arugula leaves. You need 1 prepared recipe of Basic Pizza Dough.

**Italian recipe name:** *Pizza Bianca con Rucola*

**Preparation time:** *10 minutes*

**Cooking time:** *15 minutes*

**Yield:** *4 servings*

*Olive oil for greasing pizza pans*

*¹/₄ cup flour*

*1 recipe Basic Pizza Dough*

*1¹/₂ cups shredded mozzarella cheese*

*Salt and pepper to taste*

*32 fresh arugula leaves*

*1* Preheat oven to 450°.

*2* Lightly oil two 12-inch pizza pans or 2 large baking sheets.

*3* Spread the flour on a flat surface. Press each ball of dough out to form a 12-inch circle for 2 large pies or an 8-inch circle for 4 individual pies. Transfer the dough circles to the prepared pans.

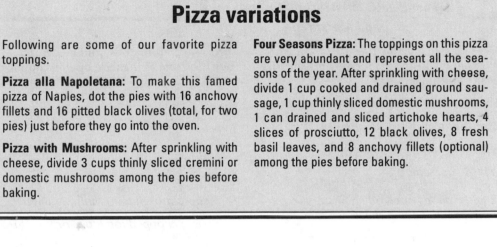

## Pizza variations

Following are some of our favorite pizza toppings.

**Pizza alla Napoletana:** To make this famed pizza of Naples, dot the pies with 16 anchovy fillets and 16 pitted black olives (total, for two pies) just before they go into the oven.

**Pizza with Mushrooms:** After sprinkling with cheese, divide 3 cups thinly sliced cremini or domestic mushrooms among the pies before baking.

**Four Seasons Pizza:** The toppings on this pizza are very abundant and represent all the seasons of the year. After sprinkling with cheese, divide 1 cup cooked and drained ground sausage, 1 cup thinly sliced domestic mushrooms, 1 can drained and sliced artichoke hearts, 4 slices of prosciutto, 12 black olives, 8 fresh basil leaves, and 8 anchovy fillets (optional) among the pies before baking.

**4** Evenly spread the mozzarella cheese over the dough circles. Season with salt and pepper and place the pans in the oven.

**5** Bake for 14 minutes, turning the pans occasionally until the cheese is bubbly and the crusts are cooked. Place the arugula leaves on top of the pizzas and serve.

# Calzone: All Folded Over

**TOQUE TIP**

A pizza can become a calzone, but a calzone can never become a pizza. A calzone is simply a circle of pizza dough that is stuffed and folded over to make a half-moon shape. Successful calzones require some attention to detail. Keep these tips in mind as you work:

- ✔ Spread the filling over just half of the stretched dough, leaving a border around the edge of the dough so that the fillings won't leak out.

- ✔ Pinch the calzone shut, making sure to seal the entire perimeter. If the dough seems to be opening in places, brush some lightly beaten egg over the dough and pinch again.

- ✔ Prick the top of the filled calzone with a fork a few times to allow steam to escape during baking.

- ✔ Wait several minutes after calzones come out of the oven before serving. When piping hot, the filling may run out. Give the filling, especially the cheese, a little time to cool off and solidify.

## Calzone with Prosciutto, Mushrooms, and Mozzarella

This classic calzone has it all — mushrooms, prosciutto, tomatoes, and mozzarella. You need 1 prepared recipe of Basic Pizza Dough. Calzone fillings are open to countless variations.

***Italian recipe name:*** *Calzone all'Italiana*

***Preparation time:*** *15 minutes*

***Cooking time:*** *20 minutes*

***Yield:*** *4 servings*

*4 tablespoons olive oil, divided, plus oil for greasing baking sheets*

*3 cups sliced cremini or domestic mushrooms*

*Salt and pepper to taste*

*¹/₄ cup flour (to spread on flat surface)*

*1 recipe Basic Pizza Dough (divided into 4 balls)*

*8 slices prosciutto or ham, julienned*

*¹/₂ cup chopped tomatoes or tomato sauce*

*2 cups shredded mozzarella cheese*

*Pinch of dried oregano*

*1* Preheat oven to 450°.

*2* Lightly oil 2 large baking sheets.

*3* Heat 2 tablespoons olive oil in a medium skillet over medium heat. Add the mushrooms and sauté, stirring often, until they've released their liquid and it has evaporated. Season the mushrooms with salt and pepper. Transfer the mushrooms to a medium bowl and let cool.

*4* Spread the flour on a flat surface. Press 1 of the balls of dough out to form an 8-inch circle. Transfer the dough to a prepared baking sheet, cover loosely, and set it aside. Repeat with the other 3 pieces of dough.

*5* Add the prosciutto, tomatoes, mozzarella cheese, and oregano to the bowl with the mushrooms. Season with salt and pepper and mix well.

*6* Spread a fourth of the filling on half of 1 dough circle, keeping it 1¹/₂ to 2 inches from the edge. Fold the other side over the filling and pinch the edges together to form a seal. Repeat this procedure with the other 3 calzones.

*7* Using a fork, poke a few holes in the top of each calzone. Drizzle with the remaining 2 tablespoons olive oil. Bake until golden brown, 15 to 20 minutes.

*Calzone with Eggs and Prosciutto: Here's a variation on the Calzone with Prosciutto, Mushrooms, and Mozzarella. For the filling, combine 8 quartered hard-boiled eggs, 10 slices of julienned prosciutto or ham, 6 tablespoons grated Parmigiano-Reggiano cheese, and 1 cup shredded mozzarella cheese (optional). Season the mixture with salt and pepper to taste. Serve baked calzones with some of the Tomato and Basil Sauce from Chapter 6.*

## Calzone with Mixed Vegetables

A selection of grilled vegetables makes a delicious calzone filling. Add some cooked sausage or leave it out to keep this dish vegetarian. You need 1 prepared recipe of Basic Pizza Dough.

*Italian recipe name: Calzone con Verdure Miste*

*Preparation time: 20 minutes*

*Cooking time: 20 minutes*

*Yield: 4 servings*

*1 small eggplant, sliced ¹/₄-inch thick lengthwise*

*1 yellow bell pepper, cored and seeded, cut into 4 long slices*

*1 red bell pepper, cored and seeded, cut into 4 long slices*

*1 zucchini, sliced ¹/₄-inch thick lengthwise*

*1 medium red onion, quartered, root intact*

*8 asparagus spears, tough ends snapped off*

*2 medium tomatoes, halved*

*3 tablespoons olive oil, divided*

*Salt and pepper to taste*

*¹/₄ cup flour (to spread on flat surface)*

*1 recipe Basic Pizza Dough (divided into 4 balls)*

*2 cups cooked ground sausage (optional)*

*1 cup shredded mozzarella cheese*

*1* Preheat oven to 450°.

*2* Brush the eggplant, peppers, zucchini, onion, asparagus, and tomato with 1 tablespoon olive oil and season with salt and pepper. Grill them, turning as necessary so that they're evenly brown and tender, but still firm. Set aside to cool.

*3* Use 1 tablespoon olive oil to lightly grease 2 large baking sheets.

*(continued)*

**4** Spread the flour out on a flat surface. Press 1 of the balls of dough out to form an 8-inch circle. Transfer the dough to a prepared baking sheet, cover loosely, and set it aside. Repeat with the other pieces of dough.

**5** Dice the grilled eggplant, peppers, zucchini, onion, mozzarella, and tomatoes and cut the asparagus into $1/2$-inch pieces. Combine them in a medium bowl. Add the sausage and, cheese and season with salt and pepper.

**6** Spread a fourth of the filling on half of 1 dough circle, keeping it $1^1/_2$ to 2 inches from the edges. Fold the other side over the filling and pinch the edges together to form a seal. Repeat this procedure with the other 3 calzones.

**7** Using a fork, poke a few holes in the top of each calzone. Drizzle with the remaining 1 tablespoon olive oil. Bake until golden brown, 15 to 20 minutes.

# Focaccia: A Flatbread with Possibilities

Focaccia, a soft flatbread that's related to pizza, is a favorite in most regions of Italy. In Florence, schoolchildren line up outside bakeries in the afternoon to grab a square of warm schiacciata, the local name for a focaccia covered with olive oil, rosemary, and coarse sea salt.

Chewy focaccia bread can be eaten as a snack, served as an accompaniment to meals, and split in horizontal halves to make sandwiches. It's similar to pizza, but different.

✔ The ingredients are basically the same, although a lot more oil is used in focaccia dough.

✔ Focaccia is thicker and has a chewy, almost spongy, texture. Pizza is thinner and crispier.

✔ Focaccia is rolled out right in the pan, not on the counter. Focaccia is usually baked in large rectangular pans, called jelly roll pans, that are about an inch deep.

✔ After the dough fills the pan, it's dimpled with your fingertips (see Figure 10-3). These dimples are perhaps what distinguishes focaccia most from pizza. Pieces of vegetables or pools of olive oil can be trapped in these dimples.

**Figure 10-3:** Dimples, or deep indentations, distinguish focaccia dough from pizza dough.

Use your fingertips to make the dimples, or deep indentations, in the top of the focaccia dough.

### Everyday Focaccia

With just olive oil and salt on top, this focaccia is the simplest and most basic. Use it to make sandwiches (just slice squares in half horizontally) or serve it as a snack. It's also great in the bread basket at a nice meal.

This basic recipe can be topped with fresh herbs, sliced tomatoes, or almost any vegetable. For example, to make Focaccia with Onions, combine 2 thinly sliced medium onions, 3 tablespoons olive oil, and salt and pepper to taste in a small bowl (see photo in color section). After making fingerprints in the dough, sprinkle as directed with kosher salt and then spread the onion mixture evenly over the dough. Bake 25 minutes at 375°.

***Italian recipe name:*** *Focaccia Tutti I Giorni*

***Preparation time:*** *30 minutes (plus rising time of $2^{1}/_{4}$ to $2^{3}/_{4}$ hours)*

***Cooking time:*** *30 minutes*

***Yield:*** *8 servings*

***Special tool:*** *17 x 11-inch jelly roll pan, standing mixer*

| | |
|---|---|
| *1 package dry yeast* | *$3^{3}/_{4}$ cups flour, divided* |
| *$1^{1}/_{4}$ cups warm water* | *$1^{1}/_{2}$ teaspoons table salt* |
| *1 teaspoon sugar* | *Cooking spray* |
| *1 cup olive oil, divided* | *2 teaspoons kosher salt* |

*1* In the mixing bowl of a standing mixer with a dough hook attachment, combine the yeast, water, and sugar. Mix for 3 minutes. Add $^{1}/_{2}$ cup olive oil, $3^{1}/_{4}$ cups flour, and the table salt. Mix at low speed until it has all come together and is smooth, about 5 minutes. If the dough is very sticky, gradually add up to another $^{1}/_{4}$ cup flour. Remove the dough and place in a large bowl that's been lightly greased with olive oil. Cover tightly with plastic wrap and allow to double in size, $1^{1}/_{2}$ to 2 hours.

*(continued)*

*2* Preheat oven to 425°.

*3* Sprinkle the remaining ¹/₄ cup flour over the dough, gently punch it down, and lightly work the added flour into the dough, 1 to 2 minutes. Place the dough in a jelly roll pan that's been sprayed with cooking spray. Roll the dough out evenly, turning the pan as necessary. Cover and allow the dough to rise for 45 minutes.

*4* Pour the remaining ¹/₂ cup olive oil into a small bowl and dip your fingertips in it. Make fingerprints ¹/₄ inch apart in the focaccia dough. Sprinkle with the kosher salt. Bake for 5 minutes. Then lower the temperature to 375° and bake until golden brown, 25 to 30 minutes.

## Focaccia with Potatoes

In some mountainous regions of Italy, flour was once scarce, and focaccia breads were made with a combination of cooked potatoes and flour. The potatoes make the dough especially light and tender. The topping includes sliced potatoes, tomatoes, anchovies, and oregano.

***Italian recipe name:*** *Focaccia con le Patate*

***Preparation time:*** *30 minutes (plus rising time of 1¹/₂ hours)*

***Cooking time:*** *1 hour, 20 minutes*

***Yield:*** *8 servings*

***Special tools:*** *Standing mixer, 17 x 11-inch jelly roll pan, ricer*

| | |
|---|---|
| *4 medium russet potatoes* | *1 tablespoon kosher salt* |
| *1 package dry yeast* | *2 small tomatoes, cut into ¹/₄-inch-thick slices* |
| *1¹/₂ cups warm water* | |
| *¹/₄ cup plus 4 tablespoons olive oil, divided, plus olive oil for greasing a bowl* | *2 teaspoons dried oregano* |
| | *8 anchovy fillets, chopped (optional)* |
| *4¹/₂ cups flour, divided* | *Cooking spray* |

*1* Place the potatoes in a medium pot and cover them with cold water. Add a touch of salt to the water and bring to a boil. Reduce the heat to a simmer and cook until the potatoes are tender when pierced with the tip of a paring knife, about 30 minutes. Drain.

*2* When the potatoes are cool enough to handle, peel them. Set aside 1 potato. Using a ricer, squeeze the flesh of the remaining 3 potatoes into a medium bowl. If you don't have a ricer, mash them with the back of a fork.

*3* In the mixing bowl of a standing mixer with a dough hook attachment, combine the yeast and water. Gently stir to combine. Add the mashed potatoes, $^1/_4$ cup oil, $3^1/_2$ cups flour, and salt. Mix at low speed until it all comes together and is smooth, about 8 minutes. Remove the dough and place it in a large bowl that's been lightly greased with olive oil. Cover the bowl tightly with plastic wrap and allow the dough to double in size, about $1^1/_2$ to 2 hours.

*4* Slice the remaining potato thinly and place it in a medium bowl. Add the tomatoes, oregano, anchovies, and the remaining 3 tablespoons olive oil. Set aside.

*5* Sprinkle the remaining 1 cup flour over the dough, gently punch it down, and lightly work the added flour into the dough, 1 to 2 minutes. Place the dough in a jelly roll pan that's been sprayed with cooking spray. Roll the dough out evenly, turning pan as necessary. Allow the dough to rise for 20 minutes.

*6* Preheat oven to 375°.

*7* Pour the remaining olive oil into a small bowl and dip your fingertips in it. Make fingerprints in the focaccia dough. Sprinkle with the kosher salt. Bake for 30 minutes and then spread the potato/tomato mixture evenly over the top. Bake for another 10 to 15 minutes, until golden brown.

# Part IV
# The Main Event

## In this part . . .

Pasta and pizza are great, but meat still matters. Italians know how to cook meat as well as poultry and seafood. Whether it's chicken cutlets flavored with lemon and white wine or grilled beef with rosemary and garlic, most Italian main courses are simple and delicious. In this part, you discover the secrets of cooking chicken, duck, turkey, rabbit, beef, veal, lamb, pork, fish, and shellfish, Italian style. In addition, this part also covers the simple vegetable side dishes that usually accompany these main courses. Dig in!

# Chapter 11

# Poultry: Fowl Fare

## In This Chapter

▶ Shopping for chicken

▶ Handling poultry safely

▶ Cooking whole birds, parts, and cutlets

▶ Going beyond chicken

Chicken has long been popular in Italy. You can't find much open land for raising cattle in Italy, so beef has always been something of a luxury, especially in the country. But anyone with a little backyard can tend chickens, something countless generations of Italians have done.

Most old-fashioned Italian chicken recipes begin by sautéing parts in fat and then adding vegetables and liquids, such as tomatoes, wine, or stock, to cook the parts through. This gentle simmering tenderizes tough parts from birds that get a lot of exercise. It also flavors the chicken and creates a rich "sauce" that you can serve over polenta or with mashed potatoes, beans, or bread.

Poultry production has changed remarkably over the past few decades. Mass-produced birds don't get any exercise, and their flesh is rarely tough. Although modern birds may not need the tenderizing effects of braising, the Italian method for cooking chicken still makes sense. Most supermarket chickens are remarkably bland. Cooking them in flavorful liquids helps give them some character.

In addition to explaining how to cook chicken parts in a covered casserole, this chapter also shows you how to turn boneless, skinless chicken cutlets into a number of quick dinners. Chicken cutlets are the ultimate convenience food, adaptable to so many types of preparation.

# Shopping for Poultry

Until relatively recently, most markets offered shoppers few choices when it came to chicken. You could choose from the store brand and perhaps a large national brand. Consumers now have many more options. Here are the kinds of birds that you're likely to find:

- ✔ **Mass-produced chickens** were the only choice until recently. These birds are raised in crowded conditions. Feeds are designed to grow birds as quickly as possible. These birds are usually quite bland, and the texture is often quite soft.

- ✔ **Kosher chickens** were always popular in urban areas with large Jewish populations. In accordance with religious law, these chickens are bathed in a saltwater bath to remove blood and impurities. All kosher chickens must be grown and processed to a standardized protocol and are clearly labeled. They are increasingly popular and are sold frozen in many supermarkets. If you aren't accustomed to cooking kosher chickens, you may need to reduce the amount of salt you add to these birds.

- ✔ **Free-range chickens** have access to the outdoors. These birds get more exercise than conventional mass-produced chickens and often have a stronger, gamy flavor. Their meat also tends to be firmer. Chefs love these birds, and many are quite good. If you want an old-fashioned chicken with a modest amount of "fowl" flavor, this is the bird for you.

- ✔ **Organic chickens** are raised without antibiotics and are fed a diet of organically grown grains. Many free-range chickens are also labeled "organic." Like free-range chickens, these birds generally have a strong poultry flavor.

# Keeping Poultry Safe

All poultry runs a high risk of contamination with salmonella or other bacteria. Some surveys indicate that as many as half of all the birds in our markets contain one or more pathogens. Safe handling and cooking is a must. Keep these simple rules in mind, and you should be fine:

- ✔ **Check sell-by dates on chickens when shopping.** Unlike meats, which are often cut by the butcher in the back of the store, chickens come to the supermarket ready for sale. The processor labels the chicken with a sell-by date that's usually two weeks after the packing date. Therefore, a chicken nearing its sell-by date can be two weeks old. Buying fresher birds is a better idea; they have at least a week left before they reach the end of their shelf life.

✔ **Get chicken home quickly and into the refrigerator.** If you're not going to cook a bird within a day or two, put it immediately into the freezer. Defrost frozen chickens on a plate (to catch juices) in the refrigerator.

✔ **Wash anything that comes into contact with raw poultry or its juices in hot, soapy water.** This include your hands, cutting boards, counters, and knives. If possible, use a dishwasher to sterilize plates, tools, or cutting boards used with raw poultry.

✔ **Don't let raw poultry or poultry juices come into contact with fruits, vegetables, or other foods that you plan on eating without cooking.** When opening packages of chicken, do this far away from other foods so that chicken juices don't contaminate other foods.

✔ **Don't let uncooked birds sit out on the counter.** Bacteria thrives in warm kitchens, but it has a harder time multiplying at temperatures close to freezing.

✔ **Handle all marinades and sauces that come into contact with raw poultry carefully.** Assume that these liquids have been contaminated with bacteria and either discard them or boil them before using to baste on birds as they cook.

✔ **Cook all poultry to an internal temperature of at least 160°.** Use an instant-read thermometer. When fully cooked, all juices should be clear, and you should see no trace of pink at the bone.

# Cooking Chicken

Chicken is so popular for a reason. It's inexpensive and so versatile. You can cook a chicken whole, in parts, or in cutlets. Like pasta, chicken works with almost any flavor. Think of chicken as a blank (or bland) canvas, ready for painting. Now arm those brushes!

## I can't believe I cooked the whole thing

Fifty years ago, most Italian homes didn't have an oven. Chickens were usually cooked in parts on top of the stove. Therefore, just a few traditional preparations for a whole bird exist.

Trussing a chicken (see Figure 11-1) is one such preparation. You should do this before adding any seasonings to the outside of the bird. Start by tucking the wings under the bird. Wrap a piece of kitchen twine around the drumsticks. Wrap a second piece of twine around the other end of the bird to hold the wings in place.

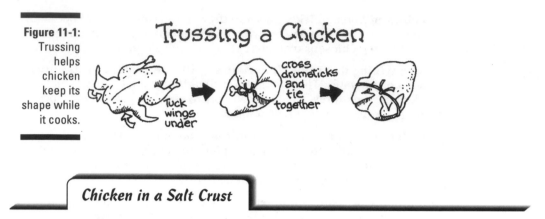

**Figure 11-1:** Trussing helps chicken keep its shape while it cooks.

## Chicken in a Salt Crust

Baking a whole chicken in a salt crust seals in its juices. Truss the chicken before coating the bird with the salt paste. You can carve the chicken in the kitchen as directed in the recipe, but for a more dramatic presentation, bring the chicken right from the oven to the table and open the salt crust before an audience.

*Italian recipe name: Pollo al Sale*

*Preparation time: 20 minutes*

*Cooking time: 1 hour, 10 minutes*

*Yield: 4 servings*

*Special tool: Aluminum foil*

*5 cups sea or kosher salt*

*6 cups flour plus flour for dusting work surface*

*3 cups water*

*4 cloves garlic, peeled*

*1 sprig fresh sage, or 1 teaspoon dried sage*

*1 sprig fresh rosemary, or 1 teaspoon dried rosemary*

*3¹/₂-pound whole chicken*

*Salt and pepper to taste*

**1** Preheat oven to 400°.

**2** In a large mixing bowl, combine the sea or kosher salt with flour and water and mix. The mixture should be moist but not wet. Set aside.

**3** Place the garlic, sage, and rosemary in the cavity of the chicken. Truss the chicken, tying the legs together (refer to Figure 11-1). Season with salt and pepper.

**4** Line a baking pan with aluminum foil. On a flat flour-dusted surface, roll out the salt dough until it's large enough to completely cover the chicken. Wrap the dough around the chicken and seal tightly. Place the chicken in the baking pan, seam side down.

*5* Bake for about 1 hour, 10 minutes. Remove from oven and crack the salt shell with a kitchen mallet or hammer. Lift away the solid pieces of dough. Transfer the chicken to a cutting board and cut into eighths. Transfer portions to each dinner plate and serve.

Another preparation for cooking whole chickens is called butterflying. In this process, the bird is flat, and the two sides of the bird are mirror images of each other, like a butterfly (see Figure 11-2).

To butterfly a whole chicken:

1. **Place the chicken, breast side down, on a cutting board.**

2. **Using a sharp knife or kitchen scissors, cut along both sides of the backbone and remove it.**

3. **Turn the chicken breast side up and spread the back apart.**

4. **Using your hands, press down on the breasts, breaking the ribs.**

   Continue pressing down until the breasts are flat like an open book.

5. **Trim off the wings to prevent them from burning.**

## Chicken Cut to Look Like a Butterfly!

Place bird, breast side down, on cutting board.

Continue pressing until it's flat like an open book.

whee!

**Figure 11-2:**
Chicken cut to look like a butterfly.

Using a sharp knife or kitchen scissors, cut along both sides of the backbone...

Turn chicken over. using your hands, press down on the breasts, breaking the ribs.

Trim off the wings to prevent them from burning!

## Chicken under a Brick

For this recipe, you remove the backbone from a chicken and then butterfly the chicken (refer to Figure 11-2). You then grill the butterflied chicken skin side down and weighted so that it cooks evenly. If you don't have any bricks, place a beat-up roasting pan on top of the chicken and then fill the pan with heavy (nonflammable) objects, such as rocks.

*(continued)*

This recipe works best with small baby chickens, also called poussins, which you can get from many butcher shops (see photo in color section). You can also use large Cornish game hens that weigh about 1½ pounds each. Serve with Sautéed Broccoli Rabe or Stewed Beans with Tomatoes, Sage, and Garlic (see the recipes in Chapter 14).

**Italian recipe name:** *Pollo al Mattone*

**Preparation time:** *20 minutes (plus 30 minutes for marination)*

**Cooking time:** *1 hour, 20 minutes*

**Yield:** *4 servings*

**Special tools:** *Two bricks, aluminum foil*

| | |
|---|---|
| 2 whole chickens (2 pounds each), cleaned | ⅓ cup olive oil |
| | Salt and pepper to taste |
| 4 to 6 cloves garlic, peeled and finely sliced | Juice of 3 lemons (¾ cup) |
| 3 tablespoons chopped sage, or 2 teaspoons dried sage | 2 cups white wine |
| | 1 pinch hot red pepper flakes |
| 3 tablespoons chopped rosemary, or 2 teaspoons dried rosemary | |

*1* Preheat grill to medium.

*2* Butterfly the chickens (refer to Figure 11-2).

*3* In a shallow pan that's just large enough to hold the chickens, combine the garlic, sage, rosemary, and olive oil. Season with salt and pepper and mix. Add the chickens to the pan, turning them over a few times to evenly coat them with the marinade. Leave them covered in the refrigerator for 30 minutes or until you're ready to grill.

*4* In a large bowl, combine the lemon juice, wine, and red pepper flakes. Set aside.

*5* Wrap 2 bricks in foil. Remove the chickens from their marinade and place them on the grill, skin side down. Place a brick on top of each. Grill for 10 minutes. Turn the chickens, placing the bricks back on top, and grill for another 10 minutes. Remove the bricks. Transfer the chickens to the bowl with the wine mixture, turn to coat the chickens with the mixture, return the chickens to the grill, and place a brick on each chicken. Grill for 10 minutes per side. Repeat this procedure 2 more times, but don't place the bricks on top during the last 10 minutes of cooking. Check the doneness of the chickens by probing the leg meat; the juices should be clear, and the meat shouldn't be at all red or pink.

## Baby Chicken with Lemon

In Italy, this dish is made with baby chickens, often called poussins in gourmet stores in the United States and elsewhere (see photo in color section). You can also use Cornish game hens from the supermarket in this recipe.

The chickens are cooked in a lot of olive oil to keep them moist. About halfway through the roasting time, the oil is discarded so that the chicken skin can crisp up. Make sure to choose a roasting pan that is deep enough to accommodate all the oil and the chickens.

***Italian recipe name:*** *Polletto al Limone*

***Preparation time:*** *20 minutes*

***Cooking time:*** *50 minutes*

***Yield:*** *4 servings*

*4 Cornish game hens or small baby chickens (about 1 1/4 pounds each)*

*Salt and pepper to taste*

*1 lemon, quartered*

*4 cloves garlic, peeled*

*2 sprigs fresh rosemary, or 2 teaspoons dried rosemary*

*1 1/2 cups olive oil, divided*

*1 lemon, sliced*

*Juice of 1 lemon (about 3 tablespoons)*

*1 cup white wine*

**1** Preheat oven to 375°.

**2** Season the hens with salt and pepper outside and inside the cavity. Place 1 lemon quarter, 1 garlic clove, and half a rosemary sprig (or 1/2 teaspoon dried rosemary) inside each hen. Drizzle the bottom of a roasting pan with 3/4 cup oil. Place the hens in the pan and drizzle the remaining 3/4 cup oil over the hens.

**3** Roast for 10 minutes, turn the hens over, and roast for another 10 minutes. Turn the hens again and cook for another 5 minutes. Drain the fat from the pan and add the lemon slices and lemon juice. Continue cooking for 10 more minutes. Add the wine. Roast until the hens are golden brown, 10 to 15 more minutes. Serve with the pan juices spooned on top.

# Take the chicken apart

Most Italian recipes begin with a whole chicken cut into eight parts — two wings, two legs, two thighs, and two breasts. Most Italian cooks do this themselves. You can now buy butchered chicken at almost any supermarket, but here are several good reasons to do this yourself:

✔ Whole chickens are considerably cheaper than chicken parts.

✔ Free-range, organic, and kosher chickens are usually sold whole. If you buy chicken parts, they usually come from mass-market birds that have the least flavor.

✔ When you cut a bird into eight parts, you're left with an extra piece — the back — that you can use to make stock. Just throw the back in a plastic zipper-lock bag in the freezer. When you have several backs, use them to make stock. (Refer to Chapter 5 for information on making chicken stock.)

Cutting up a whole chicken is easier that it looks. Just put the bird on a cutting board and get out a sharp knife. Follow these steps (see Figure 11-3), and you have the bird ready for cooking in a minute or two:

1. **Turn the chicken on its side and pull the wing away from the body.**

2. **Use the tip of a knife to cut around the joint that attaches the wing to the breast.**

   Repeat with the second wing.

3. **Turn the chicken breast side up.**

4. **While pulling the leg away from the bird with one hand, use the tip of a knife to slice the skin between the drumstick and breast.**

5. **With one hand holding the chicken, use the other hand to bend back the thigh and pop out the joint that attaches the leg to the body.**

6. **Holding the leg away from the body, cut around the joint to release the leg/thigh piece and then detach the other leg/thigh piece.**

7. **Place the leg/thigh piece skin side down on a cutting board.**

8. **Use a knife to slice through the fat line and locate the joint; after you locate the joint, cut through to separate the leg and thigh pieces; do this on both sides.**

   The joint that separates the leg and thigh is underneath a line of fat that divides the thigh and leg.

9. **Cut between the bottom of the rib cage and the back of the bird on both sides of the chicken.**

   When you're finished, the breast and back are completely separated.

   Reserve the back for making stock.

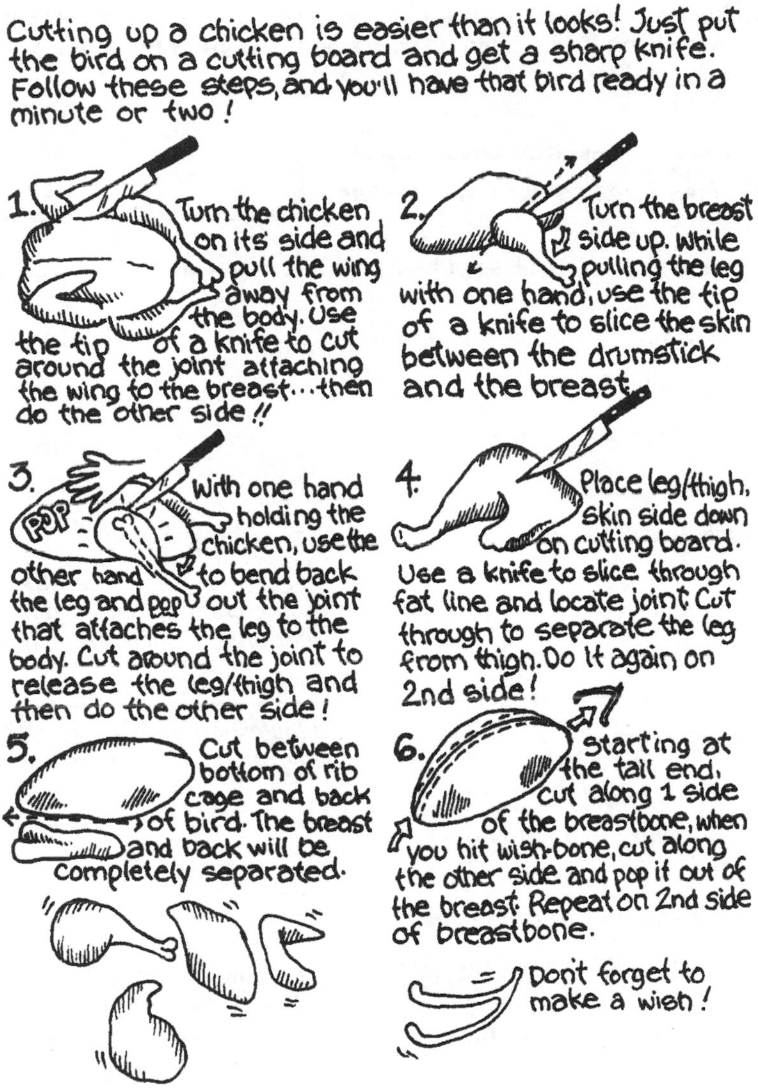

Cutting up a chicken is easier than it looks! Just put the bird on a cutting board and get a sharp knife. Follow these steps, and you'll have that bird ready in a minute or two!

1. Turn the chicken on its side and pull the wing away from the body. Use the tip of a knife to cut around the joint attaching the wing to the breast...then do the other side!!

2. Turn the breast side up. While pulling the leg with one hand, use the tip of a knife to slice the skin between the drumstick and the breast.

3. POP With one hand holding the chicken, use the other hand to bend back the leg and pop out the joint that attaches the leg to the body. Cut around the joint to release the leg/thigh and then do the other side!

4. Place leg/thigh, skin side down on cutting board. Use a knife to slice through fat line and locate joint. Cut through to separate the leg from thigh. Do it again on 2nd side!

5. Cut between bottom of rib cage and back of bird. The breast and back will be completely separated.

6. Starting at the tail end, cut along 1 side of the breastbone, when you hit wish-bone, cut along the other side and pop it out of the breast. Repeat on 2nd side of breastbone.

Don't forget to make a wish!

**Figure 11-3:**
Cutting a whole chicken into parts.

10. **Starting at the tail end, cut down along one side of the breastbone.**

11. **When you hit the wishbone, cut down along the side of the wishbone and pop it out of the breast by using your fingers or the tip of the knife.**

    Repeat on the other side of the breastbone.

Italians often braise or stew chicken parts. In most recipes, the parts are browned and then simmered with a liquid, such as tomatoes, wine, or stock, and vegetables.

## Braised Chicken with Mushrooms

Serve with grilled or toasted slices of bread rubbed with garlic and drizzled with a little olive oil.

**Italian recipe name:** *Cacciucco di Pollo*

**Preparation time:** *20 minutes*

**Cooking time:** *1 hour, 20 minutes*

**Yield:** *4 servings*

*3-to 4-pound whole chicken, cut into 8 pieces*

*Salt and pepper to taste*

*$^{1}/_{4}$ cup plus 1 tablespoon olive oil*

*8 cloves garlic, peeled and chopped*

*2 medium onions, chopped*

*1 pinch hot red pepper flakes*

*2 sprigs fresh rosemary, or 1 teaspoon dried rosemary*

*2 cups white wine*

*$1^{1}/_{2}$ pounds mixed mushrooms (shiitake, oyster, cremini, and/or domestic), quartered or sliced $^{1}/_{2}$-inch thick*

*3 cups canned plum tomatoes, chopped*

*2 tablespoons chopped fresh parsley, or 2 teaspoons dried parsley*

**1** Season the chicken with salt and pepper.

**2** Heat the olive oil in a large skillet. Add the garlic, onions, red pepper flakes, and rosemary and sauté, stirring often, for 3 minutes. Then place the chicken pieces in the skillet and cook over medium heat, turning occasionally, for 25 to 30 minutes.

**3** Drain the fat from the skillet and add the wine. Simmer to reduce the wine by half. Add the mushrooms, stir, and cook, covered, for 15 minutes. Then add the tomatoes and adjust the seasoning with salt and pepper. Simmer, covered, for 25 minutes, stirring occasionally. Mix in the parsley 3 minutes before serving.

### Braised Chicken with Tomatoes and Wine

The Italian name of this dish, "chicken, hunter's style," refers to the hearty tomato sauce flavored with wine, olives, garlic, rosemary, and hot red pepper flakes. Serve with Basic Polenta (refer to the recipe in Chapter 9).

***Italian recipe name:*** *Pollo alla Cacciatora*

***Preparation time:*** *15 minutes*

***Cooking time:*** *1 hour*

***Yield:*** *4 servings*

*3-to 4-pound whole chicken, cut into 8 pieces*

*Salt and pepper to taste*

*¹/₂ cup olive oil*

*5 cloves garlic, peeled*

*¹/₂ teaspoon hot red pepper flakes*

*3 sprigs fresh rosemary, or 1 teaspoon dried rosemary*

*1 lemon, juiced, with lemon halves reserved (about 3 tablespoons)*

*1 cup white wine*

*3 cups fresh plum tomatoes, peeled and seeded (or use canned tomatoes)*

*1 cup black or green olives, pitted*

**1** Season the chicken with salt and pepper.

**2** Heat the olive oil in a large skillet. Add the garlic, red pepper flakes, rosemary, and chicken pieces and cook, turning the pieces occasionally, for 20 minutes.

**3** Drain the fat from the skillet and stir in the lemon juice and the wine. Simmer, reducing the liquid by half. Add the lemon halves, tomatoes, and olives and simmer for 30 minutes. If the sauce becomes too dry, add a little chicken stock or water. Adjust the seasoning with salt and pepper and serve.

## Chicken, the easy way

Boneless, skinless chicken breasts, which are commonly called chicken cutlets, are easy to prepare — just open the package, rinse, and pat dry — and quick to cook. In Italian cooking, they're often used as a cheaper substitute for veal cutlets.

Like you do with veal, you may need to pound chicken cutlets before cooking. Simply place the cutlets between two pieces of plastic wrap and pound with a mallet or the bottom of a heavy pan (see Figure 11-4). Pounding ensures that the chicken cooks evenly, so don't skip this step.

**Figure 11-4:**
Chicken cutlets pounded to an even thickness.

## Chicken Cutlets Pounded to an Even Thickness

Place cutlets between two pieces of plastic wrap.

whack!

And pound with a mallet or the bottom of a heavy pan.

### Breaded Chicken Cutlets, Milan Style

For this dish, chicken breasts are coated with bread crumbs and then pan-fried in oil until crisp. This was Cesare's favorite *merenda,* or snack, growing up. He loves it hot or at room temperature. If you like, serve the chicken pieces over a salad of arugula, tomatoes, and onions.

**Italian recipe name:** *Milanese di Pollo*

**Preparation time:** *15 minutes*

**Cooking time:** *10 minutes*

**Yield:** *4 servings*

**Special tools:** *Plastic wrap, meat pounder, paper towels, aluminum foil*

$1^1/_2$ *pounds chicken cutlets (4 cutlets)*

*Salt and pepper to taste*

*2 eggs*

$^1/_2$ *cup flour*

*3 cups fresh bread crumbs, or 1 cup dry bread crumbs*

*2 cups peanut oil*

*1* Place each chicken cutlet between 2 large sheets of plastic wrap and pound them with a meat mallet (or the bottom of a heavy pan if you don't have a mallet) until they're evenly about $^1/_4$-inch thick. Lightly season with salt and pepper.

*2* In a medium bowl, lightly beat the eggs. Generously season with salt and pepper.

*3* Spread the flour over a large plate. Spread the bread crumbs over another plate.

***4*** In a skillet large enough to hold 2 of the cutlets (use 2 pans, if necessary), heat half the oil over medium heat for about 4 minutes. Don't allow the oil to smoke. Evenly coat 2 chicken cutlets with flour, shaking off the excess. Dip them, 1 at a time, in the eggs, letting any excess drip off. Then dip them in the bread crumbs, lightly shaking them to remove the excess. Slip the chicken cutlets into the skillet, making sure that they don't overlap.

***5*** Cook the cutlets for 2 to 3 minutes on one side, or until they're a rich golden brown. Turn and cook until browned on the other side, another 2 to 3 minutes. Transfer the chicken cutlets to a platter lined with paper towels and gently pat the top with paper towels. Loosely cover with foil to keep the chicken warm while you repeat this procedure with the 2 remaining cutlets.

## Breaded Chicken Cutlets in Tomato Sauce

For this dish, breaded chicken cutlets are pan-fried and then simmered in a tomato sauce flavored with garlic, anchovies, and capers.

***Italian recipe name:*** *Panate di Pollo Rifatte*

***Preparation time:*** *15 minutes*

***Cooking time:*** *30 minutes*

***Yield:*** *4 servings*

*¹/₄ cup olive oil*

*3 cloves garlic, peeled and chopped*

*Pinch of hot red pepper flakes*

*8 anchovy fillets, chopped*

*¹/₂ cup white wine*

*3¹/₂ cups (28-ounce can) plum tomatoes*

*¹/₄ cup capers, drained and chopped*

*1 cup chopped fresh parsley (about 1 large bunch), or ¹/₄ cup dried parsley*

*Salt and pepper to taste*

*Breaded Chicken Cutlets, Milan Style (refer to recipe earlier in this chapter)*

***1*** In a medium skillet, heat the olive oil, garlic, and red pepper flakes over medium heat. Cook until the garlic just starts to brown, 2 to 3 minutes. Add the anchovy fillets and wine, cooking until the wine reduces by half. Add the tomatoes and capers and simmer for 10 minutes. Then stir in the parsley and simmer for another 5 minutes. Adjust the seasoning with salt and pepper. Set aside.

***2*** Prepare the chicken cutlets. Add the cooked cutlets to the sauce and simmer for 5 minutes. Serve.

## Chicken Cutlets with Spinach

This dish is especially light and delicious.

*Italian recipe name:* Pollo alla Fiorentina

*Preparation time:* 10 minutes

*Cooking time:* 30 minutes

*Yield:* 4 servings

3 tablespoons olive oil

4 cloves garlic, peeled and crushed

1¹/₂ pounds chicken cutlets (4 cutlets)

Salt and pepper to taste

Juice of 1 lemon (about 3 tablespoons)

1 cup white wine

2 cups cooked fresh spinach, or 10-ounce package frozen spinach (thawed and drained)

14-ounce can plum tomatoes or 1 cup Tomato and Basil Sauce (refer to Chapter 6)

**1** In a large skillet, heat the olive oil and garlic over medium heat. Cook until the garlic just starts to brown, 2 to 3 minutes. Season the chicken cutlets with salt and pepper and add them to the pan. Cook until lightly browned on 1 side, 2 to 3 minutes. Turn the cutlets over and cook for another 2 minutes. Then drain any fat from the pan. Add the lemon juice and wine and continue cooking until the liquid has reduced by three-fourths, about 5 minutes.

**2** Stir in the spinach and cook for 3 minutes. Add the tomatoes and simmer for 10 minutes. Adjust the seasoning with salt and pepper and serve.

## Chicken Cutlets with Artichokes

Starting with canned artichokes hearts rather than fresh artichokes saves a tremendous amount of prep time. Serve this dish as is or use the chicken and artichokes as a sandwich filling (see photo in color section).

*Italian recipe name:* Scaloppine di Pollo con Carciofi

*Preparation time:* 15 minutes

*Cooking time:* 30 minutes

*Yield:* 4 servings

*2 cloves garlic, minced, plus 2 cloves garlic, peeled and crushed*

*2 tablespoons chopped fresh parsley, or 2 teaspoons dried parsley*

*1 medium tomato, diced*

*Two 8-ounce cans artichoke hearts, drained*

*Salt and pepper to taste*

*¹/₄ cup olive oil*

*1¹/₂ pounds chicken cutlets, pounded (4 cutlets)*

*¹/₄ cup flour*

*Juice of 1 lemon (about 3 tablespoons)*

*1 cup white wine*

**1** Preheat oven to 375°.

**2** In a medium bowl, combine the minced garlic, parsley, tomato, and artichoke hearts. Season with salt and pepper. Mix. Set aside.

**3** In a large oven-safe skillet, heat the olive oil and crushed garlic over medium heat. Cook until the garlic just starts to brown, 2 to 3 minutes. Season the chicken with salt and pepper and lightly dust them with flour. Place them in the skillet and cook until lightly browned on one side, 2 to 3 minutes. Turn the cutlets over and cook for another 2 minutes. Then drain any fat from the pan. Add the lemon juice and wine and continue cooking until the liquid has reduced by three-fourths, about 5 minutes.

**4** Stir in the artichoke mixture and cook for 3 to 4 minutes. Adjust the seasoning with salt and pepper. Cover the skillet and transfer it to the oven. Cook for 10 minutes. Serve the cutlets.

## Chicken Cutlets with Tomato and Basil Salad

This summer dish features grilled chicken breasts served with a salad of chopped tomatoes, cucumber, bell peppers, and herbs (see photo in color section). Cutlets will stick to a dirty grill, so make sure to scrape the grill thoroughly just before cooking the chicken.

***Italian recipe name:*** *Battuta di Pollo dell'Estate*

***Preparation time:*** *15 minutes (plus 30 minutes marination time)*

***Cooking time:*** *10 minutes*

***Yield:*** *4 servings*

*(continued)*

Juice of 1 lemon (about 3 tablespoons)

$^1/_4$ cup plus 1 tablespoon olive oil, divided

Salt and pepper to taste

$1^1/_2$ pounds chicken cutlets, pounded (4 cutlets)

1 medium tomato, chopped

1 small onion, finely sliced

1 yellow bell pepper, seeded and finely sliced

1 small seedless cucumber, diced

$^1/_2$ cup chopped fresh basil, or 1 tablespoon dried basil

2 sprigs fresh oregano, or 2 teaspoons dried oregano

2 tablespoons red wine vinegar

*1* Preheat grill to medium-high.

*2* In a medium shallow baking dish, combine the lemon juice, 2 tablespoons olive oil, and salt and pepper. Mix to combine. Place the chicken in the dish, turning the cutlets over a few times to evenly coat them with the marinade. Cover and refrigerate at least 30 minutes.

*3* In a large bowl, mix together the tomato, onion, yellow pepper, cucumber, basil, oregano, vinegar, and the remaining 3 tablespoons olive oil. Season with salt and pepper.

*4* Place the chicken on the grill and cook for $1^1/_2$ minutes. Rotate each cutlet 90 degrees and grill for another $1^1/_2$ minutes. Turn the cutlets over and repeat on the other side. Check to make sure that the cutlets are cooked through. If they need to cook further, move them to a cooler part of the grill, cover, and grill for another 1 to 2 minutes. Transfer the chicken to the bowl with the vegetables. Mix and serve.

## Chicken Cutlets with Balsamic Vinegar

This chicken sauté is especially quick to prepare. Use a good-quality balsamic vinegar in this recipe.

**Italian recipe name:** *Pollo al Balsamico*

**Preparation time:** *20 minutes*

**Cooking time:** *20 minutes*

**Yield:** *4 servings*

*¹/₄ cup olive oil*

*4 cloves garlic, peeled and sliced*

*1¹/₂ pounds chicken cutlets, lightly pounded (4 cutlets)*

*Salt and pepper to taste*

*¹/₄ cup flour*

*2 sprigs fresh sage, or 1 teaspoon dried sage*

*¹/₂ cup aged balsamic vinegar*

*¹/₄ cup plus 2 tablespoons chicken stock*

*1* In a large skillet, heat the olive oil and garlic over medium heat. Cook until the garlic just starts to brown, 2 to 3 minutes. Season the cutlets with salt and pepper and dust them with flour. Add the chicken and sage to the skillet and cook until lightly browned on 1 side, 2 to 3 minutes. Turn and cook for another 2 minutes. Then drain any fat from the pan.

*2* Add the balsamic vinegar and reduce slightly, about 2 minutes. Then add the stock. Cover and simmer for 10 minutes. If you want the sauce thicker, remove the chicken from the pan and simmer another 3 to 5 minutes, or to desired consistency. Adjust the seasoning of the sauce with salt and pepper. Pour the sauce over the chicken cutlets and serve.

# Beyond Chicken

When it comes to good poultry, you have more choices than just chicken. Italians also enjoy turkey and duck, which are readily available in supermarkets. Italians are also fond of small birds, such as quail, squab, and pheasant. (See the sidebar "Love those little birds" later in this chapter.)

Although rabbits aren't poultry, they're butchered and prepared in the same fashion. The meat is sweet and a bit gamy, like dark meat chicken.

## Duck

The whole ducks sold in North American supermarkets are called Pekin or Long Island ducks. Once raised on Long Island, these birds are now grown on farms around the country, and the largest producer is located in Indiana, not New York. These birds weigh about 4 pounds, perhaps 5 pounds at the most.

Don't be fooled into thinking that a duck can serve five or six people. A smaller chicken serves more people. Ducks have a larger, heavier bone structure, and they contain more fat, much of which melts away during the roasting process. A 4-pound duck feeds three, maybe four, people.

## Duck with Oranges

This recipe dates back to the 15th century. Catherine di Medici brought this dish with her to France, where it became the famed duck à l'orange. The Italian original is not nearly as sweet as the modern French preparation.

*Italian recipe name:* Ënatra all'Arancia

*Preparation time:* 30 minutes

*Cooking time:* 1 hour, 50 minutes

*Yield:* 3 to 4 servings

5-pound duck

Salt and pepper to taste

Pinch of ground cinnamon

Pinch of ground cloves

6 cloves garlic, peeled and crushed

$^1/_2$ cup olive oil

$1^1/_2$ cups white wine

2 oranges, sliced with the peel

1 cup orange juice

**1** Preheat oven to 375°.

**2** Heat a large, oven-safe skillet over medium-high heat. Add the duck and sear, turning often, to render some fat, about 5 minutes. Remove the duck from the skillet and discard the fat.

**3** Season the duck with salt and pepper. Sprinkle the cavity with the cinnamon and cloves and place the garlic inside. Heat the oil in the empty skillet over medium-high heat. When it's hot, add the duck, breast side down, and brown on all sides, about 3 to 4 minutes per side. Add the wine and reduce it by three-fourths, about 5 to 8 minutes. Arrange the orange slices on top of the duck, cover, and transfer the skillet to the oven. When you put the duck in the oven, the breast should face up. Roast for 30 minutes. Pour the orange juice over the duck and cook for another 45 minutes.

**4** Remove the skillet from the oven and allow the duck to rest for 10 minutes before separating the breast and the legs. Slice each breast in half on the bias and separate the legs from the thighs. Place a piece of breast meat and leg meat on each plate and top with the orange sauce.

# Turkey

When buying a turkey, brands are rarely an option. Many markets have one kind of fresh turkey and another kind of frozen turkey. The fresh turkeys are better, but the real issue is size.

Many cooks love the idea of roasting a 22-pound bird for the holidays. But we find that the larger the bird, the higher the likelihood that it will be overcooked. A turkey is already hard to cook, with its delicate breast meat and tougher legs. But if the bird weighs 22 pounds, it's more difficult to get the meat close to the bone cooked through without causing the outer layers to dry out and taste like sawdust.

We recommend that you buy a bird that weighs 12 to 15 pounds, gross weight. (By the time you remove the giblets and trim the neck and tail, the weight will be reduced by a pound or more.) If you're feeding a large crowd and your oven permits, think about roasting two small birds.

Although turkey is not as popular in Italy as it is in the United States, you will find the occasional recipe for roast turkey, especially in the Bologna and Verona areas. Turkey cutlets are not readily available in Italy, but they're a great way to enjoy turkey without all the work. Like chicken cutlets, they can be prepared in countless dishes. Because they're so lean, turkey cutlets are best cooked with some moist ingredients, such as wine and tomatoes.

## Turkey with Prosciutto and Cheese

This recipe comes from the city of Parma in Emilia-Romagna. The prosciutto and cheese are traditional seasonings for many local dishes, and they add flavor and richness to a piece of meat that is otherwise very bland.

***Italian recipe name:*** *Tacchino alla Parmense*

***Preparation time:*** *15 minutes*

***Cooking time:*** *20 to 25 minutes*

***Yield:*** *4 servings*

*¹/₄ cup olive oil*

*2 sprigs fresh sage, or 1 teaspoon dried sage*

*1¹/₂ pounds turkey cutlets, lightly pounded*

*Salt and pepper to taste*

*Juice of 1 lemon (about 3 tablespoons)*

*³/₄ cup white wine*

*1 cup chopped tomatoes, fresh or canned*

*6 slices prosciutto or pancetta*

*1 cup grated Parmigiano-Reggiano*

*1* Preheat oven to 400°.

*2* In a large, oven-safe skillet, heat the oil and sage over medium-high heat. Season the turkey cutlets with salt and pepper and add them to the skillet. Cook until lightly

*(continued)*

browned on 1 side, 2 to 3 minutes. Turn the turkey cutlets over and cook for another 2 minutes. Then drain any fat from the skillet. Add the lemon juice and wine and continue cooking until the liquid has reduced by three-fourths.

**3** Spoon the tomatoes over the turkey. Then top the tomatoes with slices of prosciutto or pancetta, followed by Parmigiano-Reggiano cheese.

**4** Transfer the skillet to the oven and cook for 6 to 8 minutes, until the cheese is lightly browned and bubbly.

## Love those little birds

Italians enjoy a number of small birds in a variety of recipes. These birds aren't very popular in the United States, but they're available at most butcher shops.

**Pheasant:** Of all the game birds, pheasant (*fagiano* in Italian) bears the greatest resemblance to chicken. Although wild pheasant can be dark and overpowering, the domesticated pheasant sold by butchers is light-colored and mild. Many older cooks say it reminds them of the way chicken tasted during the first half of the century, when it was mostly a local, free-range product. A whole pheasant weighs about 2½ pounds and can be cooked much like a chicken. A pheasant is ideal for two people.

**Poussin:** These baby chickens are slaughtered at 3 or 4 weeks when they weigh about 1 pound. They're preferred by restaurant chefs because of their small size, which is ideal for one person. We like them because many small chicken farms raise poussin, and they usually taste better than Cornish game hens, which are the province of mass-market operations.

Poussin are hard to find, but the trip to a specialty market or butcher is worth the effort.

**Quail:** Tiny quail (*quaglie* in Italian) have a rich flavor that is surprisingly meaty but not overly strong or gamy. They range in size from 4 to 6 ounces each. Larger quail, weighing at least 5 ounces, are easier to eat. Quail have lots of tiny bones, which can be a challenge when eating them, especially in front of strangers. Plan on serving two quail per person and encourage everyone to pick up these tiny birds with their fingers.

**Squab:** Squab (*piccioni* in Italian) are young pigeons that cannot fly because their feathers have not developed fully. They have a dark, rich, mildly gamy flavor. Most squab weigh about 1 pound, and each bird feeds one person. Domesticated squab are fairly fatty, much more so than pheasant or quail. Squab are sold whole or partially boned at the retail level. Boneless squab (the leg and wing bones remain intact) weigh about 10 ounces and are ideal for sautéing or grilling.

# Rabbit

Don't think about Bugs Bunny. Italians are not very sentimental about eating animals. And really, do you avoid eating duck because of Daffy or Donald?

Rabbit is extremely lean and low in fat, but it has much more flavor than chicken. Most rabbits weigh 2 to 3 pounds. As with chicken, Italian cooks often cut the rabbit into parts and then braise it in a covered pot. You can also roast rabbit, as long as you make sure to baste it with some wine or stock.

## Roasted Rabbit

Add potatoes to the roasting pan to make this a complete meal. The olive oil helps keep lean rabbit from drying out in the oven, as does the wine.

**Italian recipe name:** *Coniglio Arristo*

**Preparation time:** *10 minutes*

**Cooking time:** *1 hour*

**Yield:** *4 servings*

| | |
|---|---|
| *2- to 3-pound rabbit* | *1 cup olive oil* |
| *Salt and pepper to taste* | *Juice of 1 lemon (about 3 tablespoons)* |
| *4 cloves garlic, peeled* | *1 cup white wine* |
| *2 sprigs fresh rosemary, or 2 teaspoons dried rosemary* | *6 medium potatoes, peeled and cut into 1-inch pieces (optional)* |

*1* Preheat oven to 400°.

*2* Season the rabbit with salt and pepper, outside and inside the cavity. Place the garlic and rosemary in the cavity.

*3* Put the rabbit in a medium roasting pan (or a small pan if you're not preparing potatoes) and pour the olive oil over the top. Place in the oven and roast for 15 minutes. Reduce the oven temperature to 375°. Turn and roast for another 15 minutes. When the rabbit is lightly browned, pour the fat from the pan and add the lemon juice. Cook for 5 minutes. Add the wine and roast for another 25 minutes, turning midway through cooking. The rabbit should reach an internal temperature of 160°. If using potatoes, stir them into the pan 20 minutes before serving. Ten minutes before the rabbit is ready, drain the oil.

# Chapter 12

# Meat: Where's the Beef, Veal, Lamb, and Pork?

## In This Chapter

▶ Buying meat with confidence

▶ Choosing the right cut

▶ Handling and cooking meat safely

▶ Getting the skinny on scaloppine

Most Italian meat dishes are fairly simple. Presumably, everyone has already eaten an antipasto and a first course. Often, the pasta or risotto is fairly rich and contains many different flavors. Meat dishes tend to be on the plain side — some breaded cutlets sautéed in oil and served with lemon wedges or perhaps a loin of pork roasted with garlic and rosemary.

Unlike many other European cuisines, Italian cookery generally presents meat dishes without complicated or heavy sauces. Many dishes are served with their own juices as a "sauce." When sautéing cutlets or scaloppine, you make quick pan sauces by adding wine or stock to the browned bits left in the pan after you've cooked the meat.

Traditionally, most Italian homes couldn't afford large quantities of meat. So Italians served meat in small quantities, after pasta, risotto, polenta, or soup. Since the end of World War II, Italy has become a wealthy country, and Italians now eat meat in larger portions. The recipes in this chapter reflect these newer eating habits and suit most American tastes.

# Buying Meat

The meat case at the average supermarket contains hundreds of different items. If a butcher is on call, even more cuts are available for the asking. All this abundance can be confusing. Here's how to get what you want.

## Judging freshness

The only meat worth eating is fresh meat. Most markets stamp labels with a sell-by or packed-on date. Make sure to check this date before buying any meat. The sell-by date should still be several days away. A packed-on date should be recent, preferably today or yesterday. Keep these other tips in mind when shopping:

- **Look at the color of the meat.** Beef should be rosy red, not gray or brown. Lamb should be bright red as well. The color of pork and veal is lighter and doesn't indicate much about freshness.

- **Feel the meat.** It should be somewhat firm, not squishy. If the meat has been shrink-wrapped, look for excess juices in the package, a sign that the meat may have been sitting out for some time or frozen and then defrosted.

- **Look at the fat in the meat.** Why pay for external fat (all the white stuff) that you want to trim away anyway? However, internal fat is a sign that beef and lamb will be flavorful and juicy. A good steak has lots of tiny white lines, called *marbling,* that run through the meat. You may have to pay a premium for well-marbled meat, but that's money well spent.

- **Keep meat cold on its journey from the butcher case to your refrigerator.** This means buying meat (and dairy) on your way up to the checkout counter and driving home right away. (No stops at the dry cleaners, video store, or bank.) If the weather is really hot or you live some distance from your supermarket, bring a cooler along and keep meat cold with some ice packs.

## Grading

The federal government inspects all meat sold in the United States. Most other countries also have inspection programs for meat. Many packages of meat are also graded. This practice is voluntary, but most meat packagers follow the U.S. Department of Agriculture's guidelines for grading. You see three grades at the retail level:

✔ **Prime** meat is considered the highest quality and is more expensive than the other grades. These cuts have the most internal fat and presumably have the most flavor and juiciness. Prime meat rarely makes it to supermarkets. Your butcher may have prime meat, but most of it is sold directly to restaurants.

✔ **Choice** is the grade of meat most commonly found in supermarkets. It has less fat than prime meat, but it's considered to be a high-quality grade of meat.

✔ **Select** meat is a relatively new term that the government uses to indicate that the meat is especially lean. Select meat may be good for you, but it's chewier and less juicy than choice or prime meat.

You can cook prime and choice meat as you like. When using lean select meat, try moist cooking methods like braising or stewing. A grilled select steak is likely to be quite dry, but when you slice select beef into chunks and cook it in liquid, it can taste just fine.

## Choosing the right cut

Each animal — the cow, calf, lamb, and pig — yields dozens of cuts. Many of these cuts have regional names, so the terminology can be confusing. For example, strip steak, New York strip, Delmonico steak, shell steak, and top loin steak are different names for the same cut of beef.

When choosing a cut of meat for a particular dish, you must consider the cooking method. In general, you can find two types of cuts:

✔ **Tender cuts,** which often have quite a lot of fat, generally come from parts of the animal that receive very little exercise. Good examples include the beef tenderloin and veal scaloppine. You can cook these tender cuts by dry-heat cooking methods, such as grilling, roasting, and sautéing. Generally, you cook these cuts fairly quickly to maintain juiciness and tenderness.

✔ **Tough cuts** often have very little fat and come from parts of the animal that receive a lot of exercise. Good examples include the beef brisket and the lamb shoulder. These cuts are generally slow-cooked in liquid to make them tender. You don't want to grill a brisket; it's as tough as shoe leather when grilled. However, when simmered in wine, stock, and tomatoes for several hours, this cut can be tender and delicious.

Talk to your butcher about what you're making. Tender cuts are generally much more expensive than tough cuts, so if you're on a budget, consider a stew or braised dish, rather than a recipe for grilled steaks.

## Handling meat at home

Pick up the paper or turn on the television, and you're bound to read or hear about another case of food poisoning. Often, meat is the culprit. You can take a number of steps at home to minimize the risk to you and your family.

✔ **Get meat home quickly and into the refrigerator.** If you're not going to cook meat within a day or two, put it immediately into the freezer. Defrost all frozen meats on a plate (to catch juices) in the refrigerator.

✔ **Wash anything that comes into contact with meat or its juices in hot soapy water.** This includes your hands, cutting boards, counters, and knives. If possible, use a dishwasher to sterilize plates, tools, or cutting boards used with raw meat.

✔ **Don't let meat or meat juices come into contact with fruits, vegetables, or other foods that you plan on eating without cooking.** When opening meat packages, do this far away from other foods so that the meat juices don't contaminate them.

✔ **Don't let uncooked meat sit out on the counter.** Bacteria loves warm kitchens, but it has a harder time multiplying at temperatures close to freezing.

✔ **Handle all marinades and sauces that come into contact with raw meat carefully.** Assume that these liquids have been contaminated with bacteria and either discard them or boil them before using as a sauce.

## Cooking meat

Chefs may be able to tell when a piece of meat is done by touch, but the rest of us need some other clues. You can cut into meat and see what it looks like, but this is very imprecise and causes precious juices to be lost. We recommend that you cook meat by internal temperature.

If you pick up an instant-read thermometer (see Figure 12-1) at your local kitchen shop for $10, the days of overdone beef or pork will be over. When you think the meat might be done, simply stick the end of the thermometer deep into the meat (away from any bones and fat which can distort the reading) and wait about 10 seconds for the temperature to register. If the meat is not up to temperature, remove the thermometer and try again in a few minutes. Instant-read thermometers will be destroyed if left in an oven for more than a minute or two, so remember to pull them out of the meat before you close the oven door.

**Figure 12-1:** An instant-read thermometer.

Residual heat will cause the internal temperature of large cuts to rise by another 5° as the meat rests on the counter before carving. Even the internal temperature of steak will jump several degrees from the time you take if off the grill to the time you sit down to eat. If you want your beef cooked to 140°, pull it off the heat after the internal temperature reaches about 135°. Note that instant-read thermometers do not work with really thin cutlets.

Measuring the internal temperature of cooked meat is easy. Determining what temperature is right for you is another matter. Refer to Table 12-1 for a description of the terms rare, medium-rare, medium, and well-done as they apply to various types of meat. Only the temperatures at which each meat is considered palatable are listed. For example, pork is not eaten unless cooked to at least medium.

Health officials recommend cooking all meat until it is well-done. All bacteria is killed when meat is cooked to an internal temperature of 160°. This is not a problem when preparing poultry because poultry tastes best when well-done. However, a steak cooked to 160° is well-done and dry.

The choice is yours. But cooking meat to less than 160° does entail a certain amount of risk. You may not mind taking that risk yourself, but remember that children, pregnant women, the elderly, and persons with compromised immune systems from cancer, AIDS, and other diseases are much more susceptible to the effects of food-borne illnesses. If safety is your primary concern, cook all meat until well-done.

| Table 12-1 | Is It Done Yet? | |
| --- | --- | --- |
| **If You Like Meat Cooked Like This** | **Wait Until Internal Temperature Is** | **And Meat Looks Like This** |
| **Beef/Lamb** | | |
| Rare | 125° to 130° | The meat is mostly red, except for the very edges. |
| Medium-rare | 135° to 140° | The center is still pink, but the meat is slightly brown around the edges. |
| Medium | 145° to 150° | The center has a trace of pink, but the meat is mostly brown. |

*(continued)*

**Table 12-1 *(continued)***

| If You Like Meat Cooked Like This | Wait Until Internal Temperature Is | And Meat Looks Like This |
|---|---|---|
| Well-done | 160° | The meat is uniformly brown. |
| **Veal** | | |
| Medium | 145° to 150° | Milk-fed veal is mostly white with just a hint of pink in the center. Grass-fed veal is bright pink in the center and light pink elsewhere. |
| Well-done | 160° | Milk-fed veal is uniformly white. Grass-fed veal is brownish pink. |
| **Pork** | | |
| Medium | 145° to 150° | The meat is pink in the center and white around the edges. |
| Well-done | 160° | The meat is uniformly white. |

# Here's the Beef

Italy does not have the wide open plains necessary for wide-scale cattle grazing. However, cattle are raised in various spots in northern and central Italy. Perhaps the most famous Italian beef comes from Chianina cattle raised near the Val di Chiana River in Tuscany.

## Grilled Steak, Florentine Style

In Tuscany, steaks are generously coated with salt and pepper before grilling. Besides adding flavor, the salt and pepper form a crisp crust that contrasts nicely with the tender interior of the meat. T-bone steaks are the most commonly grilled cut in Florence (see photo in color section). After the steaks are grilled, the meat is removed from either side of the bone and sliced across the grain into thin pieces. You can serve these steaks this way or choose smaller rib eye or strip steaks and serve 1 to a person. Serve the steaks with a side of Stewed Beans with Tomatoes, Sage, and Garlic or Sautéed Broccoli Rabe (see Chapter 14 for those recipes).

***Italian recipe name:*** *Bistecca alla Fiorentina*

***Preparation time:*** *5 minutes*

***Cooking time:*** *20 minutes*

***Yield:*** *4 servings*

*1 tablespoon salt, divided*

*Pepper to taste*

*4 strip or rib eye steaks (about 14 ounces each), or 2 T-bone or porterhouse steaks (about 1¹/₂ to 2 pounds each)*

*1* Preheat the grill to high.

*2* When the grill is very hot, generously season the steaks with salt and pepper on 1 side only. Place the seasoned side of the steaks on the grill. Do not move them for 3 minutes; then turn them 90 degrees. When the first side is done, about 8 minutes for medium-rare and 11 minutes for medium (depending on the thickness of the steaks and the heat of the grill), season the top of the steaks and flip them over. Cook the steaks 4 to 6 minutes on the second side to desired doneness. Remove from heat and serve.

## Beef Strips with Garlic and Rosemary

This recipe is similar to a Chinese stir-fry, except with Italian seasonings and a hot skillet rather than a wok. The "sauce" in this recipe is white wine, most of which cooks off in the pan. Serve with roasted potatoes and salad or use the strips to make great steak sandwiches.

**Italian recipe name:** *Straccetti di Manzo con Aglio e Rosmarino*

**Preparation time:** *5 minutes*

**Cooking time:** *5 to 7 minutes*

**Yield:** *4 servings*

*2 pounds beef (loin, sirloin, or tenderloin), sliced ¹/₈-inch thick x ¹/₂-inch wide x 3-inches long*

*8 cloves garlic, peeled and sliced*

*2 sprigs fresh rosemary, or 1 teaspoon dried rosemary*

*5 tablespoons olive oil, divided*

*Salt and pepper to taste*

*³/₄ cup white wine*

*1* In a large bowl, combine the beef, garlic, rosemary, 2 tablespoons olive oil, and salt and pepper. Marinate in the refrigerator for up to 6 hours if you have the time or cook immediately.

*2* In a large skillet, heat the remaining 3 tablespoons olive oil over high heat. When hot, add the beef and cook, stirring occasionally, for 2 to 3 minutes.

*3* Add the wine. Stir to dissolve any flavorful particles on the bottom of the skillet. Cook for 2 to 3 minutes, adjust seasoning, if necessary, and serve.

## Meat Loaf, Tuscan Style

This is not your mother's meat loaf. Two miniature meat loaves are browned in a skillet and then simmered in a white bean stew. Cooking the meat loaves in a tomato-flavored bean stew keeps them especially moist and stretches a pound of ground beef to make 4 generous servings. This is a typical Jewish recipe from Tuscany, although the addition of grated cheese is a modern, non-Jewish addition.

**Italian recipe name:** *Hamim alla Toscana*

**Preparation time:** *15 minutes*

**Cooking time:** *1 hour, 45 minutes*

**Yield:** *4 servings*

*¹/₂ cup olive oil, divided*

*1 medium onion, chopped*

*3 cloves garlic, peeled and chopped*

*¹/₂ cup white wine, divided*

*4 medium ripe tomatoes, chopped*

*¹/₂ pound dry cannellini beans, soaked overnight in cold water and drained*

*2 quarts water*

*Salt and pepper to taste*

*1 pound ground beef*

*2 eggs*

*2 tablespoons grated Parmigiano-Reggiano*

*3 tablespoons flour*

*2 tablespoons bread crumbs*

*1 tablespoon chopped fresh parsley, or 1 teaspoon dried parsley*

*2 teaspoons chopped fresh sage, or 1 teaspoon dried sage*

*2 sprigs thyme, chopped, or 1 teaspoon dried thyme*

*1 cup chicken or beef stock*

**1** Heat ¹/₄ cup olive oil in a large saucepan over medium heat. Add the onion and garlic and cook until golden, about 3 minutes. Add ¹/₄ cup wine, the tomatoes, beans, water, and salt and pepper. Simmer until the beans are tender but still firm, 50 minutes to 1 hour.

**2** In a large mixing bowl, combine the beef, eggs, Parmigiano-Reggiano, flour, bread crumbs, herbs, and salt and pepper. With your hands, work the ingredients together to form 2 equal-sized loaves.

**3** In a medium skillet over medium-high heat, heat the remaining ¹/₄ cup olive oil. (If you're using a nonstick skillet, you can use less oil.) Brown the meat loaves on each side, about 3 to 4 minutes per side. Drain the fat from the pan. Add the remaining ¹/₄ cup wine and let it reduce for several minutes. Add the stock and let it cook for 15 minutes.

**4** Add the meat loaves to the beans and simmer for 15 to 20 minutes. Slice the meat and serve with the beans.

## Roast Beef in Bread Crust

For this unusual recipe, a roast is seared to brown the exterior and then wrapped in uncooked focaccia dough. The roast is then placed in the oven and baked. The result is a tender, juicy roast covered by a golden-brown bread crust. If you have ever had beef wellington, the effect is the same, except focaccia dough is used instead of pie pastry in this recipe.

***Italian recipe name:*** *Arrosto di Manzo Cotto nel Pane*

***Preparation time:*** *30 minutes*

***Cooking time:*** *1 hour, 40 minutes*

***Yield:*** *6 servings*

*$^1/_4$ cup plus 2 tablespoons olive oil*

*$3^1/_2$-pound boneless beef rib eye roast*

*Salt and pepper to taste*

*2 cups white wine*

*4 cloves garlic, peeled and chopped*

*2 sprigs fresh rosemary, or 1 teaspoon dried rosemary*

*2 sprigs fresh thyme, or 1 teaspoon dried thyme*

*Flour for dusting work surface*

*1 recipe Everyday Focaccia (see Chapter 10)*

*1 egg, beaten*

**1** Preheat oven to 375°.

**2** In a large skillet, heat the olive oil over medium heat.

**3** Season the rib eye with salt and pepper and add it to the skillet, searing until it is evenly browned, 3 to 4 minutes per side.

**4** Drain the fat from the pan and add the wine. Cook for 18 minutes. Transfer the meat to a platter and allow it to cool. Rub the meat with the garlic and herbs.

**5** On a flat flour-dusted surface, roll out the focaccia dough until it is large enough to completely cover the roast. Wrap the dough around the roast so that the edges of the dough meet. Trim away any excess. Brush the beaten egg along the edges to seal them. Place the dough-wrapped roast in a baking pan, seam side down, and brush the surface with the remaining beaten egg. Make three or four $^1/_2$-inch holes in the top of the crust to allow steam to escape. Bake 50 to 60 minutes. Insert an instant-read thermometer in 1 of the holes. When the roast reaches the desired temperature (refer to Table 12-1), the meat is ready. If the focaccia begins to brown before the meat is at the desired temperature, turn the oven down to 325° and cook to desired doneness. The crust should be golden brown. Let the roast sit for at least 10 minutes before serving. Slice and serve.

## Stew basics

In general, Italian beef is not as tender as beef from the United States. That's why many Italian recipes call for cooking the beef in liquid to make stews or braises.

To make a stew or braise, the meat is seared and then cooked in liquid in a covered pan. This cooking method allows the frugal cook to buy a cheap, tough cut and turn it into something tender and delicious. Most stew recipes start on top of the stove. However, after the meat has been browned and all the ingredients have been added, the pot is usually covered and placed in the oven, where the heat attacks the pot from all sides and ensures that the bottom does not burn.

Most stew recipes will taste even better the next day. Simply cool the stew and refrigerate right in the pot. The next day, skim off any fat that has congealed on the top of the stew and place the pot over a low burner or reheat the stew in a 300° oven until bubbling.

### Beef Stew

This recipe demonstrates the Italian cook's ability to turn cheap, tough beef into something delectable. This stew is fairly brothy, so serve it with lots of bread or maybe some mashed potatoes. (See Chapter 14 for the Mashed Potatoes recipe.)

***Italian recipe name:*** *Spezzatino di Manzo*

***Preparation time:*** *20 minutes*

***Cooking time:*** *4 hours, 10 minutes*

***Yield:*** *6 servings*

*¹/₂ cup olive oil*

*3 pounds beef stew meat, trimmed and cut into 2-inch cubes*

*Salt and pepper to taste*

*2 cups red wine*

*3 medium onions, sliced*

*3 carrots, sliced*

*2 celery stalks, sliced*

*6 garlic cloves, peeled and roughly chopped*

*2 sprigs fresh rosemary, or 1 teaspoon dried rosemary*

*2 sprigs fresh sage, or 1 teaspoon dried sage*

*5 cups water or beef stock, divided*

*2 cups chopped tomatoes, canned or fresh (optional)*

*1* Preheat oven to 350°.

*2* In a large ovenproof casserole, heat the olive oil. Season the meat with salt and pepper and then add it to the casserole. Brown over medium heat and then add the wine, stirring to dissolve any bits adhering to the bottom and sides of the pan. Let it reduce for 2 to 3 minutes over high heat.

*3* Add the vegetables and herbs, reduce the heat, and simmer, covered, for 10 minutes.

*4* Add $2^1/_2$ cups water or stock, bring it to a simmer, cover, and then place the casserole in the oven. Cook for 1 hour, stirring occasionally. Add 1 cup water and the tomatoes (if using), season with salt and pepper, and cook for another 2 hours. Add the remaining $1^1/_2$ cups water as necessary to keep the stew moist. The meat will be fork tender when done. Adjust the seasoning with salt and pepper, if necessary, and serve.

## Braised Beef with Vegetables and Red Wine

For this recipe, you will need a covered pan that can accommodate the meat in a single layer. The pan must also go from the stove top, where the meat is seared, to the oven, where it cooks in a mixture of red wine, tomatoes, and vegetables for several hours. A Dutch oven or round casserole with ovenproof handles or knobs should do the job.

**Italian recipe name:** *Brasato al Barolo*

**Preparation time:** *25 minutes*

**Cooking time:** *3 hours, 40 minutes*

**Yield:** *4 to 6 servings*

**Special tool:** *Food processor*

*$^1/_4$ cup olive oil*

*3 pounds beef chuck or brisket*

*Salt and pepper to taste*

*4 cups Barolo (or another full-bodied red Italian wine), divided*

*3 onions, chopped*

*4 celery stalks, sliced*

*3 peeled carrots, sliced*

*4 cloves garlic, peeled and crushed*

*4 sprigs fresh rosemary, or 2 teaspoons dried rosemary*

*Pinch of ground nutmeg*

*Pinch of ground cloves*

*Pinch of ground cinnamon*

*1 cup canned plum tomatoes, undrained*

*$^1/_4$ cup water (as needed)*

*(continued)*

*1* Preheat oven to 350°.

*2* In a medium, oven-safe casserole or Dutch oven, heat the olive oil over medium heat.

*3* Season the meat with salt and pepper and add it to the casserole. Brown the meat on all sides, cooking it over medium-high heat 3 minutes on the first side, 3 on the opposite side, and 1 minute on each of the 2 remaining sides.

*4* Drain the fat and add 2 cups wine. Simmer for 10 minutes; add the onions, celery, carrots, garlic, rosemary, and spices. Cook, stirring, for 5 minutes. Add 1 cup wine. Simmer for 5 minutes, cover the casserole, and transfer it to the oven. After 20 minutes, turn the roast, and add the remaining 1 cup wine and the tomatoes. Cook, covered, for 2$^1/_2$ hours, adding a $^1/_4$ cup water as necessary to keep the roast moist.

*5* Remove the vegetables and juices from the casserole and place them in the bowl of a food processor. Puree. Pour the puree over the roast, cover the casserole, and cook for 20 minutes in the oven.

*6* To serve, slice the meat and spoon the sauce over it.

## Braised Oxtail

The Italian name of this Roman dish loosely translates as "oxtail, butcher's style." Your average supermarket may not carry oxtail, but most butchers do. When oxtail is braised, it makes an especially hearty and delicious stew.

***Italian recipe name:*** *Coda alla Vaccinara*

***Preparation time:*** *15 minutes*

***Cooking time:*** *3 hours, 25 minutes*

***Yield:*** *4 servings*

$^1/_4$ *cup olive oil*

*10 cloves garlic, peeled and crushed*

*5 pounds oxtail, cut into 2-inch pieces*

*Salt and pepper to taste*

*2 tablespoons red wine vinegar*

*2 medium red onions, sliced*

*2 carrots, cut into* $^1/_4$*-inch pieces*

*1 cup sliced mushrooms*

*3 celery stalks, cut into* $^1/_4$*-inch pieces*

*1 cup red wine*

*2 ounces pancetta or sliced Canadian bacon, cut into 2-inch squares*

*4 cups canned whole tomatoes, crushed*

*2 teaspoons unsweetened cocoa powder*

$^1/_4$ *cup water (as needed)*

*1* Preheat oven to 350°.

*2* In a large, oven-safe skillet, heat the olive oil and garlic over medium heat until the garlic begins to brown, about 3 minutes.

*3* Season the oxtail with salt and pepper and add the pieces to the skillet. Cook over medium-high heat, turning them occasionally so that they brown evenly. Drain the fat from the skillet, add the vinegar, onions, carrots, mushrooms, and celery, and cook, stirring, for 2 minutes.

*4* Stir in the wine and pancetta. Cover and transfer to the oven. After 15 minutes, add the tomatoes and cocoa. Cook, stirring occasionally, for 3 hours; the meat should be fork tender. Add water in $1/4$ cup increments as needed to keep the stew moist.

# The Deal on Veal

Veal has gotten a bad rap. No one wants to think about baby calves, separated from their mothers, locked in cages, and then force-fed milk laced with antibiotics. Unfortunately, that's the way some veal has been produced in the United States.

In the past decade, a more politically correct form of veal has caught on with chefs and consumers. Young calves — veal comes from calves less than four months old — are allowed to graze in fields. This veal, which is called grass-fed, farm-raised, or natural veal, does not have the milky white color of the meat from calves that are caged. The color is rosy, almost like beef. Because these animals are allowed to exercise, the meat is not quite as tender either. However, many chefs believe the flavor is stronger and more interesting.

Caged calves are not much of an issue in Italy. Most Italians are happy to eat veal without questioning how the animals are raised. For the sake of authenticity, buy milk-fed veal. It's certainly easy enough to find. However, if you have given up veal because of concerns about how the animals are raised, you may want to consider the alternative. Grass-fed veal is becoming increasingly available. Many supermarkets, especially those dedicated to natural foods, carry it on a regular basis.

## Breaded and Fried Veal Chops

This dish from Milan makes a complete meal with breaded and pan-fried veal chops with a tomato and arugula salad. Rib chops may be used, but loin chops contain a juicy piece of tenderloin that the rib chops don't have and are preferred here.

***Italian recipe name:*** *Lombatina Milanese*

***Preparation time:*** *20 minutes*

***Cooking time:*** *10 minutes*

***Yield:*** *4 servings*

*4 boneless veal loin chops, cut 1-inch thick (about 2 pounds total), lightly pounded*

*Salt and pepper to taste*

*1 egg*

*1 cup packaged, dry bread crumbs*

*1 cup flour*

*1 cup peanut oil*

*4 cups arugula*

*¹/₂ cup chopped tomato*

*1¹/₂ tablespoons capers, drained*

*1¹/₂ tablespoons red wine vinegar*

*¹/₄ cup olive oil*

*1 tablespoon finely chopped shallots*

*1 lemon, quartered*

**1** Trim the chops of excess fat. Cut 3 shallow notches into the outer edge of the meat of each chop to prevent them from curling during cooking.

**2** Rub salt and pepper into the veal chops.

**3** In a shallow bowl, lightly beat the egg. Spread the bread crumbs in an even layer on a plate. Spread the flour on a separate plate. One by one, flour each chop, dip into the egg, and then roll in the bread crumbs, evenly coating the meat and shaking off any excess.

**4** In a large skillet over medium heat, heat the peanut oil. When it is hot, add the veal chops. Cook for 4 to 5 minutes, until golden brown, and then turn and cook for another 4 to 5 minutes. The meat should be almost firm when pressed with a finger. Transfer the chops to a plate lined with paper towels to drain. Repeat this procedure with the other pounded chops.

**5** In a large bowl, mix together the arugula, chopped tomato, and capers.

**6** In a small bowl, whisk together the vinegar with salt and pepper to taste. Whisk in the olive oil and chopped shallots. Pour the dressing over the salad and mix well.

**7** Place a veal chop on each plate and top it with a quarter of the salad. Serve each with a wedge of lemon.

## Veal Chops with Tomato Sauce and Mozzarella

For this dish, veal chops are cooked with the flavors of a pizza — tomatoes, basil, and mozzarella — hence the name "pizzaiola." The chops are seared, simmered in a quick tomato sauce, topped with mozzarella cheese, and then baked just until the cheese has melted. Serve with bread to sop up any extra sauce.

***Italian recipe name:*** *Cotoletta alla Pizzaiola*

***Preparation time:*** *20 minutes*

***Cooking time:*** *25 minutes*

***Yield:*** *4 servings*

*4 veal loin or rib chops (about 8 ounces each)*

*Salt and pepper to taste*

*2 tablespoons flour*

*6 tablespoons olive oil*

*6 cloves garlic, peeled*

*¹/₂ cup white wine*

*1¹/₄ cups Tomato and Basil Sauce (see Chapter 6), or 1¹/₄ cups chopped fresh tomatoes*

*1 teaspoon chopped fresh oregano*

*8 ounces mozzarella cheese, cut into small cubes*

*1* Preheat oven to 400°.

*2* Season the veal chops with salt and pepper and then dredge them in flour, shaking off any excess so that they are just dusted.

*3* In a large, oven-safe skillet, heat the olive oil. Add the garlic and cook until it just begins to brown. Add the veal chops and cook over medium heat for 5 minutes; then turn them and cook for 3 to 4 minutes on the other side. Drain the fat from the skillet. Add the wine, cooking until it almost all evaporates. Then add the Tomato and Basil Sauce and oregano. Simmer for 5 minutes. Sprinkle the mozzarella cheese over the veal chops and transfer the skillet to the oven. Bake for 8 to 10 minutes, until the cheese is bubbly.

## Venetian Style Calf's Liver

Slow-cooked onions are the secret to this recipe from Venice. Italian cooks use veal stock, but at home you can use chicken stock.

*(continued)*

*Italian recipe name:* Fegato alla Veneziana

*Preparation time:* 20 minutes

*Cooking time:* 40 to 45 minutes

*Yield:* 4 servings

$^1/_3$ cup plus 1 tablespoon olive oil, divided

4 medium onions, sliced

Salt and pepper to taste

$1^1/_4$ pounds calf's liver, cut in 2-inch x $^1/_2$-inch slices

$^1/_2$ cup flour

2 bay leaves

$^1/_2$ cup red wine

3 tablespoons white wine vinegar

$^1/_2$ cup chicken stock

**1** In a medium skillet, heat the olive oil over medium heat until hot. Add the onions, season with salt and pepper, and cook, covered, stirring frequently, until the onions are soft, about 25 minutes. Lower the heat if the onions begin to brown.

**2** Place a strainer over a bowl and spoon in the onions. Let them drain for a few minutes. Set the onions aside and pour the drained oil back into the skillet.

**3** Sprinkle the liver slices with salt and pepper and lightly dust them with the flour.

**4** Heat the oil in the skillet and add the remaining 1 tablespoon olive oil, liver, and bay leaves. Cook, stirring occasionally, until the meat is lightly browned, 5 to 6 minutes. Add the wine and vinegar. Cook for 2 to 3 minutes; add the stock and return the onions. Cook for another 5 to 7 minutes. Serve.

**TOQUE TIP**

# The skinny on scaloppine

Thin veal cutlets, called *scaloppine* in Italian or scallops in English, are the most versatile veal cut. These thin pieces can be sautéed in just a few minutes. Like chicken cutlets, they are appropriate with dozens of pan sauces. They are outrageously expensive, but veal lovers seem willing to pay the price.

Ideally, scaloppine should be cut across the grain of the top round. Cut this way, the scallops won't buckle or bend in the pan, and the entire cutlet will brown. If the surface of the cutlet is smooth, it has been cut across the grain. A bumpy or irregular surface that looks like lines indicates that the cutlets have been cut improperly.

Veal scallops should be pounded thin, either by the butcher or by you. At home, you can place the scallops between two pieces of wax paper or plastic wrap and use a meat mallet or the bottom of a heavy pan to flatten them. Ideally, the cutlets should be about $^1/_4$-inch thick after pounding.

## Veal Scaloppine with Lemon and Wine

Serve the veal with sautéed spinach and Mashed Potatoes (see Chapter 14 for the recipe).

***Italian recipe name:*** *Picata di Vitello*

***Preparation time:*** *15 minutes*

***Cooking time:*** *15 minutes*

***Yield:*** *4 servings*

| | |
|---|---|
| *¹/₄ cup olive oil* | *1 lemon, thinly sliced* |
| *1¹/₂ pounds veal scallops, thinly pounded* | *2 tablespoons capers, drained* |
| *Salt and pepper to taste* | *1 cup white wine* |
| *¹/₂ cup flour* | *¹/₂ cup chicken stock* |
| *Juice of 1 lemon (about 3 tablespoons)* | *2 tablespoons chopped fresh parsley* |

**1** In a large skillet, heat the olive oil over medium heat. Season the veal scallops with salt and pepper and dredge them in the flour, shaking off any excess. When the oil is hot, add the veal scallops to the pan. Sauté them for 2 minutes or until they are golden brown; then flip them and brown the other side for another 2 minutes. Drain the oil and discard it.

**2** Add the lemon juice, lemon slices, and capers. Mix well and cook for 1 minute. Then add the wine. Cook for 2 to 3 minutes. Transfer the veal to a serving plate. Add the chicken stock to the skillet and cook for 2 minutes. Stir in the parsley and adjust the seasoning with salt and pepper, if necessary. Spoon the sauce over the veal.

## Veal with Marsala Sauce

The Marsala wine highlights the sweetness of the veal in this fast sauté. Serve with Sautéed Broccoli Rabe and Mashed Potatoes (see Chapter 14 for recipes).

***Italian recipe name:*** *Scaloppine al Marsala*

***Preparation time:*** *10 minutes*

***Cooking time:*** *10 minutes*

***Yield:*** *4 servings*

*(continued)*

$1^1/_2$ *pounds veal scallops, thinly pounded*

*Salt and pepper to taste*

$^1/_2$ *cup flour*

$^1/_4$ *cup olive oil*

*1 cup Marsala wine*

$^1/_2$ *cup chicken stock*

*1 tablespoon chopped fresh parsley*

**1** Season the veal scallops with salt and pepper and dredge them in the flour, shaking off any excess.

**2** In large skillet, heat the olive oil over medium heat. When it is hot, add the veal scallops. Sauté them for 2 minutes or until they are golden brown; then flip them and brown the other side for another 2 minutes. Drain and discard the oil.

**3** Stir in the Marsala and cook for 2 minutes. Add the chicken stock and parsley and flip the veal over again. Cook for another 1 to 2 minutes. Transfer the veal to serving plates. Reduce the sauce to the desired consistency and spoon it over the veal.

## Veal with Sage and Prosciutto

For this Roman dish, veal scallops are rolled with a slice of prosciutto and fresh sage, secured with a toothpick, and then cooked in a lemon and white wine sauce. The name "saltimbocca" translates as "jump into the mouth," something these tasty veal scallops will surely do.

**Italian recipe name:** *Saltimbocca alla Romana*

**Preparation time:** *25 minutes*

**Cooking time:** *10 minutes*

**Yield:** *5 servings*

**Special tool:** *Toothpicks*

$1^1/_2$ *pounds veal scallops, thinly pounded (15 scallops, each 2 to 3 inches in diameter)*

*Salt and pepper to taste*

$^1/_2$ *cup flour*

*8 thin slices prosciutto, cut to fit the scallops*

*15 sage leaves*

$^1/_4$ *cup olive oil*

$^1/_2$ *cup white wine*

*Juice of $^1/_2$ lemon (about $1^1/_2$ tablespoons)*

$^1/_2$ *cup chicken stock*

*1* Season the veal scallops with salt and pepper and dredge them in the flour, shaking off any excess.

*2* Place a piece of prosciutto and a sage leaf in the center of each piece of meat. Roll the scallops tightly and secure them with toothpicks.

*3* In a medium skillet, heat the olive oil over medium heat. When it is hot, add the scallops. Cook for 2 minutes. Then turn them over and cook for another 2 minutes. Drain and discard the oil.

*4* Pour the wine and lemon juice into the skillet and swirl to combine. Cook for 2 to 3 minutes, until the liquid reduces by half. Add the stock and cook for another 2 minutes. Using tongs, place three veal scallops on each plate. Reduce the sauce to the desired consistency (it should thicken slightly) and pour it over the veal.

## Braised Veal Shanks

This hearty winter dish starts with veal shanks, round pieces of meat about 2 inches thick with a large bone in the center. The shanks are braised for several hours to make them extremely tender. Serve the shanks and their sauce with Mashed Potatoes (see Chapter 14) or Saffron Risotto, Milan Style (see Chapter 8). Many Italians consider the marrow — the gelatinous material inside the bone — to be a delicacy. If you like, give each person a small cocktail fork or demitasse spoon so that they can pull out the cooked marrow when they have eaten all the meat off the bone.

**Italian recipe name:** *Osso Buco*

**Preparation time:** *20 minutes*

**Cooking time:** *2 hours, 25 minutes*

**Yield:** *4 servings*

*2 tablespoons chopped fresh rosemary, or 2 teaspoons dried rosemary*

*2 tablespoons chopped fresh sage, or 2 teaspoons dried sage*

*4 cloves garlic, peeled and chopped*

*Salt and pepper to taste*

*4 meaty veal shanks, each about 2 inches thick*

*1 cup flour*

*$^2$/$_3$ cup olive oil*

*1$^1$/$_2$ cups white wine, divided*

*2 medium onions, chopped*

*3 medium carrots, cut into 1-inch pieces*

*3 stalks celery, cut into 1-inch pieces*

*4 cups water or chicken stock*

*3 cups canned plum tomatoes, crushed*

*(continued)*

*1* Preheat oven to 350°.

*2* In a medium bowl, mix together the rosemary, sage, garlic, and salt and pepper.

*3* Cut 2 to 3 slits in the top of each veal shank and stuff them with the herb/garlic mixture.

*4* Season the shanks with salt and pepper and dredge them in flour. Shake off any excess.

*5* In a medium, ovenproof saucepan, heat the olive oil over high heat. Add the shanks, browning them well on all sides. Drain and discard any oil remaining in the saucepan. Then add 1 cup wine, stirring to dissolve any bits that have stuck to the bottom of the pan. Add the onions, carrots, and celery. Cover the pan and reduce the heat to medium. Cook, stirring occasionally, for 8 to 10 minutes, and then add the remaining $1/2$ cup wine. Boil the wine for 2 to 3 minutes. Then add the water and tomatoes. Stir well, bring to a simmer, cover, and then transfer to the oven. Cook for 2 hours, stirring occasionally, until the meat is fork tender. Adjust the seasoning with salt and pepper, if necessary, and serve.

# On the Lamb

Although lamb looks a bit like beef, it has a much more assertive flavor that works well with a variety of seasonings. Some people shy away from lamb because they think that it is too strong. Good lamb is flavorful and rich, but not off-putting.

If you have had a bad experience with lamb, there are two possible reasons:

✔ Lamb fat has a very potent flavor, so make sure to trim away all visible fat before cooking lamb.

✔ As lamb gets older and bigger, the flavor can get quite strong. After a sheep turns two, the meat is called mutton. In general, young lamb, slaughtered at around six months, has the sweetest, most delicate flavor.

To judge slaughter age at the market, look at the size. A leg of lamb that weighs 10 pounds invariably has come from a much older animal than a leg that weighs 6 pounds.

## Braised Lamb Shanks

The shin portion of the leg is cut into round pieces with meat around the edges and a portion of bone in the center. Like other shanks, lamb shanks will soften only after prolonged cooking. Juniper berries, which are sold in the spice aisle at many supermarkets, give the sauce a pleasant resinous flavor. Serve with Stewed Beans with Tomato, Sage, and Garlic or Lentil Stew (both in Chapter 14) or with Basic Polenta (see Chapter 9).

**Italian recipe name:** *Stinco d'Agnello*

**Preparation time:** *10 minutes (plus 1 to 2 hours for marination)*

**Cooking time:** *2 hours, 20 minutes*

**Yield:** *6 servings*

*6 small lamb shanks, about 12 ounces each*

*1/2 cup olive oil, divided*

*2 cloves garlic, peeled and crushed, divided*

*2 teaspoons chopped fresh rosemary, or 1 teaspoon dried rosemary, divided*

*1 teaspoon chopped fresh thyme, or 1/2 teaspoon dried thyme, divided*

*Salt and pepper to taste*

*1/2 cup flour*

*1 carrot, peeled and sliced into 1/4-inch pieces*

*2 stalks celery, cut into 1-inch pieces*

*1 red onion, cut into large chunks*

*5 juniper berries*

*1 3/4 cups white wine*

*1 cup tomato puree*

*2 cups beef or chicken stock, divided*

**1** A few hours before cooking the lamb, rub it with 1/4 cup olive oil, 1 clove garlic, 1 teaspoon rosemary, and 1/2 teaspoon thyme. Season with and salt and pepper. Cover and refrigerate for 1 to 2 hours.

**2** Preheat oven to 350°.

**3** In a large ovenproof pan, combine the remaining 1/4 cup olive oil, 1 clove garlic, 1 teaspoon rosemary, and 1/2 teaspoon thyme and heat over medium heat for about 1 minute. Coat the shanks with flour, shaking off the excess. Increase the heat to medium-high and brown the shanks on all sides. Transfer the shanks to a plate and set aside.

**4** Pour out the excess fat from the pan and add the carrot, celery, and onion. Sauté for 5 minutes, stirring often, and then return the shanks to the pan. Mix well. Add the juniper berries and add more salt and pepper if necessary. Stir in the wine, tomato puree, and 1 cup stock. Bring the mixture to a simmer, cover, and transfer to the oven.

**5** Bake for 2 hours, turning the shanks every 20 minutes so that they cook evenly. Add the remaining 1 cup stock as needed to keep the liquid halfway up the sides of the meat. The meat will be fork tender when done; if it is still tough, bake another 30 minutes.

## Lamb with Olives

In Italy, this dish is often served with Basic Polenta (see Chapter 9) and Sautéed Broccoli Rabe (see Chapter 14). The bitter greens contrast nicely with the sweet, salty lamb.

***Italian recipe name:*** *Agnello con le Olive*

***Preparation time:*** *10 minutes*

***Cooking time:*** *2 hours, 40 minutes*

***Yield:*** *4 servings*

| | |
|---|---|
| *¹/₃ cup olive oil* | *Salt and pepper to taste* |
| *6 cloves garlic, peeled and sliced* | *Juice of 1 lemon (about 3 tablespoons)* |
| *Pinch of hot red pepper flakes* | *1 cup white or red wine* |
| *2 sprigs fresh thyme, or 1 teaspoon dried thyme* | *2 cups canned plum tomatoes, chopped* |
| *2 pounds lamb shoulder, trimmed and cut into 2-inch cubes* | *2 cups water or broth* |
| | *1 cup pitted olives* |

*1* In a medium, oven-safe saucepan, combine the olive oil, garlic, red pepper flakes, and thyme. Sauté over medium heat, stirring, for 5 minutes.

*2* Season the lamb with salt and pepper and add it to the saucepan. Cook, stirring occasionally, for 10 to 15 minutes, until the lamb has released its juices.

*3* Add the lemon juice and wine and boil for 3 to 5 minutes. Add the tomatoes, cover the pan, and simmer for 1 hour, stirring occasionally. Then stir in the water and cook another hour at a gentle simmer. Add more liquid (water or broth) as needed to keep the stew moist during the last hour of cooking. Add the olives and cook for 15 minutes. Adjust the seasoning with salt and pepper and serve.

# Cooking Today's Leaner Pork

Few fresh products have changed as much over the past 50 years as pork. At one time, a single pig generated 50 or 60 pounds of lard when it was brought to market. Breeding and leaner feeds have really slimmed down pigs. Now the average pigs yields just 8 pounds of lard at slaughter. Talk about a diet that works!

No one really misses all that lard. But these leaner pigs are yielding remarkably leaner cuts of pork. In the old days, overcooking pork was hard to do. Internal fat was in abundant supply, and the fat kept basting the meat as it cooked.

Marketers try to convince us that pork is the "other white meat." They point out that pork has almost as little fat as chicken. What they won't tell you is that pork cooked the old-fashioned way will be dry and tough. These leaner cuts must be cooked differently.

Cooking pork with plenty of liquid is one way to keep it from drying out. But don't overcook pork. Many old-time recipes call for a final internal temperature of 180°. Pork cooked this way will be about as juicy as shoe leather.

## Roast Pork Loin

To keep pork loin, which is a relatively lean cut, from drying out in the oven, it is roasted in lots of olive oil. When the roast is almost done, the oil is discarded. Given the large quantity of oil used in this recipe, you may want to economize by using pure olive oil.

To turn this into a complete meal, add several quartered potatoes to the roasting pan about 45 minutes before the roast is done. The potatoes will cook in the fat in the pan and become especially delicious.

**_Italian recipe name:_** _Arista alla Toscana_

**_Preparation time:_** _25 minutes_

**_Cooking time:_** _2 hours_

**_Yield:_** _6 servings_

_6 cloves garlic, peeled_

_3 sprigs fresh rosemary, or 2 teaspoons dried rosemary_

_1 tablespoon salt_

_$^1/_2$ tablespoon pepper_

_4 pounds pork loin (with bone)_

_$1^1/_2$ cups olive oil_

_1 cup white wine_

_**1**_ Preheat oven to 400°.

_**2**_ On a cutting board, chop together the garlic, rosemary, and salt and pepper. Mix well.

_**3**_ With a sharp knife, make narrow slits 2 inches deep in the meat. Stuff the slits with the garlic mixture. Massage any leftover garlic mixture into the meat. Place the pork loin in a roasting pan. Pour the olive oil over it and roast, uncovered, for 20 minutes.

_(continued)_

*4* Turn the roast and lower the oven temperature to 325°. Roast another 40 minutes. Add the wine. Cook for another hour, turning at 20 minute intervals. Drain and discard the oil. Let the meat rest for 5 minutes before carving.

## Sautéed Pork Chops with Tomatoes and Olives

Chops come from several places on the pig. Center loin and center rib chops are meatier and not as chewy as sirloin and blade chops (see photo in color section).

***Italian recipe name:*** *Bistecchine di Maiale in Padella*

***Preparation time:*** *10 minutes*

***Cooking time:*** *35 minutes*

***Yield:*** *4 servings*

*4 pork chops, about 8 ounces each*

*Salt and pepper to taste*

*¹/₄ cup olive oil*

*5 cloves garlic, peeled and crushed*

*2 sprigs fresh rosemary, or 1 teaspoon dried rosemary*

*¹/₂ cup white wine*

*1¹/₂ cups chopped plum tomatoes (fresh or canned)*

*¹/₂ cup pitted black olives*

*1* Season the pork chops with salt and pepper.

*2* In a large, nonstick skillet, heat the olive oil over medium heat. Add the pork chops, garlic, and rosemary. Gently shake the skillet to distribute the oil under and around the pork and then cook for 5 to 6 minutes without turning. Turn the chops over and cook the other side for 5 more minutes. Drain and discard any fat from the skillet.

*3* Add the wine, allow it to boil for about 5 minutes, and then transfer the pork chops from the skillet to a large plate.

*4* Add the tomatoes to the skillet, season with salt and pepper, and simmer for 10 minutes. Return the pork chops to the skillet and add the olives. Cook, covered, for another 5 minutes. Place a pork chop on each plate and top with the tomato/olive sauce.

## Sausage and Beans

This recipe is a good example of the Italian cook's ability to stretch a modest amount of meat to feed an entire family (see photo in color section). Here, the sausage is cooked with beans and acts more as a flavoring than the focal point of this dish. Serve this stew with good bread to soak up every drop and stretch the meat even further.

***Italian recipe name:*** *Salsiccie e Fagioli*

***Preparation time:*** *20 minutes*

***Cooking time:*** *35 to 45 minutes*

***Yield:*** *6 servings*

3 tablespoons olive oil

1¹/₂ pounds hot Italian sausage, cut into 2-inch pieces

8 cloves garlic, peeled

2 sprigs fresh sage

¹/₃ cup white wine

1 cup peeled and chopped tomatoes

5 cups cooked cannellini beans (see the sidebar in Chapter 14 for the recipe)

Salt and pepper to taste

***1*** In a large skillet, heat the olive oil over medium-high heat. Add the sausage, garlic, and sage and cook, turning occasionally so that the sausages brown evenly. Lower the heat to medium-low and continue cooking, loosely covered, until the sausages are cooked through, about 10 minutes. Drain and discard the fat from the skillet.

***2*** Add the wine and let it boil until it completely disappears, about 3 minutes. Add the tomatoes and the beans and season with salt and pepper. Simmer for 10 to 15 minutes, adding a touch of water, if necessary, to keep the mixture moist.

# Chapter 13
# Seafood, Italian Style

## In This Chapter

▶ Buying and handling fresh fish

▶ Grilling fish successfully

▶ Buying and cooking shrimp

▶ Preparing crabs and scallops

*W*hen cooking fish and shellfish, it is imperative to keep it simple. Unlike meat or even chicken, fish is so delicate that it is easily overwhelmed by complex sauces and marinades. That's not to say that some kinds of fish don't take well to aggressive seasonings, such as olives, capers, and tomatoes. Most fish just seems to taste best in relatively simple preparations.

Italians understand that fish responds best to simplicity. That's why Italian seafood recipes are so straightforward. In this chapter, we take you to the fish counter and explain how to choose the freshest specimens. We also explain how to make Italian seafood dishes at home. And we answer the burning question, "How do I know when my fish is done?"

## Fish 101

In some respects, buying fish is harder than cooking it. Great fish responds beautifully to simple cooking styles and sauces. Fish that is not perfectly fresh will always taste second rate, no matter how well it is seasoned or cooked.

So how do you know whether the fish you are buying is fresh? First and foremost, buy all seafood from a reputable store. That truck along the side of the road may have great fish, but has it been inspected by the health authorities? Will that truck be there tomorrow if the fish you buy today needs to be returned?

Keep these recommendations in mind when shopping for fish:

- **Insist on smelling any fish before you buy it.** If it smells fishy, buy something else. Good seafood should smell like the sea, briny and pleasant. If the odor is harsh or strong, the fish is not fresh.

- **Carefully inspect all fish.** If the flesh is marred or mushy, the fish is past its prime. Look for unblemished fish that looks plump and moist. You should see no signs of dryness.

- **Look at how the fish has been presented.** Stores that care about freshness will keep unwrapped fish on ice (not buried in the ice). Wrapped fish should be in a refrigerated case set at 32°.

- **Buy fish cut to order when possible.** Although the days of the old-fashioned fishmonger who would slice a tuna steak to order are fading, some shops still will cut steaks to your specifications or fillet a whole fish while you wait. This is ideal because whole fish keep better than precut fish. Getting fish cut to order also allows you to ask for the size and thickness you want.

- **Don't rule out frozen fish.** Modern technology allows fishermen to gut and flash-freeze fish at sea. If you live along the coast, you should be able to get good fresh fish. But in the many interior regions, "fresh" fish shows up in markets tired and old. Fish that is frozen at sea may, in fact, taste better than the so-called fresh fish, which was caught a week ago. When buying frozen fish, make sure that it is rock hard. At home, defrost frozen fish in the refrigerator, not on the counter.

- **Be prepared to shift gears at the market.** If you had your heart set on flounder but it looks awful, buy something else. Another thin, white fillet, such as sole, will work equally well. You can even use red snapper or sea bass. These fillets are thicker, so you may need to adjust the cooking times, but they are similar enough to flounder in terms of flavor and texture to work in most recipes. Note, though, that not all fish can be substituted for one another. Tuna or salmon are rarely well suited to a recipe designed for flounder. If you decide to buy tuna instead of flounder, be prepared to start over with a new recipe after you get home.

At home, fish needs to be handled with care. Keep fish in the coldest part of your refrigerator. To maintain optimum freshness, set wrapped fish over a bowl of ice or sandwich the wrapped fish between two ice packs. Really fresh fish that was caught yesterday will probably stay fresh on ice for several days in your refrigerator. However, you must assume that the fish you bought at the market today was caught several days ago. In that case, it must be cooked as soon as possible, preferably within hours of its purchase.

TOQUE TIP

## When is it done?

Telling when fish is done requires some practice. Some chefs cook fish by the inch, figuring that a steak or fillet will require 10 minutes of cooking time for each inch of thickness. As a broad guideline, we find that this method works. However, you still need to check the fish often and realize that an inch-thick piece of tuna may really be done in 8 minutes, while a ½-inch piece of sole may need closer to 10 minutes (not 5) in a hot oven to cook through.

The best way to judge when fish is done is to open a small hole in the thickest part of the fish with a thin-bladed knife and examine the flesh. When cooked, the fish should flake. Also, look at the color of the fish. Raw fish is translucent, and cooked fish is opaque. Because residual heat will continue to cook the fish slightly as you get it onto plates, it's best to pull fish off the heat when just a trace of translucence remains in the center.

## On the light side

Fish can be cooked in numerous ways. Because it is so low in fat and calories, many cooks like to choose cooking methods that don't add a lot of fat. Steaming or poaching (cooking in simmering water or broth) are two options.

### Fish in a Bag

You don't need to get the steamer out to steam fish. In this recipe, the fish and vegetables are wrapped in a foil pouch and steamed in the oven. The fish cooks in its own juices, sealing in flavor. Open the pouch at the table to let everyone enjoy the aroma. Or, divide the vegetables and fish among 4 individual foil packets and let each person open a pouch at the table.

*Italian recipe name:* Pesce al Cartoccio

*Preparation time:* 20 minutes

*Cooking time:* 15 minutes (plus 10 minutes waiting time)

*Yield:* 4 servings

*Special tool:* Aluminum foil

*(continued)*

2 small carrots, thinly sliced

1 yellow bell pepper, seeded and julienned

1 red bell pepper, seeded and julienned

$^1/_2$ small jalapeño chile, seeded and chopped

3 medium tomatoes, each cut into 8 wedges

2 small onions, thinly sliced

2 zucchini, cut into $^1/_2$-inch x 2-inch sticks

4 sprigs fresh thyme, or 1 teaspoon dried thyme

4 sprigs fresh parsley, or 1 teaspoon dried parsley

8 leaves fresh basil, or 1 teaspoon dried basil

$^1/_3$ cup white wine

Salt and pepper to taste

4 salmon fillets (8 ounces each)

Olive oil (optional)

**1** Preheat oven to 375°.

**2** In a large bowl, mix together all ingredients except the salmon and olive oil. Season the salmon with salt and set aside.

**3** Evenly line the bottom of an 11 x 19-inch baking pan with a sheet of aluminum foil large enough to fold over the sides of the pan. Place half the vegetable/marinade mixture on top of the foil and then lay the salmon fillets on top. Sprinkle with salt and pepper and place the remaining vegetables on top of the salmon. Cover the pan with another large sheet of foil, tightly crimping it over the pan edges to form a seal.

**4** Place the pan in the oven and bake for 10 to 15 minutes or until fish is opaque and vegetables are crisp-tender. Remove from oven and let stand 5 to 10 minutes. Open the foil wrap and transfer the vegetables and fish to individual plates. If desired, sprinkle with a good quality olive oil before serving.

## Red Snapper with Vegetables

In this recipe, red snapper fillets are cooked in a simmering broth and then served with a refreshing combination of diced raw vegetables and herbs (see photo in color section).

If you can't find red snapper at the market, try this recipe with sea bass. This dish can be served hot, warm, or at room temperature.

***Italian recipe name:*** *Dentice Primavera*

***Preparation time:*** *20 minutes*

***Cooking time:*** *8 to 10 minutes*

***Yield:*** *4 servings*

*2 medium ripe tomatoes, diced*

*3 celery stalks, diced*

*1 carrot, diced*

*1 medium onion, peeled and diced*

*1 zucchini, diced*

*5 fresh basil leaves, chopped, or
1 teaspoon dried basil*

*2 tablespoons chopped fresh parsley, or
1 teaspoon dried parsley*

*2 tablespoons olive oil*

*4 tablespoons red wine vinegar*

*Juice of 1 lemon (about 3 tablespoons)*

*Salt and pepper to taste*

*4 cups fish stock (see sidebar in
Chapter 5) or water*

*4 fillets red snapper (8 ounces each),
skin on and deboned*

*1* In a large bowl, combine the tomatoes, celery, carrot, onion, zucchini, basil, parsley, olive oil, red wine vinegar, and lemon juice. Season with salt and pepper and stir to combine. Set aside.

*2* In a large skillet, bring the fish stock to a boil. Lower the heat so that it gently simmers. Arrange the snapper in the skillet in a single layer and simmer, partially covered, for 8 to 10 minutes.

*3* Using a spatula, lift the snapper fillets out and place them on dinner plates. Top each fillet with a large spoonful of the vegetable mixture.

## Fish in Vegetable Broth

The Italian name for this dish translates literally as "fish in crazy water." No, the water is not ready for the insane asylum. The term crazy means that no real recipe exists here. Italian chefs add whatever vegetables and seasonings they have on hand. Herbs, white wine, garlic, tomatoes, and asparagus are used here, but let your imagination go . . . crazy.

***Italian recipe name:*** *Pesce in Acqua Pazza*

***Preparation time:*** *15 minutes*

***Cooking time:*** *35 minutes*

***Yield:*** *4 servings*

*(continued)*

1 onion, peeled and cut into 8 wedges

6 cloves garlic, peeled and sliced

2 whole sprigs (about 20 leaves) fresh basil, or 1 teaspoon dried basil

2 sprigs parsley, or 1 teaspoon dried parsley

1 cup white wine

¹/₄ cup white wine vinegar

¹/₄ cup water

2 medium tomatoes, quartered

Salt and pepper to taste

4 fish fillets (red snapper, sea bass, or salmon), 8 ounces each

6 asparagus spears, ends trimmed

2 tablespoons olive oil (optional)

**1** Combine all the ingredients except the fish, asparagus, and olive oil in a large skillet. Bring the mixture to a boil, and then reduce the heat and simmer, covered, for 15 minutes.

**2** Season the fillets with salt and pepper and add them to the simmering broth. Add the asparagus. Cook until the fish easily flakes, 10 to 15 minutes, depending on the thickness of the fillets. Adjust the seasoning with salt and pepper to taste. Serve the fish and vegetables with a little of the broth. Drizzle each serving with a little olive oil if desired.

# Fish in the pan

Fish responds beautifully to cooking in oil or butter. The exterior becomes crisp, while the interior remains tender and moist. The fat used to cook the fish also becomes the basis for a quick pan sauce.

## Fish with Asparagus

Flouring the fillets helps keep them from falling apart as they cook. The flour also helps to thicken the sauce.

**Italian recipe name:** *Pesce con gli Asparagi*

**Preparation time:** *20 minutes*

**Cooking time:** *20 to 25 minutes*

**Yield:** *4 servings*

*5 tablespoons white wine vinegar, divided*

*24 asparagus spears, ends trimmed and discarded*

*4 fish fillets (such as snapper, Chilean bass, or salmon), 8 ounces each*

*Salt and pepper to taste*

*$^1/_4$ cup flour*

*$^1/_4$ cup olive oil*

*4 cloves garlic, peeled and chopped*

*2 sprigs fresh thyme, or 1 teaspoon dried thyme*

*$^3/_4$ cup white wine*

*1 cup chopped tomatoes, fresh or canned*

*2 tablespoons chopped fresh parsley, or 2 teaspoons dried parsley*

**1** In a medium saucepan, bring 2 quarts salted water to a boil. Add 4 tablespoons vinegar. Cut the tips off of the asparagus and slice the spears into $^3/_4$-inch pieces. Blanch the asparagus for 3 minutes in the water-vinegar mixture. Drain and set aside.

**2** Season the fish with salt and pepper.

**3** Spread the flour out on a large plate and coat each fillet with flour, shaking off any excess.

**4** Place the olive oil and garlic in a large skillet and cook over medium heat for 2 minutes. Place the fish fillets and thyme in the pan and cook for 3 minutes. Then turn the fish over and cook for another 3 minutes.

**5** Pour any excess oil out of the skillet and then add the remaining 1 tablespoon vinegar. Cook for 30 seconds. Add the wine and let it reduce for 2 to 3 minutes. Add the tomatoes and season with salt and pepper. Cook over low-medium heat, partially covered, for 6 to 8 minutes. Add the asparagus and parsley during the last 4 minutes of cooking.

**6** Using a spatula, lift the snapper fillets out of the pan and place them on dinner plates. Top each fillet with a large spoonful of the asparagus and tomato sauce.

## Halibut with Peas and Scallions

This simple spring recipe is a meal-in-one, with peas and halibut cooking together (see photo in color section). Not only is this efficient, but the fish and peas flavor each other for a delicious result.

***Italian recipe name:*** *Halibut con Piselli e Cipolline*

***Preparation time:*** *15 minutes*

***Cooking time:*** *25 minutes*

***Yield:*** *4 servings*

*(continued)*

4 halibut fillets (8 ounces each)

Salt and pepper to taste

$^1/_4$ cup olive oil

10 scallions, cut into 1-inch pieces

2 sprigs fresh thyme, chopped, or
1 teaspoon dried thyme

1 cup white wine

1 pound fresh peas (removed from
pods), or 1 pound frozen peas

2 medium tomatoes, skin and seeds
removed, chopped

$^1/_4$ cup chopped fresh basil

**1** Season the halibut with salt and pepper.

**2** Heat the olive oil in a large skillet. Place the halibut and the scallions in the skillet and
cook over medium heat for 3 minutes. Turn the fish, add the thyme, and cook for
another 3 minutes.

**3** Pour any excess oil from the skillet and add the wine and the peas. Cook for 5 minutes,
shaking the skillet occasionally. Transfer the halibuts to plates or a serving platter and
cover to keep warm. Add the tomatoes, season with salt and pepper, and continue
cooking, partially covered, for 10 minutes. Add the basil 2 minutes before serving. If
the skillet looks dry, add 2 tablespoons water.

## Grouper, Livorno Style

For this recipe, the fish is cooked right in a tomato sauce. The fish and tomato sauce
are especially good served over some plain polenta. If you can't find grouper, use sea
bass or cod.

**Italian recipe name:** Cernia alla Livornese

**Preparation time:** 15 minutes

**Cooking time:** 40 to 45 minutes

**Yield:** 4 servings

$^1/_4$ cup olive oil

1 small red onion, peeled and thinly sliced

4 cloves garlic, peeled and chopped

$^1/_4$ teaspoon hot red pepper flakes

1 cup white wine

2 cups crushed canned tomatoes

2 cups fish stock (see sidebar in Chapter
5) or water

$^1/_3$ cup pitted black olives

$^1/_4$ cup capers, drained

3 tablespoons chopped fresh parsley, or
2 teaspoons dried parsley

4 grouper fillets (6 ounces each)

Salt and pepper to taste

*1* Combine the olive oil, onion, garlic, and red pepper flakes in a large skillet. Cook over medium heat, stirring occasionally, until the onion and garlic begin to brown, about 5 minutes.

*2* Add the wine to the skillet, let it reduce for about 3 minutes, and then add the tomatoes, fish stock, olives, capers, and parsley. Simmer the sauce, stirring occasionally, until it's rich and thick, about 25 to 30 minutes.

*3* Season the grouper fillets with salt and pepper and add them to the skillet. Cook, covered, until the grouper easily flakes when probed with a knife, 8 to 10 minutes. Serve the fish topped with the tomato sauce.

## Salmon with Fresh Tomato Sauce

Plum tomatoes are used in this recipe to make a quick pan sauce for seared salmon.

*Italian recipe name:* Salmone con Pomodoro Fresco

*Preparation time:* 15 minutes

*Cooking time:* 20 minutes

*Yield:* 4 servings

| | |
|---|---|
| *3 tablespoons olive oil* | *4 salmon fillets (8 ounces each)* |
| *1 medium onion, peeled and quartered* | *Salt and pepper to taste* |
| *4 cloves garlic, peeled and crushed* | *1 cup white wine* |
| *1 sprig fresh thyme, or 1 teaspoon dried thyme* | *4 medium tomatoes, cut into 1-inch cubes* |
| *2 sprigs fresh parsley, or 1 teaspoon dried parsley* | *8 basil leaves, chopped, or 2 teaspoons dried basil* |

*1* Heat the olive oil in a large skillet over medium heat. Add the onion, garlic, thyme, and parsley. Sauté for 2 minutes. Drain and discard the oil.

*2* Season the salmon with salt and pepper. Add it to the skillet and cook over medium-high heat for 3 to 4 minutes. Then turn the fillets over and cook for 3 minutes.

*3* Add the wine, tomatoes, and basil to the skillet and season with salt and pepper. Cook, covered, over low-medium heat for 8 minutes. Serve each salmon fillet topped with a generous spoonful of tomato sauce.

## Swordfish with Tomatoes and Oregano

This flavorful, quick dish comes from the island of Sardinia (see photo in color section). It is refreshing and light —perfect for summer.

**Italian recipe name:** *Pesce Spada all'Isolana*

**Preparation time:** *10 minutes*

**Cooking time:** *20 minutes*

**Yield:** *4 servings*

*4 swordfish steaks (8 ounces each)*

*Salt and pepper to taste*

*¹/₄ cup olive oil*

*5 cloves garlic, peeled and crushed*

*Juice of ¹/₂ lemon (about 1¹/₂ tablespoons)*

*1 cup white wine*

*1¹/₂ pounds cherry tomatoes, cut in half*

*2 teaspoons dried oregano*

*1 cup pitted black olives*

**1** Preheat oven to 375°.

**2** Season the swordfish with salt and pepper.

**3** Heat the olive oil in a large, oven-safe skillet over medium heat. Add the garlic and the swordfish steaks and cook for 3 to 5 minutes, or until lightly browned. Turn the steaks over and cook for another 3 minutes. Drain and discard the oil.

**4** Add the lemon juice and wine to the skillet and let it reduce by half. Gently stir in the tomatoes, oregano, and olives. Simmer for 2 minutes on the stovetop and then transfer the skillet to the oven. Bake for 6 to 8 minutes. Place the swordfish steaks on individual plates and top each with a generous spoonful of the sauce.

## Sea Bass with Mushrooms

In Italy, this recipe is usually made with fresh porcini mushrooms. Shiitake mushrooms are more readily available in other places and have a similar meaty texture. Sea bass has a fairly strong flavor that matches up well with shiitake mushrooms. The stems on shiitake mushrooms are tough and cook up rubbery. Just use the caps in this and other recipes.

**Italian recipe name:** *Branzino con Funghi*

**Preparation time:** *20 minutes*

**Cooking time:** *45 to 50 minutes*

**Yield:** *4 servings*

*¹/₄ cup olive oil, divided*

*3 cloves garlic, peeled and minced*

*1 teaspoon chopped fresh oregano, or ¹/₂ teaspoon dried oregano*

*2 teaspoons chopped fresh parsley, or 1 teaspoon dried parsley*

*4 cups sliced shiitake mushrooms*

*1 cup white wine, divided*

*Salt and pepper to taste*

*1 cup chopped canned tomatoes*

*4 sea bass fillets (7 ounces each)*

*Juice of 1 lemon (about 3 tablespoons)*

**1** Heat 2 tablespoons olive oil and the garlic in a medium skillet over medium heat. Sauté until the garlic just begins to brown, 1 to 2 minutes.

**2** Add the oregano and parsley and cook for 20 to 30 seconds, stirring. Then add the mushrooms. Sauté the mushrooms over medium-high heat, tossing or stirring occasionally, for 3 to 4 minutes. Add ¹/₂ cup wine, season with salt and pepper, and cook for 2 to 3 minutes. Stir in the tomatoes and cook, covered, for 15 minutes. Add 1 to 2 tablespoons water, if necessary, to keep the mixture moist.

**3** Season the fish with salt and pepper.

**4** In a large skillet, heat the remaining olive oil over medium heat. When it is hot, add the fish. Cook for 3 minutes. Then turn the fillets over and cook for another 3 minutes. Drain any excess oil from the skillet and add the lemon juice and remaining ¹/₂ cup wine. Shake the skillet to incorporate the liquid and simmer for 2 minutes.

**5** Add the sauce to the skillet and simmer, covered, for 3 to 5 minutes. Serve the fish topped with the sauce.

# *The Basics of Shellfish*

Shellfish requires some slightly different buying and cooking procedures than fish. Clams, oysters, and mussels are usually purchased alive in the shell. If these bivalves are in good shape, you should have trouble prying apart their shells. They usually respond to a light tapping by closing their shells.

TOQUE TIP

---

# How to grill fish

Most Italian homes don't have an outdoor grill, so fish has traditionally been prepared inside. Cooking fish in a pan also allows the cook to make a sauce for the fish. However, grilling fish is appealing. If you hate the smell of fish and don't have very good ventilation in your kitchen, then grilling is definitely the way to go.

Although grilling is fairly easy, many novice cooks have trouble with fish on the grill. Nothing is worse than spending $20 on tuna steaks and then having them stick to the grill. So how do you prevent this kind of culinary disaster?

Start with the right kind of fish. Really thin, tender fillets, such as sole or flounder, are not meant for the grill. Their flesh is not firm enough to withstand the rigors of grilling. Thick, firm steaks are best for the grill. Fillets can work if they still have skin on one side.

Cook the fish, skin-side-down, for several minutes before turning them.

Fish responds best to a hot — but not blazing hot — fire. You should be able to hold your hand several inches above the grill for several seconds. After the grill is hot, scrape the grate clean with a wire brush. It's a good idea to lightly brush the fish with a little olive oil right before it goes onto the grill. Don't go overboard, or you can cause flare-ups. However, a light coating of oil will keep the flesh from sticking.

When grilling fish, keep the flavors and sauces fairly simple. A brush of olive oil and a squirt of lemon juice is enough for really good fish. You can add simple sauces (some diced raw tomatoes flavored with herbs works well with most fish), but don't go overboard.

---

WARNING!

Mollusks need to breathe, so don't store them (or buy them) in a closed plastic bag. Refrigerate mollusks in a bowl covered with a damp cloth until you are ready to use them.

Mussels may have small weedy protrusions, called "beards," which need to be removed. See Figure 13-1 for an illustration of the technique for removing the beards.

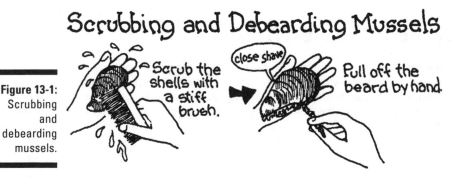

**Figure 13-1:** Scrubbing and debearding mussels.

## Tuscan Fish Stew

Almost every region in Italy makes a hearty fish stew. The version in this recipe comes from Tuscany and contains mussels and clams, as well as shrimp, squid, and fish. Make sure to buy squid that has already been cleaned. Doing this yourself is messy and very time consuming, and cleaned squid is very inexpensive. Fish stock gives this stew an especially rich flavor, but you can use water instead.

**Italian recipe name:** Cacciucco

**Preparation time:** 20 minutes

**Cooking time:** 50 to 55 minutes

**Yield:** 6 servings

*1 tablespoon chopped fresh rosemary, or 1 teaspoon dried rosemary*

*1 teaspoon chopped fresh sage, or 1 teaspoon dried sage*

*1 teaspoon hot red pepper flakes*

*1 medium red onion, peeled and chopped*

*8 cloves garlic, peeled and crushed*

*¹/₄ cup olive oil*

*¹/₂ cup white wine*

*8 squid, cleaned and cut into 4 pieces each*

*2 dozen mussels, scrubbed and debearded*

*2 dozen clams (place in a bowl under cold running water for 5 minutes to remove any sand)*

*1 pound plum tomatoes (fresh or canned), pureed*

*3 cups fish stock (see sidebar in Chapter 5) or water*

*6 large shrimp, peeled and deveined*

*1 pound boneless fish (any mixture of monkfish, salmon, tuna, grouper, or halibut)*

*Salt and pepper to taste*

*4 slices Tuscan or Italian bread, toasted and rubbed with a clove of garlic*

*1* In a large soup pot, sauté the rosemary, sage, red pepper flakes, onion, and garlic in olive oil over medium heat. When the onion becomes soft, after about 5 minutes, add the wine and cover the pot. Cook until the wine is completely reduced, 5 to 7 minutes.

*2* Add the squid and cook, stirring occasionally, for 10 minutes. Add the mussels and clams and cook, stirring occasionally, for 8 minutes. Add the tomatoes and water or fish stock and simmer for 15 minutes, stirring occasionally. Add the shrimp, fish, and salt and pepper to taste and simmer for 8 minutes. Adjust the seasoning with salt and pepper, if necessary. Discard any clams or mussels that don't open. When you are ready to serve, spoon the stew into soup bowls and top with the toasted bread.

# Shrimp

The vast majority of shrimp in the marketplace has been frozen and then thawed at the store. If you like, buy frozen shrimp (it's pretty high-quality) and defrost it yourself. Or buy shrimp that has been thawed by the fishmonger. Just be suspicious of any store that claims to sell "fresh" shrimp.

Thousands of species of shrimp exist. For the cook, the most important difference is size. Larger shrimp are quicker and easier to clean, but they are expensive. Really tiny shrimp are cheaper but can be difficult to clean. They also are easy to overcook. That's why medium shrimp (about 20 per pound) are your best bet for value and ease of cleaning.

Buying shrimp that have been peeled and deveined may seem appealing, but they usually are not as firm and sweet-tasting as shrimp that you peel yourself. You can leave the shells on during cooking. Shrimp are often served in their shells in Italian restaurants. However, many Americans balk at removing shrimp shells at the table.

For this reason, you may want to peel shrimp before cooking them. You can also devein the shrimp at the same time. The black vein that runs down the back of the shrimp is edible, but most chefs remove it for aesthetic reasons, and so do we. A plastic deveiner makes quick work of the peel and vein. However, you can peel and devein shrimp by hand. Simply rub and pull the shell off by hand (rinsing the shrimp under cold running water as you do this); then use a paring knife to make a slit down the back of each shrimp; and then wash away the black vein.

## Shrimp with Beans

Shrimp and beans is a favorite combination in many parts of Italy. The type of bean used will vary from region to region. The use of a high-quality extra-virgin olive oil is important in this dish, which is served at room temperature and makes an excellent summer meal.

***Italian recipe name:*** *Sparnocchi e Fagioli*

***Preparation time:*** *10 minutes*

***Cooking time:*** *5 to 7 minutes (excluding cooking time for beans)*

***Yield:*** *4 to 6 servings*

2 pounds medium shrimp, peeled and deveined

3 cups cooked, drained cannellini beans (see the sidebar in Chapter 14 for the recipe) or thoroughly rinsed canned beans

3 tablespoons red wine vinegar

$^1/_2$ cup olive oil

2 medium tomatoes, diced

8 fresh basil leaves, coarsely chopped, or 1 teaspoon dried basil

Salt and pepper to taste

**1** In a medium saucepan, bring 3 quarts lightly salted water to a boil. Add the shrimp and simmer until they are just pink and firm, 2 to 3 minutes. Drain.

**2** In a large bowl, mix together all the remaining ingredients. Add the shrimp to the bowl and toss or stir to combine. Serve hot or at room temperature.

# Soft-shell crabs

Springtime means soft-shell crabs. Starting in May and continuing through the summer, Atlantic blue crabs molt and shed their tough outer shells. Before a larger shell can grow back, the crab is tender and completely edible. It is at this precise moment that the crab is removed from the water and shipped to market.

Soft-shell crabs must be alive at the fish market. Because they will stay alive out of water for just a couple of days, soft-shell crabs are often cleaned and frozen. Defrost these crabs in the refrigerator at home and use them as you would cleaned fresh crabs.

Cleaning soft-shell crabs is not for the squeamish (see Figure 13-2). You need to snip off the eyes and mouth, remove the gills just under the top shell on either side of the crab, and pull off the little flap, called the *apron,* at the back of the crab.

**Figure 13-2:** Cleaning soft-shell crabs.

## Grilled Soft-Shell Crabs with Salad

Soft-shell crabs are a favorite in Venice. In this recipe, they are either grilled or roasted and served over salad greens for a light summer meal (see photo in color section).

**Italian recipe name:** *Granchi Teneri alla Griglia con Insalata*

**Preparation time:** *20 minutes (plus 3 hours marination)*

**Cooking time:** *10 minutes*

**Yield:** *4 servings*

**Special tool:** *Plastic wrap*

*$^1/_2$ cup olive oil, divided*

*$^1/_2$ cup white wine*

*1 tablespoon salt*

*8 soft-shell crabs*

*4 garlic cloves, peeled and sliced*

*3 sprigs rosemary, leaves stripped off branches, or 2 teaspoons dried rosemary*

*2 tablespoons red wine vinegar*

*1 tablespoon capers, drained*

*Salt and pepper to taste*

*1 head of radicchio, thinly sliced*

*4 leaves Romaine lettuce, thinly sliced*

*2 scallions, trimmed and sliced*

*$^1/_2$ yellow bell pepper, seeded and sliced into matchstick-sized slices*

*1* In a small bowl, mix $^1/_4$ cup olive oil, wine, and salt. Place the crabs in a shallow baking dish. Spoon the marinade over the crabs and sprinkle them with the garlic and rosemary. Cover the dish with plastic wrap and refrigerate for 3 hours.

*2* When you are ready to cook the crabs, remove the plastic wrap and preheat the grill or the oven to 450°. If grilling, remove the crabs from the marinade and grill for 3 to 4 minutes per side. If roasting, drain the marinade, place the crabs in a baking dish, and cook in the oven for 8 to 10 minutes (if large crabs) or 5 minutes (if small crabs), or until the meat is white when the crabs are cut open.

*3* In a large bowl, mix the remaining $^1/_4$ cup olive oil, vinegar, capers, and salt and pepper. Add the radicchio, romaine, scallions, and yellow pepper and toss to coat evenly. Arrange the greens in neat mounds on individual plates. Top each salad with 2 crabs and serve.

# Scallops

Like oysters, clams, and mussels, scallops are bivalves. However, scallops are shucked at sea and just the meaty white muscle makes it to market. Scallops come in several varieties. Sea scallops are large and plump. In most markets, they are the best choice.

Tiny bay scallops are an especially delicious variety, but they have become increasingly hard to find. They come from the waters off Nantucket and Long Island and are the width of a wine cork and about half as long. If you can find bay scallops, buy them. They are a rare treat.

Many calico scallops (an inferior species from warmer waters) are labeled bay scallops in the market. If the price is less than $12 a pound, you are not buying bay scallops, no matter what the sign says. Calicos are often sold for as little as $4 or $5 a pound. They are usually smaller than bay scallops and tend to overcook and become tough. Their flavor is also second-rate.

Most scallops have a small tendon on the side. It usually is a slightly different shade of white than the rest of the scallop. This tendon can trap some sand and will cook up a bit tough. With your fingers, peel this tendon off and discard it before cooking the scallops.

## Scallops with Porcini Mushrooms

Fresh porcini mushrooms are a delicious component in the following recipe. Unfortunately, they are hard to find. Luckily, cremini mushrooms are readily available and a perfectly fine substitute in this recipe. If you can find bay scallops, use them whole.

**Italian recipe name:** *Cappesante con Funghi Porcini*

**Preparation time:** *15 minutes*

**Cooking time:** *15 minutes*

**Yield:** *6 servings*

*30 ounces sea scallops, tendons removed and scallops cut in half crosswise*

*3 cups fresh porcini mushrooms, sliced $1/4$-inch thick*

*4 cloves garlic, peeled and sliced*

*1 sprig fresh thyme, or 1 teaspoon dried thyme*

*2 tablespoons chopped fresh parsley, or 2 teaspoons dried parsley*

*2 tablespoons olive oil*

*Juice of 1 lemon (about 3 tablespoons)*

*$1/2$ cup white wine*

*Salt and pepper to taste*

*1* Preheat oven to 375°.

*2* Combine all ingredients in a baking dish. Place the dish in the oven and bake for 6 to 8 minutes. Drain the liquid from the scallops and return them to the oven for another 2 to 3 minutes; they should spring back when touched. If you want your mushrooms more tender, remove the scallops from the dish and continue cooking for 5 minutes. Serve warm with salad greens, such as arugula.

# Chapter 14

# Vegetable Side Dishes

## In This Chapter

▶ Defining the contorno

▶ Cooking Italian-style vegetables

▶ Creating your own contorni

▶ Soaking and simmering dried beans

*T*he vegetable course, which is usually served along with the main course, is called the contorno (con-**tour**-no). This word derives from the Italian word for "contour." The idea is that the vegetable course, by reminding you of the season, gives shape or definition to the meal. Asparagus is a sure sign of spring, just as eggplant signals the height of summer.

Many Italian contorni start with familiar vegetables like potatoes, spinach, or onions, but use cooking techniques or flavorings that may be new to you. Other contorni begin with what might be called Italian vegetables — broccoli rabe, fennel, artichokes, and the like.

This chapter shows you how to give old favorites a new and distinctly Italian twist. We also show you how to handle some vegetables that you may never have cooked before. Be flexible when planning the contorno and shop with your eyes open for something new or something especially fresh and appealing.

## Cooking Vegetables, Italian Style

Italian vegetable side dishes are usually quite simple to prepare. Ingredient lists are mercifully short, and the emphasis is on the vegetable itself. Although other cuisines may consider the flavor of the vegetable to be incidental (or something that must be hidden in some fashion), Italian cooking celebrates vegetables on their own terms.

In general, that means few cream or cheese sauces, which tend to drown out delicate vegetable flavors, are used in Italian vegetable dishes. Seasonings are used sparingly. In some cases, vegetables are seasoned with nothing more than olive oil and salt.

Note that restrained seasoning means that the vegetables themselves must taste good. A stick of butter can camouflage almost anything. However, if a recipe relies on just garlic, salt, and olive oil, the vegetable itself must taste like something. That means buying fresh vegetables. (Spinach and peas are the only frozen vegetables that Italians regularly use.) When we say fresh, we don't mean vegetables that were picked a week ago.

For the best results, you must be a picky shopper. If your supermarket produce aisle looks like a vegetable graveyard, then go to a farmers' market, a gourmet store, a produce shop, or anyplace where they care about the quality of the produce they sell.

## Al dente is for pasta

Blame trendy nouvelle French chefs, blame gung ho American chefs, blame somebody for the sorry state of vegetable cookery in most restaurants. We are tired of eating almost-raw carrots and asparagus that have more spring than a rubber ball. Vegetables are not meant to be cooked al dente.

Italians have always known that undercooking vegetables does them an injustice. If you want crisp vegetables, make some dip or put them in a salad. But please don't serve almost-raw vegetables with a steak.

If you're going to cook your vegetables (and you should if you're serving them as side dish with cooked meat, poultry, or fish), then really cook them. Italians aren't afraid to let green beans or broccoli get tender. This doesn't mean you should overcook your vegetables and make them soggy or limp. But don't be afraid to cook the vegetables until tender, when their texture will marry well with the other cooked elements on the plate.

## Flavoring is the key

We know of two general approaches to flavoring vegetables. The vegetables can be cooked and then flavored, or they may be flavored as they cook. Some vegetables are always prepared the first way, some are always prepared the second way, and some can be prepared either way.

Recipes that call for cooking and then flavoring vegetables usually start with steaming or boiling. The vegetables may be fully cooked and then drizzled with some vinaigrette, or partially cooked and sautéed, usually in some olive oil with garlic, herbs, hot red pepper flakes, onions, and so on. Cooking and then flavoring works well with many green vegetables, including broccoli, green beans, and asparagus. It's also appropriate with cauliflower and potatoes.

When vegetables are cooked in water, enhancing or changing their flavor is hard. The water should be salted, but steaming or boiling is mostly about changing the texture of the vegetable, not the flavor.

Recipes that call for simultaneous flavoring and cooking favor dry-heat cooking methods like sautéing, roasting, grilling, or broiling. In the absence of water, the vegetables will brown, a process that brings out their natural sugars and adds flavor. In Italy, vegetables are cooked in a flavorful fat, usually olive oil but sometimes butter. Often flavorful ingredients, such as pancetta, garlic, onions, and herbs, are added to the pan as well.

Simultaneous flavoring and cooking works well with vegetables that have natural sugars that can caramelize, such as onions or fennel, or with vegetables that tend to be watery, such as zucchini, eggplant, or mushrooms. The dry heat evaporates much of the moisture in these vegetables and helps concentrate their flavor.

The broccoli rabe and mashed potato recipes in this chapter are examples of cooking and then flavoring. The remaining recipes call for flavoring the vegetables as they cook.

## Serve as you like

You can serve most vegetable side dishes hot, but they're almost all good at room temperature. When trying to coordinate several dishes, this is a real blessing. Concentrate on getting the fish, meat, or chicken to the table hot. If the vegetable has cooled down a bit, that's fine.

# Favorite Italian Vegetables, A to Z

We could write a whole book about preparing vegetables in the Italian manner. (And several people have.) Unfortunately, we don't have enough space in this book to give a recipe for every vegetable that is commonly used in Italy.

We don't want you to feel cheated, so we put together this list of the most popular vegetables in Italy along with some information on how to ready them for cooking, as well as suggestions about cooking methods and flavorings. We also include some of our favorite vegetable recipes.

# Artichokes

This strange-looking vegetable takes a lot of effort in the kitchen, but the results are worth the wait. An artichoke is actually the flower bud of a Mediterranean thistle plant. Much of an artichoke is inedible. In fact, only the base of the leaves, the heart, and the interior part of the stem are fit for human consumption. You can boil or steam whole artichokes and then eat around the inedible parts. Pull off leaves and scrape them between your teeth to get the tender part in your mouth. This is how artichokes are usually served in France, with a vinaigrette or dipping sauce as an appetizer.

In Italy, artichokes are often cleaned and sliced before cooking. The tough, inedible parts are often removed before cooking. Basically, anything that is dark green must go, including the exterior of the stem, the outer layer of the leaves, the top half of the remaining leaves, and the furry choke in the center. The remaining artichoke heart can be sliced and then cooked until tender. Because an artichoke will turn brown when the flesh is exposed to air, make sure to rub all cut surfaces with a halved lemon as you work. Take the other half of the lemon and squeeze it into a bowl of cold water. Drop the cleaned artichoke pieces into the bowl while you take apart the next artichoke (see Figure 14-1).

After all the artichokes are in the bowl, drain them and cook. Cleaned, sliced artichokes are best braised — that is, cooked in olive oil and then simmered in liquid. Flavor the olive oil with onions and/or garlic and cook the artichokes in stock or chopped canned tomatoes.

# Asparagus

Asparagus are easy to prepare for cooking. Simply break off the tough ends and steam or boil the remaining part of the spears until tender. Drain the asparagus and season with some lemon vinaigrette or a drizzle of olive oil and some salt. You may also put boiled or steamed asparagus spears in a buttered dish, sprinkle them with grated Parmesan cheese, and then run them under the broiler just until the cheese melts.

## Cleaning Artichokes

**Figure 14-1:**
Cleaning artichokes.

Remove several layers of leaves by hand...

Cut off tips of remaining leaves with a knife.

Rub cut surfaces with half a lemon.

Peel the skin off the stem with a vegetable peeler.

Slice the artichoke into quarters and scoop out fuzzy choke with a spoon!

all clean, cook me!

In addition to boiling and steaming, asparagus can be coated with olive oil and sprinkled with salt and then roasted in a very hot oven or grilled. When the asparagus spears start to brown, they're done.

## Beets

Beets will stain everything in their path, so exercise some caution when working with them and don't wear nice clothes. Snip off all but the last inch of the stem, but leave the narrow root tip and rootlets in place. Boil the bulbs until a skewer glides easily through them. Depending on the size of the beets, this can take as long as 30 minutes. Drain the beets and when they're cool enough to handle, use a paper towel to rub the skins off, snap off the roots and cut off the stem. Slice the beets and drizzle with olive oil or a vinaigrette. Beets are quite sweet and are often served at room temperature.

## Broccoli

Like other green vegetables, broccoli is usually steamed or boiled. It can be drizzled with olive oil or vinaigrette or sautéed in garlicky olive oil after it has been cooked. You can trim away and discard the stalks, but thrifty Italian cooks often peel the stalks and then cut the broccoli into long spears.

## Broccoli rabe

This slightly bitter green (see Figure 14-2) looks like broccoli but tastes more like kale or collard greens. The tough, thick parts of the stalk should be snapped off and discarded. The thin stalk, leaves, and florets are the parts you want to cook. Broccoli rabe should be blanched and then sautéed in oil.

**Figure 14-2:**
Broccoli
rabe.

## Sautéed Broccoli Rabe

Broccoli rabe has a slightly bitter flavor that stands up nicely to the garlic and hot red pepper flakes in this recipe (see photo in color section). You can prepare broccoli, spinach, kale, Swiss chard, turnip greens, and other leafy greens in the same fashion.

**Italian recipe name:** *Rapini Saltati*

**Preparation time:** *15 minutes*

**Cooking time:** *15 minutes*

**Yield:** *4 servings*

*2 pounds broccoli rabe, washed, tough stems removed and discarded*

*¹/₄ cup olive oil*

*4 cloves garlic, peeled and sliced*

*Pinch of hot red pepper flakes*

*Salt and pepper to taste*

**1** In a large pot, bring 4 quarts lightly salted water to a boil. Add the broccoli rabe, cover, and cook, stirring occasionally, until the broccoli rabe is tender but still firm, about 5 minutes.

**2** Drain into a colander, pressing out the excess water with the back of a spoon.

**3** Heat the olive oil and garlic in a medium skillet over medium heat. When the garlic begins to brown, add the red pepper flakes and broccoli rabe. Cook 5 minutes, stirring occasionally. Season with salt and pepper. Serve.

# Cabbage

Savoy cabbage, with its crinkly green leaves and nutty flavor, is popular in Italy. Red cabbage is also eaten. Italians generally cut cabbage leaves into thin strips and then sauté them in butter, oil, or the rendered fat from pancetta. Cabbage cooks down quite a lot, so you will need to start with a small mountain of shredded cabbage to feed four.

# Cauliflower

To prepare cauliflower for cooking, remove the leaves and central core and then break the head into bite-sized pieces. Cauliflower is cooked like broccoli, either by boiling or steaming. It has a much milder flavor than broccoli and can tolerate a range of seasonings, from olives and capers to olive oil and salt. Steamed cauliflower is especially delicious when coated with bechamel sauce and grated Parmesan cheese and baked.

# Eggplant

**TOQUE TIP**

The challenge with eggplant is cooking it, not preparing it. We don't bother peeling or salting eggplant, as many sources suggest. In general, we don't mind a little bitterness in eggplant. Really big eggplant can be excessively watery and bitter, so try to buy smaller eggplant, certainly nothing that weighs more than 1 pound. Simply remove the green top, slice or dice the eggplant, and cook.

Eggplant acts like a sponge, soaking up whatever medium it's cooked in. This can be a good thing because eggplant picks up the flavors of the other ingredients it's cooked with. However, eggplant also soaks up almost as much oil as you give it. It actually seems to absorb less oil when fried rather than sautéed. If you're concerned about fat intake, lightly brush eggplant slices with oil and then grill, broil, or roast them until golden brown.

# Endive

This salad green also can be served as a contorno. To prepare endive as a vegetable side dish, halve it lengthwise, making sure to keep the stem end intact so that the leaves don't separate. Cooking mellows the bitter flavor of endive. It can be brushed with olive oil and roasted or braised. To braise endive, sauté pieces in oil or butter, add a little stock or white wine to the pan, cover, and simmer until tender.

# Escarole

This salad green has enough stamina to withstand some cooking. Wash the leaves to remove any grit and then shake them dry. Add the damp escarole to a deep pot that has been lightly oiled with some olive oil. (If you like, you may cook garlic, onions, or hot red pepper flakes in the oil before adding the escarole.) Throw the lid on the pot and wait several minutes until the leaves are tender. Like all greens, escarole will cook down quite considerably.

# Fennel

With its assertive licorice bite, raw fennel (shown in Figure 14-3) is a delicious addition to the salad bowl. However, you can cook fennel. The texture becomes silky, and the flavor mellows considerably. Fennel can be rubbed with olive oil and grilled or roasted. It can also be braised like endive. To prepare fennel, lop off the feathery fronds (they can be minced and used like a fresh herb in some recipes) and the celerylike stalks. The white bulb is the main attraction. Remove any bruised or brown portions from the bulb and then slice it into wedges, slices, or thin strips.

**Figure 14-3:**
Fennel.

## Green beans

Green beans are usually blanched in salted water or steamed and then drizzled with olive oil or a flavorful vinaigrette. This method preserves their bright green color and some texture. You can also cook beans in tomato sauce or other liquids, but they'll turn a drab olive color and become quite soft. Either way, the tips of the beans should be cut off with a knife or popped off with your fingertips before cooking.

## Mushrooms

Contrary to popular wisdom, mushrooms may be washed to remove dirt. Just don't let them soak in water, or they'll become soggy. After you clean the mushrooms, dry them thoroughly. The ends of the stems are usually tough and should be removed. The whole stem on a shiitake or portobello mushroom is tough and should be removed.

Small mushrooms, including the standard white button, the brown cremini, the silky oyster, and the meaty shiitake, can be cooked in the same fashion. These mushrooms are best sautéed in oil or butter. Oversized portobello mushrooms may be sliced or diced and sautéed or left whole and brushed with olive oil and grilled, roasted, or broiled. (See Figure 14-4 for an illustration of a variety of mushrooms.)

**Figure 14-4:**
A variety of
mushrooms.

## Sautéed Mixed Mushrooms

The contrasting flavors and textures of cremini, shiitake, and oyster mushrooms make this recipe especially good. However, you can prepare this recipe with just one or two of these mushrooms, if you like.

These mushrooms make an excellent accompaniment to most any meat dish. You may also serve them as a pasta sauce or spooned over polenta.

***Italian recipe name:*** *Funghi Misti Trifolati*

***Preparation time:*** *10 minutes*

***Cooking time:*** *25 to 30 minutes*

***Yield:*** *4 servings*

*¹/₄ cup olive oil*

*5 cloves garlic, peeled and chopped*

*1 teaspoon chopped fresh oregano, or 1 teaspoon dried oregano*

*2 teaspoons chopped fresh parsley, or 1 teaspoon dried parsley*

*15 cremini mushrooms, sliced ¹/₄-inch thick*

*20 oyster mushrooms, sliced ¹/₄-inch thick*

*20 shiitake mushrooms, sliced ¹/₄-inch thick*

*¹/₄ cup white wine*

*1 cup chopped canned plum tomatoes*

*Salt and pepper to taste*

***1*** In a medium skillet, heat the olive oil. Add the garlic and cook over medium heat until golden, about 2 minutes. Add the oregano and parsley, cook another 30 seconds, and then add the mushrooms.

***2*** Sauté the mushrooms over medium-high heat, tossing or occasionally stirring, for 2 to 3 minutes. Add the white wine and tomatoes, season with salt and pepper, and cook, covered, at a simmer for 15 to 20 minutes. Add 2 or 3 tablespoons water, if necessary, to keep the mushrooms moist. The mushrooms should be tender. Serve warm.

# Onions

Onions are often braised (as in the following recipe) or baked and served as a vegetable side dish. Large whole onions can be stuffed and left whole or sliced. Small pearl onions are usually left whole, as are cipolline, small Italian onions with flattened sides and a mild flavor.

## Sweet and Sour Onions

Small white pearl onions have a pesky skin that requires some work to remove. You can use frozen pearl onions in a pinch, but they tend to be less flavorful and a bit mushy. If you can find cipolline, use them in this recipe.

**Italian recipe name:** *Cipolline in Agrodolce*

**Preparation time:** *10 minutes*

**Cooking time:** *40 to 45 minutes*

**Yield:** *4 servings*

*1 pound pearl or cipolline onions, peeled and trimmed (about 1¹/₂ pounds unpeeled)*

*2 tablespoons olive oil*

*3 tablespoons red wine vinegar*

*3 tablespoons balsamic vinegar*

*¹/₄ cup white or red wine*

*1¹/₂ to 2 tablespoons sugar, divided*

*Salt and pepper to taste*

*1¹/₂ cups water, divided*

*1* Place the onions in a medium bowl and add enough hot water to cover them. Let them sit for 5 minutes and then peel them. Dry with paper towels.

*2* Preheat oven to 375°.

*3* In a medium skillet, combine the onions and oil and cook over medium heat for 12 minutes, tossing or stirring frequently.

*4* Add the wine vinegar, balsamic vinegar, wine, 1¹/₂ tablespoons sugar, and pinch of salt and pepper. Cook, simmering, for 15 minutes, and then taste and decide whether you want to add the remaining ¹/₂ tablespoon sugar.

*5* Stir in 1 cup water and transfer the pan to the oven. Bake for 10 minutes, stirring occasionally. Add more water, if necessary. Serve hot or at room temperature.

# Peas

Fresh peas are a delicious treat. Unfortunately, peas lose much of their sweetness almost as soon as they're picked. That's why frozen peas are so popular. Fresh and frozen peas can be boiled until tender (just cook frozen peas for less time) and then seasoned with olive oil or herbs. You can also cook peas in a covered pan in a small amount of stock or other liquid.

# Peppers

Bell peppers should be cored, seeded, and sliced before cooking. Most recipes call for sautéing the strips of bell pepper until tender. In many cases, tomatoes or other liquids are added to the pan, and the peppers are stewed until quite soft.

## Stewed Peppers

This was a favorite dish of Cesare's grandfather, Beppe. He used to eat peppers in the morning before going to work in the fields. But in the country, bell peppers were available only during the summer. Every August, to keep Grandpa Beppe happy, Grandma Maria would make jars and jars of Peperonata so that they could eat it all through the winter. You can serve Peperonata at room temperature as an antipasto or spooned over toasts or crostini (see photo in color section). The peppers are also delicious hot, served as a side dish or tossed with a pasta or risotto. If you serve the peppers with pasta, add a tablespoon of grated Parmesan cheese to each serving.

**_Italian recipe name:_** _Peperonata_

**_Preparation time:_** _15 minutes_

**_Cooking time:_** _50 minutes_

**_Yield:_** _4 servings_

_6 cloves garlic, peeled and crushed_

_2 medium onions, sliced_

_2 red bell peppers, seeded and sliced into strips_

_2 green bell peppers, seeded and sliced into strips_

_2 yellow bell peppers, seeded and sliced into strips_

_3 tablespoons olive oil_

_2 sprigs fresh sage, or 1 teaspoon dried sage_

_1 cup white wine_

_Salt to taste_

_2 cups chopped tomatoes (about 3 medium tomatoes)_

_2 tablespoons capers, drained_

_2 tablespoons chopped fresh parsley, or 1 teaspoon dried parsley_

_$^1/_2$ cup chopped fresh basil, or 2 teaspoons dried basil_

**_1_** Place the garlic, onions, bell pepper slices, and olive oil in a large skillet and cook over medium heat, stirring occasionally, until the onions are soft, about 8 minutes.

_(continued)_

**2** Add the sage and wine and season with salt. Cover and cook for 8 minutes at a low simmer.

**3** Stir in the tomatoes and capers. Cover and cook for 25 to 30 minutes. If the mixture dries out, add 2 or 3 tablespoons water. The peperonata should be moist.

**4** Add the parsley and basil and stir well. Cook for 2 minutes. Serve warm or at room temperature.

## Potatoes

Potatoes can be mashed or stewed (see the recipes that follow) or diced, coated with olive oil and salt, and roasted in a hot oven until golden brown. In Italy, roasted potatoes are often seasoned with garlic and rosemary. To keep the garlic and herbs from burning, add them to the potatoes about 15 minutes before you think the potatoes will be done.

### Mashed Potatoes

If you like really smooth mashed potatoes, use a ricer (as shown in Figure 14-5). You can mash the potatoes with a potato masher, but invariably a few small lumps will remain.

*Italian recipe name:* Pure di Patate

*Preparation time:* 15 minutes

*Cooking time:* 40 minutes

*Yield:* 4 to 6 servings

*4 to 5 medium potatoes (2 pounds)*            *1 cup warmed milk*

*Salt and pepper to taste*                            *Pinch of ground nutmeg*

*4 tablespoons butter*

**1** Place the potatoes in a medium pot and cover them with cold water. Add a touch of salt to the water and bring to a boil. Reduce the heat to a simmer and cook until the potatoes are tender when pierced with the tip of a paring knife, about 35 to 40 minutes. Drain.

**2** When the potatoes are cool enough to handle, peel them. Using a ricer, squeeze the potato flesh back into the pot. If you don't have a ricer, place the potatoes back in the pot and mash them.

**3** Using a wooden spoon, whip in the butter. Slowly add the milk, beating with each addition, until the potatoes are smooth and moist; you may require only ²/₃ cup milk depending on the moisture of the potatoes. Season with salt and pepper and nutmeg and serve immediately.

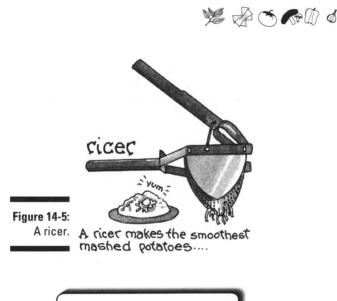

**Figure 14-5:**
A ricer.

A ricer makes the smoothest mashed potatoes....

### Stewed Potatoes

Potatoes are cooked in the oven in a mixture of vegetables and wine (see photo in color section). Sometimes sausage or boiled beef is added to this dish to turn it into a main course.

Ideally, this dish should be prepared in an ovenproof saucepan. If your saucepans have plastic or wooden handles and can't go into the oven, scrape the vegetable and wine mixture into a roasting pan, add the potatoes, and cover the pan with foil.

***Italian recipe name:*** *Patate al Tegame*

***Preparation time:*** *15 minutes*

***Cooking time:*** *45 to 55 minutes*

***Yield:*** *4 servings*

*(continued)*

*¹/₄ cup olive oil*

*5 cloves garlic, peeled and crushed*

*2 medium onions, peeled and cut into 8 wedges each*

*2 medium carrots, cut into 1-inch pieces*

*5 celery stalks, cut into 1-inch pieces*

*Pinch of hot red pepper flakes*

*2 sprigs fresh sage, or 1 teaspoon dried sage*

*1 cup white or red wine*

*6 medium potatoes, peeled and cut into 1¹/₂-inch cubes*

*2 cups chopped tomatoes, canned or fresh*

*Salt and pepper to taste*

**1** Preheat oven to 375°.

**2** In a medium ovenproof saucepan, heat the olive oil over medium heat. Add the garlic, onions, carrots, celery, red pepper flakes, and sage. Cook over medium heat, stirring often, until the vegetables soften, about 20 minutes. Lower the heat, if necessary, to prevent browning.

**3** Add the wine and cook for 2 to 3 minutes, until the wine has mostly evaporated.

**4** Place the potatoes and tomatoes in the saucepan. Stir to combine. Season with salt and pepper. Cover the pan and transfer it to the oven. Cook for 45 to 50 minutes, stirring occasionally. The potatoes should be very tender but still intact.

# Radicchio

Like endive, this bitter salad green can be cut into wedges and cooked as a vegetable side dish. Make sure to slice the radicchio through its stem so that the leaves will remain attached at the bottom. Brush wedges of radicchio with olive oil and grill, roast, or sauté.

# Spinach

This tender leafy green may be prepared like broccoli rabe and other tougher greens (blanched and then sautéed), or you may skip the blanching step and simply add damp leaves to a pot with some olive oil and seasonings. Throw the cover on, and the spinach will steam in the water attached to the leaves. Cook just until the leaves have wilted, no more than 5 minutes.

# Swiss chard

Swiss chard has large crinkly green leaves and a pleasant, earthy flavor. Swiss chard comes in two varieties — one has white stalks, and the other has red stalks — but they taste pretty much the same. To prepare Swiss chard for cooking, tear the leafy green portions away from the stalk, discard the stalk, wash the leaves, shake dry, and then cook as you would cook spinach.

## Winter squash

Hard squashes, such as butternut, are a winter staple in Italian cooking. Peeling a winter squash can be tricky (see Chapter 8 for more information), but the sweet, yellow flesh is worth the effort. To serve squash as a side dish, cut the peeled flesh into cubes, coat them with olive oil, and roast in a hot oven until tender. Winter squash is also used in risotto dishes and as a filling for pasta.

## Zucchini

Zucchini comes in a variety of sizes. In general, smaller zucchini (no more than 6 or 8 ounces) have fewer seeds and are less watery than really large zucchini. Small zucchini also tend to have a better flavor. Zucchini can be diced and sautéed in olive oil with garlic, onions, herbs, and/or lemon zest. Zucchini can also be cut lengthwise into strips that can be brushed with olive oil and grilled, broiled, or roasted.

Because zucchini grows so close to the ground, bits of sand can become embedded in the skin. Run your hand over the zucchini after washing it. If you feel little bumps, soak the zucchini in a bowl of cold water for 10 to 15 minutes to loosen the sand.

# Cooking Legumes

Legumes — dried beans and lentils — are part of the extended family of vegetables. Like vegetables, beans may be served as a contorno. You can also use beans in salads, soups, or pasta sauces.

## Dried beans

Home-cooked beans are generally superior to canned beans. They generally have a firmer texture and better flavor because you can season them as you wish. Dried beans are not hard to prepare, but they do require some planning.

---

# How to cook cannellini beans

Rinse the cannellini beans, removing any stones and shriveled beans. Place the beans in a large bowl and cover with cold water. Soak them for at least four hours (and preferably overnight). Drain the beans and place them in a medium saucepan with a sprig of sage, two celery stalks, and three cloves of crushed garlic. Cover with fresh cold water and bring to a boil. Reduce the heat and simmer until tender, about 1¼ hours. Cool beans and refrigerate them in their cooking liquid until needed, up to four days. Drain the beans and discard the sage, garlic, and celery stalks before using in recipes.

Other dried beans may be prepared in the same fashion. Cooking times will vary depending on the freshness, size, and type of beans. One cup of dried beans yields about 2 cups cooked beans.

---

Dried beans should be soaked in cold water before cooking. Soaking cuts cooking time and also leaches out some of the compounds that can cause gas when beans are eaten. Beans must be soaked for at least four hours (and preferably overnight).

The beans are then drained and cooked with fresh cold water and aromatics, such as garlic, herbs, carrots, onion, and/or celery. After the beans are tender, cool and refrigerate them in their cooking liquid. They'll keep for several days. When needed, simply drain the beans.

Home-cooked beans are so delicious that they may be seasoned simply, perhaps with just olive oil, salt, and fresh herbs. Canned beans are often very mushy and salty. They may be fine in soups or dips where the beans are pureed. However, in simple bean dishes, make your own beans, and you will notice a big difference.

Cannellini beans (or white kidney beans) are extremely popular in Italy. However, other beans are also used in Italian dishes. Chickpeas, also called garbanzo beans, are round, golden beans with a mild, nutty flavor. They're popular in southern Italy. Brown borlotti beans and speckled white-and-red cranberry beans are also used in many Italian recipes.

## Stewed Beans with Tomatoes, Sage, and Garlic

The Italian name of this Tuscan recipe translates as "beans in the style of little birds." Game birds are often seasoned with the same tomato, sage, and garlic sauce, hence this curious name.

*Italian recipe name:* Fagioli all'Uccelletto

*Preparation time:* 5 minutes (excludes preparation of beans)

*Cooking time:* 45 to 50 minutes (excludes cooking of beans)

*Yield:* 6 to 8 servings

| | |
|---|---|
| $^1/_4$ cup olive oil | 5 cups cooked cannellini beans (see the sidebar "How to cook cannellini beans") |
| 5 cloves garlic, peeled and crushed | Salt and pepper to taste |
| 2 sprigs fresh sage, or 1 teaspoon dried sage | 1 cup chicken stock or water |
| 1 teaspoon hot red pepper flakes | 1 loaf Tuscan, Italian, or French bread, sliced |
| 3 cups whole canned tomatoes | |

*1* In a medium saucepan over medium-high heat, combine the olive oil, garlic, sage, and red pepper flakes. Cook, stirring, until the garlic turns golden, about 3 minutes.

*2* Add the tomatoes and their juice. Cook for 15 minutes. Then add the beans, reduce the heat to simmer, and stir.

*3* Season with salt and pepper. Add the chicken stock or water. Stir. Cook for 25 to 30 minutes over low heat, stirring occasionally. Serve with Tuscan bread.

# Lentils

Unlike other dried legumes, lentils don't need to be soaked and can be cooked rather quickly, in about half an hour. Lentils may be flavored as they cook (as in the following Lentil Stew recipe), or they can be boiled with aromatics, drained, and then used in salads (see Chapter 4). Like other dried legumes, lentils will double in volume when cooked.

## How to cook lentils

To cook lentils, combine 2 cups lentils, 4 cups vegetable stock or water, 1 halved onion, 2 small carrots, 2 cloves crushed garlic, and 1 sprig sage in a medium saucepan. Bring to a boil, reduce heat, and simmer for about 30 minutes, until the lentils are tender but still firm. Cool the lentils and refrigerate them in their cooking liquid until needed, up to four days. Drain the lentils and discard the vegetables and herbs. Add to recipes as directed.

Lentils come in several varieties. Brown lentils are the most common choice in supermarkets. They hold their shape reasonably well, but are a bit bland. Red or orange lentils will fall apart when cooked and are not used in Italian cooking. If you can find green lentils (sometimes called French lentils or lentils du Puy or lenticchie Castelluccio), buy them. They cook up much firmer than brown lentils and have an earthier, sweeter flavor. Look for them in gourmet shops, natural food stores, and better supermarkets.

## Lentil Stew

This lentil dish is delicious as a bed for grilled sausages or as a side dish with meatloaf.

*Italian recipe name: Lenticchie in Umido*

*Preparation time: 10 minutes*

*Cooking time: 45 to 55 minutes*

*Yield: 4 to 6 servings*

*3 tablespoons olive oil*

*4 celery stalks, finely chopped*

*1 medium carrot, finely chopped*

*1 medium onion, finely chopped*

*3 cloves garlic, peeled and finely chopped*

*1 sprig fresh sage, or 1 teaspoon dried sage*

*6 slices of pancetta or bacon, finely chopped (optional)*

*2 cups dried green or brown lentils, rinsed or briefly soaked*

*1 cup white wine*

*Salt and pepper to taste*

*3 tablespoons tomato paste*

*3 cups water or broth, divided*

**1** Heat the oil in a medium saucepan over medium heat. Add the celery, carrot, onion, garlic, sage, and pancetta. Stir frequently over medium heat for 10 minutes or until the onion is soft and slightly brown.

**2** Stir the lentils into the sautéed vegetables and cook for about 2 minutes. Pour the wine in the pan, stirring to blend ingredients. Cook, reducing the wine, for 3 minutes. Season with salt and pepper.

**3** Stir in the tomato paste and 1¹/₂ cups water or broth. Bring the mixture to a gentle simmer. Cover the pan and cook very slowly for 20 minutes. Adjust the seasoning with salt and add another cup water or broth and cook for another 10 minutes; the lentils should be tender but still firm enough to hold their shape. If necessary, add the remaining liquid as necessary and cook for another 5 to 10 minutes.

# Part V
# La Dolce Vita

## The 5th Wave    By Rich Tennant

"We're making ladyfingers for the tiramisù, why?"

# In this part . . .

What's a meal without dessert? Even if it's just a few biscotti and a good cup of espresso, Italians know how to finish a meal with style. This part shows you how to prepare the best Italian desserts — everything from the famed tiramisù to cakes, tarts, and cookies. This part also shows you how to make all those trendy Italian coffee drinks, including espresso, cappuccino, and latte.

# Chapter 15
# Desserts: Tiramisù and Beyond

## In This Chapter

▶ Making the most of fruit

▶ Serving tiramisù at home

▶ Cooling off with gelato

▶ Baking simple cookies and biscotti

▶ Mastering the art of Italian cakes and tarts

*I*talians are rightly famous for their desserts. Some evidence indicates that Italians invented ice cream, or *gelato* as it's called in Italy. Even if ice cream originated elsewhere, the Italians have surely perfected the art and science of making frozen desserts.

There's no doubt that the Italians invented biscotti. These crunchy cookies have become all the rage at coffee bars and restaurants. They're perfect for dipping into a mug of joe, but they also make a great dessert when paired with fruit or ice cream.

Tiramisù, a creamy puddinglike concoction made with ladyfingers and chocolate, is one of the top restaurant desserts of the 1990s. (Crème brûlée and warm chocolate brownie cake are the other contenders.) The popularity of tiramisù shows no signs of decreasing. In this chapter, we show you how to make this dessert at home.

In addition to these popular Italian desserts, we also introduce some recipes that don't get as much attention as they deserve. Italians know that good fruit often makes the best desserts. We show you how to turn fruit into dessert. Lastly, Italians love a showy cake or tart. These desserts require some work, but the results are worth the effort.

# Fruit First

The world's first desserts were made with fruit. Starting with the apple given to Adam by Eve, humans have savored fruit as a light, sweet way to end a meal. Because the traditional Italian meal contains so many courses, fruit is the traditional dessert. Cookies might make an appearance as well, but cakes, tarts, and other rich desserts are reserved for holidays and special occasions.

In many homes, a bowl of fruit is set out on the table. Everyone takes what he or she likes, peeling the fruit, if necessary. The fruit bowl can contain almost anything that you can eat out of hand, from grapes and berries to oranges and apples. Dried fruits and nuts in the shell can also be part of the fruit bowl.

You can also dress up the fruit a bit and turn it into a real dessert. The following recipes show some of the possibilities.

## Prunes in Red Wine

Dried prunes are subjected to a 2-step process in this recipe. First, you need to soak them in water to make them soft. Second, you cook them in red wine flavored with sugar, cinnamon, and citrus to season them. You serve the prunes in the red wine mixture, which acts as a syrupy sauce. If you like, add a scoop of vanilla ice cream to each bowl.

*Italian recipe name:* *Prugne al Vino Rosso*

*Preparation time:* *10 minutes (plus 2 hours soaking time and 2 hours cooling time)*

*Cooking time:* *15 minutes*

*Yield:* *6 servings*

| | |
|---|---|
| *1¹/₂ pounds dried prunes* | *1 cinnamon stick* |
| *1 quart good quality red wine* | *1¹/₄-inch-thick orange slice* |
| *1 cup sugar* | *1¹/₄-inch-thick lemon slice* |

*1* Place the prunes in a medium bowl, cover them with water, cover the bowl, and set aside for 2 hours.

*2* In a medium saucepan, combine the remaining ingredients. Drain the prunes and add them to the pan. Simmer for 10 minutes.

*3* Cool to room temperature or chill in the refrigerator for several hours. Serve prunes and some of the cooking liquid in dessert bowls.

## Roasted Fruit

This recipe is very easy to prepare (see photo in color section). The fruit is sliced, sprinkled with sugar and some grappa, and then roasted in the oven. (See the sidebar in Chapter 16 for an explanation of grappa.) Roasting concentrates the flavor of the fruit, making it especially sweet and juicy. If you like, use brandy or a fruit-flavored liqueur (Grand Marnier would be good) rather than the grappa. You can also roast other fruits, including peaches, plums, and nectarines.

***Italian recipe name:*** *Frutta Arrosto*

***Preparation time:*** *10 minutes*

***Cooking time:*** *25 minutes*

***Yield:*** *4 servings*

***Special tool:*** *Aluminum foil*

*2 medium oranges, sliced with peel intact*

*2 apples, peeled, cored, and sliced*

*2 pears, peeled, cored, and sliced*

*2 bananas, peeled and sliced*

*$1/4$ cup grappa or sweet liqueur, divided*

*5 tablespoons sugar, divided*

*1* Preheat oven to 400°.

*2* Cover a baking sheet with aluminum foil.

*3* In a large bowl, mix the fruit with 2 tablespoons grappa and 1 tablespoon sugar. Spread the mixture on the foil-lined baking sheet.

*4* Place another sheet of foil over the fruit and crimp the edges together to form a large pouch. Bake for 10 minutes.

*5* Open the foil and sprinkle the fruit with the remaining $1/4$ cup sugar. Bake for another 10 to 15 minutes, or until the fruit is slightly caramelized (sort of brown). Spoon the fruit into serving dishes, drizzle with the remaining 2 tablespoons grappa, and serve.

# Dessert on a Spoon

There's something so comforting about a creamy dessert. The texture is smooth and rich, and the flavor of all that cream and eggs is just divine. The following desserts are all meant to be eaten with a spoon.

## Tiramisù

This creamy puddinglike concoction starts with ladyfingers (sponge cake) soaked in cold espresso. (Ladyfingers are sold in most supermarkets. They're golden brown and shaped like long ovals, or the fingers on a lady's hand.) You layer the soaked cakes in a baking dish and cover them with a mixture of beaten eggs, sugar, and Mascarpone cheese. Then, you spoon this mixture over the cakes and dust them with some cocoa powder or grated bittersweet chocolate (see photo in color section).

Because you don't cook the eggs in this dish, you may not want to serve this dish to children, the elderly, or people with compromised immune systems. If you're concerned about eating raw eggs, replace the eggs, sugar, and vermouth in this recipe with Zabaglione (see next recipe). Cool the Zabaglione to room temperature, fold in the Mascarpone, and use this mixture to cover the layers of soaked cakes.

**Italian recipe name:** *Tiramisù*

**Preparation time:** *25 minutes (plus several hours chilling time)*

**Cooking time:** *None*

**Yield:** *8 servings*

**Special tool:** *Standing mixer*

*7 eggs, separated*

*7 tablespoons sugar*

*¹/₄ cup sweet vermouth or liqueur (such as Kahlua)*

*2¹/₂ cups Mascarpone cheese*

*³/₄ cup cold espresso or strong black coffee*

*24 ladyfingers*

*3 tablespoons good quality cocoa powder, or 4 ounces bittersweet chocolate, grated*

**1** In a large bowl, beat the egg yolks and sugar with a standing mixer until pale and thick, about 5 to 6 minutes. Add the vermouth and Mascarpone and beat until the mixture is thick and smooth.

**2** Clean the beaters and thoroughly dry them. In another bowl, beat the egg whites until they are stiff and form peaks. Fold the egg whites into the Mascarpone mixture.

**3** Pour the espresso into a shallow dish. Dip a ladyfinger in, turning it quickly so that it becomes wet but does not disintegrate, and place it on the bottom of an 8-x-8-x-2-inch dish. Repeat until the entire bottom of the pan is covered with soaked ladyfingers. Spoon half the Mascarpone mixture over the ladyfingers. Repeat with another layer of soaked ladyfingers and cover with the remaining Mascarpone mixture. Level the surface with a spatula and then sift the cocoa powder over the top. Cover. Chill for several hours before serving.

## Zabaglione

Zabaglione is a frothy, eggy custard flavored with sweet wine. To prevent the eggs from curdling, you need to cook them in a bowl suspended over simmering water. Spoon the Zabaglione over a slice of dry cake or serve with ladyfingers or fresh berries.

***Italian recipe name:*** *Zabaglione*

***Preparation time:*** *5 minutes*

***Cooking time:*** *5 minutes*

***Yield:*** *4 servings*

*6 egg yolks*

*6 tablespoons sugar*

*1 cup white wine (Moscato or any sweet wine)*

*1* Fill a 3-quart saucepan ¹/₃ full with water. Bring it to a simmer over medium heat.

*2* In a large metal bowl, beat together the egg yolks and sugar. Whisk in the wine. Set the bowl over the simmering water, taking care that it doesn't touch the water. Whisk for 3 to 5 minutes, removing the bowl from the heat for a moment or two if it heats too quickly (you want to warm the eggs, not cook them). The mixture should be foamy and somewhat thick. Serve immediately in small serving bowls.

## Crème Caramel

For this recipe, you pour a rich eggy custard into small ceramic ramekins (see Figure 15-1) that have been filled with homemade caramel sauce. The custards are then baked, chilled, and inverted onto individual plates. This is the Italian version of the Spanish dessert called flan.

You can prepare this recipe fairly quickly, but a number of the steps are tricky. When making the caramel, stay close to the stove. Burning the caramel is easy, and burnt caramel doesn't taste very good. If possible, prepare the caramel in a light-colored pan so that you can easily judge the color of the caramel against a shiny or white background. To keep the custard from curdling in the oven, set the ramekins in a large, deep baking pan, place the pan in the oven, and then add enough hot water to come halfway up the sides of the ramekins. The water moderates the harsh oven heat and keeps the custards from overcooking. Be careful when adding the water. You don't want to splash any into the ramekins.

*(continued)*

**Italian recipe name:** *Crema Caramellata*

**Preparation time:** *10 minutes*

**Cooking time:** *40 minutes*

**Yield:** *6 servings*

**Special tools:** *Six 4-ounce ramekins or heat-proof custard cups, pastry knife or small knife*

*1 teaspoon vegetable oil for greasing the ramekins*

*1 cup sugar, divided*

*$1^1/_2$ tablespoons water*

*2 cups milk*

*$^1/_4$ vanilla bean, or $^1/_4$ teaspoon vanilla extract*

*3 eggs*

*2 egg yolks*

**1** Preheat oven to 350°.

**2** Lightly grease the ramekins with the vegetable oil.

**3** Prepare the caramel: Combine $^1/_2$ cup sugar and the water in a small, heavy saucepan and cook over medium heat until the mixture is thick, bubbling, and light brown in color. Do not overcook.

**4** Pour the hot caramel into the 6 ramekins. The caramel should be about $^1/_8$-inch deep. Wearing oven mitts, swirl the ramekins to coat the bottom and part of the sides with caramel. Set aside.

**5** Prepare the custard: Pour the milk into a small saucepan. Cut the vanilla bean in half lengthwise and scrape the seeds into the pan. Add the bean to the pan. Cook, uncovered, over medium heat, stirring, until mixture is hot. Remove from heat. Whisk the eggs and egg yolks together with the remaining $^1/_2$ cup sugar just until smooth. While stirring, very gradually pour the hot milk into the egg mixture. Discard the vanilla bean and pass the custard through a fine strainer. Pour the custard into the caramel-coated ramekins.

**6** Set the ramekins into a larger baking pan and pour enough hot water into the pan to reach halfway up the sides of the ramekins.

**7** Bake for 25 to 30 minutes until the top of the custard is firm to the touch. Let cool at room temperature and then refrigerate for at least 2 hours.

**8** To serve, unmold the crème caramel by running a small knife or spatula along the sides of the ramekin to loosen the custard from the sides. Invert each onto a dessert plate.

**Figure 15-1:**
A ceramic
ramekin.

ceramic ramekin

## Cream Puffs

For this dessert, tender pastry balls are piped with a creamy filling. You can serve them as is or with your favorite chocolate sauce and whipped cream.

**Italian recipe name:** *Bignè*

**Preparation time:** *15 minutes (plus cooling time)*

**Cooking time:** *30 minutes*

**Yield:** *4 servings*

**Special tools:** *Handheld mixer, pastry bag with round tip (see Figure 15-2)*

| | |
|---|---|
| *1 cup water* | *1¹/₄ cups flour* |
| *1 cup butter (2 sticks) plus butter for greasing baking sheet* | *Pinch of baking soda* |
| | *6 room-temperature eggs* |
| *1 teaspoon vanilla extract* | *3 tablespoons heavy cream* |
| *1 tablespoon sugar* | *¹/₂ recipe Pastry Cream (see recipe later in this chapter)* |
| *Pinch of salt* | |

*1* Preheat oven to 375°.

*2* In a medium saucepan, heat the water with the butter, vanilla extract, sugar, and salt. When the butter has melted, beat in the flour and baking soda. Cook over low heat, stirring constantly, for about 5 minutes. Remove from heat.

*3* Add the eggs one at a time, beating with a handheld mixer after each addition.

*4* Lightly grease a baking sheet. Using 2 spoons or a pastry bag fitted with a round tip, squeeze the mixture out onto the tray in small 1¹/₂ to 2-inch balls, leaving 2 to 3 inches of space between each. Bake for 20 to 25 minutes, or until golden brown. Remove from the oven and cool on a wire rack before filling.

*5* While the cream puffs bake, prepare the filling: In a medium bowl, whip the heavy cream until it has soft peaks. Fold the whipped cream into the Pastry Cream. Using a pastry bag fitted with a round tip, poke a hole in the side of each cream puff and gently squeeze the pastry bag until the puff is filled. You can also slice each cream puff in half, spoon the filling into the top and bottom halves and sandwich the halves back together.

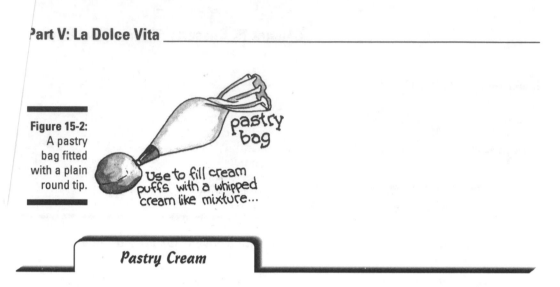

**Figure 15-2:**
A pastry
bag fitted
with a plain
round tip.

Use to fill cream puffs with a whipped cream like mixture...

## Pastry Cream

This thick, eggy cream has many uses in the pastry kitchen. You can lighten it with whipped cream and use it as a filling for cream puffs or between cake layers. Or you can line a baked tart shell (see Pastry Dough recipe later in the chapter) with Pastry Cream and then cover the cream with fresh berries. Pastry Cream keeps in the refrigerator for several days.

**Italian recipe name:** *Crema Pasticcera*

**Preparation time:** *10 minutes (plus cooling time)*

**Cooking time:** *10 minutes*

**Yield:** *2¹/₂ cups*

**Special tool:** *Plastic wrap*

| | |
|---|---|
| *2 cups milk* | *¹/₂ cup sugar* |
| *Grated zest of 1 lemon* | *1 teaspoon vanilla extract* |
| *3 egg yolks* | *¹/₄ cup flour* |
| *1 egg* | |

**1** In a medium saucepan, bring the milk and lemon zest to a slow simmer over medium heat, stirring constantly. Do not boil.

**2** In a medium bowl, beat the egg yolks and egg with the sugar and add the vanilla extract and flour. Beat vigorously for 1 minute.

**3** Add a ladle of the hot milk (about ¹/₃ cup) to the bowl, mix, and then add the contents of the bowl to the milk in the saucepan. Place over low heat and cook, stirring, until the mixture boils and thickens, 3 to 5 minutes. Cook another minute and remove from heat.

**4** Transfer the Pastry Cream to a bowl, cover it directly with plastic wrap (to prevent a skin from forming on the top), and allow it to cool.

# Chilly Desserts

Culinary historians can't agree about the source of the first frozen, or more likely partially frozen, ices. Possible candidates include China, Egypt, India, and various Middle Eastern or Arabic locations. However, the first European written record about ices comes from a 16th-century Italian physician. Undoubtedly, the Italians are responsible for introducing ices to other European countries, including France and England.

Whatever their pedigree, frozen desserts have a long history in Italy. Italians love their *gelato* (gel-**lot**-oh), Italian-style ice cream. Locals and tourists line up around the block to sample the dozens of flavors at the top ice cream shops in cities like Rome and Florence.

Gelato is a lot like American ice cream, with one important difference. Italian gelato is usually much more intensely flavored. Strawberry gelato tastes first and foremost of berries. Many American ice creams are more about the dairy, especially because they contain more heavy cream than gelato. With gelato, the flavor is the thing.

You can find dozens of common gelato flavors. In addition to the basics, like vanilla and chocolate, many uniquely Italian flavors exist. Here are some of the more unusual gelato flavors that you may see in a good *gelateria,* or Italian ice cream shop:

- **Castagna:** Chestnuts make an especially rich, creamy gelato.

- **Fichi:** Italians use fresh figs in season.

- **Gianduja:** Italians use this intense combination of chocolate and hazelnut to flavor many desserts. It's extremely popular in Italy.

- **Limone:** Citrus fruits, such as lemon, are a popular flavoring for gelato. Orange, called *arancia,* is also common.

- **Nocciola:** Italians love hazelnuts, and this is one of the most popular gelato flavors in Italy.

- **Panna:** This is ice cream (panna means cream) without any flavorings — basically vanilla ice cream, minus the vanilla.

- **Riso:** A little cooked arborio rice is added to a plain vanilla ice cream base for an unusual gelato that resembles frozen rice pudding.

## Real Italian ice

In addition to gelato, Italians make another kind of frozen dessert called a *granita* (grah-**knee**-ta). Granite (plural for granita) are scraped ices, much like the Italian ices sold by street vendors in North America. They have a granular, icy texture, somewhat like a Sno-Kone. The ingredients are processed by hand and not in a machine, making them ideal for people who don't own an ice cream machine. Granite usually don't contain any dairy products, so most are nonfat as well.

The classic technique for making granite calls for pouring the flavorful base (fruit juice, fruit puree, or espresso, mixed with sugar and other flavorings like lemon juice or liqueur) into a shallow pan and occasionally scraping the mixture with a spoon as it hardens in the freezer. This scraping/freezing process continues for several hours or until small, distinct ice crystals form.

The term granita comes from the Italian word for grain or kernel. A well-made granita consists of tiny, individual, shimmering crystals of flavored ice. With so little sugar and no dairy products, granite should taste of fruit (or espresso) and not much else. The idea is to distill the essence of an orange or some berries into a frozen ice.

To make 4 servings of granita, pour 2 cups of a highly flavorful liquid into a 13-x-9-x-2-inch ceramic or glass pan. Place the pan in the freezer for 30 minutes. Using a large metal spoon, stir frozen crystals from around the edges of the pan back into the liquid. As the mixture continues to freeze, scrape the spoon against the sides and bottom of the pan to loosen and break up frozen crystals. Repeat this scraping process every 30 minutes or so until the mixture is frozen and a bit creamy, about 3 hours total. Scoop the crystals into individual bowls or goblets and serve immediately.

As for the liquid, here are some ideas:

- **Fresh Berry Granita:** Puree 3 cups fresh berries with 1½ cups cold water. Press the mixture through a fine sieve to remove any skins or seeds. Sweeten with ⅓ cup sugar or to taste.

- **Espresso Granita:** Combine 2 cups brewed espresso with ¼ cup sugar. Add a tablespoon or so of your favorite liqueur, if desired.

- **Caffe Latte Granita:** Combine 1 cup espresso with 1 cup milk and ¼ cup sugar.

- **Lemon Granita:** Combine ½ cup freshly squeezed lemon juice with 1½ cups water, ½ cup sugar, and a teaspoon or so of grated lemon zest.

- **Orange Granita or Pink Grapefruit Granita:** Combine 1½ cups freshly squeezed orange juice or pink grapefruit juice with ½ cup water, ⅓ cup sugar, and a teaspoon or so of grated orange or grapefruit zest.

### Vanilla Ice Cream

When making the custard for the ice cream, don't let the mixture come to a boil. To prevent this from happening, cook the custard over medium-low heat and remove from heat as soon as the custard is thick enough to coat the back of a spoon.

*Italian recipe name:* Gelato di Crema

*Preparation time:* 5 minutes (plus several hours chilling and freezing)

*Cooking time:* 10 minutes

*Yield:* 6 to 8 servings

*Special tool:* Ice cream machine

| | |
|---|---|
| 7 egg yolks | 1 cup cream |
| ²/₃ cup sugar | 1 vanilla bean, or 1 teaspoon vanilla extract |
| 3 tablespoons light corn syrup | |
| 2 cups milk | Pinch of salt |

**1** In a mixing bowl, cream the egg yolks, sugar, and corn syrup together until pale and thick.

**2** Combine the milk and cream in a medium saucepan. Cut the vanilla bean in half lengthwise and scrape the seeds into the pan. Add the bean and salt. Cook, uncovered, over medium heat, stirring, until mixture simmers. Remove from heat, discard the vanilla bean, and add about ¹/₃ cup milk/cream mixture to the mixing bowl. Stir. Slowly add the contents of the mixing bowl to the saucepan, stirring constantly. Place the pan over low-medium heat and cook, whisking, until the custard is thick and coats the back of a spoon, about 3 minutes. Cover the custard directly with plastic wrap (to prevent a skin from forming on the top) and allow it to cool at room temperature. Then refrigerate it, covered, until chilled.

**3** Freeze in an ice cream machine according to manufacturer's directions.

# Biscotti and Cookies

The word biscotti (biss-**cot**-tee) translates as "twice-cooked" and refers to the fact that you bake these Italian cookies twice. You usually form the dough into long logs and bake them until firm. You then slice the logs on the diagonal into individual cookies, which are baked again. The finished cookies are dry and hard. You can eat them as is, but they're best when dunked in a mug of coffee or even a glass of milk.

Biscotti make a great afternoon snack. However, you can also serve them as dessert, even at the end of a fairly fancy meal. Biscotti are often served with sweet dessert wine for dunking. (Vin santo is the most common choice, but any good dessert wine is fine.) Biscotti are also a nice way to dress up ice cream or fresh fruit.

## Biscotti

This recipe is for the classic almond biscotti that comes from Tuscany (see photo in color section). Traditionally, a little vin santo is added to the dough. You can use Marsala or white wine if you like.

***Italian recipe name:*** *Biscotti*

***Preparation time:*** *20 minutes*

***Cooking time:*** *40 to 45 minutes*

***Yield:*** *20 to 28 cookies*

***Special tools:*** *Parchment paper, serrated knife*

*$^1/_2$ cup sweet butter (1 stick)*

*1 cup sugar*

*2 tablespoons vin santo*

*Grated zest of 1 lemon*

*3 eggs*

*$^1/_2$ cup milk*

*2 cups flour plus flour for dusting work surface*

*1 teaspoon baking powder*

*Pinch of salt and pepper*

*2 cups whole almonds, toasted*

*1* Preheat oven to 350°.

*2* In a mixer or a large bowl, whip or beat the butter and sugar together until creamy. Add the vin santo and lemon zest and blend well. Add the eggs, 1 at a time, beating with each addition. Mix in the milk. Then slowly work in the flour, baking powder, and salt and pepper. Add the almonds, stirring until they're well dispersed.

*3* Divide the dough in half. On a floured surface, shape the dough portions into smooth, baguette-shaped logs (about 3 inches wide). Line a baking pan with parchment paper and then place the dough on top. Bake for 20 to 25 minutes, until light brown, and then remove from the oven and transfer the baked dough to a cutting board. Let cool for 5 minutes.

*4* Using a serrated knife, cut slices (cookies) on the bias, about $^3/_4$-inch thick. Lower the oven temperature to 300°. Place the cookies back on the lined baking pan in one layer and bake for another 15 to 20 minutes to dry them out slightly. Remove from the oven and cool them on a wire rack.

## Raisin Cookies

This recipe comes from northeastern Italy. These cookies are fairly dry and are often served with dessert wine.

*Italian recipe name:* Passulate

*Preparation time:* 20 minutes (plus 2 hours soaking time)

*Cooking time:* 30 to 35 minutes

*Yield:* 20 cookies

*Special tools:* Rolling pin, parchment paper

2$^1$/$_2$ cups raisins

2 cups chopped almonds

2 cups chopped walnuts

$^3$/$_4$ cup honey

Pinch of ground cinnamon

Pinch of ground cloves

Pinch of salt and pepper

Grated zest of 1 lemon

2 cups flour plus $^1$/$_4$ cup to roll the dough

*1* Place the raisins in a medium bowl, cover with water, and let them soak for 2 hours.

*2* Preheat oven to 350°.

*3* Drain the raisins in a strainer, lightly pressing them to remove excess water. Return them to the bowl along with the remaining ingredients (except the $^1$/$_4$ cup flour to be used when rolling the dough). Stir until the mixture forms a dough and then transfer the dough to a flat, flour-dusted surface.

*4* Using a flour-dusted rolling pin, roll the dough until it is a $^1$/$_4$-inch-thick square. Incorporate flour as needed to prevent the dough from sticking to the pin.

*5* Cut the dough into 1$^1$/$_2$-inch squares and place them on a baking sheet lined with parchment paper. Bake for 30 to 35 minutes, until evenly browned. Remove and cool the cookies on a wire rack.

# Let Them Eat Cake

Often, you may want to serve something impressive for dessert. Cake fits the bill, especially if you're serving a crowd.

Unlike other European cakes, which tend to be rich and buttery, Italian cakes often are quite dry. They're designed to be moistened with wine, Pastry Cream, or Zabaglione.

## Hazelnut Cake

This recipe comes from the Piedmont region in northwestern Italy. You can serve it on its own, but it's better with a dollop of Zabaglione. Add a glass of Moscato d'Asti for a real Piedmontese dessert.

**Italian recipe name:** *Torta di Nocciole*

**Preparation time:** *20 minutes (plus cooling time)*

**Cooking time:** *40 to 45 minutes*

**Yield:** *6 servings*

**Special tools:** *Standing mixer, 9-x-2-inch round cake pan, rubber spatula*

$^1/_2$ cup plus 3 tablespoons butter plus butter for greasing pan

2 cups flour plus flour for dusting pan

3 eggs, separated

1 cup sugar, divided

$1^1/_2$ teaspoons baking powder

$^1/_4$ teaspoon salt

1 cup toasted and finely chopped hazelnuts

*1* Preheat oven to 350°.

*2* Grease and flour the round cake pan, tapping any excess flour out of the pan.

*3* In the bowl of a standing mixer, beat the egg whites on low speed until frothy. In a slow, but steady stream, add $^1/_2$ cup sugar. Gradually increase the speed to the highest setting. Beat until the whites are dense and stiff, about 10 minutes.

*4* In a large bowl, combine the egg yolks and remaining $^1/_2$ cup sugar. Beat until they're well combined. Stir in the baking powder and salt. Add the beaten egg whites, flour, melted butter, and hazelnuts. Using a rubber spatula, gently fold the ingredients together until just incorporated.

**5** Transfer the batter into the prepared cake pan, smoothing out the top with the spatula.

**6** Bake until the cake is lightly browned and a knife inserted in the center comes out clean, about 40 minutes. Let the cake cool in the pan for 5 minutes. Then turn it out onto a wire rack and let it cool for at least 2 hours.

## Layer Cake

This cake can be split in half horizontally to make 2 layers (see Figure 15-3). You can fill the layers with Pastry Cream (see recipe earlier in the chapter) that has been lightened with a little whipped cream, some cooled Zabaglione, or a favorite chocolate sauce.

**Italian recipe name:** *Torta Margherita*

**Preparation time:** *20 minutes (plus cooling time)*

**Cooking time:** *40 minutes*

**Yield:** *6 servings*

**Special tools:** *9-x-2-inch round cake pan, handheld mixer, serrated knife, rubber spatula*

| | |
|---|---|
| *Butter for greasing cake pan* | *2 egg yolks* |
| *1 cup flour plus flour for dusting cake pan* | *Pinch of salt* |
| *4 room-temperature eggs* | *$^3/_4$ cup sugar* |

**1** Preheat oven to 375°.

**2** Grease and flour the cake pan. Bring a large pot half full of water to a simmer.

**3** In a large bowl, beat the eggs, egg yolks, salt, and sugar together with a handheld mixer on medium speed for 1 minute.

**4** Place the bowl on the large pot of simmering water. Whisk until the egg mixture is warm and then remove from heat. Whip on high speed until the mixture has lightened in color and increased in volume four times.

**5** Sift the flour into the mixing bowl and gently fold it into the batter by using a rubber spatula. When well incorporated, pour the mixture into the prepared cake pan. Bake until a knife inserted in the center comes out clean, about 40 minutes. Let the cake cool in the pan for 5 minutes. Then turn the cake out onto a wire rack and let it cool for at least 2 hours.

**6** Slice the cake in half horizontally and fill as desired.

**Figure 15-3:**
Use a serrated knife to slice the cooled cake in half to make two layers.

Use a serrated knife to slice the cooled cake in half to make two layers.

# Queen of Tarts

Italians use a rich pastry dough to make a wide array of nut and fruit tarts.

Unlike American pie dough, the following pastry is quite rich and sweet. In fact, it can be rolled thick, cut into small pieces, sprinkled with sugar and chopped nuts, and baked into cookies. For tarts, you're going to want to roll the dough thinner.

 Pastry isn't hard to handle as long as you keep it cold. That means refrigerating the dough for at least half an hour before rolling it out. Also, don't handle the dough too much. Your hands are hot and can melt the butter in the dough.

## Pastry Dough

This recipe makes enough pastry for 2 tarts. Bake 1 and put the other (unbaked) in the freezer for a later day. Pastry Dough keeps in the freezer for a month. Simply defrost it overnight in the refrigerator before rolling.

*Italian recipe name:* Pasta Frolla

*Preparation time:* 5 minutes

*Cooking time:* None

*Yield:* Two 9-inch tart crusts

*Special tools:* Standing mixer or handheld mixer, plastic wrap

*1 cup room-temperature butter (2 sticks)*

*1 cup sugar*

*3 room-temperture eggs*

*2 teaspoons vanilla extract*

*3 cups flour*

*1¹/₂ teaspoons baking powder*

*Pinch of salt*

*1* In the bowl of a standing mixer or in a large bowl using a handheld electric mixer, whip or beat the butter and sugar together until creamy.

*2* Add the eggs, 1 at a time, beating with each addition. Stir in the vanilla extract. Then slowly mix in the flour, baking powder, and salt. Mix for about 45 seconds, until the dough comes together and all ingredients are combined.

*3* Remove the dough from the bowl and divide in half. Using your hands, shape each half into a smooth disk. Wrap them in plastic wrap and refrigerate for at least half an hour before using. When ready to use, roll out on a floured surface with a rolling pin to approximately 11 inches in diameter.

## Walnut Meringue Tart

This tart is similar to a pecan pie, except the filling is much lighter because it's made from *meringue*, or egg whites beaten with sugar. To get the maximum volume from the egg whites, make sure that you separate them carefully from the yolks and bring to room temperature. Even just a speck or two of yolk (or any trace of oil on the bowl or beaters) makes properly whipping the whites impossible.

**Italian recipe name:** *Torta di Noci*

**Preparation time:** *20 minutes*

**Cooking time:** *40 minutes*

**Yield:** *6 servings*

**Special tools:** *10-inch springform pan (see Figure 15-4), parchment paper or waxed paper, standing mixer, rubber spatula*

*¹/₂ recipe Pastry Dough (see recipe earlier in the chapter)*

*Butter for greasing pan*

*Flour for dusting pan*

*6 room-temperature egg whites*

*¹/₄ teaspoon salt*

*1 cup minus 1 tablespoon sugar*

*2 cups walnut halves*

*Grated zest of 1 lemon*

*(continued)*

*1* Preheat oven to 325°.

*2* Butter a 10-inch springform pan and line the bottom with parchment paper or waxed paper.

*3* On a flour-dusted surface, roll out the Pastry Dough until it's 11 to 12 inches in diameter. Fit it into the bottom of the springform pan, cutting away the excess.

*4* In the bowl of a standing mixer, beat the egg whites and the salt on low speed until frothy. In a slow, but steady stream, add the sugar. Gradually increase the speed to the highest setting. Beat until the whites are dense and stiff, about 10 minutes. Fold in the walnuts and lemon zest. Mix thoroughly. Using a rubber spatula, turn the mixture into the prepared pan. Bake for 35 to 40 minutes, until lightly browned and the meringue is cooked. Cool the tart in the pan. Remove the side of the pan. Cut cake into wedges to serve.

**Figure 15-4:**
A springform pan.

A springform pan has a latch on the side and a detachable bottom.

## Blueberry Tart

Pastry Dough, Pastry Cream, and fresh summer fruit make an unbeatable combination. You can use any fresh berries or sliced stone fruits (peaches, plums, nectarines, or apricots) in this recipe.

Here, you bake the crust empty and then fill it when cooled. To keep the empty crust from bubbling up in the oven, prick it all over with a fork and then line the crust with a piece of foil. Weigh down the foil with metal pie weights or dried beans to keep the crust in place as it bakes.

**Italian recipe name:** *Crostata di Mirtilli*

**Preparation time:** *10 minutes (plus cooling time)*

**Cooking time:** *30 minutes*

**Yield:** *6 servings*

**Special tools:** *9-inch tart pan with a removable bottom, aluminum foil, metal pie weights or dried beans*

*Butter for greasing pan*

*Flour for dusting work surface*

*$^1/_2$ recipe Pastry Dough (see recipe earlier in this chapter)*

*2 cups fresh blueberries, rinsed and dried*

*2 tablespoons sweet liqueur (such as Grand Marnier)*

*$^1/_2$ recipe Pastry Cream (see recipe earlier in this chapter)*

*1 tablespoon confectioners sugar*

*1* Preheat oven to 375°.

*2* Lightly grease the tart pan.

*3* On a flour-dusted surface, roll out the Pastry Dough to about 12 inches in diameter, $^1/_8$- to $^1/_4$-inch thick. Carefully center the dough in the tart pan, lightly lifting and pressing the dough so that it conforms to the bottom and sides of the pan. Trim the edges leaving a 1-inch overlap around the pan. Fold this dough forward, toward the inside of the pan, and crimp it decoratively.

*4* Prick the bottom of the tart dough all over with a fork. Loosely lay a piece of aluminum foil over the dough and place dried beans or pie weights on the foil. Bake on the center rack of the oven for 15 minutes.

*5* Remove the foil and the beans or weights and continue baking the dough for another 10 to 12 minutes until lightly browned. Remove the pan from the oven and cool the tart dough in the pan on a wire rack.

*6* In a medium bowl, mix together the berries and the liqueur.

*7* Evenly spread the Pastry Cream on the bottom of the tart shell. Neatly arrange the blueberries over the top. Carefully separate the bottom from the sides of the tart pan and place the tart (on the pan's bottom) on a serving plate. Sprinkle with confectioners sugar and serve.

## Mantuan Almond Tart

This simple tart comes from the city of Mantua in Lombardy. It's very crisp and hard, more like a cookie than a conventional tart, especially because it has no filling. Because this tart is so crisp, you should break the tart into pieces by hand instead of slicing it. This tart is fairly dry and is meant to be served with wine. In Mantua, cooks traditionally use lard in this recipe, but you can make it with butter instead.

*(continued)*

**Italian recipe name:** *Sbrisolona*

**Preparation time:** *20 minutes (plus cooling time)*

**Cooking time:** *40 minutes*

**Yield:** *4 servings*

**Special tool:** *9-inch tart pan with removable bottom*

*¹/₂ cup room-temperature butter plus butter for greasing tart pan*

*1 cup flour plus flour for dusting pan*

*1 cup sugar*

*2 egg yolks*

*1 teaspoon vanilla extract*

*2 teaspoons grated lemon zest*

*1 cup cornmeal*

*Pinch of salt*

*1 cup chopped almonds*

*1* Preheat oven to 350°.

*2* Lightly grease the tart pan and then dust it with flour, lightly tapping the bottom of the pan to remove any excess flour.

*3* In a large mixing bowl, cream together the butter and sugar. Add the egg yolks, beating to incorporate. Stir in the vanilla extract and lemon zest.

*4* Add the flour, cornmeal, and salt. Mix until well combined and then stir in the almonds.

*5* Pour the batter into the prepared pan. Place the pan on the center rack of the oven and bake for 30 to 40 minutes; when the tart is done, a cake tester or paring knife should come out clean after being inserted in the center. Cool the tart in the pan on a wire rack. Break into pieces and serve.

# Chapter 16
# Coffee and After-Dinner Drinks

. . . . . . . . . . . . . . . . . . . . . . . . . . . . . . . . . . . . . . . . . .

## In This Chapter

▶ Making perfect espresso

▶ Foaming milk for cappuccino

▶ Ordering Italian coffee in America

▶ Deciding what to serve after dinner

▶ Getting a grip on grappa

. . . . . . . . . . . . . . . . . . . . . . . . . . . . . . . . . . . . . . . . . .

*E*spresso and cappuccino are the latest Italian inventions to conquer the world. After decades of decreasing consumption, we're drinking more and more coffee, and we can thank the Italians for that. A quick peek at most any television sitcom tells the story. Characters seem to spend all day hanging out in coffee bars, downing lattes and cappuccinos. Americans have discovered two things Italians have always known about coffee — it's fun, and it can taste good when made right.

Unfortunately, making good espresso is very different from making good coffee. It's also much harder. Even if you don't want to make espresso at home, ordering coffee out has gone beyond the simple "milk or sugar" question. A visit to the local java joint can quickly become a test of your hipness, with everyone speaking a highly specialized coffee bar language.

In this chapter, we show you how to make good Italian coffee drinks at home. We also explain all the terminology and etiquette, and we cut through some of the hype. If nothing else, you'll be able to order a latte and know what you're talking about. The chapter ends with a look at some Italian after-dinner drinks that you can often serve with espresso.

# Coffee, Italian Style

Italians love espresso. Big cities and small villages alike are dotted with bars, where patrons stand at the counter to down a shot of espresso and maybe munch on a breakfast pastry. Many Italians make several pit stops during the day, ducking into a coffee bar every few hours for a refill. Unlike American coffee bars, which often have couches and tables for relaxing, most Italian coffee bars aren't designed for hanging out. A quick sip, and Italians are off. Meeting someone at an Italian coffee bar for a date is pretty hard to imagine. People usually crowd around the counter, often two or three deep. Think happy hour at an American bar on a Friday evening.

Italians like their espresso black, usually with lots of sugar but no milk. The exception is in the morning, when drinks like cappuccino and latte are popular. However, ordering a cappuccino after dinner in an Italian restaurant is considered odd. Italians are not big milk drinkers and don't understand why you would want something so rich and filling after a big meal.

---

## American coffee bar lingo

If you think that following the medical dialog in an episode of *ER* is tough, try ordering at an American coffee bar. Unless you want to look foolish, you need to learn the lingo. Here's our crash course.

Most places list coffee drinks by their Italian names (see the sidebar "Italian coffee drinks" for more information). But then the *barista* (the Italian word for a person who works behind the counter at a coffee bar) and many customers use shorthand to explain the size, type of milk, whether the milk should be steamed or frothed, and the caffeine status. We've heard some pretty silly names and combinations, such as a Half Caf Double Short Skinny Latte or Short Skinny Sleeper Cappuccino. Here are some of the most common terms:

✔ **Short:** A small latte or cappuccino, usually about 6 ounces.

✔ **Tall:** A large latte or cappuccino, usually about 12 ounces.

✔ **Grande:** An extra-large latte or cappuccino, usually about 16 ounces.

✔ **Double Short/Double Tall/Double Grande:** Two shots of espresso in a coffee drink.

✔ **Short/Tall/Grande Skinny:** Coffee drink made with skim milk.

✔ **Short/Tall/Grande Two:** Coffee drink made with 2 percent milk.

✔ **Short/Tall/Grande Breve:** Coffee drink made with half-and-half instead of milk.

✔ **Half Caf:** Coffee drink made with half regular espresso and half decaf espresso.

✔ **Sleeper:** Coffee drink made with decaf espresso.

# *What is espresso?*

You make brewed coffee by letting water drip or percolate through ground beans. The process takes several minutes and produces a beverage that has the same consistency as water. Espresso is made by forcing almost-boiling water under pressure through finely ground coffee. The process takes just seconds.

Espresso has more body than brewed coffee. Fans also say that this extraction process captures more bean flavor in the cup, and we agree. Recognizing a good espresso is easy: The top of the espresso should be covered by a thick, light brown blanket of tiny bubbles called *crema*. Crema is essential because it adds smoothness and creaminess — without it, espresso is just strong coffee.

If the crema is not well defined (it should be thick enough to briefly trap sugar crystals sprinkled over an espresso), you need to use different coffee or adjust your espresso-making technique. (See the section "Using an espresso machine," later in this chapter.) Good espresso begins with freshly ground coffee beans that have been roasted medium or dark. (Lightly roasted beans make insipid espresso.) Look for dark brown (but not black) beans — beans can be roasted too much, and black beans make burnt-tasting espresso — that have an oily sheen. Dry or cracked beans are past their prime.

If you're concerned about optimum quality, grind the beans yourself. Unfortunately, inexpensive blade grinders don't really grind beans fine enough for espresso. You really need a burr grinder (the beans are crushed between metal plates rather than chopped, as in a blade grinder), and they cost at least $50, if not more. That's why many people ask their coffee roaster to grind the beans.

The downside to having your coffee ground at the store, rather than at home, is that beans begin to lose freshness as soon as they're ground. If you're a connoisseur — that is, the kind of person who isn't satisfied with anything but the absolute best — or if you plan to nurse a bag of coffee over a period of a month or two, buying ground coffee is a problem.

For normal folks, buying ground coffee is fine as long as you use it up in a few weeks (consider buying coffee by the half pound) and properly store it. Store whole beans or ground coffee in airtight containers away from sunlight. Whole beans do best at room temperature. Ground coffee is fine on the counter for a few days, but put it in the freezer if you plan to take a week or two to go through your coffee supply.

# Italian coffee drinks

Italian coffee bars rarely have a menu or printed sign listing all their coffee drinks. So it helps to know what you like. Here are descriptions of the major Italian coffee drinks. And, yes, we finally explain the difference between a latte and a cappuccino.

✔ **Espresso:** A single shot of espresso, measuring 1½ ounces. Served in a warmed demitasse — a small cup that holds about 3 ounces. To take the chill off ceramic demitasse cups, fill them with hot tap water while waiting for the espresso machine to heat up. Fancy machines have a built-in warming plate for cups.

✔ **Espresso Doppio:** A "double" shot of espresso, measuring about 3 ounces. Served in a large demitasse cup or a very small coffee cup.

✔ **Espresso Ristretto:** A "short" or "restricted" espresso of about 1 ounce. Made by cutting short the water flow when brewing. Very syrupy and intense.

✔ **Espresso Lungo:** The opposite of a ristretto, made by adding an ounce or two of hot water to a single espresso to make a milder or "long" cup. When diluted with 3 or 4 ounces of hot water, this drink is sometimes called an *Americano,* because it has a similar intensity as American-style brewed coffee.

✔ **Espresso Macchiato:** A single espresso "marked" by a tablespoon of frothed milk. Perfect when you don't want all the milk used in a cappuccino or latte but aren't ready for plain espresso.

✔ **Espresso con Panna:** A single shot of espresso with a small dollop of whipped cream. Very decadent and very delicious. Especially popular in the afternoon in Italy.

✔ **Espresso Romano:** Espresso served with lemon peel. Italians turn up their noses at this American invention for good reason — the acidity in the lemon peel detracts from the flavor of the espresso. Real Italian restaurants serve espresso as is, with the sugar bowl on the side and nothing else.

✔ **Espresso Corretto:** A single espresso that has been "corrected" with a splash of brandy, grappa, or other spirit. Some Italians have this for breakfast. Not recommended if you want to keep your job elsewhere in the world.

✔ **Cappuccino:** A single espresso topped with equal amounts of steamed milk and frothed milk. Steamed milk has been heated; frothed milk is both heated and aerated and has a stiff, foamy consistency. Often dusted with cocoa powder or ground cinnamon. Nutmeg, a common duster in America, is rarely used in Italy.

✔ **Caffe Latte:** This translates as "coffee with milk" and is similar to the French *cafe au lait* or the Spanish *cafe con leche.* In Italy, the latte is a morning drink consumed at home rather than in coffee bars. It's usually made with brewed coffee (rather than espresso) and steamed milk. It doesn't contain any foam. Americans have adopted this drink as their own, partly because it's easier to charge $3 for a coffee drink in a large cup. Most American coffee bars use espresso and add much more milk than they do in Italy. Some American coffee bars also add frothed milk. A thin crown of frothed milk makes this drink similar to a cappuccino. When a lot of foamy milk is added, this drink is indistinguishable from a cappuccino.

✔ **Caffè Mocha:** Italian companies make dozens of syrups that are traditionally used to make sodas. A shot of syrup is poured into a tall glass that is then filled with soda water or fruit juice. American coffee bars have adopted these flavorings, adding them to espresso, something most Italians would consider disgusting. A caffè mocha is made by adding about half an ounce of chocolate syrup to a single espresso. The flavored espresso is then topped with several ounces of steamed milk. We understand the appeal of adding chocolate syrup to coffee. Adding vanilla, almond, or hazelnut syrup makes some sense, but we would never consume coffee drinks made with them. But why would anyone want to add raspberry or orange flavor to a coffee drink?

## Types of espresso machines

Of course, you can ruin great coffee by placing it in the wrong espresso machine. (Bad technique can ruin good coffee used in a good espresso machine, too. More on that in the upcoming section "Using an espresso machine," we promise.) Here, we tell you about four types of machines commonly used to make espresso (see Figure 16-1). Only two of them build enough pressure to make *real* espresso. Despite what their manufacturers may claim, the other two make strong coffee, not espresso.

**Figure 16-1:** Different types of coffee makers used in Italian homes.

Coffee Makers
electric pump
moka
ciao!
piston lever espresso machine

The moka is the standard coffee maker used in Italian homes. For espresso, you need a machine with an electric pump or piston lever.

✔ **Electric steam espresso machine:** The cheapest type of electric espresso machine relies on steam pressure. We don't think these machines are worth the expense, no matter how minimal. Often sold for $50 or less, these machines produce a weak brew that has no more body than regular coffee and lacks the all-important crema. Machines sold with a glass carafe use steam pressure. Avoid them at all cost. Real espresso is always brewed directly into demitasse cups.

✔ **Moka:** The *moka* is a nonelectric device used in most Italian homes to turn out *caffe*. A moka is usually made of brushed aluminum and comes in three parts. Water goes into the bottom chamber. A coffee filter rests at the top of this chamber. A second chamber is then screwed on top. The moka is set over a burner, and within a few minutes, the pressure from the steam forces the hot water up through the grounds and into the top chamber.

A moka doesn't produce enough steam to make real espresso. Also, you must buy a separate steaming wand if you want to froth milk. (Most Italians just heat the milk on the stove to make real lattes.) Despite these drawbacks, you may want to invest in a moka. The coffee is good and strong, and the price is right, usually about $20. Mokas come in various sizes, capable of making 3 to 10 cups of coffee at a time.

✔ **Electric pump espresso machine:** The moka makes strong Italian-style coffee, but for espresso you need a machine that can generate much more pressure. The majority of good machines on the market use electric pumps to push hot water through the grounds. Pumps can generate much more pressure than steam alone. The cheapest electric pump espresso machine costs about $150. We've seen machines designed for home use that run more than $1,000, and professional models can cost thousands more.

✔ **Manual pump espresso machine:** Another type of machine relies on a manual pump. These old-fashioned units have a large handle in front. The lever controls a piston that forces hot water through the grounds. Although these machines are the most complicated to master, some espresso buffs like them because they give the user more control.

How fast or slowly the water is pushed through the grounds affects the flavor and consistency of the espresso. At espresso bars in Italy, you can order a *ristretto* (a super-concentrated espresso with extra viscosity) or a *lungo* (a slightly diluted espresso, which is ideal for iced coffee). Piston machines cost at least $400 and are a small part of the U.S. market because they are both expensive and difficult to use.

You can't alter the length of time that the water takes to pass through the grounds when using an electric pump machine. However, as long as the manufacturer has calibrated the machine properly (and most do), it should be capable of producing superior espresso.

In the end, the idea of the piston machine is better than the reality, and we recommend electric pumps to friends and family who want to make real espresso and cappuccino at home.

## Using an espresso machine

Percolators and drip coffee machines are nearly idiot-proof, but espresso machines require some practice and skill to operate. In fact, Starbucks and other chains train their workers for weeks. Some companies even run their own "coffee colleges."

Home cooks don't want to go to school just to learn to make coffee. Thankfully, machines are becoming easier to use as manufacturers try to simplify things for the home market. And making great espresso at home is cheaper than ever before. You can find literally hundreds of models on the market, and prices have been falling steadily as competition increases.

Buying a good espresso machine is no guarantee to making good espresso at home. First, you have to buy quality beans that have been freshly roasted. Next, the coffee must be ground correctly, either at the coffee store or at home. If the coffee is too coarse, the water runs through the grounds without extracting enough flavor. If the coffee is too fine, the water takes too long to pass through the grounds and picks up some bitter notes. On most grinders, the "fine" setting delivers the right results.

After you grind the coffee, you must spoon it into the filter basket. A single espresso requires 7 grams of coffee. (Most machines come with a spoon that holds the right amount.) You must then tamp or press the coffee into the filter. If the grounds are too loose, the water runs through too quickly. If you tamp too much, the water gets stuck in the grounds. Grounds that are a bit coarse should be tamped more than grounds that are a bit fine. Tamping is an art and takes practice.

Lukewarm espresso is pretty bad, so we suggest warming everything that comes into contact with the coffee, including the demitasse cup and filter holder. You can fill the cup with hot tap water or use the warming tray that comes with some expensive espresso machines. As for the filter holder, try running some hot water through the machine with the empty (that is, without coffee) holder in place.

Needless to say, you can mess up this process in plenty of places. But it can be mastered, though not on the first try. That's why many companies are turning to pod technology. Like tea bags, *pods* contain ground coffee enclosed in a filter paper. You simply pop a pod into a pod-friendly espresso machine, press the button to activate the electric pump, and wait a few seconds for a perfect cup of espresso. In addition to being idiot-proof, you don't have any messy, wet grounds to dispose of. Simply toss the used pod into the garbage. For more on pods, see the sidebar "The pod people are coming."

## The pod people are coming

Most experts believe that espresso pods will eventually dominate the North American consumer market. Pods are so much easier and cleaner to use that this logic makes sense to us. A few years ago, early prototypes required the purchase of specific pods from the manufacturer of the espresso machine. But that's all changing now.

Illycaffè, Italy's leading espresso company, has relinquished its patent on paper pods. Most espresso manufacturers are designing machines that accept the "easy serving espresso" (ESE) pods, which are based on the original Illycaffè design. This type of generic pod is identified by an ESE logo, which also appears on packing cartons for espresso machines. The idea is that the pods will be available everywhere coffee is sold so that consumers can buy pods at their local roaster instead of relying on the machine manufacturer to also sell them the coffee. If you do buy a machine that accepts pods, make sure that it can also accommodate ground coffee. Not all do.

All this convenience does come at a cost. Although more and more reasonably priced models accept the pods, the pods cost about twice as much to use as ground coffee. However, prices are coming down as pods become more widely available. In a few years, pods may cost just a little more than ground coffee.

## Foaming milk 101

In addition to making espresso, a good espresso machine should be able to steam milk to make a cappuccino or latte. At the very least, the steaming wand should have enough power to double the volume of cold milk, without either scorching it or leaving it tepid.

Each manufacturer suggests a different technique for getting the optimum results with its steaming wand. Some manuals suggest submerging the wand deep into a pitcher of milk, but others say that the tip of the wand should go just below the surface of the milk.

We suggest that you follow the directions that came with your espresso machine. However, you should remember two important points when steaming milk with an espresso machine:

- ✔ **The milk must be cold.** Don't pour milk into a hot container for steaming. You might even consider chilling the container in the refrigerator.

- ✔ **Fresh milk is essential.** As milk approaches its expiration date, getting the milk to foam properly becomes tougher, because the milk sugars are breaking down into *lactic acid* (the stuff that causes milk to taste sour), and lactic acid prevents the milk from trapping air. Even before milk tastes sour, its ability to foam can be compromised. The upshot of all this science: fresh, cold milk foams best.

You can foam any type of milk — skim, lowfat, or whole. Skim milk creates drier foam, and whole milk makes the creamiest, richest foam. Don't try to foam half-and-half or cream at home. The fat clogs the nozzle on most home machines. Even when using milk, the steaming wands clog without regular maintenance. When you finish steaming the milk, open the steam valve into an open container to blow out any milk. Then wipe the wand to remove any particles before they harden. After the milk cools, it becomes quite difficult to remove.

 If you like steamed milk for regular coffee but don't want to spend $150 on an espresso machine, you have another option. You can heat milk in a saucepan on the stove until hot but not boiling. Whirr the milk in a blender for a few seconds, and the result is steamed milk that's a bit foamy. To create real froth or foam (the stiff stuff on top of a real cappuccino), you need to invest in an electric milk steamer. Most models are simply a boiler with a steaming wand that's more powerful than the steaming wands on most reasonably priced espresso machines. You pour water into the boiler, plug in the steamer, and in a few minutes you will have enough steam for a cappuccino and a facial.

# After-Dinner Drinks

Italians often enjoy a *digestivo* after a meal. As the Italian name implies, these alcoholic beverages are thought to aid in digestion. We can't vouch for the science here, but we do know that sipping an after-dinner drink is a very civilized way to prolong a meal and keep the conversation going. Serve the drinks with coffee or after coffee.

## Cordials

Sweet digestivi are called *liquori,* or liqueurs, in Italian. In English, these potent drinks are more likely called *cordials.* Italian cordials are often quite sweet. Here are some of the most widely available options. Serve them straight, on the rocks, or diluted with some seltzer.

- **Amaretto:** The most popular of the Italian cordials, this almond-flavored liqueur is also used frequently in baking. Some brands are made from almonds, but most are actually made from apricot pits, which have a strong almond flavor.

- **Anisette:** This clear cordial has an intense licorice flavor. It's made from anise seed and is often served with coffee.

- **Frangelico:** This syrupy cordial has an intense hazelnut flavor. It's used to flavor desserts or is served on its own. It's sold in a bottle shaped like a monk and is named for a 17th-century Italian hermit.

- **Galliano:** This sweet, bright yellow cordial is blended from a variety of herbs, spices, and berries. The flavor of licorice is pronounced, and it has more than a hint of vanilla. It comes in a tall bottle featuring its namesake, Major Giuseppe Galliano, a hero of the Ethiopian War.

- **Sambuca:** This clear cordial has a very strong, sweet licorice flavor. Unlike anisette, it's made from the berries of a small shrub, not anise seeds. You usually serve sambuca with coffee. Sometimes, sambuca is served *con le mosche,* or "with the flies." A few whole coffee beans are dropped into the glass of sambuca, which is then ignited to create a blue flame. The heat releases some of the coffee flavor into the sambuca. Of course, wait until the flames die before drinking the sambuca and make sure to keep your arms and table linens at a safe distance.

- **Strega:** This mild, golden liqueur is made from herbs, flowers, and spices. The color comes from saffron, and the flavor of vanilla is especially noticeable. The name translates as "witch."

Italians also enjoy bitter digestivi called *amari.* Some of these strong drinks were thought to have medicinal purposes. You can serve them straight or on the rocks with some seltzer water. The latter preparation is best for novices. Amari are hard to find outside of Italy. These two are the most widely available:

- **Averna:** This popular amaro comes from Sicily. It's bitter but still drinkable, with hints of chocolate and spice.

- **Fernet Branca:** This minty, bitter drink tastes like bad medicine. It's definitely an acquired habit, although some Italians are passionate about their Fernet.

## Dessert wines

If a potent cordial doesn't seem appealing, you may want to consider serving a dessert wine. Some are fortified, so they're slightly more alcoholic than regular wine. However, none come close to the potency of grappa or even amaretto.

Most dessert wines taste best chilled. We often serve them with cookies, cheeses, and berries. Here are some of our favorites:

- **Asti Spumante:** The Italian equivalent of Champagne, Asti Spumante is sweeter and quite bubbly. You serve it as an aperitif with antipasti or with cheeses, fruits, and plain cakes after a meal.

- **Marsala:** Sicily produces numerous styles of Marsala. Some are syrupy and sweet, others dry and light. The drier wines are best for cooking. Sweet Marsala makes a nice after-dinner drink. Marsala wines are produced around the world, including California. Most of these wines are quite cheap and rough, and you should use them only for cooking. If you're serving Marsala on its own, look for a quality wine from Sicily. Marsala is particularly good with fruits and nuts.

- **Vin santo:** This amber Tuscan wine is mildly sweet but not cloying. Traditionally, you serve it with almond biscotti. The biscotti are dipped into the wine to soften them up. Vin santo varies greatly in quality and price, depending on how long it has been aged. Good vin santo has been aged in wood barrels for at least three years.

## Ending it right

Italians love coffee drinks and liqueurs for many reasons. Sure, they taste great. But they're also the perfect way to make an enjoyable meal last well into the night. If you are tired of sitting at the table, why not serve coffee and drinks out on the patio or maybe by the fire? It's a casual, definitely Italian way to end a great meal.

## Grappa: For tough guys and gals only

*Grappa* is a clear brandy, not a liqueur. However, it's often served the same way, either on its own after dinner or with coffee. Grappa is made from the skins that remain after grapes have been pressed to make wine. The skins are mixed with water and then distilled. The result is a fiery drink that most newcomers to grappa find unpalatable.

Grappa was once a peasant drink, but it has become incredibly trendy. We have been in hip bars and nightclubs in New York, London, and Los Angeles that stock a half dozen brands of grappa. Some brands are now being made from grapes mixed with wine to mellow some of the fire. Flavored grappas are also a new development in the export market. The beautiful, clear Venetian glass bottles certainly have helped boost sales as well. The bottles are works of art that look great behind the bar. Some bottles of grappa now retail for $500 or more, as much an indication of the bottle's craftsmanship as the quality of contents.

# Part VI
## Menus for Every Occasion

The 5th Wave    By Rich Tennant

@RICHTENNANT

"Relax - another helping of vermicelli, and I'll be done with your precious shredder."

## In this part . . .

Great recipes (and this book is filled with them) are the building blocks for great meals. But you have to know how to put individual dishes together. Memorable meals don't just happen; they take some planning. In Chapter 1, we explain the philosophy behind creating an Italian menu. In this part, we give you some concrete examples, using recipes from this book to create dozens of menus, both elegant and simple. Whether you're planning an Italian Christmas Eve celebration or a quick weeknight dinner for the family, we've got it covered.

# Chapter 17

# When Company Calls

● ● ● ● ● ● ● ● ● ● ● ● ● ● ● ● ● ● ● ● ● ● ● ● ● ● ● ● ● ● ● ● ● ● ● ● ● ● ● ●

### In This Chapter

▶ Cooking for a crowd

▶ Planning a holiday get-together

▶ Entertaining friends in style

▶ Dining for love

● ● ● ● ● ● ● ● ● ● ● ● ● ● ● ● ● ● ● ● ● ● ● ● ● ● ● ● ● ● ● ● ● ● ● ● ● ● ● ●

*F*ace it. Sometimes, you have to cook. You can't really order take-out pizza for Christmas dinner. If you want to have friends and family to your house (and you want them to come back), Italian food is a natural choice. Italian food is popular, relies on many inexpensive ingredients, and allows for a fair amount of flexibility, especially because you traditionally serve many dishes at room temperature.

This chapter envisions a number of social situations — everything from a bridal shower luncheon to dinner for your kid's soccer team — and offers some strategies and menus for serving good food without killing yourself with work.

## Preparing for Success

Although most of these menus are easy enough to follow, they're not necessarily quick. (For simple weeknight menus, see Chapter 18.) But you can cut down on the amount of work by following a few suggestions.

> ✔ **Try to do as much preparation and cooking as you can in advance.** Rely on your refrigerator and freezer to keep dishes waiting for company.
>
> ✔ **Enlist help.** Spouses and children should pitch in. Think about getting a friend or neighbor to split the cooking duties. A party can certainly have two hosts.
>
> ✔ **Remember that these menus are suggestions.** Of course, you can make substitutions or eliminate a dish or two.

✔ **Consider letting professionals do some of the cooking.** Buy appetizers or desserts at a good gourmet shop or Italian bakery. That way, you can still serve a multicourse menu without feeling like you're training to become a caterer.

✔ **Know your limitations.** Before settling on a particular menu, read all the recipes twice and make sure that you have the time, energy, and money that's required. If you have any doubt, figure out how to simplify the work or simply choose another menu.

# Cooking for a Mob, Italian Style

Your kid's soccer team is coming over for dinner, or maybe it's your turn to host the neighborhood potluck. Italian cooking is a natural for entertaining a crowd. Most people like Italian food, and you can keep costs down, especially if you plan a meal around pasta or chicken rather than beef or fish. The following menus rely on crowd-pleasing recipes that you can double or triple as needed.

## Pasta night

This menu starts with the theory that everyone likes pasta. (As theories go, this one seems pretty sound to us.) You can dress up this menu by adding a selection of appetizers. Or keep it simple by serving just pasta, salad, and dessert.

You can make batches of the sauce in advance and keep them in the refrigerator for a few days. When the time comes to cook the pasta, add up to $1\frac{1}{2}$ pounds of spaghetti to one pot, using as many pots as needed. For example, to serve 12, cook 3 pounds of pasta in two pots.

We like to serve the crunchy and sweet fennel and orange salad after this pasta dish, but you may serve a large leafy salad if you choose. The tiramisù is a good dessert because it feeds a lot, and you can prepare it in advance.

✔ Pasta with Tomato and Basil Sauce (Chapter 6)

✔ Fennel and Orange Salad (Chapter 4)

✔ Tiramisù (Chapter 15)

## Summer barbecue, Italian style

Italians love to eat outdoors, or *al fresco*. Foods from the grill combined with room-temperature dishes make a perfect summer party. This menu starts with a room temperature eggplant relish that you can serve with toasts or raw vegetables. Grilled T-bone steak, seasoned and cooked Florentine style, is the main course. Because it's summer, we've chosen some vegetable salads to act as the *contorno*. After all this eating, we suggest roasted fruit for dessert.

- ✔ Sicilian Eggplant Relish (Chapter 3)
- ✔ Grilled Steak, Florentine Style (Chapter 12)
- ✔ Italian Potato Salad (Chapter 4)
- ✔ Mushroom Salad (Chapter 4)
- ✔ Roasted Fruit (Chapter 15)

## Lunch for the ladies

This menu is light and summery, ideal for a bridal shower or other midday get-together. The tomato, mozzarella, and basil salad takes just minutes to assemble. The chicken is delicious straight from the grill, but you can serve it at room temperature. (We suggest that you grill the chicken an hour before your guests arrive and then jump into the shower.) The blueberry tart is an impressive but simple dessert that even the guys — if they're invited — will love.

- ✔ Tomato and Mozzarella Salad, Capri Style (Chapter 4)
- ✔ Chicken under a Brick (Chapter 11)
- ✔ Blueberry Tart (Chapter 15)

# Holiday Fare

You don't have to be Italian to enjoy Italian food around the holidays. Who doesn't like lamb for Easter or a seafood extravaganza for Christmas Eve? The following menus represent the best of Italian cooking. Because they're designed for holidays, these menus are fairly elaborate and require advance work.

## Easter, Italian style

Because Easter is such a festive holiday, we suggest spending some extra time to make spinach ravioli. Of course, if you live near a good pasta shop or gourmet store that makes its own fresh pasta, you can always let someone else do the hard work and just cook and sauce the ravioli yourself.

- Bruschetta with White Beans (Chapter 3)
- Spinach Ravioli (Chapter 7)
- Braised Lamb Shanks (Chapter 12)
- Mashed Potatoes (Chapter 14)
- Layer Cake (Chapter 15)

## An Italian Passover

Jews have lived and cooked in Italy for centuries. In Rome, for example, a Jewish neighborhood along the Tiber River has several excellent restaurants. Many popular dishes, such as *carciofi alla guidia* (deep-fried whole artichokes), have their roots in Italy's Jewish cuisine. The following menu takes its inspiration from this cuisine. You don't eat leavened bread during Passover, so spread the chicken livers over matzoh instead.

- Crostini with Chicken Livers (Chapter 3)
- Grouper, Livorno Style (Chapter 13)
- Sautéed Mixed Mushrooms (Chapter 14)
- Stewed Potatoes (Chapter 14)
- Prunes in Red Wine (Chapter 15)

## A seafood dinner for Christmas Eve

Traditionally, Italians don't eat meat on Christmas Eve. Church doctrine has changed to permit the consumption of meat on Christmas Eve, but the custom lives on. Some menus call for as many as seven or eight kinds of seafood. We start with mussels as an antipasto and then move on to a simple salmon salad, followed by spaghetti with clams, and then swordfish.

- Peppered Mussels (Chapter 3)
- Salmon Salad (Chapter 4)
- Spaghetti with Clams (Chapter 6)
- Swordfish with Tomatoes and Oregano (Chapter 13)
- Lentil Stew (Chapter 14)
- Sautéed Broccoli Rabe (Chapter 14)
- Walnut Meringue Tart (Chapter 15)

# Special Meals for Friends

Some of our favorite menus are those designed for a small gathering of friends. The intimate dinner party, with four to eight people, is a chance to try dishes you would never make for a crowd because the ingredients are so expensive or the preparation is just too complicated. The following menus enable you to show off your culinary skills. Make sure to serve these dishes with good wines for an evening to remember.

## A taste of Tuscany

Small dinner parties provide the perfect opportunity to create a regional menu. You can impress your guests with your in-depth knowledge of Italian food. This hearty menu takes its cue from the cooking of Tuscany.

- ✔ Bruschetta with Tomatoes (Chapter 3)
- ✔ Rigatoni with Sausage and Peas (Chapter 6)
- ✔ Tuscan Fish Stew (Chapter 13)
- ✔ Biscotti (Chapter 15)

## New Year's Eve with friends

Staying at home on New Year's Eve can be fun, especially if you have good food, good wine, and good company. This menu can help you and your friends ring in the new year with plenty of cheer.

- ✔ Vegetables with Hot Anchovy Dip (Chapter 3)
- ✔ Spaghetti with Clams (Chapter 6)
- ✔ Sea Bass with Mushrooms (Chapter 13)
- ✔ Stewed Potatoes (Chapter 14)
- ✔ Hazelnut Cake (Chapter 15)

# Cucina d'Amore: Cooking for Two

The link between sex and food is as old as humankind. Why do you think mothers have told daughters that good cooking is the quickest way to win a man's heart? Take it from two guys, Mother was right. And take it from two men with a lot of experience in the kitchen, good cooking is also the quickest way to win a woman's heart.

The following menus are designed for two. We've chosen recipes that you can scale down — no vats of stew or cakes that serve ten.

## Dinner by the fireplace

This winter menu is perfect for a romantic dinner for two, especially for Valentine's Day or maybe New Year's Eve. If oysters, scallops, beef, and silky crème caramel can't seduce your partner, then nothing will.

- Stuffed Oysters, Taranto Style (Chapter 3)
- Scallops with Porcini Mushrooms (Chapter 13)
- Beef Strips with Garlic and Rosemary (Chapter 12)
- Crème Caramel (Chapter 15)

## Spring fling

This light spring menu takes advantage of seasonal produce to create a memorable meal that won't leave you too full to go out dancing after dinner. If you can get your hands on some good tomatoes, serve the salmon. If the peas look good, then try the halibut. Either way, make sure to save room for the *zabaglione,* a frothy custard spiked with Marsala. Serve the zabaglione over fresh berries. This menu is so good that your partner may spoon-feed you dessert.

- Asparagus with Parmesan (Chapter 3)
- Trenette with Pesto, Genovese Style (Chapter 6)
- Salmon with Fresh Tomato Sauce or Halibut with Peas and Scallions (both in Chapter 13)
- Zabaglione (Chapter 15)

## Summer love

Food can be an aphrodisiac, but in the summer you want to keep things light. Room-temperature dishes, such as the prosciutto and fruit and the *panzanella* (a vegetable and bread salad from Tuscany), are especially appropriate. If you choose the Biscotti for dessert, this menu can go to the beach or park for a picnic. If you're staying at home, eat dinner on the patio and go for the ice cream.

✔ Prosciutto with figs or melon (You don't need a recipe for this; just serve thinly sliced prosciutto with halved fresh figs or chunks of peeled cantaloupe or honeydew melon; see photo in color section.)

✔ Tuscan Bread Salad (Chapter 4)

✔ Shells with Uncooked Tomato Sauce (Chapter 6)

✔ Vanilla Ice Cream or Biscotti (Chapter 15)

## Foolproof first date menu

Say you've invited someone special over for dinner. Or maybe it's your first date, and you want to ensure a second date. You need a menu that works. You're also pretty nervous, so you need a simple menu that won't add more stress to an already dicey situation. This menu should do the trick.

The chicken and mushroom recipe is a one-dish main course, and it can sit on the stove simmering away as you hop in the shower. The salad takes less than five minutes to prepare, and you have to make the tiramisù in advance because you serve it chilled. We've also chosen foods, such as tomatoes and chicken, that most everyone likes. (Wait for the second date to prepare calf's liver.)

✔ Tomato and Mozzarella Salad, Capri Style (Chapter 4)

✔ Braised Chicken with Mushrooms (Chapter 11)

✔ Tiramisù (Chapter 15)

# Chapter 18

# Everyday Meals

### In This Chapter

▶ Feeding a family on a budget

▶ Cooking when the clock is ticking

▶ Keeping down fat but not flavor

*W*hen you entertain, you often plan the menu weeks in advance. When you make dinner for the family, the menu often just happens. Face it, most people don't do their best culinary thinking after a long day of working or tending children. In this chapter, we help you answer the dreaded question — what's for dinner? — with style and ease.

## Planning a Weekday Supper

Tuesday night supper isn't the time to try out a traditional, five-course, Tuscan extravaganza. Here are some general thoughts about planning a weekday supper:

✔ **Keep it simple.** A weekday menu should consist of no more than three dishes. Ideally, one or two dishes do the trick.

✔ **Don't hesitate to let your local gourmet store or supermarket do some of the cooking.** Prepared desserts, appetizers, and even side dishes can help. Or buy a whole roasted chicken and then add some sides or a salad that you make yourself.

✔ **Keep your pantry and refrigerator well stocked.** If you can skip an early evening run to the supermarket (when the lines are long and slow), you'll have more energy for cooking. Think about picking up a few items at lunchtime when stores are less crowded.

✔ **Try cooking in bulk.** On Sunday night, prepare a double batch of white beans and use them throughout the week in salads and side dishes. If you're making a simple tomato sauce on Monday, you can easily double the recipe and save some for later in the week.

> ✔ **Try to have fun in the kitchen.** Cooking can be relaxing. All that chopping can let you work out the day's stress and anxiety. Good music and some nice wine can also help.

With these guidelines in mind, we've devised menus for several weekday scenarios that may play out in your house.

# Save Those Lire: Feeding Four for Less Than $15

If money is a concern (and when isn't it?), then look no further than this book. All budget-conscious shoppers need some Italian dishes in their repertoires. After all, how many nights a week can you eat tuna noodle casserole?

Many Italian dishes taste expensive but are not, because Italian cooking relies on big flavors — like garlic, onions, and fresh herbs — that pack a lot of punch for a little money. You generally use expensive ingredients, such as olive oil, in small amounts that add just pennies to the cost of a dish.

We've put together three menus that rely on pasta, soup, and chicken. All three are inexpensive to prepare but still tremendously satisfying. Best of all, you can eat like royalty and still pay the mortgage.

## Pasta night on a shoestring

At just pennies a pound, pasta is a must for any budget-minded cook. To save money, choose sauces with tomatoes and vegetables rather than those with seafood or lots of cheese. Meat sauces work as well, satisfying the carnivores in your family without breaking the budget.

When serving pasta as a main course, try to choose something hearty. We like orecchiette — a small, ear-shaped pasta — with broccoli rabe because this dish is quite substantial and offers a vegetable as well as the pasta. (If you can't find orecchiette, try penne or ziti in this recipe.) We suggest a simple potato salad to accompany the pasta and greens. (Italians love their starches and don't mind serving potatoes after pasta. In fact, in northern Italy, they sauce pasta with potatoes.) If you have more time and money, follow the pasta with either Breaded Chicken Cutlets in Tomato Sauce or Turkey with Prosciutto and Cheese (both in Chapter 11) instead of the potato salad.

Other pasta dishes that you might consider as main courses include Penne with Tomatoes, Capers, Anchovies, and Olives (the capers and olives require an initial outlay of cash, but they last forever in the refrigerator, and you need very little to get a lot of flavor); Spaghetti with Garlic, Oil, and Chiles; or Rigatoni with Eggplant. (All three of these pasta recipes are in Chapter 6.)

- ✔ Orecchiette with Broccoli Rabe (Chapter 6)
- ✔ Italian Potato Salad (Chapter 4)

## Soup's on

Soup is good food. Soup is also cheap food. Many Italian soups begin with water (which is free) rather than beef or chicken stock. If the soup is hearty enough, you can build a meal around it. Pasta and Bean Soup (see Chapter 5) fits the bill. We like to serve soup with some focaccia, which you can buy or make yourself. Add a simple leafy green salad or the Salmon Salad (see Chapter 4) to round out the meal.

- ✔ Pasta and Bean Soup (Chapter 5)
- ✔ Everyday Focaccia (Chapter 10)
- ✔ Salmon Salad (Chapter 4)

## Chicken in a pot

Chicken used to be cheap. But with the cost of boneless breasts now rivaling that of beef, many parts of the bird are no longer a bargain. However, if you buy a whole bird and cut it up yourself (or if you buy bone-in parts), you can still get a good deal.

We like to cook bone-in, skin-on chicken parts in a pot with vegetables to make a complete dinner. You cook Braised Chicken with Tomatoes and Wine (see Chapter 11), which has a nice thick sauce that you can serve over polenta, with rice, or with Stewed Potatoes (see Chapter 14).

- ✔ Chicken Stewed in Tomato Sauce and Wine (Chapter 11)
- ✔ Basic Polenta (Chapter 9) or Stewed Potatoes (Chapter 14)

# Cucina Rapida: Fast Cooking

Cooking during the week usually has to be fast. Most people have no time to prepare a dozen vegetables or simmer a sauce for an hour. We've designed the following meals to be on the table 30 minutes after you walk into the kitchen.

## Pasta night, 1

You can prepare dozens of pasta sauces in the time it takes to bring the water to a boil and cook the noodles. The following summery menu is especially quick if you make the pesto in advance and keep it in the refrigerator or freezer.

To store pesto, place it in an airtight container and pour a thin film of oil over the sauce. If freezing pesto, leave out the cheese and stir it in after you defrost the pesto.

> ✔ Fennel and Orange Salad (Chapter 4)
> ✔ Trenette with Pesto, Genovese Style (Chapter 6)

## Pasta night, 2

This second pasta menu features quick-cooking shrimp and a simple mushroom salad. This menu is fancy enough for impromptu entertaining, but simple enough to become a standard in your home.

> ✔ Mushroom Salad (Chapter 4)
> ✔ Spaghetti with Shrimp (Chapter 6)

## Cutlets in the pan, 1

Cutlets, also called scaloppine, are a favorite item for weeknight meals. These boneless, skinless cuts are thin enough to cook through in just minutes on top of the stove. We like to remove the cooked cutlets from the pan and then make a quick pan sauce. The sauce can be as simple as wine or lemon juice, or you can make it more elaborate (and heartier) by adding vegetables.

This menu starts with veal, but chicken (see the following menu) or pork cutlets are other possibilities. The simple flavors of lemon and wine work nicely with the broccoli rabe. If you have time, add some mashed or roasted potatoes.

> ✔ Veal Scaloppine with Lemon and Wine (Chapter 12)
> ✔ Sautéed Broccoli Rabe (Chapter 14)

## Cutlets in the pan, 2

You can assemble prosciutto and melon in minutes (just drape thin slices of prosciutto over wedges of cantaloupe or honeydew melon — see photo in color insert), making an elegant starter for this simple meal. Follow with chicken cutlets and some sautéed mushrooms. If you have the time and energy, add a steamed or *blanched* (or boiled) green vegetable, such as broccoli or green beans.

✔ Prosciutto with Melon (Chapter 3)

✔ Chicken Cutlets with Balsamic Vinegar (Chapter 11)

✔ Sautéed Mixed Mushrooms (Chapter 14)

## Seafood in a flash

Like cutlets, thin fish fillets cook through in minutes on top of the stove or on the grill. You can start the meal with some simple toasts covered with white beans. Or, if you can go outside to use the grill, start the meal with grilled shrimp or grilled squid instead.

✔ Bruschetta with White Beans (Chapter 3)

✔ Halibut with Peas and Scallions (Chapter 13)

# Lean Cuisine: Meals to Cut Fat, Not Flavor

Italian cooking is very diet-friendly. Many recipes contain a lot of vegetables, which are high in flavor and fiber but almost free of fat and calories. Many recipes also use olive oil rather than butter or cream. Olive oil contains very little saturated fat and delivers a lot of flavor in every tablespoon.

Throughout the book, we give recipes that combine fish, chicken, or pasta (all of which are low in fat) with an abundant amount of vegetables. Not only is this a healthy way to eat, but these dishes are complete meals, so it's an easy way to cook.

Note that some recipes in this section may contain more oil than your diet permits. However, the oil is incidental in these recipes (it adds flavor but isn't essential for cooking), and you can significantly reduce the amount, if you like.

## Fish is your friend

Seafood is a natural when you're trying to cut calories and fat. We particularly like dishes that combine fish and vegetables to make complete, light meals. The red snapper dish that we recommend here contains zucchini, celery, carrots, onions, arugula, basil, and parsley. You sauté the fish and vegetables, so make sure you use just enough oil to lightly coat the bottom of the pan. Use a nonstick pan to cut the amount of fat needed to cook the fish even further. Another diet-friendly seafood dish is Salmon with Fresh Tomato Sauce (see Chapter 13). The toasts with white beans start the meal on a light, healthy note.

- ✔ Bruschetta with White Beans (Chapter 3)
- ✔ Red Snapper with Vegetables (Chapter 13)

## The skinny on chicken

Cooking chicken on the grill is a perfect way to keep the amount of fat in check. We particularly like Chicken Cutlets with Tomato and Basil Salad (see Chapter 11). The tomatoes keep the chicken breasts moist, and the basil adds a burst of freshness and flavor. You won't feel like you're dieting.

To round out the meal, brush some vegetables, such as zucchini, eggplant, onions, peppers, or asparagus, lightly with olive oil and grill them until lightly browned.

## Pasta is almost perfect

Ripe summer tomatoes are so juicy that they form their own sauce for pasta. No cooking — just dicing — is required. Because tomatoes are so moist, you need to add only oil for flavor. Again, fresh herbs really perk up the flavors in this dish.

- ✔ Shells with Uncooked Tomato Sauce (Chapter 6)
- ✔ Fennel and Orange Salad (Chapter 4)

# Part VII
## The Part of Tens

The 5th Wave          By Rich Tennant

"I'm pretty sure it's pizza dough that gets tossed, not pasta dough."

## In this part . . .

This part of our book distills the important points of good Italian cooking into ten easy rules. For those of you who want to get an advanced degree in Italian cooking, we provide a listing of Web sites and other places to find out more about food, wine, and other aspects of Italian culture. Finally, we cover some all-important Italian phrases.

# Chapter 19

# Ten Commandments of Italian Cooking

*In This Chapter*

▶ The golden rules of Italian cooking

*W*e know. Rules are meant to be broken. But if you can tame your rebellious streak and try to follow these guidelines (doesn't that sound friendlier than rules?), your life will be easier and your cooking will be better. We promise.

## Start with Fresh, High-Quality Ingredients

Freshness is next to godliness in the Italian kitchen. That means using fresh herbs, not dried, and ripe, local tomatoes, not rock-hard orbs that have been picked green, shipped thousands of miles, and then gassed to create a faux red color.

In addition to using fresh herbs, eggs, breads, fruits, and vegetables, buy high-quality oils, vinegars, pastas, and rices. Most Italian dishes rely on a few key ingredients, and those ingredients must taste good in order to produce good food.

Pasta with garlic, olive oil, and hot chiles provides a good example of what can happen when you use inferior or superior ingredients. Use powdered garlic, tasteless olive oil, and wimpy hot red pepper flakes, and this pasta dish doesn't create much interest. However, if you take a minute or two to mince the garlic yourself, add a good extra-virgin olive oil (it can be spicy, floral, or fruity — your choice here), and use a dried red chile with some heat, this quick pasta is delicious. So good, in fact, that we promise that if you make it the right way, this dish will become a staple in your house.

So how do you recognize good ingredients? When choosing fruits and vegetables, freshness is always important. Place of origin is key as well. Strawberries from a local farm are almost always better than berries shipped from Mexico or elsewhere, because fruits and vegetables shipped around the world must be bred to withstand the rigors of travel. (If you think travel is tough on you, just think about what it does to a strawberry.) Many commercial operations also focus on appearance, with flavor considered last, if at all. In contrast, farmers who sell locally usually plant varieties that taste good. Nothing else matters, especially to farmers who sell by the roadside and have to face their customers every day.

As for pantry items like olive oil and balsamic vinegar, you must taste several brands to find one that you like. Italian brands are usually good, but domestic brands can compete in some categories (especially pasta), usually at some cost savings. After you taste a range of oils or vinegars or olives, you begin to develop personal preferences. Maybe you like a spicy oil that burns the back of your throat. Or maybe you like something more fruity. Neither is better than the other — just different.

One note about money. Don't make every decision based solely on cost. A liter of extra-virgin olive oil from Tuscany or Liguria may cost $25, compared to $10 for a supermarket brand. That may seem like a sizable difference in cost (and it is). But the $25 oil costs about 35 cents per tablespoon, compared to about 14 cents per tablespoon of the cheaper oil. If you're drizzling a tablespoon of oil over grilled fish (four pieces of swordfish can cost $20 or more), the better oil (and the extra 20 cents) may make the difference between a good dish and a great one. Sounds like the $25 oil is a good deal after all.

For more on ingredients, see Chapter 2.

# Simpler Is Always Better

We've eaten in some of the finest restaurants around the world, from family-run trattorias in the Tuscan countryside to the glitziest eateries in New York, Vancouver, Sydney, and Los Angeles. In our experience, the best meals are usually the simplest. We love restaurants, but the food is often overwrought. It has been stacked, stuffed, and so overworked that sometimes we find it hard to know what we're eating.

Good Italian food is always simple, accessible, and easily recognized. Many chefs approach cooking as if it were mad science. They think that if they throw enough ingredients and flavors together, something new and wonderful will emerge. Most of these chef-made creations are new, but like the Frankenstein monster, they can be hideous monstrosities.

The Italian chef knows that good dishes begin with good ingredients. The preparation and cooking coaxes the natural flavors from these ingredients. Sometimes, chefs pair certain foods for contrast or emphasis — for example, salty, creamy prosciutto with sweet, unctuous figs. At other times, chefs choose each ingredient to work together to create a specific flavor or sensation.

Although most Italian recipes have short ingredient lists and require minimal preparation, don't be lulled into thinking that you can cook Italian food without concentrating on the job at hand. Often the taste of a dish relies on a basic technique. For example, you must sauté the garlic over moderate heat until golden for most pasta sauces. If you don't cook the garlic enough, its flavor is raw and harsh. But let the garlic turn dark brown, and it imparts a bitter flavor to the pasta sauce.

When cooking Italian food, be suspicious of any dish that seems overly complex. If the preparation requires a staff of chefs, the recipe probably isn't authentically Italian.

## Cook with the Calendar

When planning meals, let the calendar guide you. Shells with Uncooked Tomato Sauce (see Chapter 6) is a summer dish, which you should make only with ripe tomatoes. Likewise, Butternut Squash Risotto (see Chapter 8) is ideal in November but odd in July. In Italy, cooking seasonally is relatively easy, because you can't find tomatoes in markets during the winter, and squash appears locally only when it's in season (during the fall and early winter).

In America, most food is grown far from urban centers, in places like California's Central Valley or the farm belt of the Midwest. Food is shipped thousands of miles, and most shoppers have no relationship with the people who produce their food. The fact that more and more of the produce sold in America is actually grown abroad, in places like Mexico, Chile, or New Zealand, makes the connection between farmer and cook even more tenuous.

For Italians, cooking seasonally comes naturally, because they maintain close contact with local farming cycles. In Italy, most food is grown locally. Although supermarkets in Boston look much like markets in Chicago or Montreal, the produce available in Venice is often very different from the produce available at markets in Sicily, because agriculture, at least in some respects, remains a local business. Of course, Italians have access to the same out-of-season produce that we see in our markets — pineapples jetted in from Hawaii or mangoes from Jamaica. But for the most part, Italians buy their vegetables at outdoor markets or small stands that local farmers supply.

When planning a meal, the typical Italian cook shops for the produce first. The meal takes its cues from the items that catch the attention of the cook. These foods are fresh and usually taste good. Too often, North American cooks end up disappointed in the food that they prepare because their vegetables and fruits are mediocre.

So what can the cook who doesn't live in Italy do? Try shopping at green markets and farm stands, which usually rely on local produce. Cooking seasonally is much easier if the produce at the market is actually in season. If you shop at a supermarket that carries both in-season and out-of-season vegetables, you have to be more discriminating. Those tomatoes from Holland or Israel might look good, but do they ever really taste like tomatoes? Ask the produce manager where specific items come from and try to pick the fruits and vegetables that have been grown closest to home.

Also, try to think of your mother's or grandmother's cooking. For a July meal, would she have made zucchini or brussels sprouts? The answer is zucchini, unless you live on the other side of the equator, where July means winter.

## Get to Know Your Vegetables

You can't cook real Italian food without spending some time in the produce aisle. Italians don't use canned or frozen vegetables, except in these two situations:

- ✔ They often use frozen spinach to flavor homemade pasta or fill ravioli; however, Italians would never serve frozen spinach as a side dish.

- ✔ They may also use frozen peas. Fresh peas have a short season and don't hold up well in supermarkets because they lose their sweetness almost as soon as they're picked. If you really like peas, grow your own or buy from a local farm; otherwise, stick with frozen.

Other than spinach and peas, use only fresh vegetables. If you think that you don't like vegetables, you need to try different vegetables or new cooking techniques. As far as we're concerned, you can make every vegetable taste delicious as long as it's fresh and then properly seasoned and cooked.

As you cook more and more Italian food, you may become pickier about the quality of vegetables that you buy. Natural-food stores and specialty markets often offer a better and fresher selection than standard supermarkets. Prices may be slightly higher, but vegetables are generally so inexpensive that you'd be happy to trade a little extra money for better flavor.

# Make Friends with Your Local Cheese Vendor

Authentic Italian cooking depends on high-quality cheeses. With few exceptions, this means Italian cheese. Canned grated Parmesan cheese can never compare to the real thing — aged Parmigiano-Reggiano.

Read labels. Fontina from Italy is a semisoft cheese (not quite as runny as brie, but pretty close), with a nutty, buttery flavor. Fontina made elsewhere in Europe and in North America is usually much firmer, with a rubbery texture and little flavor. Italian fontina is a wonderful cheese, worth seeking out. The impostors aren't much better than sliced singles of American cheese.

Nowadays, supermarkets do a better job of stocking Italian cheeses, especially Parmigiano-Reggiano, but finding a source that carries a wide selection of Italian cheeses is worth the effort. If you live near a decent cheese shop or an Italian market, great. If not, gourmet stores likely have a wider and fresher selection of Italian cheeses than local supermarkets have.

In addition to buying good cheeses, discover how to handle them. Parmesan, Pecorino, and other hard cheeses lose flavor fairly quickly when grated, so grate cheese yourself rather than buying it already grated. For more information on purchasing and handling cheese, see Chapter 2.

# Experiment with Recipes

Following a recipe is an important skill. Especially when baking, you need to measure precisely and follow directions exactly. But most Italian cooks prepare dishes from memory, changing quantities and procedures ever so slightly each time. After you figure out how to make a dish, you can follow this model, substituting parsley for basil in a pasta sauce or using Pecorino instead of Parmigiano-Reggiano in a frittata.

Sometimes, you may want to make changes to accommodate a personal preference. However, most Italian cooks make minor changes to favorite dishes because they either do or don't have a particular ingredient on hand. If basil is out of season (or your local market has sold out), make a tomato sauce flavored with parsley, or perhaps tarragon or even mint. The result may not be what the author of the recipe had in mind, but don't worry. Some of the best Italian cooking comes from improvisation.

In addition to making subtle changes in ingredients, you can also change the cooking procedure to vary the result. Maybe you want the onions in a dish to be finely minced and cooked only until softened. Prepared this way, the onions fade into the background of a tomato sauce. But if you take the same onion, slice it into long, thin strips, and then sauté those strips until they're a rich golden brown color, the effect is quite different. Cutting the onions into strips makes them visually and texturally more prominent. Cooking them longer makes their flavor sweeter and more intense.

As you gain more confidence in preparing Italian dishes, you can customize dishes to suit personal preferences. Before you know it, you'll be cooking like a real Italian, relying on your senses and intuition rather than a written recipe.

## Taste as You Cook

Cooking without tasting is impossible. No one but you knows how salty or spicy you like your food. We recommend that you season most dishes throughout the cooking process and then adjust the seasoning just before serving. If you wait to add salt until just before serving, the salt doesn't have time to blend with the other ingredients and bring out their full flavors. If a dish has several components, we suggest that you season each part of the dish and then adjust the seasonings after you combine everything.

We like the clean, clear flavors of kosher or sea salt. Unlike regular table salt, these salts don't contain any additives. We recommend that you keep salt in a small bowl or salt cellar near the stove. Use your fingers to pick up the crystals and sprinkle them evenly over foods. Eventually, you can gauge how much salt you use without measuring spoons.

In addition to salt, Italians season many foods with ground black pepper, hot red pepper flakes or dried chiles, and fresh herbs. Italians use these seasonings to support and enhance the flavor of foods. The focus is rarely, if ever, on these seasonings. For example, Italians use dried chiles to add depth and boldness, but the heat should never be overpowering. Dishes that require liquid or carbohydrate "chasers" to dull the sting of chiles aren't Italian.

## Work at Building Flavor

Many Italian recipes begin with this seemingly innocuous direction: "Sauté the onions, carrots, and celery until softened." Some recipes may omit one of these aromatic vegetables or add garlic or parsley to the pan. Traditionally, the frying medium was lard. Today, most Italian cooks rely on olive oil.

These aromatic vegetables are called the *battuto*. The word translates as "beaten" and refers to the fact that these vegetables have been chopped quite fine, as if they had been pounded. The size of the vegetables is important. They should almost melt into the dish so that they're not immediately visible. However, the effect of the battuto is quite prominent.

On occasion, you don't cook these vegetables before the other ingredients in a dish are cooked. If added along with the veal and mushrooms for a veal stew, their flavors are clearer and fresher, but not as rich. Sometimes, you add these ingredients, especially the garlic and parsley, toward the end of the cooking time without cooking them at all. *Gremolata,* a mixture of parsley, garlic, and lemon zest sprinkled over *osso buco* (veal shanks) at the table, is a good example. Using a battuto this way produces the strongest flavor.

However, in most recipes, you sauté the battuto over moderate heat to deepen the flavors of the vegetables. This occurs before you add any other ingredients to the pan. The vegetables release their flavors into the fat, which flavors ingredients that you add subsequently to the pan. In this way, every bite of a tomato sauce has a hint of onions or garlic, or every spoonful of soup has been tinged by the sweetness of the carrots or the grassy flavor of the celery.

When you cook the battuto, it becomes a *soffritto.* Spanish cooking relies on a similar cooking process and uses the same name (but spelled *sofrito*) to describe a mixture of onions and tomatoes, which you can flavor with leeks, bell peppers, herbs, carrots, celery, or garlic. The Italian word *soffritto* roughly translates as "underfried" and refers to the fact that you shouldn't cook the vegetables too quickly. The soffritto is rarely browned, but rather is cooked until the onions are golden. Applying moderate heat transforms the raw, harsh flavors of the vegetables into a richer, sweeter, more harmonious flavor base.

# Be Frugal

For most of the first half of the 20th century, food was scarce in many parts of Italy. The two World Wars had a devastating effect on the Italian economy. Although the Italian economy has grown tremendously since the end of World War II (Italy now has the world's seventh largest economy), Italian cooks haven't abandoned the thrifty culinary practices of their grandparents.

The Italian cook finds a use for almost every food item, even things that most American cooks may discard. Italian cooks recycle stale bread as croutons in soups or in salads. They save rinds from Parmigiano-Reggiano cheese to flavor water-based soups.

Most parts of the vegetable get used. You can purchase beets with their leafy tops attached. You can cook the beets themselves one day and then save the leafy greens to use in salad or in place of spinach in a pasta filling. Likewise, you usually remove the tough stalks from Swiss chard before cooking the leaves. However, you can keep the thick white (or red) stalks for several days in the refrigerator and then use them to make a simple gratin by adding a Bechamel Sauce (see Chapter 7) and grated cheese.

Although throwing out some scraps is fine (you can't do much with potato peelings), be as frugal as possible in cooking. Don't assume that more is better and keep adding more ingredients to a dish that doesn't taste right. Excess rarely produces the best results. Think about what you don't like about the dish on the stove and then take a considered step to remedy the problem. Even if you may not want to save hunks of stale bread to make your own bread crumbs (although you really should), you should practice this kind of frugality when approaching Italian cooking.

# Enjoy Yourself

Even if the food is fantastic, we don't consider a meal to be a success if we haven't enjoyed ourselves. Italian food is meant to be shared and savored. Enjoy the food as well as the cooking process. All that time in the kitchen may seem like a chore, but try to focus on the benefits. As the cook, you get to relieve some stress by chopping onions into submission. Cooking also stimulates the senses. We find the aroma of garlic cooking in olive oil to be almost as seductive as the dishes that the garlic flavors. If you can appreciate the entire process, from shopping to the presentation of finished dishes, cooking can become an integral part of your life. Like most Italian cooks do, you'll look forward to spending time in the kitchen.

And remember, good food isn't necessarily an end unto itself. Food is a stimulus, a way for us to connect with our families and friends. Even if the food wouldn't merit rave reviews from the local restaurant critic, if the meal enables you to enjoy the company and conversation of others, it has served its purpose.

Most Italian families mark the end of every week with a Sunday feast. Brothers and sisters, aunts and uncles, cousins and grandparents all gather around the table. And although the food is usually fresh and delicious, it's the company, not the food, that keeps the family coming back week after week.

# Chapter 20

# Ten Resources to Find Out More about Italy and Its Food

### In This Chapter
▶ Surfing the World Wide Web for Italian food sites
▶ Reading up on Italy in books and magazines

This book should answer all your basic questions about Italian cooking. We also tackle numerous specialized topics in detail. However, you can always find out more about Italian cooking.

The following books, magazines, and Web sites are particularly noteworthy because they provide in-depth, specialized information. Think of it this way: If you read this book, you earn a bachelor's degree in Italian cooking. Check out the following sources carefully, and you may earn that Ph.D.

## The Magazine of La Cucina Italiana

Italy's leading food magazine, *La Cucina Italiana*, is available in an English-language version, called *The Magazine of La Cucina Italiana*, which is published in the United States and customized for the North American market. The American publishers run an excellent Web site, with hundreds of recipes in the data bank, as well as a good glossary of Italian cooking terms and ingredients. The Web site also features significant excerpts from the magazine and contains information on subscribing. The Web address is www.piacere.com. To start a magazine subscription by phone, call (888) 857-7016. An annual subscription (six issues) costs $24.

## DolceVita

The tagline for this Web site is "on the net Italian style," and the site lives up to this billing. This Italian online zine, which *Tribunale di Milano* operates and translates into English, covers a wide range of subjects, including fashion, design, travel, art, and cuisine. Stories on restaurants in Milan, the origins of balsamic vinegar, and springtime recipes for artichokes give readers a hip, current look at the Italian food scene. The graphics are stylish, and long essays, such as one on Sicilian cooking, have been translated by a pro. This site is very practical but also lots of fun to visit. The Web address is www.dolcevita.com.

## Italy for the Gourmet Traveler

If you're traveling to Italy, this book by Fred Plotkin is a must. If you can't leave home, you can curl up on the couch and read about where to find the finest prosciutto in Florence or the freshest fish in Venice. The book is organized by region, and each section of the book describes the best and most typical food for that area. The book covers more than 300 cities and villages. In addition to a listing of 800 restaurants, you can find extensive information on other food outlets, including butcher shops and coffee bars. The listings take you off the beaten path to places not covered in traditional tourist guidebooks. *Italy for the Gourmet Traveler* was published by Little, Brown and Company in 1996 and retails for $19.95.

## Journal of Italian Food & Wine

Believe it or not, this American magazine devoted to Italian cooking has no affiliation with an Italian publication. The *Journal of Italian Food & Wine* is a "small" magazine, clearly run on a tight budget. However, the articles are generally well written and comprehensive. No one writes as lovingly about the markets of Bologna or restaurants in the countryside near Lucca. The magazine comes out six times a year, and an annual subscription costs $16.97. For more information, call (888) 656-6669.

# Everything Florence

If you're passionate about the Duomo, the David, and Tuscan white beans, then you need to know about this Web site devoted especially to the city of Florence. The Florence tourist board maintains the site, but the site contains a wealth of information beyond the standard listings. In addition to restaurant and hotel listings, you can find extensive information about the art, history, churches, and people who have made this city so famous and beloved. You can also enjoy more than 100 traditional Florentine and Tuscan recipes, including pasta and bean soup and bread salad. The Web address is `www.arca.net/florence.htm`.

# Ottaviana's Kitchen

The Web is home to thousands of personal sites that enable surfers around the globe to enter someone else's home or life. This site opens with a sepia-toned photo of Maria, the Web site author's mother and culinary inspiration. In her home page, Ottaviana, who was born and raised in the United States, says she has no children and has created this Web site as a way of passing on her mother's recipes. Most of the 50 or so recipes are fairly authentic (fried cardoons and tripe in tomato sauce), but some are Italian-American. The tone is warm and friendly. The Web address is `www.geocities.com/NapaValley/6750`.

# Antique Roman Dishes

For something completely esoteric, you can check out some unusual Roman dishes that date back 2,000 years or more. The author, who appears to be a history or anthropology scholar at Carnegie Mellon University in Pittsburgh, has translated two dozen recipes from an ancient Roman manuscript. The author has included an interesting listing of native Roman ingredients, such as *defritum* (a thick syrup made from figs) and *liquamen* (a salty fish sauce). You probably won't want to cook from these sketchy descriptions, but it's fun to read about rolls made with unfermented juice or pancakes made with honey and black pepper. The Web address (and it's a long one) is `www.cs.cmu.edu/~mjw/recipes/ethnic/historical/ant-rom-coll.html`.

# Cucina Online

This Italian online zine has been translated into English and offers a wealth of information about gourmet shopping and Italian restaurants in the United States, as well as weekly menus from an Italian chef. One of the best things about this site is the extensive glossary, which covers hundreds of culinary topics with definitions and pictures of everything from Mediterranean fish varieties to the preparation of gnocchi. If you read Italian, check out the complete text of Pellegrino Artusi's *La scienza in cucina e l'arte di mangiar bene*, the Italian equivalent of *The Joy of Cooking*. You can read some interesting essays, such as the text of a talk given at the Italian Cultural Institute in New York on the history of pasta. The Web address for the English-language home page of this site is `www.cucina.italynet.com/default2.htm`.

# Eating in Italy

Faith Heller Willinger is an American food writer who has lived in Italy for more than 25 years. Few people who write in English are as knowledgeable about Italian food. If you're thinking of traveling to northern Italy (either literally or vicariously), check out her book, *A Traveler's Guide to the Gastronomic Pleasures of Northern Italy*. Willinger covers Italy's 11 northern regions, explaining the local dishes, wines, and traditions particular to each. She gives you extensive restaurant listings, as well as fun sections, such as a description of various gelato flavors (dozens exist) and some arcane Italian food terminology. The book was published by William Morrow and revised by the author in 1998. (Make sure that you get the new version.) It retails for $20.

# Treasures of the Italian Table

This little book is perfect for bedtime reading. Burton Anderson is one of the world's leading wine writers. He lives in Tuscany, and in this volume, he turns his attention to the food of his adopted country in a collection of long essays. You won't find any recipes here, just detailed and moving descriptions of Italy's most important foods, including white truffles, pasta, olive oil, pizza, Parmigiano-Reggiano cheese, risotto, balsamic vinegar, and espresso. Anderson also does a good job of depicting the lives of the artisans who grow and make these foods. *Treasures of the Italian Table* was published by William Morrow in 1994 and retails for $20. Although several years old, the book is by no means dated. Italians have been making most of these ingredients the same way for centuries. Local bookstores should be able to order this somewhat-hard-to-find title, or you may want to try one of the Web booksellers (such as Amazon.com at `www.amazon.com`).

# Chapter 21

# Ten Italian Phrases to Impress Your Date

## In This Chapter

▶ The first and last words to use in Italian restaurants

*W*e've sprinkled Italian words throughout the book. We like the way they look and sound, and we also think that they can help when reading food labels or restaurant menus.

Here, we give you a list of Italian phrases that can make you sound like a real Roman. Use them when shopping at your local Italian deli (you may get better service) or try them out in an Italian restaurant. They're sure to impress your date and might just get you some special attention from the waitstaff.

When trying to pronounce Italian words, sound everything out. You'll come across very few silent letters, and most words sound like they're written. All those vowels may throw you at first, but they sure sound sexy.

We have added our own pronunciation key in parentheses. Linguists may laugh, but we think these phonetic clues (instead of the standard linguistic symbols, which we find confusing) can help you pronounce these important words like a real Italian. Emphasize the syllables in bold.

## Buonasera

Most dates are for dinner, so when you walk into an Italian restaurant at night, saying "good evening" to the maitre d' or host is a nice touch. *Buonasera* (**bwone**-a-**sair**-a) is the standard greeting in Italy after siesta time, used both in the late afternoon and the early evening. When it's time to say "good night," switch to the phrase *buonanotte* (**bwone**-a-note-tay).

## Per Favore

Your mother was right. Add the word *please* to the end of any request, and people, especially waiters, are more likely to do as you ask. *Per favore* (pear fav-**or**-ay) literally translates as "for favor," but use this phrase like the English word *please*. *Per piacere* (pear pia-**chair**-ay) translates as "if you please" and is sometimes used in place of *per favore*.

## Mille Grazie

Why say thank you, or *grazie*, when you can offer someone "a thousand thanks" by saying *mille grazie?* The phrase *mille grazie* (**me**-lay **grat**-zee-ay) is akin to saying "thank you very much" in English. It also makes you sound like a connoisseur of all things Italian.

## I Primi, I Secondi

Many Italian restaurants divide the menu into courses. You probably recognize *antipasti* and *dolce* as appetizers and desserts. But many English speakers get confused by the words *i primi* (e **pre**-me) and *i secondi* (e sa-**cun**-dee). *I primi* translates as "the firsts" and refers to traditional Italian first courses, such as pasta, rice, polenta, and gnocchi. *I secondi* translates as "the seconds" and refers to the traditional second courses, such as meat, poultry, and fish. The custom in Italy is to order both — the first course is very small. In the United States, restaurants usually turn most *primi* into a main course if you ask.

## Vino Rosso, Vino Bianco

What's a date without wine? *Vino* (**vee**-no) is the Italian word for wine. *Vino rosso* (**vee**-no **row**-so) is red wine, and *vino bianco* (**vee**-no bee-**ahn**-co) is white wine. Although Chardonnay and other white wines popular in the rest of the world are produced in Italy, you're more likely to see Pinot Grigio (**Pea**-no **Gree**-gee-oh), Soave (**Swa**-vay), and Vernaccia (Ver-**notch**-ah). As for popular reds, look for Dolcetto (Dol-**chet**-toe), Barolo (Bar-**roll**-oh), and Chianti (Key-**ahn**-tee).

# Cin Cin

After the waiter brings your wine, you may want to make a toast. The Italian equivalent to cheers is *cin cin* (chin chin). Clink glasses and say these words as an expression of camaraderie. This salute can certainly help break the ice at the beginning of an awkward date.

# Per Due

There's something romantic about sharing a T-bone steak, often called *bistecca Fiorentina* (bee-**stake**-ah Fee-or-en-**teen**-ah) on Italian restaurant menus, or other entree in a restaurant. When ordering, you can slip *per due*, which means "for two," into the conversation. It's easy to pronounce (pear **dew**-ay), and this phrase lets the waiter know that you and your date are a hot item.

# Mio Amore

If the evening is going well, you may want to sprinkle this Italian phrase for "my love" into the conversation. The words *mio amore* (**me**-oh ah-**more**-ay) should roll off your tongue. Of course, if you're on a first date and realize there's no chance of a second one, hold back.

# Ancora un Po' di Pane

This is a pretty advanced phrase, but it comes in handy, so you may want to try to manage this mouthful. *Pane* (**pahn**-ay) is Italian for bread, and you should use this entire phrase to ask the waiter for more bread. The first part of the phrase, *ancora un po' di* (ahn-**core**-a oon poe dee) translates as "some more." You can add almost any noun to the end of this phrase to ask for more wine (*vino*), water (*acqua* or **ah**-kwa), or even cheese (*formaggio* or for-**mah**-joe). To be polite, add the Italian word for please (*per favore*) after the noun, or *ancora un po' di pane, per favore*. If you can spit this all out, you're ready for Beginners Italian II.

## *Il Conto*

Asking for the check in a restaurant can be awkward, especially at the end of a romantic meal. Do you start flailing your arm in the air? We've seen people snap their fingers, even whistle, to get the waiter's attention. If you're on a date, don't start with these gestures. They only make you look silly. Wait for the waiter to come by and then ask for the check by saying *il conto* (ill **con**-toe). Again, it's nice to add *per favore* (please) to the end of this phrase.

# Part VIII
# Appendixes

The 5th Wave     By Rich Tennant

"What 'ya mean you don't want espresso?"

# In this part . . .

Don't know the difference between simmering and boiling? Can't remember how many teaspoons are in a tablespoon? Want to order some aged balsamic vinegar by mail? Then this part is for you. Appendix A succinctly defines important cooking terms. Appendix B lists some common substitutions, abbreviations, and equivalents. Appendix C contains notes about our favorite mail-order sources for Italian cooking equipment and ingredients.

# Appendix A

# Glossary of Italian Cooking Terms and Ingredients

• • • • • • • • • • • • • • • • • • • • • • • • • • • • • • • • • • • • • •

*W*e have tried to use as little jargon as possible when writing this book. But it's impossible to write a cookbook without using some common cooking terms like boil or sauté. Just in case you didn't graduate from cooking school, we have gathered all the terms that you may see in this book and defined them for you.

**adjust:** To taste a dish just before serving and add more seasonings, especially salt and pepper.

**al dente:** To cook until tender but still firm.

**bake:** To cook in the oven.

**baste:** To add moisture and flavor to food as it cooks by brushing with pan drippings, melted butter, or a sauce. Also, to spoon liquid over food to baste.

**beat:** To mix ingredients briskly with a wooden spoon or electric mixer so that they become smooth.

**blanch:** To partially cook food in boiling water. Blanching sets color in green vegetables and helps loosen skins on fruits, such as peaches and tomatoes.

**blend:** To combine ingredients, usually until smooth, with a spoon, spatula, whisk, or electric mixer.

**boil:** To bring water or other liquid to a temperature of 212° at sea level. The surface of the liquid will be covered with large bubbles when boiling. Also, to cook food in water or other liquid that is at 212°.

**braise:** To brown food in fat, cover with liquid, cover the pot, and cook over low heat until tender. Long, slow cooking tenderizes tough cuts of meat. Foods can be braised on top of the stove or in the oven.

**bread:** To coat a piece of food with bread crumbs to seal in moisture and to add a crunchy texture to the exterior. Many foods are first dipped in beaten eggs or other liquids to help make the crumbs adhere. *See also dredge, dust, flour.*

**broil:** To cook under the broiling element in an oven.

**brown:** To cook food quickly over high heat, usually in a pan on top of the stove but sometimes in a pan in the oven, under the broiler, or on the grill.

**brush:** To coat the surface of food with a liquid ingredient, such as melted butter, using a small pastry brush.

**butterfly:** To cut a piece of food almost in half horizontally, leaving a seam that joins the two pieces together. When opened, the food item will resemble a butterfly or two pages in an open book.

**caramelize:** To cook food until the natural sugars cause the exterior to brown. Often refers to onions.

**chop:** To cut food into uniform pieces, usually about $1/2$ inch in size.

**cream:** To beat butter, often with sugar, until smooth and light.

**crumble:** To break up or crush food into small pieces with your fingers.

**cube:** To cut food into square pieces. Size is usually designated in recipes.

**dash:** A small amount of seasoning, less than $1/8$ teaspoon (also known as a *pinch*).

**deglaze:** To add liquid to a hot skillet or roasting pan. Use a wooden spoon to lift off browned bits clinging to the bottom of the pan and make a sauce.

**devein:** To remove the intestinal tract from the back of shrimp.

**dice:** To cut into equal-sized pieces, usually less than $1/2$ inch in size.

**drain:** To remove liquid from a food by pouring it into a colander or strainer. Also, to spoon off fat from a pan.

**dredge:** To coat food with flour, breadcrumbs, or cornmeal. ***See also*** *bread, dust, flour.*

**drizzle:** To pour a liquid in a slow, steady stream.

**dust:** To coat a work surface or food lightly, usually with flour or confectioners sugar. ***See also*** *bread, dredge, flour.*

**flour:** To coat a work surface, pan, or piece of food with flour. To flour a greased baking pan, add several tablespoons of flour, and turn the pan to coat the bottom and sides with flour. Tap out excess flour. ***See also*** *bread, dredge, dust.*

**fold:** To gently combine two mixtures or ingredients by using a rubber spatula. Often used to describe the motion for adding beaten egg whites or heavy cream into a thicker mixture.

**fry:** To cook food in very hot fat. Deep-fried foods are completely submerged in fat.

**grate:** To rub food, especially cheese, against holes on a grater to cut the food into tiny pieces.

**grease:** To coat a pan or baking dish with fat. Fat may be sprayed on, brushed on, or wiped on with a paper towel.

**grill:** To cook on a rack over very hot coals or a gas grill.

**knead:** To work bread dough with the palms of your hands, a food processor, or a stand mixer until the dough is smooth and elastic.

**line:** To cover the bottom of a pan with a piece of parchment or waxed paper or aluminum foil to prevent sticking and make cleanup easier. If necessary, use scissors to cut paper or foil to fit.

**marinate:** To soak and season food in flavorful sauce or liquid. Refrigerate perishable foods while they marinate. The seasoning liquid is called a *marinade.*

**mash:** To press cooked food, often potatoes, into a soft puree with a masher or ricer.

**melt:** To heat solid food over low heat until it liquefies. Usually refers to butter or chocolate.

**mince:** To cut into equal-sized pieces, usually less than $1/4$ inch in size.

**peel:** To remove the skin from food, usually fruits or vegetables, with a peeler, paring knife, or your hands.

**pinch:** A small amount of seasoning, less than $1/8$ teaspoon (also known as a *dash*).

**poach:** To cook food in simmering liquid, usually in a covered pan on top of the stove.

**pound:** To flatten meat between two sheets of waxed paper or plastic wrap with a mallet or heavy saucepan.

**preheat:** To turn on the oven, grill, or broiler before cooking. Set the temperature as indicated in the recipe and wait for the oven, grill, or broiler to reach that temperature before cooking food.

**prick:** To stick tines of a fork into food.

**puree:** To mash or grind food into a smooth paste by using a ricer, food processor, or blender.

**reduce:** To cook liquid over high heat so that it evaporates and the original volume decreases. As liquid reduces, consistency thickens, and flavor concentrates.

**roast:** To cook in the dry heat of an oven. Usually refers to meat, chicken, fish, or vegetables. Similar to the term *bake* except that roasting implies savory foods and browning of the exterior.

**sauté:** To cook food in a small amount of fat in a pan or skillet set over high heat.

**sear:** To brown the exterior of food very quickly in a hot oven, under a broiler, on a grill rack, or in a pan on top of the stove.

**season:** To flavor food with salt and pepper, herbs, and spices. Taste before seasoning and add flavorings as desired.

**shred:** To cut into long, thin strips.

**shuck:** To remove the meat from bivalves, such as clams, oysters, and mussels, and discard the shells.

**sift:** To pass flour and other dry ingredients through a fine mesh sifter to remove lumps and to lighten the texture.

**simmer:** To bring water or other liquid to a temperature just below boiling, usually about 190° at sea level. The surface of the liquid will be covered with tiny bubbles when simmering. Also, to cook food in water or other liquid that is just below the boiling point.

**skim:** To remove fat or bits of food that rise to the surface of soup, stock, or stew as it cooks. Use a mesh skimmer or a spoon.

**sliver:** To cut food into long, thin pieces. Usually applies to garlic cloves.

**steam:** To cook food on a rack or in a basket set above boiling water in a covered pan.

**stew:** To cook food in simmering liquid for a long period of time. Similar to braise.

**stir-fry:** To cook food over very high heat, constantly stirring to make sure that the food does not burn. Usually occurs in a wok, but food can be stir-fried in a skillet.

**stock:** A strained, flavorful liquid made by cooking meat, poultry, vegetables, and/or fish in water. Used to make soups, sauces, and stews.

**strain:** To remove liquid from a food by pouring it into a colander or strainer. Similar to *drain*.

**stud:** To insert seasonings, usually garlic or herbs, into the surface of food. Often, a paring knife is used to make small holes in meat for seasonings.

**stuff:** To fill a food cavity, such as a chicken or a hollowed-out vegetable.

**toast:** To lightly brown food, especially nuts, in a dry skillet or on a baking sheet in the oven. When toasting nuts, remove them as soon as they are fragrant and very lightly colored.

**toss:** To combine ingredients quickly by using two spoons, two forks, or a spoon and fork.

**whip:** To beat air rapidly into food, such as cream or eggs, with a whisk or electric mixer until light and fluffy.

**whisk:** To combine ingredients with a looped wire kitchen utensil, usually until smooth.

**zest:** To remove the outermost colored skin (not the bitter white pith just beneath the skin) from citrus fruits. Use a grater, vegetable peeler, or specially designed zester, which removes skin in long, thin strips.

# Appendix B
# Common Substitutions, Abbreviations, and Equivalents

●●●●●●●●●●●●●●●●●●●●●●●●●●●●●●●●●●●●●●●●●●●●●●

*T*hings don't always go as planned in the kitchen. Even pros get caught shorthanded once in a while. We can't tell you how many times we thought that we had a specific ingredient only to find out halfway through making a recipe that this ingredient had mysteriously vanished.

This chapter can help get you out of these jams. Sometimes, you can't use a substitute for an ingredient. For example, you can't make a cake recipe that calls for flour without the flour. However, many times you can make some adjustments. For example, vegetable oil can almost always replace olive oil. The flavor may not be as good, but the recipe works. Likewise, you can surely make a recipe that calls for walnuts using pecans or almonds instead.

Here are some not-so-obvious substitutions that you can make when in a pinch. Remember, it's always best to follow a recipe. But when you can't, turn to this list for help.

For thickening soups, stews, and sauces:

- 1 tablespoon (15 milliliters) cornstarch or potato starch = 2 tablespoons (30 milliliters) all-purpose flour
- 1 tablespoon (15 milliliters) arrowroot = $2^{1}/_{2}$ tablespoons (37 milliliters) all-purpose flour

For leavening agents in baked goods:

- $^{1}/_{4}$ teaspoon (1 milliliter) baking soda + $^{1}/_{2}$ teaspoon (2 milliliters) cream of tartar = 1 teaspoon (5 milliliters) double-acting baking powder
- $^{1}/_{4}$ teaspoon (1 milliliter) baking soda + $^{1}/_{2}$ cup (125 milliliters) buttermilk or plain yogurt = 1 teaspoon (5 milliliters) double-acting baking powder in liquid mixtures only; reduce liquid in recipe by $^{1}/_{2}$ cup (125 milliliters)

For dairy products:

- 1 cup (250 milliliters) whole milk = $^1/_2$ cup (125 milliliters) evaporated milk + $^1/_2$ cup (125 milliliters) water

  or 1 cup (250 milliliters) skim milk + 2 tablespoons (30 milliliters) melted butter

  or $^1/_4$ cup (50 milliliters) powdered milk + 1 cup (250 milliliters) water

  or 1 cup (250 milliliters) soy milk

For eggs:

- 2 egg yolks = 1 whole egg
- 4 extra-large eggs = 5 large eggs

For sweetening:

- 1 cup brown sugar = 1 cup (250 milliliters) granulated sugar + $1^1/_2$ tablespoons (22 milliliters) molasses

Miscellaneous substitutions:

- 1 tablespoon (15 milliliters) prepared mustard = 1 teaspoon (5 milliliters) dried mustard
- 1 cup (250 milliliters) broth or stock = 1 bouillon cube dissolved in 1 cup (250 milliliters) boiling water
- 1 square (1 ounce/28 grams) unsweetened chocolate = 3 tablespoons (45 milliliters) unsweetened cocoa + 1 tablespoon (15 milliliters) butter, margarine, vegetable shortening, or oil
- 1 ounce (28 grams) semisweet chocolate = 3 tablespoons (45 milliliters) unsweetened cocoa + 2 tablespoons (30 milliliters) butter, margarine, vegetable shortening, or oil + 3 tablespoons (45 milliliters) granulated sugar

Suppose that a recipe calls for 1 pound tomatoes, and you don't own a kitchen scale. (You should, you know.) Or maybe you can't remember how many tablespoons are in a cup. Table B-1 lists common equivalent measures. Table B-2 deals with food items, giving cup and weight measures for some often-used ingredients. All measurements are for level amounts. Note that some metric measurements are approximate.

| Table B-1 | Conversion Secrets | |
|---|---|---|
| *This Measurement . . .* | *. . . Equals This Measurement . . .* | *. . . Equals This Measurement* |
| Pinch or dash | less than $1/8$ teaspoon | 0.5 mL |
| 3 teaspoons | 1 tablespoon | 15 mL |
| 2 tablespoons | 1 fluid ounce | 30 mL |
| 4 tablespoons | $1/4$ cup | 50 mL |
| 5 tablespoons + 1 teaspoon | $1/3$ cup | 75 mL |
| 8 tablespoons | $1/2$ cup | 100 mL |
| 10 tablespoons + 2 teaspoons | $2/3$ cup | 150 mL |
| 12 tablespoons | $3/4$ cup | 175 ml |
| 16 tablespoons | 1 cup | 250 mL |
| 1 cup | 8 fluid ounces | 250 mL |
| 2 cups | 1 pint or 16 fluid ounces | 500 mL |
| 2 pints | 1 quart or 32 fluid ounces | 1 L |
| 4 quarts | 1 gallon | 4 L |

| Table B-2 | Food Equivalents | |
|---|---|---|
| *This Measurement . . .* | *. . . Equals This Measurement . . .* | *. . . Equals This Measurement* |
| 1 pound all-purpose flour | 4 cups sifted | 1 L sifted |
| 3 medium apples or bananas | approximately 1 pound | 500 g |
| 2 slices bread | 1 cup fresh bread crumbs | 250 mL |
| 1 pound brown sugar | $2^{1}/4$ cups packed | 550 mL packed |
| 8 tablespoons butter | 1 stick | 125 mL or $1/2$ cup |
| 4 sticks butter | 1 pound | 454 g |
| 6 ounces chocolate chips | 1 cup | 250 mL |
| 1 pound confectioners sugar | $4^{1}/2$ cups sifted | 1.125 L sifted |

*(continued)*

### Table B-2 *(continued)*

| *This Measurement . . .* | *. . . Equals This Measurement . . .* | *. . . Equals This Measurement* |
|---|---|---|
| 1 cup dried beans | 2 cups cooked | 500 mL |
| 1 large garlic clove | approximately 1 teaspoon minced | 5 mL minced |
| 1 pound granulated sugar | 2 cups | 500 mL |
| ¹/₂ pound hard cheese (such as Parmesan) | approximately 2 cups grated | 500 mL grated |
| 1 cup heavy whipping cream | 2 cups whipped | 500 mL whipped |
| 1 medium lemon | 3 tablespoons juice, 1 to 2 teaspoons grated peel | 45 mL juice, 5 to 10 mL grated peel |
| 4 ounces nuts | approximately ²/₃ cup chopped | 150 mL chopped |
| 1 large onion | approximately 1 cup chopped | 250 mL chopped |
| 1 pound pasta | 4 cups raw, 8 cups cooked | 1 L raw, 2 L cooked |
| 3 medium potatoes | approximately 1 pound | 500 g |
| 1 cup raw rice | 3 cups cooked | 750 mL cooked |
| 1 large tomato | approximately ³/₄ cup chopped | 175 mL chopped |
| 3 medium tomatoes | approximately 1 pound | 500 g |
| 1 28-ounce can whole tomatoes | 3 ¹/₂ cups | 875 mL |

# Index

*(continued)*